About the Authors

Katharine Anne Ommanney is a pioneer in educational dramatics, having selected the high school as her chosen field in the early twenties. She has been fortunate in combining her quarter century as dramatics teacher at North High School, Denver, with extensive teaching and lecturing at the university level, acting on the stage and in radio, and professional directing of all types of productions. Her advanced specialized training includes an M.A. from Stanford as well as study at the Royal Academy of Dramatic Art and the Oxford Summer School of Speech in England and at the American Academy of Dramatic Art. She was *Billboard* correspondent for several years and has also contributed numerous articles to *Theater Arts* and other drama and educational magazines.

Katharine Ommanney has received widespread recognition, including listing in *Who's Who of American Women* and *Leaders in Education,* honorary membership in Zeta Phi Eta and Alpha Phi Gamma, and service on boards such as those of NET (now ATA), WPA Federal Theater (Colorado), and drama sections of NEA conventions. She was a delegate to the 1970 Governor's Conference of the Year 2000 in Honolulu and to the Association of Women of the Pacific in Australia.

In 1972, Katharine Ommanney received The Founders' Award of SSTA Secondary Division of ATA. Since her early retirement, she has been active in the theater of Hawaii, where she has taught at Maunaolu College, Maui, and produced various current plays and productions. For seven years she was on the Executive Board of the Hawaii State Theater Council under the State Foundation on Culture and the Arts and is active with the long-standing Maui Community Theater. She has ''pursued the drama around the world'' all her life seeing plays and theater festivals, lecturing and directing on all the continents.

Harry H. Schanker is a dedicated teacher-director of high school dramatics. He has a wide background of training and experience in all phases of classroom and production activities and is a devoted student of the drama.

He earned a B.S. degree in Language Arts from Kansas University and an M.A. degree in Secondary Education from the University of Colorado. He has taught English, speech, drama, and stagecraft in the Denver Public Schools for almost three decades. He has received the Distinguished Teacher Award and twice has received an Honorable Mention as Colorado Teacher of the Year. He also served two years as State Director for the International Thespian Society. He is the editor of *Dramatic Comedy,* an anthology of ''classic'' comedies and a part of the McGraw-Hill Patterns in Literary Arts series.

Harry Schanker originated the Summer High School Theater in Denver and served as its first director; he has produced its summer musicals with great success. He has also supervised the auditorium and backstage areas and equipment in the Thomas Jefferson High School, where he has made an enviable reputation as teacher and producer, having directed well over a hundred productions and handled the technical work for at least that many.

FIFTH EDITION

The Stage & the School

KATHARINE ANNE OMMANNEY
HARRY H. SCHANKER

WEBSTER DIVISION, McGRAW-HILL BOOK COMPANY
New York, St. Louis, San Francisco, Dallas, Atlanta, Toronto

Title Page: *Mark Antony pays tribute to Brutus: "This was the noblest Roman of them all." The conclusion in* Julius Caesar, *from the New York Shakespeare Festival production.*

To My Students

whose enthusiasm and companionship in my daily classwork in Dramatics inspired me to write this book fifty years ago.

Acknowledgments on pages v–viii are an extension of this copyright page.

Editorial Development:	John Rothermich
	Lorraine Labate
Editing and Styling:	Linda Richmond
Design:	Ben Arrington
	Valerie Scarpa
Production:	Judith Tisdale
Photo Research:	Alan Forman
Cover Photo:	Jerry Goodstein
Frontispiece:	George Joseph

This book was set in 11 pt. Times Roman by Typographic Sales, Inc. The color separation was done by Beaumont Graphics.

Library of Congress Cataloging in Publication Data

Ommanney, Katharine Anne.
  The stage and the school.

  Bibliography
  Includes index.
  Summary: Outlines the history of drama and aspects of dramatic interpretation and production.
  1. College and school drama. 2. Amateur theatricals. 3. Drama. 4. Theater. [1. Amateur theatricals. 2. Drama. 3. Theater] I. Schanker, Harry H. II. Title.
  PN3175.045   1982   792'.0222   81-4658
  ISBN 0-07-047671-3   AACR2

1   VHVH 90 89 88 87 86

Acknowledgments

We wish to thank the following authors, publishers, and agents for granting us permission to include copyrighted materials.

WALTER H. BAKER COMPANY for the excerpt from *Neighbors* by Zona Gale. Reprinted by permission of Baker's Plays, Boston, Mass.

BANTAM BOOKS, INC., for excerpts from *Daisy Miller* by Henry James, *The Master Builder* by Henrik Ibsen, and *Secret Service* by William Gillette from *50 Great Scenes for Student Actors*, edited by Lewy Olfson. Copyright © 1970 by Bantam Books, Inc. Reprinted by permission of the publisher. All rights reserved.

JAMES BALDWIN for the excerpt from *The Amen Corner* by James Baldwin. From *The Young Actor's Workbook* by Judith Roberts Seto, © 1979, Doubleday, New York. Copyright by James Baldwin. Reprinted by permission of the author.

MRS. PHILIP BARRY for an excerpt from *The Philadelphia Story* by Philip Barry. Courtesy of Mrs. Philip Barry.

DODD, MEAD & COMPANY, INC., for the following: Excerpt from *Trifles* by Susan Glaspell. Reprinted by permission of Dodd, Mead & Company, Inc., from *Plays* by Susan Glaspell. Copyright 1920 By Dodd, Mead & Company, Inc. Copyright renewed 1948 by Susan Glaspell. Excerpt from *Whose Life Is It Anyway?* by Brian Clark. Reprinted by permission of Dodd, Mead & Company, Inc., from *Whose Life Is It Anyway?* by Brian Clark. Copyright © 1978 by Brian Clark. Excerpt from ''Work'' published in *The Hour Has Struck* by Angela Morgan.

DOUBLEDAY & COMPANY, INC., for the following: Excerpt from *Blithe Spirit* by Noel Coward. Copyright 1941 by Noel Coward. Reprinted by permission of Doubleday & Company, Inc. Excerpt from *Pride and Prejudice* by Helen Jerome. Reprinted by permission of Doubleday & Company, Inc.

DOME PRODUCTIONS for the excerpt from *The Belle of Amherst* by William Luce.

DRAMA BOOK SPECIALISTS for the excerpt from *The Fantasticks*[1] by Tom Jones and Harvey Schmidt. Reprinted from *The Fantasticks/Celebration* by Tom Jones and Harvey Schmidt by permission of Drama Book Specialists (Publishers). Copyright, as an unpublished work, 1960 by Tom Jones and Harvey Schmidt. © Copyright 1964 by Tom Jones and Harvey Schmidt.

MARI EVANS for ''The Rebel'' from *I Am a Black Woman*, published by Wm. Morrow & Company, 1970, by permission of the author. No biographical material to be used without permission of the writer; no birth date to be used.

Table of Contents

Prologue

The Golden Jubilee Edition of *The Stage and the School* is the coordination of the five preceding volumes plus the results of a survey of teachers using the 1972 edition. The subject matter has been curtailed and expanded into only four parts— "Interpreting the Drama," "Appreciating the Drama," "Producing the Drama," and "A Treasury of Scenes and Monologues." There is greater emphasis on the techniques used in the actual production of the latest types of plays and musicals as well as on such popular forms of acting as mime and improvisation.

The evolution of high school dramatics is a vital step in American education. It was about 1920 when the subject was introduced at the secondary level in response, I think, to the tremendously popular little theater movement, in which I was deeply involved. I voluntarily left the field of drama instruction and production at the university level to teach drama in the high school. The impetus to write the book came when I was working on the course of study in dramatics for the Denver high schools and found there was no textbook at the secondary level that covered all aspects of drama and its interpretation. Teachers of English were having to teach dramatics without specialized training and were seeking help in such areas as voice and diction, pantomime, and directing and staging plays. Before the twenties, high school productions were almost entirely worthless farces or lightweight operettas, usually given to raise money for athletics! The lasting result of the success of the subject has been its development from the kindergarten to the university. The response of theater enthusiasts to the book published in 1932 has brightened my life these fifty years!

In the introduction to the first edition, I wrote that the chief purpose of the book was "to inspire creative activity on the part of young people and to present ample subject matter affording an intelligent appreciation of drama and offering sound technical training in its interpretation, and experience in the presentation of plays." I mentioned that the course should achieve such educational values as "the complete enlistment of all the faculties in the enjoyment of aesthetic effort, the creation of ideals, and the rehearsing of later life activity." The purpose of the present edition is the same, but I am sure the students are better prepared to achieve the individual development than they were before creative dramatic work became a part of the elementary grades.

Naturally, many of my favorite sections of past editions have become expendable in making room for practical techniques of production. Among these are: "Living the Drama with Shakespeare"; "The Student Playwright"; "Motion Pictures, Radio and T.V."; "The Photo Essay *A Play Is Born*"; and *Poor Maddalena* by Louise Saunders, the finest one-act play for classwork I know featuring realism and fantasy, humor and pathos, fascinating characters, fine writing, and a splendid theme for students of creative arts.

Reviewing the five volumes has been a most gratifying experience because they represent not only changing attitudes toward education along theatrical lines but also the appearance of newly coined words and old words that now mean what they didn't fifty years ago!

The most important changes and developments in contemporary theater in America are those involving the general public. Centers of the performing arts are being erected across the country, many with separate buildings fully equipped for community and repertory theaters and musical auditoriums. The movement began in 1935 with the organizing of ANTA leading to the development of Arts Councils in cities and smaller regions in many states. Today the National Endowment for the Arts is helping to finance promising theater groups and talented individuals. Whether the United States should have a National Theater, similar to those in most European countries, is being seriously considered, since the Kennedy Center of Performing Arts in Washington is reported to be the only one supported largely by private enterprise of all the great cultural centers of the world. The growth of the Youth Theater has become a vital force in most communities where children and adults are working together to produce worthwhile productions of all types.

One of the welcome trends today is the growing interest in public education in developing the potentials of the gifted child. That has been perhaps the most vital attainment of high school dramatics. I am sure every teacher with a number of years in the subject receives many letters of appreciation from former students stating that no other experience brought them to the fullest realization of their potential, which ultimately helped them achieve success and happiness.

Harry Schanker is responsible for bringing this edition up to date. He is actively engaged in teaching drama in the high school and producing plays on the stage that he designed. His productions, especially those in the summer terms staged with students from all the Denver high schools, prove his ability and experience. His excellent chapter "The Musical Play" is, I am sure, the best presentation guide available anywhere for teacher-directors in that difficult field. His charts and sketches of materials and arrangement of equipment for all productions will be of vital value to backstage workers, who today are more important than ever before.

Mr. Schanker and I hope, as we did ten years ago, that we have been helpful to students, directors, and technicians involved in high school dramatics. Our continuing wish is that *The Stage and the School* will bring "knowledge and appreciation of the enduring values of drama which have brought entertainment, inspiration, and enlightenment for 2,500 years to countless men and women in the theater around the world."

My personal message to students and teachers alike is to make the theater a part of your life. I have pursued it around the world these fifty years and have seen glorious productions in the famous theaters of the great cities and on the streets of far-off villages. I urge you to study both here and abroad and plan your lives to understand the customs, ideals, and ways of life of all nations by being familiar with their drama. Mr. Schanker is already taking students abroad whenever possible. Here, far from the mainland of the United States, the theater of Hawaii has enriched my life. That creative, talented people of all ages and ethnic backgrounds are keeping me a part of our remarkably successful Maui Community Theatre by naming their annual awards "The Kitty-Awards" so that my name will live is my great delight. You young people studying this book can find the high school stage one of your most rewarding experiences.

I wish at this time that I could thank the hundreds of persons who have given me the inspiration and material which have kept *The Stage and the School* flourishing for so long. I could list them in the early editions but not in the later ones as their numbers multiplied. Now I can only extend my deepest appreciation to Harry Schanker, John Rothermich, and Lorraine Labate, who have made this Jubilee Edition possible.

—*Katharine Anne Ommanney*
Kula, Maui, Hawaii
October 1980

Overleaf: *A scene from the play* Custer.

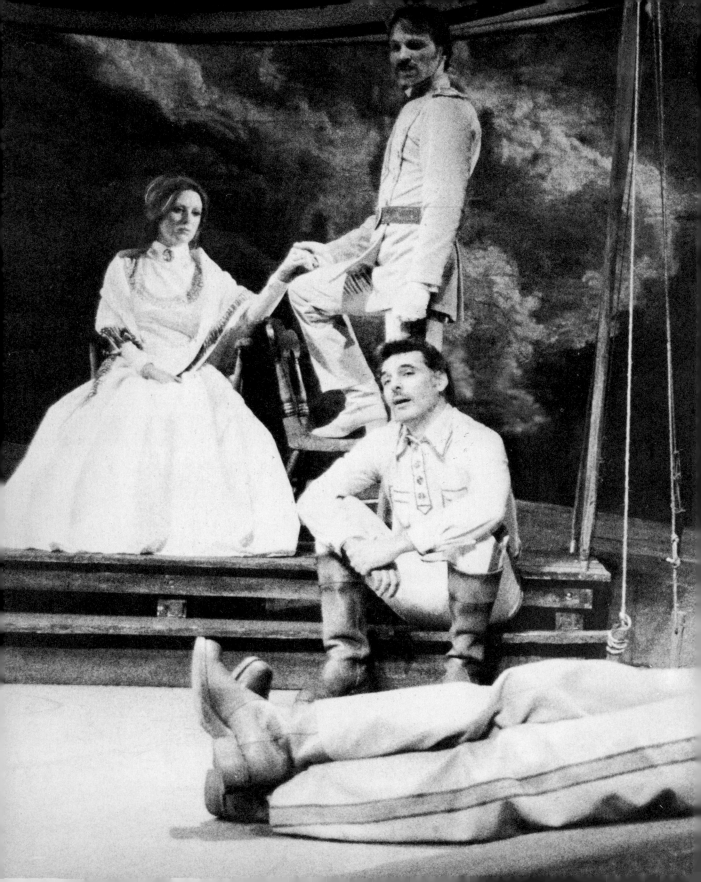

PART ONE

Interpreting the Drama

CHAPTER ONE

The Student of Drama

Whether its setting has been the marble columns of ancient Greece, the crude carts of the Middle Ages, the cobbled inn yards of Elizabethan England, the glittering showboat on the Mississippi, the proscenium stages of the last 30 years, or the intimate, offbeat showplaces for our experimental theater, the stage has always had a remarkable fascination for the average individual. Radio and television have brought the drama into our homes, and the school has brought it to the student.

RELATION BETWEEN THE STAGE AND SCHOOL

As a student approaching dramatics in the high school, you have a background no other young people have had. As a child you spent hours before the television watching, fascinated, the lives of other people involved in exciting happenings. You grew up in the days of the wide screen and stereophonic sound of the motion picture. In elementary school, you have probably already enjoyed creative dramatics, with simple improvisations freeing your mind and body for expressive action. In junior high school, you may have appeared in public performances of plays and musicals. You are now prepared to approach drama as a composite art form that has had a universal appeal for countless generations.

Therefore, the classwork and public performances will open the world of the theater to you. You will experience the delights of both the actor and the spectator. At the same time, you will develop yourself as an individual. The search for identity is an urgent need of young people. The acting of a role in a scene or in a play demands an understanding of your own internal resources and those of the character. Also, in the reading and the witnessing of plays, you involve yourself empathetically with the problems of other people. Empathy is a vital phase of theater, as well as of all the arts, because it means that a person identifies with an object, situation, or individual outside of himself or herself. Thus, through empathy, you gain a sympathy and sensitivity for the emotions and attitudes of other people, which carries over into your daily life. The study of the techniques of acting—the effective use of the tools of your voice and body—is the practical means by which you improve your physical and emotional expressiveness. This experience in self-development and social adjustment is a reasonable means of finding the individual identity so sought after today.

Thus, you can take advantage of the three phases of this course: a study of the theater as one of the chief divisions of art and literature; the actual acting and producing of plays; and the development of your personality, a natural outcome of a wholehearted absorption in the other two phases.

The world of the theater also fosters a delightful use of the leisure time that modern affluence and shorter working hours will bring into your adult life. A multitude of experimental and community groups are welcoming enthusiastic amateurs, the lovers of the drama, into active participation. Also, since most successful plays are immediately published, even in paperback, you can spend many hours in imaginative and fascinating reading of the most exciting form of

Students from a New Mexico Native American school learn that creating a role in a scene or a play demands an understanding of their own internal resources and those of their characters.

literature. As a result of this intimate study of the theater you are about to undertake, you will keep yourself alive to current movements, and you will develop a critical judgment and enjoyment of plays you are seeing on stage, motion-picture screen, and television.

In this course, you will be brought into contact with some of the finest examples of the old and the new theater. You must take advantage of opportunities to attend the repertory, road-show, summer stock, and amateur productions available and judge them intelligently. Perhaps you will have the invaluable experience of appearing in your school's public productions. Today high school standards are as professional as the age and appearance of the cast will permit.

You will, therefore, become a part of the knowledgeable theater-going public, which can affect the ever-changing drama of today. With discrimination you will seek out the best of stage, screen, and television productions and not waste time in apathetic gazing at repetitious, worthless, and tasteless offerings. More important, you will face whatever life holds for you with a quickened imagination, a better-developed voice and body, and a keener appreciation of art and humanity.

THE DEVELOPMENT OF THE INDIVIDUAL

The changing world of the theater is typical of the changing world you will be facing in the immediate and distant future. Never have so many opportunities for creative experience been available. The limitless expanses of space, the new frontiers of oceanography, the "great globe itself" to its farthermost outposts are within your reach. Constant breakthroughs in every field—electronics, medicine, aviation, and all the others—are making life more meaningful and exhilarating. Consequently, the relationships of individuals and nations to each other are of utmost importance in controlling these changes and their effects on modern existence.

Thus, your development as an individual is of vital significance not only to you but also to society. Your growth is, of course, the goal of all your subjects. But dramatics deals with you personally more than any other subject does because of your relation to the parts you play and to the other members of the class. Dramatics is distinctly a group activity, where you need all the patience, sportsmanship, tact, and good nature you can muster. Nothing is more trying on the nerves and disposition than putting on a play; you may already have discovered this. Your ability to accept criticism, to get along with others, and to lose yourself in the success of class projects and productions determines your value to that success. You must be prompt, dependable, and responsive if you are to gain and give all you should.

In no other art is the individuality of the student so important. You, as the actor, have two persons involved in the creative experience whom you must understand—yourself and the character you are portraying. The internal and external

Dramatics is a group activity for which you need patience, sportsmanship, tact, and good nature.

resources of these two individuals determine the response of the audience and thus the success of the performer. Your improvement mentally, emotionally, socially, and physically will give you the most enduring satisfactions of the course.

Today you can appreciate that Shakespeare knew what he was talking about when Jaques says in *As You Like It,* "All the world's a stage and all the men and women merely players." Today the term *role-playing* is popular. Each of you plays a part as you encounter differing situations and people involved in daily living. You seem to become different personalities depending on whether you are at home or at school or involved with jobs or social groups. Such chameleonlike personality shifts are worthy of self-analysis.

In one of his plays, Philip Barry states that emotion is the only real thing in human life. Certainly one who never experiences deep emotion never really lives. The loss of self in another individuality, which comes when a person acts a part sincerely or watches a play intensely, is one of the chief values of a dramatics course. This vicarious living of a life apart from one's daily experience is the chief appeal of the stage in both school and theater.

If you wish to get the full value of the dramatics course, you will make every play you read, in and out of class, a source of experimentation by playing all the parts at home without an audience. Establish a regular schedule for vocal, physical, and interpretation practice, and follow it conscientiously. Enter into all phases of the classwork enthusiastically, whether or not the particular assignment appeals to you. Be as interested in watching the work of the other members of the class as in performing yourself. Try to catch the spirit of every scene you work up. You will be surprised that you have acquired a keener sense of humor, a more alert interest in life, and a broader sympathy for people and their problems.

As in all activity, you will get from the dramatics class only what you put into it. The very nature of the subject matter demands an intensity of effort and enthusiasm of interest few courses draw forth. In this way, in classwork or in public production, you may experience the ultimate achievement of the actor—holding an audience spellbound with your emotional appeal as you reveal the true nature of the role you are playing.

READING PLAYS FOR PERSONAL ENJOYMENT

Reading plays is one of the most satisfying ways to spend your leisure hours. Modern playwrights publish their plays as well as seek their production, and most publishing houses have excellent reissues of classics and of the most interesting dramas of the past and present. If you browse among the drama bookshelves in public libraries, you will find thousands of volumes, including everything from various translations of the ancient Greek and Roman dramas to the latest Broadway and off-Broadway productions.

Reading plays is less time-consuming than reading novels, for the playwright must find the exact word or phrase to advance the plot, characterize the people, and bring out the theme—all through dialogue alone. The playwright seldom has time for long descriptions or philosophical passages to explain ideas. As the course advances, you will learn to appreciate the skills demanded in the creation of a first-class play. You will find that the secret of reading drama is to visualize the persons, settings, and action and let the development of the plot carry you along with its suspense and conflict.

As you read a play, you have time to think about what is being said without needing to keep pace with rapid action onstage. You can decide what is accomplished for the plot in every situation, analyze the characters in relation to their problems, and, best of all, take time to relish the humor and enjoy the dialogue. The deepest satisfaction lies in the fact that you can trace the development of the theme and notice the dramatist's methods of bringing it out and pointing it up. After so many years of watching the fleeting impressions of television and motion pictures, you will be able to quietly live the lines and enjoy them.

READING SCENES ALOUD

Group reading of scenes from plays is an excellent first step in acting, particularly for characterization. Select a scene in which people have strong feelings and express themselves convincingly. You may choose one from this book or from your own reading. In choosing your scene, imagine the appearances, moods, and personalities of the characters. Since this may be your first appearance before the class, your choice of scene should be the best possible introduction you can find— a scene that you really like and that you feel you can interpret effectively.

Perhaps your teacher may prefer to assign roles for this exercise, expecting you merely to express the meaning of your character's lines and suggest the personality. Or you may have to carefully rehearse a piece of work. Your teacher may want you to read from your seats and focus only on the actual reading or may encourage you to take several days to work up the scene to present in front of the class with thought-out facial expressions and movements. At the end of the term, it might be interesting to do the same scene again and compare that reading with your first.

In preparing your role, the first thing to do is to read the scenes very carefully and, if possible, to read the entire play. Then you must visualize the character's appearance—age, size, clothing, and vocal and bodily responses. The character's internal resources—goals, emotions, attitudes, and inner reactions to the other persons—are even more important. Try also to understand the character's motivation in this particular scene and the changes in mood so that you can express effectively the reasons for your character's behavior.

Next, read the entire scene aloud, including all the characters, to appreciate their relationships and the main issues involved in their reactions. You must also determine the high point of the action and how to work up to it. Move about, if you want to, as you catch the spirit of the situation, and let your face and body express the emotions the words imply.

DISCUSSION

1. Where did you first become interested in the theater?

2. What plays have you read? Have you enjoyed them as much as novels and other forms of literature?

3. Why is the use of leisure becoming a more serious problem today than ever before?

4. Why do you think the search for identity has grown to be of such concern today?

5. What are likely to be some of the best qualities of young people interested in dramatics? Some of the less admirable?

6. Do you agree that we play different roles in our social relationships?

7. How do you explain the universal appeal of the drama?

CHAPTER TWO

Improvisation

Are you ready to act? The approach that should help you gain confidence "on the boards" is called *improvisation*. Improvisation is the impromptu portrayal of a character or a scene. You will make up character, lines, and action as you go along, without a formal script. You will have a lot of fun as you are learning some of the fundamentals of acting and getting better acquainted with your classmates. Imagination is the key to improvisation. You must learn to "say the most with the least," that is, you must convey personality and physical traits, conflicts and desires, age and dress with a minimum of aids. Sometimes you may be allowed to use a few props, but character must be conveyed by voice, posture, and bodily movement.

Drama is the link between thought and expression. It depends upon words and action rather than upon words alone. Drama began as pantomimed descriptive action, became stylized dance, and then was ritualized into formal dramas. Words could not convey the full excitement of the great hunt or battle, and so bodily movements were added by the actor-storyteller. The playwright must turn action into words, and the actor must turn those words into action. When improvising, however, you must create both words and action, remembering Shakespeare's advice to the Players: "Suit the action to the word, the word to the action." As a result of your improvising, you should have a better understanding of what goes into a play and should develop a keener appreciation of clever lines, good action, effective blocking, well-developed characters, and strong plots.

Spontaneity and freshness at each performance are the goals of the director of a play, the challenge to the cast, and the pleasure of the audience. However, after weeks of rehearsal or after many performances, the "illusion of the first time" is sometimes difficult to capture, and a play becomes stale. Improvisations are enjoyable in their you-never-know-what's-coming-next freshness. They should help you appreciate the sparkle that comes with a first-time performance. You will appreciate the most important factor in the execution of lines or action—timing.

8

Play casts may rehearse for weeks to achieve the kind of fresh, natural timing that may come as you improvise.

FOUNDATION OF INTERPRETATION

Improvisation is the foundation of interpretation just as pantomime is the foundation of acting. It is the first step in learning to laugh and cry at will. At the heart of theater is discipline, especially self-discipline. It demands physical and mental control, adaptability, acceptance of and positive response to criticism, "directability," and cooperation with others.

Drama began as pantomimed descriptive action, became stylized dance, and then was ritualized into formal dramas. An improvised stage such as this one was common in England during the 1600s.

Although improvising emphasizes the creative—doing rather than telling—the beginning performer often wants to experience the actual emotion rather than to portray it. The student must always bear in mind that a person may go only so far and still be acting. Beyond that point, the actor *is* rather than *is pretending to be*. This is where the discipline enters in. The character, like makeup and costume, must be removed by the actor after the scene is over. As an actor, you should grow as a result of the performance, but you must never let a characterization engulf your own identity. When that happens, you are no longer an actor.

"What is happening now" is the keynote of improvisation. Improvisation focuses your attention on natural actions and reactions and should force you to concentrate on immediate responses. All action should be motivated only by what you already know about the characters and situation and by what is brought forth as you improvise. You do not have the advantage—or disadvantage—of knowing what lines come next in a script. You must play it as it develops. You will learn how a scene may change direction as the result of a single line or action. You may even find it necessary to meet one of the toughest challenges that faces an actor: to "do nothing effectively"—that is, to be on the stage, visible, but not playing an active part in the scene. In such cases, you must get the audience to accept your presence without being distracted. To call attention to your presence would be scene-stealing. You will learn to appreciate the interrelationships of the characters and how essential it is that an actor be a member of the team.

You will appreciate even more a well-written script, which is the finished product of many improvisations that passed through the author's mind while designing the action. In fact, the trial run of most plays is a form of improvisation where the playwright sees "how it plays" and makes necessary changes in the script before the big opening. You will also realize why it is said that a well-written play has no wasted words. Sincere characterization will develop during improvisation to become deeper and more convincing as you proceed toward formal acting. You will begin to feel the role and sense when you are only impersonating the character and when you or a fellow actor is "putting on the cloak but not the soul" of the part.

When your character is described, no matter how simply, you should immediately ask, "Who am I? What kind of person am I? When does this action take place? How should the audience react to me? How am I different from the other characters?" "What are the fewest things I can do to convey the most?" and, finally, "What does my character want?" You will soon learn that a raised eyebrow, a silent stare, a one-word response, or a groan may convey more than a dozen sentences. Try also to determine the mood of the scene. Ask yourself how your character can contribute to the complication and resolution of the idea to be presented.

This mime troupe knows that relaxation is the first step toward believable improvisation.

In your characterization, do not yield to the common impulse to "play the character down." Shallow characterizations are weak characterizations. Luigi Pirandello said that a person plays a "game of masks" in life, putting on a different mask for each person or occasion faced. Seldom does a person want anyone to see what is really behind the mask. The convincing actor lets the audience see the various outer masks of a character, but also allows them to see what is behind, even if only for brief moments. When this is carefully worked out, the audience sees a well-rounded, thoroughly developed personality.

Improvisation provides you with your first opportunities to hold up the masks, but it should also teach you the dangers found in a characterization that is as thin as a single mask. There are certain "masks" that are identifiable in theater. As you read about the commedia dell'arte, the humours, and the stock characters (Chapter 9), you will see how these personality types can give you an insight into character analysis and help you in more complex improvisations.

The improvised approach to acting is being adopted by many directors, and most directors encourage improvising while the actor is working toward the development of a character. Some directors are using a completely improvised approach. This creative experience has certain benefits for the developing actor, but the production usually suffers from a lack of direction, unity, and coherence. A combination of inner-developed improvisation and outer-lead direction usually brings out the best in theater.

IMPROVISATION WARM-UPS

1. *The Mirror.* This is a fundamental exercise in acting training. Two persons face each other. One is the activator; the other, the responder. The activator moves the hands, the head, and eventually, any part of the body while pretending to look in a mirror. The responder matches the actions of the activator without making physical contact. The goals are to learn to work smoothly with a partner and to feel the single impulse of an action. Keep your movements steady and fluid. You are not to trick your partner.

2. *Join Me.* Two persons begin pantomiming separate activities, such as painting a wall or shooting a movie. Each works independently, trying to catch on to what the other person is doing. The first to make that discovery joins the other person, so that together they complete the task.

3. *The Machine.* This is group improvisation that puts your imagination to the test. One person starts the machine by performing a physical action, such as pumping the arm or lifting a knee. Another person joins the first piece of the machine by linking a different physical action to the first. This continues until as many members of the group as possible become part of the machine.
   Variation 1. Make the machine a manufacturing process, so that raw materials are turned into a finished product.
   Variation 2. Add sound to the action. Each new action must be accompanied by its own new sound.

4. *Sock It to Me.* The class divides into groups of two persons each. One partner tosses a small imaginary ball to the other partner. The responder catches the ball, reacting to its weight, velocity, and location, and then throws it back. After the ball has passed back and forth at least three times, either partner may change the size, weight, velocity, or direction of the ball. This may continue through basketballs, shot puts, medicine balls, and so on, each change occurring after a minimum of three passes.
   Variation 1. The ball may be changed to a different object on every third exchange.
   Variation 2. The ball may be propelled by another object, such as a racquet.

5. *The Exchange.* The class divides into groups of two persons, each facing the other. One partner begins moving toward the other partner, performing a simple task, such as pushing a wheel barrow, bouncing a ball, or throwing newspapers. As quickly as possible, the responder must pick up the action and imitate it, moving toward the activator. When both partners meet, they mirror the action of the other.
   Variation 1. Each partner separately pantomimes any physical action, such as skipping rope. When the partners meet, they exchange actions and move away, performing the new action.
   Variation 2. This is the same as Variation 1, but each person has a sound as well as an action that is exchanged.

CONCENTRATION ACTIVITIES

1. Each student is given a simple measurement task to perform. While the class watches, the student engages in the completion of the assigned task. This activity focuses attention on a specific action in view of an audience. Some sample actions are below.

    Measure a room.   Measure a window.
    Measure a chair.   Measure the floor.
    Measure a door.   Measure a desk.

2. Each student chooses a personally familiar action to perform. Simple props are necessary. In acting out this action, there must be a sense of urgency within the student motivating her or him to perform the action and complete the task *now*. After completing the action, each student explains the reason behind the urgent need to rush. Some sample actions are below.

    Hem a skirt.   Apply makeup.
    Photograph a subject.   Write a letter.
    Change a bicycle tire.   Hide a valuable.

3. Building on Activity 2, as the student performs the action, a second student comes into the scene. This second student also has an action to perform. Neither student, however, must be distracted by the other's behavior.

4. Building on Activity 3, conversation is added to the scene. Both students continue to perform their actions. However, they now talk to each other or mutter to themselves. Concentration on the actions must be maintained in spite of the complication of talking.

5. Pairs of students are assigned a simple location and a relationship. The relationship could be between brother and sister. The location could be in the family's garage. One student is already in the garage engaged in an activity, such as painting a chair. That student is in a certain mood. The second student arrives from a specific location and is in a specific mood. The scene builds around the two moods, the relationship, and the location of the present action.

IMPROVISING SCENES

Before you begin working with a partner on an improvised scene, there are a few *dos* and *don'ts* to keep in mind. Following these simple rules will free your imagination and keep your improvisation moving.

Dos

1. Take your cues from your scene partner.
2. Play your scene from moment to moment.
3. Allow your intuition to be your guide.
4. Be spontaneous in your actions.

Don'ts

1. Never deny anything your scene partner says about you or the situation. If your partner says you have lovely yellow eyes, accept the statement as true and allow your imagination to help you respond.

2. Avoid asking questions. Make statements about your feelings and observations. Questions turn an improvisation into a question-and-answer routine.

3. Avoid explanations about situations and feelings. If you are happy, show it. If you are afraid of the dark, show that. *Telling* is storytelling, not acting. Acting is *doing*.

With the class divided into groups of two persons each, select one incident around which to build your scene, and decide whether it will be the opening event, the climax, or the conclusion of an imagined play. You can get your material from any source you wish. Some suggestions are the pictures in this book, newspaper clippings, cartoon captions, and anecdotes from magazines; events in your own or your parents' and friends' lives; or historical and literary sources. The suggestions at the end of this chapter may be of use.

Decide on the main idea you want to put over and on the general mood. You may do any kind of scene you want—comic or sad, fanciful or realistic—but each character must be a distinct type, totally different from the others. You should avoid such generalized scenes as those involving students in a dormitory or members of a basketball team. The greater the difference in age, personality, and type among the characters, the more contrast your scenes will contain.

Work out your stage setting carefully, knowing just where the entrances will be. You probably will have nothing more than a table and a few chairs to work around. You will not use any doors, windows, or heavy props. Suggest entrances and major props by what you do. You may carry any small articles you need since this is improvisation, not pantomime. In turning the classroom into a street, a ballroom, a theater dressing room, an office, or whatever you choose, you are developing not only your own imagination but also that of the rest of the class. They will see whatever you make clear to them, first by your explanation and then by your performance.

Visualize your character in detail and try to feel emotions. Make up dialogue that you feel will be appropriate to your character and to the situation. Before you enter, take on the physical attitude of your character in accordance with the character's age, size, and mood. Walk in character as you enter, and remember that your audience is out front.

Onstage, talk loudly enough to be heard and do not hide behind other people or pieces of furniture. Try not to stand beside your scene partner all the time. Move about freely. Take plenty of time to speak and move, so that you can create a definite impression. Most important, keep in character all the time. Listen and speak as the character would in the situation, and lose yourself in appropriate actions and reactions.

As you get more practice in improvising scenes, you can begin to learn some of the subtleties of acting. You will find that you can stand still without fidgeting and that you can make definite gestures when you feel the need, avoiding the little, aimless ones. When you must move to a chair or toward another person, learn to go straight there without rambling. If you are to pick up an article, actually see it before you touch it. By observation you will learn that the head usually reacts first (sometimes the eyes), then the torso, and then the rest of the body.

INDIVIDUAL IMPROVISATIONS

After working with a partner, you can try to develop individual characters in definite situations, reacting to imaginary persons or crowds, or showing particular moods. It is harder to work by yourself than with another person, but you can, by yourself, take more time to create a personality and to feel more deeply.

In these improvisations, keep relaxed and have fun. Do not allow yourself to feel embarrassed by the reactions of other students. Do not let classmates who seem to fall right into a character without apparent effort discourage you from trying to do the same thing.

INDIVIDUAL EXERCISES USING A MIRROR

Your teacher will provide a full-length mirror to help you prepare for the following improvisational exercises.

1. You or your teacher will furnish props, such as canes, umbrellas, fans, glasses, and books. You will use one of these props. After 30 seconds of preparation time before the mirror, you will present a 30-second pantomimed characterization built around the prop you used. It is recommended that the mirror be located away from the class's view so that you can concentrate alone. While one person performs, another can be preparing.
    Variation 1. Use the prop you have chosen for something other than its normal function. Improvise a character using the prop's new function. For example, you could change a cane into a laser beam.

2. You or your teacher will furnish a costume item, such as a hat, gloves, a coat, a scarf, a shawl, or a vest. Again, use the mirror to see how the costume can help convey a character. Then, using the costume item as a key to revealing your character, present a 1-minute character pantomime.

3. Bring a mask to class. It can be a Halloween mask or other commercial mask or a mask you have made for yourself. Use the mirror for preparation. Pantomime the character the mask suggests for 30 seconds.

Variation 1. Place all the masks brought to class on a table. Two or three persons may choose someone else's mask and take it to the mirror to work out a character. After 1 minute of preparation, improvise a scene around the new masked character that you created.

Variation 2. Add sounds or speech to any of these exercises.

If you keep practicing all sorts of characterizations on the spur of the moment at home, you will find doing improvisations in class much easier. Try being all sorts of people—Joan of Arc at her trial, a star during a television interview, an Olympic champion after a big event, and so on. Get yourself into all sorts of emotional states, laughing out loud and even crying if you can. With no one around, you will not feel silly. And the practice will show in your classwork because you will be more responsive and sensitive to changing moods and situations. You will find your voice and body becoming more flexible and expressive and your impersonations much better.

Remember: Improvise! Fill the "gaps" made by your own or another performer's actions or lines, and make "gaps" for others to fill. Feel free to experiment, using motivation as your impelling force. Imagination will be the key to characterization, so make every look, every line, and every action count. Every now and then, you will realize that you have caught another personality, if just for a moment, and will know what it is to feel like an actor.

APPLICATIONS

The following suggestions for improvisations provide a step-by-step progression from simple emotional responses to the improvised writing of a play.

Emotional Responses

1. Express the following feelings through, first, a facial response and, second, a facial response combined with a bodily reaction. Try to recall a personal experience that caused you to experience these feelings.

love	jealousy	grief	shock
hope	ecstasy	embarrassment	sympathy
fear	kindness	understanding	patience
bitterness	scorn	irritability	fickleness
skepticism	rebuke	disbelief	mockery
longing	sarcasm	pleading	courage
greed	happiness	mourning	surprise

2. Place the following items in individual paper sacks. Each member of the class must reach into a sack, feel the object that is in it, say "one thousand one" silently, and then convey the sensation received by a facial expression and a one-sentence reaction. After experiencing the sensations of sight, sound, touch, smell, and taste associated with the objects in the following list, practice recalling your sensory

Pantomime

1. Act like the following:

a tear drop	a raspy hinge
a floating cloud	an animated doll
a clock	a weather vane
a delicate snowflake	a spinning top

2. React bodily to the following:

a sharp slap	a pin prick	a stubbed toe
a driving rain	a piercing siren	frostbitten fingers
a biting wind	a moonless night	hay down your back
sticky tape	rain on the roof	scorching pavement

3. React facially to these words:

red	twilight	butterfly	springtime
here	encourage	perpetual	tranquility
friend	fool	Sunday afternoon	loneliness

4. Create a place by pantomiming the use of three objects associated with the setting. Some sample settings are below.

a cemetery	a pet shop	an amusement park
a bus	a toy store	a restaurant
a flower shop	a train station	a dentist's office

   Variation 1. Write the names of objects on slips of paper. Fold the slips of paper, and place them in a hat or a box. Each student takes a slip of paper and begins to create the object for the class by using that object in pantomime.
   Variation 2. Write activities, places, situations, or characters from a play on slips of paper. Through pantomime, act out whatever is written on the paper.

5. Play "living statues." Work with a partner. One person shapes the other into a position expressive of an emotion.

Vocal Responses

Make up a list of statements similar to the examples below. Exchange your list with that of a classmate, and react to one statement as five different people.

Examples of statement:	You have just said, "I don't like asparagus!"
Respond as:	Your mother, your doctor, your waiter, your hostess, your little daughter
Statement:	You have just said, "I've been asked to the prom!"
Respond as:	Your best friend, a jealous rival, your ex-boyfriend, the teacher whose class you have interrupted, your father, your mother, your sister, your brother

Improvisation is the foundation of interpretation. These student clowns entertain harried commuters at a Chicago railroad station.

impressions without handling the real object. Such sensory recall is an essential tool for the actor. There will be times when you must drink hot coffee onstage without the luxury of real hot coffee. The heat, the taste, and the smell of the coffee must come from your imagination.

sandpaper	cold cream	raisins
cooked spaghetti	feathers	knitting yarn
a cotton ball	a flower petal	cracker crumbs
rough tree bark	a piece of lettuce	a marble
a pickle	crumpled cellophane	an ice cube
sawdust	a baby's pacifier	a piece of fur
a sprig of parsley	steel wool	wet paper
an English walnut	a grape peel	a sardine
burlap	whipped cream	a spring

3. React to the following sentences with one gesture or bodily stance.

Your face is red!	Do you always look like that?
I hate you!	I think you're frightened.
You have pretty eyes.	You're standing on my toe.
I love you.	How much do you really weigh?
Who do you think will win?	Did you understand what I said?
Relax, and count to ten.	Does the medicine taste so bad?

Change of Command

Two to five persons will begin improvising a scene based on a simple situation. One person, either your teacher or a member of the class, will act as director. As the scene develops, the director will call out various emotions to specific members of the performing group. As each individual is called, that person must immediately assume the emotion mentioned. The improvisation is to continue without pausing as the emotions are called out.

Variation. Other elements, such as age, situation, weather, time (day, year, historical period), or mood, may be changed.

I Want

This is a good two-person activity to develop a sense of conflict within a scene. Each student wants to fulfill a specific objective. One student may want the other's shoe, while the other student wants to leave the room. The object of the improvisation is to get what you want without asking for it.

Variation. Improvise the above activity as a well-known stock character, comic-strip character, or television character. Stock characters might be such types as hypochondriacs, wealthy snobs, athletic stars, misers, domineering individuals, intellectuals, and so on.

Famous People

1. Make up a list of quotations, real or imaginary. Improvise the situation leading up to the quotation and end with the quotation.

   Examples: "Et tu, Brute?"

   "Give me liberty, or give me death!"

   "Damn the torpedoes, full speed ahead!"

   "Ask not what your country can do for you, but what you can do for your country."

   "You may fire when ready, Gridley."

   "Which way did they go, George?"

2. With a single stance, a single gesture, or a combination of the two, portray the following:

   Leonardo da Vinci painting the "Mona Lisa"

   Ben Franklin flying his kite

   Your favorite star accepting his or her first Oscar

   Annie Sullivan teaching Helen Keller sign language

   Nero playing his lyre while Rome burned

   Betsy Ross sewing the American flag

   Now create your own list from contemporary situations and people.

3. Improvise the dialogue and actions of famous people in the historical situations for which they are remembered.

4. Repeat your improvisation of Exercise 3, but change the ending.

5. Have several famous personalities respond in character to the same imaginary situation.

Scripts

1. From a description of the following situations, characters, or both, develop some scripts.
   a. Two salesclerks are discussing a department manager they dislike. The manager appears and accuses one of them of having stolen a necklace that has disappeared. Work out your own solution.
   b. A father meets his 15-year-old daughter in the hall at midnight on her return from a party that ended at ten-thirty. Show what happens when they meet.

2. The microcosm is ''the world on the head of a pin''—people from varied walks of life are thrown together by chance to face the same situation.
   a. An elevator is caught between floors. Work out your own characters, their reactions, and the conclusion.
   b. Do the same thing with people in a lifeboat together, in a taxi stuck in a traffic jam, and on a subway during a power failure.
   c. Read some works of literature having a microcosmic structure—for example, ''The Outcasts of Poker Flats'' or ''The Ambitious Guest''—and improvise a similar situation.

3. Read about the stock characters in the commedia dell'arte in Chapter 10, and write your own scripts using these characters.

Literary Sketches

1. Improvise a scene from ''The Devil and Daniel Webster'' by Stephen Vincent Benét.

2. Improvise a scene from one of Guy de Maupassant's short stories, such as ''The Necklace'' or ''A Piece of String.''

3. Improvise a scene from ''The Lady or the Tiger'' by Frank R. Stockton.

4. Improvise a scene where the Fox and the Cat tell Pinnochio of the wonders of Candyland.

5. Improvise the Mad Hatter's tea party or the trial scene from *Alice's Adventures in Wonderland*.

6. Improvise Dorothy's first meetings with the Scarecrow, the Tin Woodsman, and the Cowardly Lion in *The Wizard of Oz*.

7. Improvise a scene from a Greek myth, such as ''Jason and the Golden Fleece.''

8. Improvise one of Aesop's fables.

9. Improvise one of James Thurber's fables.

10. Improvise a Bible story, such as David and Goliath, Joseph and his brothers, or Samson and Delilah.

If You Were . . .

After deciding what roles each person will play in the scene, reenact some event, real or imaginary, such as the following:

1. You are members of the Roman Senate when Julius Caesar has just been stabbed to death. Each of you must recall something Caesar did to you that makes you support or reject the conspirators.

2. At lunch, someone rushes in with the news that a spaceship has just landed in City Park. Speculate on ship, occupants, origin, and so forth.

3. Just given an engagement ring, tell the world about it, including your ex-boyfriends and your fiancé's former admirers.

4. The Duke Godiva and his court are together when word is brought in that Lady Godiva has just ridden through the streets.

5. You are the only five survivors at the Alamo.

Rumors Are Flying

Begin with a simple rumor and expand it, each person adding a new detail, character, twist, and so on. Tell the next person about it by improvised action until you have created a working script.

Potpourri

Now, after everyone has been in at least two improvisations, dream up new situations, rewrite scripts you have previously used, or make new scripts from news articles or works of literature. Use some of the characters the class has created, and let them play out the new situations.

Creating the Improvised Play

Divide the class into groups of five to eight persons. In a discussion, each group is to work out a script that could be made into a simple, improvised play. Decide on the theme of your play, the characters, the basic conflicts, and the style. After improvising the script several times to establish some blocking, lines, and workable scenes, fill in your outline until you have a skeletal script. Improvise two or three more times, and you will be able to set down a written script created by the improvised approach to acting.

BIBLIOGRAPHY

Rockwood, Jerome: *The Craftsmen of Dionysus: An Approach to Acting,* Scott, Foresman, Glenview, Illinois, 1966.

Spolin, Viola: *Improvisation for the Theater: A Handbook of Teaching and Directing Techniques,* Northwestern University Press, Evanston, Illinois, 1963.

CHAPTER THREE

Pantomime and Mime

Pantomime is the art of telling a story without speech. Pantomime is often called the "art of silence." Because all actors are seen before being heard or understood, the art of acting without using speech is the first technical phase of your interpretive training. It was also the first form of acting. Pantomime preceded the drama in ancient times, kept pace with it through the Middle Ages and Renaissance, and threatened to overshadow it in the first quarter of the twentieth century with the silent picture. Throughout the ages, pantomime has gone hand in hand with dancing and was the forerunner of classical ballet.

Traditional pantomimes have delighted European and Asian audiences for centuries. Traditional pantomimes attained their highest form in the commedia dell'arte of Italy in the sixteenth century. Emphasizing polished bodily response in formalized scenes, the famous characters of Harlequin, Columbine, Pantaloon, Pierrot, and Pierrette have survived in many popular one-act plays. It was Marcel Marceau who made Americans aware of the acting power of mime. His cross-country tours of full-evening programs onstage and his appearances as guest star on television introduced many people to this ancient art form. If you ever see him in person or on film, watch carefully every expression and movement, for they are perfect examples of the original art.

Much of current drama is pantomimic. *Stop the World—I Want to Get Off*, *Rosencrantz and Guildenstern Are Dead*, *Pippin*, and *The Fantasticks* use pantomime a great deal.

VALUE OF PANTOMIME

A course in pantomime is often the introduction to acting study. Courses in mime, movement, and bodily coordination—under various labels—are a part of the training in all specialized schools of drama and in many universities.

You, of course, must remember that technique in acting is never an end in itself. It is only a valuable means of making your stage movements and facial expressions effective and your voice and speech audible. Acting techniques will help you communicate more effectively, not only in acting but also in daily living. Because the trend in modern theater is for action to take the place of words, directors are looking for actors who can communicate physically.

Your work with pantomime logically follows your experience with improvisation. It will give you the technical means by which gesture and movement may become pictorially effective. As a student of drama, you should make every effort to develop a sound technique in the efficient and flexible use of your body. By so doing, you will be able to meet the inner demands of a sensitive role while under the stress and strain of performance before an audience.

PURPOSE OF PANTOMIME

A responsive, expressive body is an actor's greatest asset today. For most people, physical coordination and poise are more a matter of training than heredity. The purpose of pantomime is to encourage meaningful movement, significant gesture, and animated facial expression. These can be acquired through daily exercise to keep your muscles supple.

The Kabuki theater of Japan is a stylized form of pantomime. Kabuki actors are rigorously trained to use bodily coordination, gesture, and facial expression to tell classical Japanese tales.

The purpose of pantomime is to encourage meaningful movement and gesture and animated facial expression.

Pantomime demands a flexible and expressive body. Because of the close relationship between physical and emotional attitudes, it is important that you learn to use your body correctly and effectively by conscious exercise until the right habits are set up and become automatic. All forms of correct physical exercise are important, especially those that develop muscular coordination and freedom of movement.

To some extent the body is the outer expression of the inner personality. But the inner personality is also partly the result of physical attitudes. Physical exhaustion after acting with intense emotion, performing while ill, and weeping at moments of great joy or sorrow all show the close relationship of our internal and external responses.

Since an actor's personal appearance is a large part of character portrayal, the first work in pantomime deals with normal posture, movement, and gesture. Gracefulness is the happy medium between overrelaxation or flabbiness and overtension or rigidity. Perfect coordination of all parts of the body is a basic requirement of bodily poise and expressive movement.

PHYSICAL TRAINING FOR PANTOMIME

Any exercise that develops physical coordination is valuable for you as you prepare to perform. Fencing and dancing are required courses in most drama schools. Tennis, golf, swimming, and skiing are good hobbies. And jogging, isometric exercises, which can be practiced at any time, and the deep breathing of yoga are among the many forms of physical exercise recommended. Whenever possible, do not take a car, an elevator, or a bus—walk. This is still one of the best exercises.

At all times, your body should move or sit as a whole. From the top of your head to the tips of your fingers and toes, your body should be expressive. As a matter of fact, it always is expressive, but not always in the way you might desire. For example, a slovenly walk, a rigid or slouching posture, irritatingly aimless gestures, or a wooden face reveal your personality just as clearly as do purposeful, vigorous movements and a radiant, mobile face. Nine times out of ten, the world will take you at your "face value." You are judged first by your appearance and manner, only much later by what you say and how you say it.

Relaxation

Behind bodily poise and skill in action is relaxation. This is a matter of inner composure and mental awareness as well as physical flexibility. Successful actors, like athletes, must not be tense, emotionally "uptight," or physically stiff. You should learn right away to let go consciously all over, from the top of your head to the soles of your feet, whenever you feel a sense of strain on the stage or in real life. A few deep breaths and loosening muscles all over also help.

Before starting a daily practice of physical exercises, you must get your body relaxed. The following exercises will help you relax. Repeat each exercise four times—first to the right and then to the left, or forward and then backward.

1. Raise, lower, and rotate your head without moving your shoulders. Let it roll freely, without the slightest tension.

2. Rotate your shoulders up and down, forward and back, and in circles.

3. Move your arms in wide circles, first close to the body and then at shoulder height.

4. Rotate your lower arms from the elbow, toward and away from the body. Hold your arms straight down and slightly away from your body.

5. Rotate your hands from the wrists.

6. Move your arms horizontally and vertically, with wrists leading.

7. Shake your hands vigorously, keeping them completely relaxed.

8. Open and close your fists, stretching the fingers apart and draw them together.

9. Do the five-finger exercises. Hold your hands out in front of you. Place the heels of your hands side by side with the open palms facing you. Make each hand into a fist. Roll back each finger one at a time—little, middle, ring, first, and thumb. Alternate one finger of the right hand with one finger of the left hand. Return hands to fists, closing one finger at a time.

10. Bend your body forward, back, and to each side.

11. Clasping your hands together, push your arms vigorously above your head. Then rotate your body, keeping your head within your arms.

12. Rotate each leg in circles, kick as high as possible, and swing each leg forward and back.

13. Rise on your toes, bend your knees, and sit on your heels.

14. Rotate each foot at the ankle.

15. Pick up marbles with your toes.

A complete process for relaxation is given on pages 55 to 58 for your voice work. It is advisable for you to practice this after the above exercises.

Posture

Your posture is fundamental, not only to your health but also to your personal appearance. Often good posture offsets a plain face, and certainly in the theater it is of far greater importance. Therefore, the next step in training the body deals with normal posture, movement, and gesture.

To stand properly, hold your body easily erect with chest high, chin up, back flat, and arms and legs straight but not tense. Keep one foot slightly in front of the other, the weight centering on the ball of the forward foot. The following exercise will help you develop good posture. It should be repeated many times.

1. Stand easily erect with your weight on the balls of your feet.

2. Bend forward, perfectly relaxed, with your loosely hanging arms almost touching the floor.

3. Place your right hand on your chest and your left hand at the small of your back.

4. Raise your body to an upright position, expanding the torso so that you feel your hands being pushed apart.

5. Bring your head to an upright position last in the sequence of moves. Hold the chin at right angles to the throat.

6. Drop your arms to the sides. Shift your weight to the ball of one foot and move forward. Keep your chest high, head erect, and the small of your back flat.

Walking

In walking, maintain good posture and a sense of exuberant alertness. Face the world squarely with high chest, erect body, and direct glance. ''Thinking yourself tall'' may help you carry yourself gracefully. Although the heel strikes the ground a fraction of a second before the toes, your movement should spring from the balls of your feet, and it should be easy, poised, and rhythmical.

The length of your step will be modified by many elements, such as your height, build, and physical energy. However, avoid striding, mincing, plodding, or tottering. Toeing straight ahead with your weight on the balls of your feet is the natural way to walk, and walking in a straight line keeps the moving silhouette narrow. Except when playing parts that call for it, never place your feet more than two inches apart. Your body should swing easily from the hips, and your arms should swing in easy opposition to your legs. Beware of habitually looking at the ground.

When you turn, rotate on the balls of your feet, shifting your weight from one foot to the other. Never turn on your heels or cross one foot over the other, tripping yourself. Turn your entire body, including your head.

Your posture is important in maintaining good stage presence. Miriam Colon shows great dignity in her easily erect stance.

When walking, maintain good posture and a sense of alertness. Even in this still photograph, you can feel the aliveness of the actresses as they move across the stage.

Remember to hold yourself easily erect when standing or walking. Avoid the common habits of leaning forward, holding one shoulder higher than the other, looking down as you walk, dragging your feet, walking on your heels, keeping your feet apart as you walk, or tensing any part of your body.

These exercises from daily life are designed to help you stand and walk in the right way.

Imagine you are standing:

1. At the microphone in your auditorium, ready to give a speech.
2. In the doorway of a potential employer, waiting for an interview.
3. In the garden, watching a cardinal.
4. At the curb, waiting to dash across the street when the lights change.
5. At the airport, waiting for friends to arrive.

Imagine you are walking:

1. On a sandy beach with a fresh wind blowing over the waves.
2. On Fifth Avenue in New York City, with the skyscrapers and church spires rising above you.

3. In a forest of tall trees on a lovely fall day.
4. On a ballroom floor at a formal dance.
5. On the stage, trying out for a part.

Walking up and down stairs is an excellent exercise. Place one foot in front of the other, and lift your weight from the balls of the feet. Think yourself tall and vigorous, keeping a high chest and head. Rest your hand lightly on the banister. Try not to look at the stairs.

Sitting

Getting to, into, and out of a chair is often a problem. First, decide where and why you are being seated. What is the best way to the chair, stool, or bench you will occupy? Normally you walk directly there, but sometimes you have to plan how to get around people and obstacles on the way. When you arrive, you turn and back up until the calf of your leg touches the chair and you can sit.

When sitting, maintain an erect position. Keep the base of your spine at a 90° angle to the seat, and lean easily against the back of the chair. Your hands will ordinarily rest in your lap or on the arms of the chair. Crossing your arms on your

When sitting, keep an erect position. Good sitting posture makes these actresses appear relaxed and in control of the moment.

chest or folding them restricts your breathing and looks tense. Avoid playing with buttons, jewelry, or your hair. Just sit easily erect against the chair. Your feet may be crossed at the ankles, or one foot may be placed slightly in front of the other. Avoid crossing your legs, spreading your feet apart, and resting your hands or elbows on your knees.

In rising, let your chest lead, not your head. Keep your weight balanced on the balls of your feet, placing one foot slightly forward and using the rear one as a lever in pushing yourself up. Never hang on to the arms of the chair or push yourself up from them. Take a deep breath while rising. This relaxes the throat, gives a sense of control, keeps the chest high, and leads into a good standing position.

Crossing and Turning

The middle area of the stage is called center, the front is downstage, and the back is upstage. The actor's right is stage right and his or her left, stage left as the actor faces the audience. To cross means to move from one position to another. On entering the stage, the actor leads with the upstage foot to turn the body toward the audience. Normally all turns are made to the front. When making turns, rotate on the balls of your feet.

Try these exercises in crossing and turning, walking, sitting, and rising.

1. Enter stage right to speak at a microphone downstage center. Cross to center and turn downstage. Stand with your right foot slightly advanced and weight forward. To leave, turn right, shift weight to left foot, and go off right.

2. Enter stage right and cross to center. Remember that you have forgotten something and turn front, rotating on balls of the feet. Go back right.

3. Enter left and walk diagonally upstage to up center where there is an imaginary bookcase. Get a book and go off right.

4. Enter right to wait for someone at a store entrance up center. Turn front and look around. Then turn and pace up and down, looking into the windows on both sides of the entrance. Each time you reach center, turn to look around. Finally give up and go off left.

5. Enter stage right as if to meet a friend. Cross to chair at left center. Without looking at chair, turn front, touching chair with calf of upstage leg. Shift weight to upstage foot and lower body into the chair, keeping head and chest high. See your friend approaching stage left. Rise, pushing with the upstage leg. Shift your weight to forward foot and step with back foot. Move to front center. Meet your friend and exit left.

6. Enter a living room. Greet the hostess and be seated on a couch. Rise to greet a person of influence and be seated again. Rise, bow, and leave.

Falling

Some roles will require you to fall onstage. Practicing the following exercise will enable you to fall safely and convincingly.

1. Relax, and sway or stagger backward.

2. Sway forward, dropping the hands and arms.

3. Relax from the ankles and bend the knees.

4. Pivot slowly and, as you do so, go closer and closer to the floor. Lower the shoulder that is closest to the floor and slide down.

5. Land on the side of the leg. Roll on the hip. Catch your weight on your forearm.

6. Lower the head to the ground.

Gesture

Gesture is the movement of any part of the body to help express an idea. It may be a lift of the eyebrow, a toss of the head, or a sweeping movement of the arm and hand. A change of attitude is usually expressed first by the eyes, then by the response of the mouth and facial muscles, then by the reaction of the torso, and lastly by the motion of the arm, hand, and finger tips. These movements are so rapid that they seem simultaneous, but in training exercises you must try to follow their natural sequence.

Gesture is the movement of any part of the body to help express an idea. What words might have accompanied this gesture?

A few practical suggestions regarding the use of the arm and hand may help you develop controlled gestures. However, you should remember that all technical practice must eventually become second nature if your gestures are not to appear artificial and affected.

Use exercises to free your tight muscles and establish habits of graceful coordination. Every movement of the arm should begin at the shoulder, pass through the elbow and wrist, and "slip off" the ends of the fingers. It is most important that every arm gesture finish at the finger tips. Nothing is more ineffective than an arm movement in which the fingers are curled flabbily at the ends. The movement should be from the body, and the wrist should lead in horizontal and vertical gestures. Every gesture must have a definite purpose. If there is no purpose, there should be no gesture. Since the sole purpose of a gesture is to emphasize or clarify a thought or feeling, it is better to do nothing at all than to make meaningless movements. Try to cultivate definite, clear-cut, telling gestures.

When doing the following exercises, use your entire body, but focus your attention on the objects mentioned. See the object, touch it, and finally react. Let your eyes, eyebrows, and mouth show your reactions. Lift your arms from the shoulder, letting the movement pass through the elbow and hand and end in the tips of your fingers. Show the shape, weight, and size of any object you pick up. After you have shown that you have picked it up, be sure to hold it or put it down definitely.

1. You are walking in a garden. Pick flowers from plants, bushes, and vines, and pull weeds. Select fruit from a tree, taste it, and throw it away. Select another piece and eat it.

2. You go into the garage and find a flat tire. Fix it.

3. You arrive at an airport shortly before take-off time. You are carrying a suitcase, an umbrella, a box of candy, and magazines. You drop your suitcase and everything spills out. Put down everything else you are carrying in the process of recovering the contents of your suitcase. Retrieve everything and lift the suitcase last of all.

4. You are wandering around a department store. You feel the fabrics, smell the perfume, and look at costume jewelry without buying anything. You see a display of hats. Try on several. Buy one and wear it out, adjusting it in a mirror before leaving the store.

ACTING WITHOUT WORDS

Pantomime is the basis of characterization, which in turn is the basis of acting. People express themselves in their bodily actions before they speak, so it is natural that the first step in acting is to create personalities without the use of words.

The interdependence of bodily response and feeling begins at birth and continues through life. For example, if you habitually slump as you walk, draw down your face, and look at the ground, you will soon become physically and mentally lazy and emotionally listless. Note that listless people do slump, draw down their face, look at the ground, and drag their feet. If, therefore, you want to impersonate such a character, you can do those things and give a pretty good imitation. However, it would be better dramatically to imagine you are so utterly lazy, bored, and weary with life that your chest will naturally slump, your face droop, and your feet drag.

In other words, try to feel the emotion first and allow it to gain control of your body, but then consciously respond from your head to your feet. You will probably respond awkwardly at first. Then apply the technical principles and train yourself to respond not only sincerely but artistically as well.

General Principles

General principles of the techniques of pantomime are based on what human beings do physically in response to emotional stimuli. Your richest source of authentic material for pantomimes is careful observation of people in daily life, on the stage and screen, and individually or in crowds. Watch facial expressions, mannerisms, gestures, and ways of walking. You may find it profitable to analyze the movements of television, movie, and stage actors. Also note how your own bodily responses reflect your feelings.

A responsive and expressive body is an actor's greatest asset. Alfred Lunt and Lynn Fontanne in Durrenmatt's The Visit.

There are two phases of your work with pantomime. You have studied the first—exercises to relax your muscles and free your body for quick expression of feeling. The second phase is the creation of characterizations in which feeling prompts a bodily response. Both activities demand concentration of thought and interest in detail. You will find it takes a great deal of time and practice to create the exact effect you desire.

Studying technical principles and applying them mechanically will limber the body and train it to react effectively. If you practice the physical exercises and then work out pantomimes, you will realize suddenly that you are carrying yourself better and reacting to your ideas with spontaneous facial expressions and gestures as you have never done before.

Physical Principles

There are a few established principles that affect acting. They are based on what people often do in real life as well as on the best way to communicate a feeling or idea. The following are some of these principles. Try to apply them as you work out your pantomimes.

1. The chest is the key to all bodily action.

2. The wrist leads most hand gestures.

3. Keep the arms away from the body when gesturing. Except on specific occasions when it is necessary for communication purposes, do not gesture above the head or below the waistline.

4. Arms and hands should always be moved in curves, never in straight lines, unless you are deliberately trying to give the impression of awkwardness or being ill-at-ease.

5. Positive emotions, such as love, honor, courage, and sympathy, expand the body and tend toward a high chest and head, free movement, broad gestures, and animated gestures.

6. Negative emotions, such as hate, greed, fear, and suffering, contract the body and tend toward a shrunken chest, tense movement, restricted gestures, and drawn features.

7. Facial expression—the use of the eyes, eyebrows, and mouth—usually precedes action.

8. Whenever possible, make all gestures with the upstage arm, the one away from the audience, and avoid all tendency to cover the face.

9. Some exaggeration of bodily response is essential to being clearly understood.

In J. B., Archibald MacLeish's contemporary play based on the Book of Job, J. B.'s face clearly expresses anguish as he implores God to tell him why he must suffer. This play is an allegory. The actors are Lane Bradbury and Pat Hingle.

10. Always keep the audience in mind and direct reactions to it.

11. All action must be definite in concept and execution, and all movement must be clearly motivated.

Standard Pantomimic Expressions

The suggestions below are standard pantomimic expressions. After you have familiarized yourself with them, choose one that stimulates your imagination and create a character and situation to fit it.

Body as a Whole

1. Feet together, weight on both feet, and body passive represent timidity, indifference, or trained self-control.

2. Weight carried to the front foot with the body leaning slightly forward represents interest, persuasion, sympathy, enthusiasm, and positive emotions.

3. Weight carried to the rear foot represents fear, hesitation, deep thought, amazement, and negative emotions.

4. Shrunken chest and bowed head represent old age, envy, greed, and negative emotions.

Hands and Arms

1. Arms extended, palms up, are appropriate for pleading, presenting ideas, and offering sympathy. Let movement reach fingertips.

2. Arms drawn up or back with palms down are appropriate for negation, refusal, condemnation, fear, horror, and negative ideas.

3. Clenched fists represent anger and effort at control.

4. Pointed finger and extended arm are useful for pointing out, commanding, and directing.

Feet and Legs

1. Feet apart with legs straight denotes arrogance or stolidity.

2. Feet apart with legs bent denotes lack of bodily control, old age, great fatigue.

3. Tapping the foot depicts irritation, impatience, nervousness.

4. Twisting one foot denotes embarrassment.

5. Feet apart, head high, and arms akimbo represent conceit, scorn, contempt, and self-assertiveness.

Head and Face

1. Head raised, eyebrows lifted, eyes wide, and mouth open represent fear, horror, joy, and surprise.

2. Head raised, eyebrows lifted, and mouth drawn down depict comic bewilderment or a quizzical state.

3. Head down, eyebrows down, and mouth set or twisted by biting lips show worry, meditation, and suffering.

4. Twisted mouth and eyebrows can show petulance, irony, anger, pain, sophisticated attitudes, and various subtle emotions.

5. Raised eyebrows, wide eyes, smiling or open lips may depict innocence, stupidity, or coquetry.

Characterization

Characterization in pantomime involves placing a character in a situation and showing that character's feelings through nonverbal expression. This entails two mental processes—imitation and imagination. You must develop a memory bank of emotions by carefully observing other people. When you see a person involved in a highly emotional situation, observe facial expressions, gestures, and body language. Draw upon your observations when creating parts to be sure your characterization is true to life. However, this is only the beginning, for you must use your imagination to place and maintain yourself in the part you are playing.

After you have put on some comfortable clothes that leave your body free for action, run through the relaxing and other practice exercises. Then imagine yourself in situations such as the following:

1. You are alone in your home. Go to the television set and adjust it. You find that you are watching the climax of a horror picture. Suddenly you hear a sound at the window. As you listen, the sound continues. The window slowly opens and a hand appears. You seize a book and hurl it at the hand, which promptly disappears. You tiptoe to the window, lock it, and fall into a chair, exhausted.

2. Practice falling several times (see page 31). Then imagine yourself in the following situations.

    a. You have been wounded in the shoulder. Fall from loss of blood.

    b. You have stubbed your toe on roller skates left on the floor. Fall, get up, and put away the skates, limping from a sprained ankle.

    c. You suddenly feel faint and fall. Then you recover, get up, and stagger to a chair.

    d. You are walking downstairs. You slip and fall down several steps.

3. Relating each to an imagined situation, show fear, agony, appeal, embarrassment, hate, sympathy, indecision, power, weariness, and joy. First use

Carol Channing recording Ludwig Bemelman's Madeline *for Caedmon Records. Notice that, though she has no audience, Ms. Channing reacts to the reading with her whole body.*

your face, next your hands, and then your feet. Finally, express these emotions with your entire body.

Showing Emotional Responses

Emotion affects our bodies in various ways. In practicing the exercises below, be sure that you feel the emotion first. Then let your face and body respond.

1. You have quarreled with your girlfriend or boyfriend. You are standing by a window, looking out, frowning, and biting your lip. Your chest is sunken; your body is slumped. The phone rings. Your face lights up, with eyes wide and lips smiling. Your chest is up. You wait expectantly to hear your name called. Then you run to the phone and lift the receiver, holding it in your upstage hand. Let your face reflect the conversation. When you hang up, you show by your movements whether the quarrel is over or not.

2. You are a feeble old man or woman coming out to sit in the sun. You walk with short, uncertain steps. Your head is down, and your face, drawn. You sit down slowly with great effort and gradually relax as the sun warms you. Someone calls you, and you express your irritation by frowning and shaking your head. Then you rise, pushing yourself up from the arms of the chair. Hurry away as fast as your stiffness of limbs will allow, expressing worry and agitation.

3. Pantomime individual speeches from selections in this book. Pick selections with contrasting emotions.

INDIVIDUAL PANTOMIMES

Now you can begin working out real pantomimes involving careful planning, rehearsing, and presentation before the class. The individual pantomimes may well be divided into imitations of people you know and imaginary characterizations.

Preparation

In your pantomime of a real person, you should first determine that individual's chief characteristics. Is that person friendly? Timid? Boisterous? Suspicious? Glamorous? Physically vigorous? Discontented? Next, note mentally the details of the person's habitual facial expression, especially the eyes and mouth. Observe how that person holds the head, moves the hands, and walks. Decide what makes that person different from any other human being. Then place your character in a situation. (You need not have actually seen your character in such a situation, but you must be able to imagine how that person would react to it.) Take plenty of time to think through the exact reactions to your imaginary situation. Visualize them as if you were watching your character on a television screen. Finally, imitate what you have imagined your character would do.

In your imaginary characterizations, you should follow much the same procedure. You will, however, have to begin by inventing the details that will characterize the person you plan to play. What is your character's age? What are the physical traits? How does your character dress? What makes your character a distinctive individual? Only when you can see your character as clearly as someone you actually know will you be able to make your character live.

Whether your character is real or imaginary, you must work out in detail the situation in which you plan to place your character. Have your character enter a definite environment in a clear-cut state of mind and body. Invent something that will change the mood. The conclusion of your pantomime should leave no uncertainty in the mind of your audience about the mental state of the character when leaving the stage.

You will also need to visualize in detail the setting of your pantomime. Be sure you know the exact position of the doors, windows, furniture, and props you will employ. Make the location of things clear to your audience. Always put objects back where you got them. Use your body as the reference point for the objects you use. For example, relate to the things in your setting as being eye-, chest-, waist-, or knee-high.

Size, shape, weight, resistance, texture, and condition are important elements in pantomime. Show your audience the exact *size* of an object wherever possible. In conveying its size to your audience, consider the height, length, and width of the object. Small objects, such as cups, books, and food, can be outlined with the hands. Large objects, such as furniture or shrubbery, require the involvement of your whole body. Extremely large objects, such as trees or houses, need to be outlined through eye and head movements.

Objects have different shapes. Some are round; some are square. Other common shapes are ovals, rectangles, and triangles. Convey *shape* as you do size, through the use of eyes, hands, and whole body.

Every item you handle has *weight*. A sack of popcorn does not weigh the same as a sack of sugar. A cement brick weighs more than a sack of sugar but far less than a gold brick. Through your pantomimed muscular tension, you convey an object's weight. Never let the audience have a vague notion of weight. For example, the idea that "something is being carried" is not specific enough. You must show that "a small, lightweight square box" is being carried, picked up, or put down.

Objects also have a quality called resistance. *Resistance* is the firmness or solidity of an object. An ice cube will become smaller as it melts. A balloon blown up changes in solidity when it bursts in your hands. A down-filled pillow gives far more when it is grasped in your hands than does a basketball. Pushing a baby carriage demonstrates less resistance than pushing a stalled automobile. Resistance also involves the object's response to your actions. If you pull a rope, does something go up or come toward you? If you pull an artificial rose petal, does it come off easily or must you yank at it?

The surfaces of objects have a definite texture. Determine the *texture* of your object. Is it rough or smooth? Jagged or rounded? Is the surface sandy? Pebbly? Prickly? Concentrate on that texture as you touch your object. Allow your senses to respond to what you are touching. The more sensorily involved you become with your object, the more expressive your reactions will be to that object. And you will convey through your facial expressions and body language your sensory reactions to your object. Touching a velvet cushion is very different from touching a cactus.

Many ideas or things that you use in your pantomimes will be in a particular state or have a particular condition that must be expressed through your actions. For example, changing states or conditions are hot to cold, solid to liquid, or youth to age. Specific degrees of a state or condition are sweetness, sourness, spiciness, brightness, or loudness. Motion is a condition you must also remember. Youth and the aged move differently. An antelope moves with grace as compared to a gorilla, which moves awkwardly. Planes are propelled into the air at takeoff, while ships glide away from a pier at launching time.

Last of all, assume the physical appearance of your character as nearly as you can. Feel yourself to be your character's age and size. Let your character's state of mind take possession of you until your face, hands, and feet are reacting as your character's would in the imagined situation.

While working out your individual pantomime, keep the following directions constantly in mind.

1. Set your mental stage in detail, knowing exactly how much space you are to use, the location of the furniture, and the shape, weight, and position of every imaginary prop you will be using. If you move an object, make very clear its shape, weight, and new position. After you have made your audience see your setting and props, you must remember not to break the illusion by shifting an article without clear motivation and action.

2. Visualize the appearance and emotional state of your character in minute detail.

3. Imagine yourself to be dressed in the clothes of your character. Make your audience see the weight, shape, and material of each garment and its effect upon you in your particular mood and situation.

4. Remember that in all dramatic work, the thought comes first—think, see, and feel before you move. Let your eyes respond first, then your face and head, and finally, the rest of your body. This is a *motivated sequence.*

5. Keep your action simple and clear-cut. Pantomime should not be a guessing game.

6. Keep every movement and expression visible at all times to your entire audience.

7. Never make a movement or gesture without a reason. Ask yourself: "Does it make clear who I am, how I feel, or why I feel as I do?" Take time to make every movement clear and definite.

8. Try out and analyze every movement and gesture until you are satisfied that it is the most truthful, effective, and direct means of expressing your idea or feeling.

9. Make only one gesture or movement at a time, but coordinate your entire body with it and focus the attention of the audience upon it.

10. Rehearse until you know that you have created a clear-cut characterization and that the action began definitely, remained clear throughout, and came to a conclusion.

11. Plan your introduction very carefully. It may be humorous or serious, but it must arouse interest in your character and the situation in which your character is placed. It also must make clear all the details of the setting and preliminary situation.

12. Plan the ending very carefully. You should either leave the stage in character or come back to your own personality and end with a bow or a smile.

SUGGESTIONS FOR INDIVIDUAL PANTOMIMES

If you find it difficult to get started, the following suggestions may help you. At first, it is not a bad idea to run through them all in rather rapid succession to get yourself limbered up physically and imaginatively. Then select one and work it out in detail, elaborating on mannerisms and concentrating on details. After creating a single study that satisfies you with its clarity, build up a sequence of events that brings about a change of mood and situation. Finally, build up to a definite emotional climax and conclusion. Such a pantomime will require hours of preparation before it will be ready for class presentation.

1. Standing erect, with your feet close together, suggest the following:

    a. A butler or maid
    b. A model waiting to display the latest fashions
    c. A critical older person contemptuously watching the behavior of the younger generation

2. With legs wide apart and a comfortable posture, represent the following:

   a. A warm-hearted host standing in front of the fireplace beaming at the guests
   b. An activist student addressing a mass meeting
   c. A contented farmer smoking a pipe and standing in the doorway studying the weather

3. With alert posture, one foot somewhat ahead of the other and your weight definitely placed on the ball of the forward foot, represent the following:

   a. A high school student watching a football game
   b. An energetic cheerleader addressing a mass meeting

4. With a similar posture, except that the weight is definitely shifted to the rear foot, impersonate the following:

   a. An old lady afraid to cross the street
   b. A mother disgusted with the caterpillar her child is showing her
   c. A student hesitating to ask a favor of the teacher
   d. A hunter terrified at seeing a snake swinging from a tree

5. Cross the room, suggesting by your posture and walk the following:

   a. A burglar stealing across an unfamiliar, dark room
   b. A vigorous athlete walking across the campus
   c. A Native American looking for enemies in the forest
   d. A murderer stealing up on a victim with uplifted knife
   e. A tired soldier marching in a parade
   f. A weary worker returning from a long, hard day at the office
   g. A criminal in the death cell awaiting a last-minute reprieve

6. Walk across the room, kneel, and kiss a lady's hand in the manner of the following:

   a. A knight of the Middle Ages in armor
   b. A cavalier of the court of Charles II, with a long curled wig, a stiff, outstanding coat with ruffled sleeves, and a plumed hat
   c. A modern boy burlesquing a romantic lover

7. Walk across the room and curtsy in the manner of the following characters:

   a. A colonial lady at a formal party in a full-skirted gown and towering headdress
   b. A beauty of the old South during the Civil War
   c. A timid country girl at the squire's house
   d. A naughty little girl at dancing school

8. Cross the room, sit in a chair, and rise as the following characters:

   a. A criminal in the witness box at the trial
   b. A coquettish old lady flirting with a handsome young man
   c. A miser counting money and listening for eavesdroppers

    d. A middle-aged gossip retelling the latest scandal

    e. A parent at the bedside of a sick child

    f. A king or queen dismissing his or her court

    g. A sleepy child trying to keep awake

    h. A teenager at a dance

    i. A frightened substitute teacher in the first class of the school year

    j. An angry traffic cop

9. Suggest, by smiling, the following characters:

    a. A seasick traveler trying to appear sociable

    b. A Sunday school teacher greeting some new students

    c. A tired clerk trying to sell a product to a fussy customer

10. Suggest, by facial expression, the following situations:

    a. A diner opening a rotten egg

    b. A small child taking a nasty-tasting medicine

    c. A junior high school student watching a sentimental movie on television

    d. A butler or maid admitting unwelcome guests

11. Assume the following characters as completely as you can. Sit or walk, as you choose, and include enough action to show them in a real situation:

    a. An egotistical, self-confident businessperson

    b. A conceited rock star

    c. A swaggering campus leader

    d. A distinguished society leader

    e. A patient trying to gain courage before going into a dentist's office

    f. An energetic and jovial stenographer

    g. A person bothered by a mosquito while trying to read

GROUP PANTOMIMES

Group pantomimes should follow your individual ones and eventually lead you into the acting of a short play. They will, therefore, demand even more careful planning and rehearsal time than you have devoted to your individual pantomimes. They may be based on plays, novels, stories, or such secondary sources as photographic magazines, newsreels, and films. Feel free, also, to draw upon the daily life about you.

Plan your story as you would a one-act play. Center it around one interesting situation that has a carefully worked out exposition, rising action, a climax, and a logical and clear-cut conclusion. Create an interesting setting and five or six strongly contrasted characters. Be sure that each character is a real personality. Motivate all entrances, exits, and side action, and be sure that all characters can be seen at all times. Avoid bunching, huddling behind furniture, or standing in stiff lines. Your stage picture should be well balanced and attractive, and attention should always be focused on the center of interest. Rehearse together until you have a unified whole in which each character is a living, breathing person. Do not rush your action, for the audience must be able to follow the development of all the roles. Take plenty of time to tell your story effectively and pictorially. Remember that you are limited to visual means of presenting your ideas. Try to build your plot around an emotional situation with considerable human interest. Avoid trite material. Be original, imaginative, and painstaking.

SUGGESTIONS FOR GROUP PANTOMIMES

The suggestions below may be useful to you. Be sure you plan the entrances and exits carefully and keep the action clear and unhurried. See that each character is a distinct personality and that the stage picture is well balanced at all times.

1. A boy and a girl quarrel and make up.

2. Several old soldiers recount their adventures in World War II.

3. A typical "character" actress, a leading man, and a leading woman are awaiting their cues in the greenroom (the room offstage where actors and actresses rest and chat between appearances).

4. A young married couple tries to play matchmaker by setting up a blind date with the husband's brother and the wife's ex-college roommate.

5. A group of six children play hide-and-go-seek. One must be chosen to be "it." The others hide.

6. Several persons apply to a personnel director for a position.

7. A babysitter takes charge after the parents have departed.

8. A photographer takes a family picture of four generations.

9. A shy young man pays his first call on a girl, who does not know how to put him at ease.

APPLICATIONS

1. Write on separate pieces of paper twenty suggestions for pantomimes that can be presented by a single person. Four should show just one mood. Four should reveal a transition from one mood to another. Four should require a definite entrance and exit. Four should necessitate sitting and rising. Four should require falling down and getting up again. Bring these suggestions to class and mix them up. Let each class member draw one and present it in class.

2. Give as many individual and group pantomimes as possible before the class. Analyze each performance to see whether it has convincing characterization, clarity, reality, and effectiveness. These questions, among others, should be discussed:

   a. Has the pantomime been carefully prepared?

   b. Are the characters interesting, lifelike, and vivid? Do you become emotionally involved with them?

    c. Do the gestures and movements seem sincere, convincing, clear, and properly motivated?

    d. Does all the action help flesh out and clearly represent the characters and their situation for you?

    e. Is the action clear-cut, realistic, prolonged sufficiently, and exaggerated enough to be seen by the whole audience?

    f. Can you visualize the setting, the props for the characters, and the clothing of the characters?

    g. Does the pantomime have a definite beginning and ending?

3. Pantomime scenes involving deep emotion or light comedy from the selections in this book.

MIME

Mime, a special art form, is an offspring of pantomime. Mime is abstract and highly stylized. Because it is abstract, mime often lacks preciseness. In fact, it is through that lack of exactness that its greater meaning is conveyed. Mime replaces exactness with *conventions*—abstractions that communicate symbolic or literal meanings. For example, the mime does not walk as we ordinarily do. None of the mime walks—and there are several—look like normal walking. The mime walk is an *illusory walk,* giving only the idea of walking.

Pantomime deals with reality, while mime goes beyond reality. Thus, mime is not limited by the real world. A mime may look at the world from the point of view of a cat. This does not mean that the mime is acting out being a cat. Through catlike actions and behavior, the mime may help us see, think, and feel from the cat's point of view.

A mime is concerned with a theme not an impersonation. Some mime themes might be expressed in a few simple words: "Loneliness," "Young Dreams," or "A Born Loser." Or the theme may be expressed in a phrase or a statement: "Old Friends Are Gone, Only the Birds Remain," "I'm Young, and I Can Do Anything," or "Down Inside, I Know That No Matter How Well Things Seem to Be Going, I'll Fail in the End."

In mime, the action conveys the theme. In pantomime, the action conveys only action. For example, simply flying a kite can be a fine pantomime. But snagging it on a tree after struggling to get it soaring high in the sky may be a mime's way of saying: "Our aspirations often become entangled with the things of this world."

The mime is not concerned with the element of time. Mime is frozen in time— the present. The mime concentrates on a sequence of actions in time, each action performed in its proper sequence and completed before moving on to the next. The mime must know the physical and dramatic origins of each mimic action. What muscle groups and body parts are necessary to perform the action? When in the sequence of dramatic events is this action needed?

Each primary mime action is preceded by a preparatory action. This preparatory action is usually a movement opposite to the action the mime wishes the audience to follow. It is much like the windup of a baseball pitcher prior to the delivery of the ball. For instance, the mime, before reaching out for an object, would first draw the arm back somewhat. This exaggerates the action and focuses the audience's attention on the action.

Both the pantomimist and the mime work with imaginary objects—a flower, a glass, or a ball. But the mime may also use parts of the body or the whole body to become an object or express an idea. The opening of the hands forms a butterfly or a book; the clasping of the arms and hands around the body becomes the hugging of a friend or lover; the writhing of the entire body becomes the motion of a snake. Pantomime is always silent, but mime may use nonverbal sounds, such as escaping air, a telephone busy signal, or the screech of tires.

Everything in mime must be exaggerated. This exaggeration lifts mime above simple repetition of an action. Most hand actions are executed with a *setting* of the action. Mimes refer to this setting as *the click*. For example, if you were to take a drinking glass, at the moment at which the glass is grasped, your fingers should ''snap'' around the glass. This snap establishes the glass's shape, size, and resistance in one action. The setting of the action is seen quite readily when a mime suggests the presence of a wall. Each hand snaps into place from the wrist as contact with the wall is made. The snap shows the wall, its flatness, and its resistance.

Conventional Mime Actions

Mime is made up of many traditional conventions. One of the most basic mime conventions is that of the *illusory walk*. There are several mime walks that are commonly used. The simplest is done in the following manner. Stand with your feet pointed out at a 45° angle. Place your weight on your right foot. Lift your left heel so that you are on the ball of the left foot. Then, shift your weight to your left foot by dropping the left heel and at the same time raising the right heel. Once you have the feet shifting rhythmically, add an arm swing. The arms swing in an exaggerated, but not overdone, manner. The illusion of walking appears when you move opposite arms and feet. Swing the right arm when you lift the left foot and the left arm when you lift the right foot.

A second illusory walk begins with the same starting position. The left foot is lifted and stretched out away from you at a 45° angle and then brought back toward you in a sliding motion. The third illusory walk is much like the second except that when the left foot is brought back to the starting position, the knee is turned inward and the foot is lifted behind and away from you with a snap. At the same time that the left knee is turned inward, the right knee is turned out to prepare for its step. Although the third illusory walk is difficult to master, the illusion is quite effective. It is also the walk you may have seen used by many of the famous mimes.

In all the mime walks, there should be a lifting of the body just as the weight is shifted from one foot to the other. This is very important to the illusion. The exaggerated arm movement is also important. Speeding up the walk, leaning the body forward, and swinging the arms across in front of the body (much like in ice skating) will create the illusion of running.

Another mime convention is the *rope pull*. Stand with your body facing "two o'clock" with your left foot forward, knee bent, and your weight on it. Reach out as far as you can with your left hand, and grasp a 1-inch rope. Take the rope with your right hand just in front of the left hip. Now *pull*. Your weight shifts to your right foot, and the left hand is in front of your right hip. The rope should be straight through the two hands, which are parallel to the floor. The rope should maintain its diameter throughout the pull. Now comes the tricky part! Let go with the right hand, reach over the left, and grasp the rope about a foot in front of the left hip. Then, with a quick movement, shift your weight back onto your left foot as you reach out as far as you can with your left hand to take the rope for another pull. It is the quick "one-two" of the right hand-left hand switch that creates the illusion of pulling a large rope.

Another mime convention is the *ladder climb*. Remember that the rungs of a ladder form a sort of picture frame that can help you create the illusion as the audience "sees" your face move from frame to frame. When you climb a ladder, your arms and legs work together on the same side. Bend the elbows slightly, raise your arms above your head, and grasp the rung of the ladder with both hands. Now lift your left foot. Then lower it. As you lower your left foot, bring your left arm straight down. The left hand is still grasping the rung of the ladder. Look up, see the next rung, take it with your right hand, lift the right foot, and bring hand and foot down together, watching the rung as it passes before your eyes. Coming down is a little more challenging because there is more illusion to create. Place your hands on the ladder rungs as before. Lift the left foot and suspend it on the rung. Look down (about shoulder level) at the rung you are going to grasp. Let go with the left hand and take the rung below as you step down. As the left hand comes down, the right hand must go up to the "rung above" position, and the right foot must be lifted ready to step down. Obviously, the hands are passing each other, but the illusion is that of descending.

Still another mime convention is *climbing up and down stairs*. First go up the stairs. Use the first mime walk for this illusion. Grasp the handrail about eye level with your right hand. If you are not sure about the size of the rail, take hold of your left wrist, get the feel of that size, and use that for the rail. Now, as you walk—usually taking three steps—bring the hand down past your body at the angle of the rail until your hand is just past your hip. Then reach up and take the rail again. Remember the click before each new action starts. Continue up the stairs. Coming down the stairs is easy, too. Just reach down in front of you at a comfortable distance (about midthigh), grasp the rail lightly with the right hand, and move the hand up beside you to about the midchest level. As you bring the arm up, extend the elbow out. This will enable you to keep the rail straight.

Conventional Mime Makeup

Another convention associated with mime is the makeup. The classic mime tries to neutralize the face by painting it a white mask, stopping at the jawline, hairline, and in front of the ears. The detailed makeup is individualized by each mime, but all mimes make up the eyes and mouth, the two most expressive parts of the face. Some draw in brows, some add a tear, a flower, a star, or other character feature somewhere on the face. Most classic mimes still use the conventional makeup, but there are many who perform without the white mask. The choice is yours.

Conventional Mime Costume

Costume for mime is also a convention. However, there are many kinds of mime dress. The most important item of clothing is a flexible shoe, such as a ballet shoe. Some mimes perform in leotard and tights or dance pants. Others wear jump suits. Some wear bib overalls and striped knit shirts. Professional mimes often use specially made costumes consisting of fairly tight stretch pants and a matching short-waisted jacket worn over a knit shirt. Marcel Marceau's Bip is one of the few to use a character costume.

In recent years, a Swiss-trained mime troupe called Mummenschanz opened the doors of mime to the use of special props and nontraditional subjects. Many of their props were really costumes, such as stretch sacks. However, their imaginative style and creative mimes challenged other mimes to expand the form of mime beyond the ''costumeless, propless'' tradition of classic mime.

Mime Exercises

Mime exercises are of three types: inclinations, rotations, and isolations (separations). An *inclination* is a bending of the body to the front, the side, or the rear. *Rotations* are a turning or pivoting of some part of the body, such as the head or chest. *Isolations* separate parts of the body for individual development and expression.

The classic mime neutralizes the face by making it a white mask. The white makeup stops at the jawline, hairline, and in front of the ears.

Mime exercises begin with the heels close together and the toes pointing out at a 45° angle. The mime thinks of the body as being divided into six major parts: head, neck, shoulders, chest, waist, and hips. These may be further subdivided for more refined exercises. Complete each movement before moving to the next. Do not rush.

Inclinations (Move each body part one at a time)

1. Incline the head, the neck, the shoulders, the chest, the waist, and then the hips to the right. As the hip inclines right, slide the left foot along the floor away from the body. Straighten up one step at a time. Then repeat the action to the left. Remember to slide the right foot out for the hip inclination.

2. Do a vertical inclination, keeping the body relaxed. Drop the head forward. Next, the neck. The chin should be resting lightly on the chest. Now the shoulders. You will look very round-shouldered. Now drop the chest forward. Feel as if the chest has caved in just above the stomach. Now drop at the waist. This should put the back in a position parallel to the floor. Finally, drop from the hips. Depending upon your physical flexibility at this time, you should be touching your toes, the floor, or perhaps you can even place your hands flat on the floor. Now go back to your standing position, doing your inclinations slowly in reverse order.

3. Following the same steps, incline to the rear.

Rotations (Move each body part in sweeping arcs)

1. To rotate the head and neck, start by dropping the chin on the chest. Rotate the head and neck to the right, back, left, and front. Raise the head.

2. To rotate the shoulders, add a sweeping motion of the shoulders to the head rotation.

3. To rotate the chest, broaden the sweeping motion by adding the chest to the head rotation.

4. To rotate the waist, broaden the sweeping motion even more by bending from the waist as you rotate the head.

5. When rotating the hips, freely swing from the hips as the sweeping motion reaches its broadest arc. All six body parts are now involved.

6. Reverse directions and rotate to the left. Follow each step as described above.

Isolations

1. Isolate the head by moving it straight forward, then straight back, to the left, and to the right. Keep the head level; do not incline it. Now rotate the head to the right, then to the left.

2. Isolate the right shoulder. Raise it up; lower it; move it forward; move it back. Rotate the shoulder forward. Rotate it to the rear.

APPLICATIONS

1. Line up as two teams facing each other for a rope pull. Your teacher will call out which team pulls. Remember, when one team pulls, the other team must "give" by leaning forward.

2. You are in a box. Show the size and shape of the box.

3. Get a kite into the air. Tug on the string to get it higher and higher. The string breaks, and the kite drifts away. Watch it and then walk off stage sadly.

4. Design a mime. Give it a title. Write your title on a large piece of paper or cardboard, and set it up before the class. Turn in your mime statement and the outline of your mime to your teacher before you begin. Then present your mime to the class. You may enter from the wings, or you may begin from a neutral standing position (head up with eyes directed forward.)

BIBLIOGRAPHY

Alberts, David: *Pantomime: Elements and Exercises,* University of Kansas Press, Lawrence, Kansas, 1971.

Decroux, Étienne: *Mime: The Art of Étienne Decroux,* Pratt Adlib Press, New York, 1965.

Enters, Angna: *On Mime,* Wesleyan, Middletown, Connecticut, 1965.

Fast, Julius: *Body Language,* Lippincott, New York, 1970.

Kipnis, Claude: *The Mime Book,* Harper & Row, New York, 1974.

Shepherd, Richmond: *Mime, the Technique of Silence,* Drama Book Specialists, New York, 1971.

CHAPTER FOUR

Voice
and
Diction

An expressive voice and clear, correct speech are not only indispensable tools for the actor, they are also assets in every walk of life. Personnel directors list them among the assets needed for positions that involve meeting the public and sharing ideas. As Shaw so amusingly points out in *Pygmalion,* social standing and educational background are judged by the way a person talks.

The lack of communication between people—individuals and groups—is the cause of much of the confusion of this generation. As you watch on television the confrontations between sectional and racial segments of our own United States or try to follow international diplomacy, you realize the importance today of clarity in speech and accuracy in choice of words. Since drama is one of the arts of communication, drama class can be a good way to improve your personal speech.

There is more faultfinding from the public and the professional critics concerning the lack of voice clarity and the sloppiness of diction on the part of American actors than of any other phase of acting. Especially in comparison with the British players who appear in the best Broadway and television plays, this criticism appears justifiable. With the popularity of intimate family plays, Westerns, and the rapid-fire spots of dialogue on many television specials, our American speech becomes indistinct in comparison with that of the British. In fact, bodily action is being played up and the spoken word overlooked in many stage shows where audience involvement rather than communication is stressed.

You will find, however, that directors in regional and repertory companies, which produce classics and important contemporary dramas of ideas, are expecting young actors to speak clearly and correctly. These directors do not accept mumbling and provincial pronunciations. As Americans in the superjet age are traveling more and more, they themselves are becoming more conscious of the American nasality of tone and lack of clarity in speech criticized by foreigners for years as a very real handicap. Therefore, no matter how your life works out, you will find that clear speech will be an asset in whatever lifework you undertake.

The artificial use of "stage diction" is not suitable for average young Americans. It becomes an affectation in general communication, but, if you go into the theater professionally, you will pick it up naturally. Familiarity with stage diction will increase your value in many plays and also your pleasure in understanding the English plays that are now a part of our American theater.

In the drama class, a simple, practical daily routine of exercises and constant attention to your speech are necessary. If you understand the fundamental principles explained in this chapter and practice the exercises regularly, you can improve your vocal and speech habits.

DEVELOPING AN EFFECTIVE VOICE

There is nothing mysterious or complicated about developing an effective voice. It depends primarily upon bodily relaxation and good posture. Few people

On a television show, Orson Welles reads a scary Halloween script so well that it lures a monster (Alan Sues) out of the woodwork.

realize the close relationship between the voice, the emotions, and the body. The voice of a person who is ill, tired, worried, angry, nervous, hurried, or tense reflects those feelings. The voice becomes high-pitched, monotonous, or colorless. On the other hand, a person who is poised, self-confident, and healthy is likely to have a pleasing voice. Consequently, your first efforts should be directed toward building a vigorous, well-controlled body and a cheerful disposition.

Voice is produced by the air from the lungs passing over the vocal folds, which are thin curtains of muscles with delicate edges. These folds respond instantly and set up vibrations, or waves. The vibrations become sounds and are amplified when they strike the resonating chambers of the throat, head, nose, and mouth. Exactly what sounds are produced depends upon the shape of the resonating chambers, and this shape is determined by the position of the tongue, soft palate, lips, and lower jaw. For correct speech and voice production, it is necessary for you to have deep central breathing; an open, relaxed throat; flexible tongue and lips; and a relaxed lower jaw.

Human beings breathe and make sounds correctly at birth, using the vocal apparatus in a relaxed, natural way. Unfortunately, as the environment surrounding infants, dependent largely upon the attitude of parents and associates, closes in, tensions set in. Then the throat muscles tighten, affecting speech habits by the time young children start talking. Therefore teenagers have frequently already established poor vocal habits. These can be eliminated within an amazingly short time by regular exercise and constant vigilance when speaking.

Specialized drama schools include required courses in speech and diction, and more and more attention is being paid in high schools to developing clear, correct communication techniques. In your dramatics class homework, you should spend about half an hour a day, when you are feeling fresh and relaxed, in establishing good speech habits by regularly doing the exercises in this chapter.

Breath Control

Breath control determines the carrying power of your voice and the intelligent reading and speaking of words combined into thought groups. The first exercises should, therefore, deal with central breathing, consciously controlled.

No one can teach you how to breathe, for you have done so successfully since your birth, and you can breathe correctly when you are asleep or perfectly relaxed. There is some difference, however, between regular breathing and breathing for speech. In regular breathing, the inhalation (breathing in) and exhalation (breathing out) periods are of equal length. Breathing for speech requires a very brief inhalation period and a slow, controlled exhalation period. This is true because, for all practical purposes, speech is produced only when the breath is being exhaled. In breathing for speech, therefore, you should inhale through the mouth,

(Left) *Actors in the French and English Restoration period were masters of crisp articulation, vocal inflection, and breath control.*

(Right) *The actor in the center is Gandval, who plays the part of Glorieux.*

since this allows for more rapid intake of breath than does inhalation through the nose. You should work for a prolonged and controlled exhalation so that the outgoing breath will match your needs for sustained vocal tone. Controlled breathing is more important to the actor than deep breathing, for the tone of the voice depends upon it.

The first exercises for you to try in training your voice are those that will focus the breathing process in the center of your body and those that will strengthen and control the breath stream once it has been centered where it belongs. Practice these exercises every night and morning until central breathing gradually becomes automatic.

1. Place your hands on either side of the lower part of the rib cage. Now pant rapidly, laugh silently, and sniff in the air in tiny whiffs. Lie down and breathe deeply and regularly. Keep your hands in the same position.

2. Stand straight with an easy, well-balanced posture. Inhale slowly, making sure from the feeling under your hands that the whole rib cage is expanding. Hold your breath without straining for a count of six. Then exhale slowly and

evenly while you mentally count, first to fifteen and then to twenty, twenty-five, and thirty. Be particularly careful to avoid muscular tension.

3. Repeat Exercise 2, gauging the evenness of your exhalation either by whistling or by making a soft sound as you breathe out, such as the sound of *s* or *ah*. If the sound is jerky or irregular or fades at the end, repeat the exercise until you can keep the sound smooth and regular.

4. Use a favorite poem or prose passage for practice in breath control. Take a deep breath and see how far you can read in the selection before you have to take a second breath. Do not strain, and be sure to relax after each effort. Your breath control will improve.

Relaxation

The degree of relaxation determines the beauty of the voice and the carrying power of the vowel sounds, which are made with an open, relaxed throat, a relaxed jaw, and flexible lips. Therefore, before any period of voice exercises, you must relax, consciously letting go both mentally and physically. Yawn! Stretch your whole body as an animal does after a nap. (Incidentally, watching a cat relax and move is an excellent exercise in itself for bettering your own reactions.) Feel the big muscles of your back, legs, and arms ease first. Imagine that a warm, relaxing shower is falling over your head. Imagine it passing over your forehead and wiping out the frown lines. Imagine it releasing the tension of the little muscles around your eyes, nose, mouth, and especially your cheeks, so that the lower jaw and lips are loose.

Next roll your head forward and backward and to the sides until both the inner and outer throat muscles are relaxed. Then imagine the shower pouring over your whole body, relaxing your arms and fingertips, your chest, lungs, diaphragm, and even your toes. You should be yawning by this time, and that is one of the best voice exercises. With practice, you can learn to run through this process imaginatively when you are waiting to make a speech or standing in the wings before an entrance on the stage. You will also find it an excellent cure for stage fright. Also run through the posture exercises on page 26, and then do the breathing exercises on page 54 before you begin vocal work. The importance of an erect, easily relaxed body should not be underestimated.

Practice of the exercises below demands careful use of your vocal apparatus.

For Relaxed Jaw

1. Let your head fall forward on your chest. Lift it up and back, letting the jaw remain loose. Drop it again and slowly roll the head over the right shoulder, back, over the left shoulder, and forward, describing a circle.

2. Drop your head forward again. Place your hands lightly on your cheeks and lift your head with your hands, keeping the jaw relaxed and being careful to avoid using the jaw muscles. When your head is lifted, the jaw should hang open. It helps sometimes to try to make your face as expressionless as possible. Looking blank will help relax the muscles.

3. Babble like a baby, saying *dä-dä-dä-dä lä-lä-lä-lä* brightly, and feeling relaxed and happy, moving only the tip of the tongue. (In these and following exercises, refer to the list on page 83 for pronunciation of vowel sounds.)

For Open Throat

1. Yawn freely, getting the feeling of an open, relaxed throat.

2. Take in a deep breath, relax your jaw, think of your throat as large, and exhale slowly.

3. Say: "I can talk as if I were going to yawn. Hear me talk as if I were going to yawn."

4. Say *lō-lā-lē-lä-loo,* gradually increasing the energy for each repetition. Give the vowels fullness and roundness, and relax your jaw. Sing the syllables on one note. Increase your volume by breathing deeply, but do not tighten your throat. Use the tip of your tongue for the *l*'s.

5. Repeat the following expressions, keeping the throat open: *lä-lä-lä-laughs, lä-lä-lä-lose, lä-lä-lä-loaves.*

For Flexible Lips

1. Say *oo-ō-ô-ŏ-ä,* opening your lips from a small circle to a large one. Then reverse, saying *ä-ŏ-ô-ō-oo.* These sounds may be sung with the piano, taking them all on one note. Keep the tongue flat in your mouth with the tip at the lower teeth. Keep your throat well open and your jaw relaxed.

2. Say *mē-mō-mē-mō-mē-mō-mē-mō.* Then sing these sounds with the piano.

For Flexible Tongue

1. Say rapidly: *fŭd-dŭd-dŭd-dŭd-däh-fŭd-dŭd-dŭd-dŭh-däh-fŭd-dŭd-dŭd-dŭd-däh-frill.* Trill the *r* in *frill.*

2. Keeping your jaw well relaxed, repeat the following sounds, watching with a hand mirror to see that your tongue is slowly arched as you go from one position to the next: *ä-ŭ-ēr-ä-ă-ĕ-ā-ĭ-ē.*

3. Say *ĭra-ĭra-ĭra-ĭra-ĭra-very.* Trill the *r* in *very.*

For Resonance

Resonance is the vibrant tone produced when sound waves strike the chambers of the throat, head, nose, and mouth. The best practice for resonance is humming with an open, relaxed throat. The nasal passages must be kept open for vibrations to be set up in them, so exhale through the nose using the *m-n-ng* positions. The cavities of the head will vibrate automatically if you hum while throwing the voice forward. If the nasal passages are closed by a cold or raised soft palate, the sound is denasalized. The much-criticized nasal twang of many American voices is due to nervous tension, which tightens the throat and raises the soft palate, thus closing the nasal cavities, cutting down resonance, and leaving the voice flat.

1. To locate your larynx and feel the vibration of the vocal cords, place your fingers lightly on your Adam's apple and say *b*. Then say *p* and *d*, then *t* and *v*, then *f* and *s*, and then *z*. Note the vibration on the *b*, *d*, *v*, and *z*. Also note the vibration on the vowel sounds *ā*, *ē*, *ī*, *ō*, and *ū*.

2. To feel the effect of obstructing the resonators, sing the word "hum" and then repeat it while you pinch your nose closed. Say "good morning," opening your mouth and your throat. Say it as if you were on the verge of tears and were swallowing them. Say it holding your nose closed. Say it with your teeth tightly set. Say it while drawing your tongue back in your mouth.

3. Place your fingers gently on your lips and on your nose and hum, feeling the vibration. Place the palm of your hand on the top of your head and hum. Try to feel the vibration. Repeat with your fingers at the back of your head. Repeat the exercise using a piano and noting where on the scale the vibration is strongest.

4. Sing the sounds of *m-n-ng*, using a piano. Then combine each of them with the vowel sounds in Exercise 4 of "For Open Throat" and repeat.

5. Say the following words with full resonance: *ring, sing, ding-dong, bells, wind*.

For Speech and Breathing

1. Breathe in, relaxing your throat and lower jaw. Count "one" as you exhale. Repeat and count "one, two." Continue until you can count to twenty on one breath. Be careful not to tighten up. It may take you several weeks before you can reach twenty, but take time so that you can do it without straining. Any tension is bad.

2. Breathe in. Relax your throat and lower jaw. Say "Hong Kong" as you exhale, prolonging the vowel and *ng* sounds.

3. Breathe in. Relax your throat and lower jaw. Say ''Hear the tolling of the bells—iron bells'' as you exhale, prolonging the vowels and the *ng* and *n* sounds.

4. Breathe in. Relax your throat and lower jaw. Without straining, try to retain the position of your diaphragm as you exhale, saying slowly, ''Roll on, thou deep and dark blue ocean, roll.''

5. Again read the selection used for breath control. This time do not try to see how far you can read on one breath, but read it naturally, inhaling as you have to between the phrases. Form the vowels accurately and sound the *m's, n's,* and *ng's* carefully.

VOICE CHARACTERISTICS

There are four characteristics of the voice that must be used correctly if you are to become an effective and expressive speaker. These are quality, pitch, volume, and rate. Their development constitutes voice training.

Quality

Quality is the individual sound of your particular voice. Its beauty and richness can be improved by keeping the resonating chambers of your throat and head open. Your daily speech habits are most important. Never speak with a tight throat, and always try to use a low, clear tone. Relax your throat frequently with a yawn, and breathe through your nose when you are not speaking. Never strain your voice.

The quality of your voice depends, for the most part, upon resonance and the correct formation of vowel sounds by the speech organs.

The vowel sounds, so important in the quality of your tone, are all made with the lower jaw relaxed. The position of the lips and tongue determines the sound. In pronouncing all vowels, you must keep the tip of the tongue at the base of the lower teeth. *Ah* is the most open sound, with the tongue flat and lips loose. By rounding the lips, you produce the sounds of ŏ *(ŏn)*, ô *(lôrd)*, ō *(ōh)*, o͞o *(look)*, and o͞o *(lo͞ose)*. Keep the tip of the tongue at the base of the lower teeth and the jaw and lips relaxed. Allow the middle of the tongue to arch up and forward until it almost touches the roof of the mouth to produce the sounds of ŭ *(ŭp)*, ēr *(makēr)*, ă *(ăt)*, ĕ *(lĕt)*, ā *(āte)*, ĭ *(ĭt)*, ē *(bē)*. Practice making these sounds without tightening the throat, concentrating on the tone so that it leaves the mouth and passes beyond the lips and is not muffled or ''swallowed.'' In this way, you keep a pure tone in every syllable and word that you utter, and the quality of your voice is at its best.

It is important for the actor to remember that voice quality is definitely affected by emotion. Perhaps you have already realized that your voice responds instantly

Speaking with a relaxed throat produces the resonant, clear tone so important to the interpretation of Shakespearean dramas. James Earl Jones (left) as Timon in Shakespeare's Timon of Athens *is a powerful actor known for his resonant voice and good articulation.*

to your inner feelings. For example, the voice may quiver with fear, sweeten with sympathy, and harden with anger. If you wish to develop a flexible, responsive voice for acting, you must cultivate your imagination to the point where your tone becomes that of your character experiencing various moods. In addition, the age of your character will affect the quality of the voice. For instance, with old age the vocal apparatus is usually less flexible and the disposition has been obviously affected for better or worse by life's experiences. These things must be made apparent in your characterizations. A good way to help yourself is to listen very carefully as you meet a new person and try to judge that person's temperament and mood by the tone of voice. Note also voices of your friends and family.

APPLICATIONS

Practice the following exercises aloud, first feeling the appropriate emotion and then speaking.

1. Repeat a single word—*no, yes, dear, of course, really*—conveying the following emotions: surprise, scorn, irritation, sarcasm, boredom, suspicion, eagerness, love, doubt, weariness, exaltation, determination, horror, pain, despair, and joy.

2. Assume the character of a happy child, a cross elderly person, a dictatorial employer, a discouraged job-seeker, an eloquent minister, a distinguished actor, a

plotting criminal, and a hysterical survivor of an earthquake. Speak the following sentences as each of these characters would.

a. Now is the time to make your choice.

b. Oh, what a beautiful morning!

c. Whatever will be will be.

d. Stop! Think it over before you do anything rash!

3. Say the following words, recalling personal experiences to give them "color," the special tone quality resulting from feeling and imagination: *home, icy, flag, ocean, roar, sunset, welcome, golden, jingle, melancholy, magnificent, dog, star, glamorous, eternal, enemy, splendid, horrible, brilliant, glory, sobbing, autumn, whisper, shot, scream, terrific.*

4. Read the following selections, concentrating mainly on the vowel sounds. Try to make each vowel in an accented syllable as full and rich as possible. Sound these vowels alone many times, and then put them back in the words. (Note: In these and in all other excerpts and passages, the student is urged to read the complete work, if possible, in order to understand fully the mood and meaning of the selection.)

a.

[JULIET:]

> The clock struck nine when I did send the Nurse;
> In half an hour she promised to return.
> Perchance she cannot meet him—that's not so.
> O, she is lame! Love's heralds should be thoughts,
> Which ten times faster glides than the sun's beams,
> Driving back shadows over low'ring hills.
> Therefore do nimble-pinioned doves draw love,
> And therefore hath the wind-swift Cupid wings.

Romeo and Juliet
by William Shakespeare

b.

[PROSPERO:]

> Our revels now are ended. These our actors,
> As I foretold you, were all spirits, and
> Are melted into air, into thin air:
> And, like the baseless fabric of this vision,
> The cloud-capp'd towers, the gorgeous palaces,
> The solemn temples, the great globe itself,
> Yea, all which it inherit, shall dissolve
> And, like this insubstantial pageant faded
> Leave not a rack behind.

The Tempest
by William Shakespeare

c.

[THE GHOST OF HAMLET'S FATHER:]
> I am thy father's spirit;
> Doom'd for a certain term to walk the night,
> And, for the day, confin'd to waste in fires
> Till the foul crimes done in my days of nature
> Are burnt and purg'd away. But that I am forbid
> To tell the secrets of my prison-house,
> I could a tale unfold whose lightest word
> Would harrow up thy soul. . . .

Hamlet
by William Shakespeare

Pitch

Pitch is the relative highness or lowness of the voice at any given time. Each person's voice has a characteristic pitch level from which it moves up and down. Women's voices are pitched on a higher level than those of men, and children's voices are higher still. Pitch is determined by the rapidity with which the vocal folds vibrate. This vibration, in turn, is influenced by the length of the vocal folds, their elasticity, the degree of tension in them, their thickness, and the amount of breath pressure applied.

Most persons use only four or five notes in ordinary speaking, but a good speaker can use two octaves or more. Many girls and women pitch their voices, consciously or unconsciously, at too high a level, not realizing that a low voice is far more musical and easily heard. As a rule, therefore, girls should do their vocal exercises on the lower pitch levels.

The pitch of the voice gives meaning to speech. When speakers are excited, interested, and enthusiastic in conversation, they unconsciously lift the pitch on important words to emphasize them and lower the pitch on unimportant words to subordinate them. In repeating conversations, they lower or raise the voice in imitation of various people. Pitch gives life to reading aloud and speaking. It depends largely upon a vital interest in living and in what you are saying and doing. For a colorful and interesting voice, keep your mind alert as you talk, read, and think.

As you speak, you often alter your pitch. There are two primary ways of doing this. In the first, the *step,* you shift abruptly from one pitch level to another between words, parts of sentences, or sentences to express a distinct break in thought or feeling. In the second, the *inflection,* you gradually raise or lower the pitch level within a word or sentence. A rising inflection shows incompleteness of thought or uncertainty and is often used in asking a question. A falling inflection indicates completeness and definiteness and is often used in answering a question. The rising-falling inflection is used to convey both subtle shades and sharp differences of meaning within words.

Variety in pitch, called modulation or inflection, makes the voice musical. Monotony in pitch, resulting either from speaking continuously on one level or from giving every sentence exactly the same inflection, is a fatal flaw in speaking. Without variety in pitch, speakers are unable to hold the attention of their audiences. Ministers, teachers, and lawyers sometimes fall unconsciously into pitch patterns and monotonous inflections, which lessen their influence to a marked degree. Monotony in pitch may be due to two technical deficiencies: a person's inability to hear pitch changes, or a lack of vocal flexibility. The former is probably caused by a defect within the hearing mechanism and should be discussed with a speech correctionist, who may administer a test for *tonal deafness*. Lack of flexibility, however, can be overcome by practice and conscious attention. It is due largely to lack of vitality and enthusiasm in thought and feeling or in vocal and bodily response.

As a student of dramatics, you must learn to control the number, length, and direction of pitch changes and the modulation of your voice as you interpret a part. In doing exercises for improving your pitch range and flexibility, a tape recorder is

In Home *by Samm-Art Williams, Charles Brown and Michele Shay use good vocal pitch, intense volume, and varied speaking rates to make this Southern dialect play completely intelligible to the audience.*

of great value, for it helps to train your ears as well as your voice. Today almost all schools have tape recorders. If you use one, you will be able to hear your voice in scenes and check on your skill in doing interpretative work. In any case, you must learn to go as low and as high in pitch as you can without straining. Try to notice your own and other people's changes in pitch in normal conversation and how these changes affect the communication of thoughts and feelings. Notice what anger, exhaustion, irritation, worry, joy, and excitement do to the pitch of people's voices. You will find that the pitch is usually higher when a person is angry, that dominant people use falling inflections for the most part, and that timid ones use brief, rising inflections. Sneering and sarcasm are often shown by rising-falling inflections, which convey subtle meanings.

The reading aloud of plays or lively conversations from stories is extremely helpful in daily practice for pitch variation. When reading aloud, you may find that a complete poem or single passage in prose has a predominant mood. An idea that is lofty and inspiring may need little range in pitch and will be best expressed by long, falling inflections. A passage that is comic, exciting, lyrical, and vital will have a wide range with many short, changing inflections. In all interpretative work, keep asking yourself, ''What am I saying?'' and then answer the question in the author's words.

APPLICATIONS

1. Count from one to ten, beginning as low as you can and going as high as you can without strain. Then reverse the count and come down. Be sure that it is pitch and not loudness that makes the difference in each count.

2. Count slowly from one to ten, giving the vowel in each number a long falling inflection. Repeat with a long rising inflection on each. Then alternate the two exercises.

3. Using the alphabet, talk as if you were preaching a sermon, explaining a geometry problem, describing a horrible accident you just saw, putting a little child to sleep, and speaking to someone who is hard of hearing.

4. Take a nursery rhyme and recite it as a parent, an old-fashioned elocutionist, a bored teenager, and a frightened child.

5. Read the following sentences with the widest possible range. Put emphasis on the important words and syllables by raising the pitch, using both the step and inflection shifts. Drop definitely on unimportant words.

   a. What a glorious sunset!
   b. To speak effectively, you must raise your voice on the important words.
   c. In direct conversation we change the pitch of the voice constantly.
   d. Did you hear what I said? Then go!
   e. No, I will not go!

    f. Look, that plane is exploding!

    g. I shall never, never, never believe you again!

6. Stand behind a screen or curtain and give the following lines, having someone check on your variations in pitch.

    a. No, never. Well, hardly ever.

    b. To be or not to be, that is the question.

    c. Do unto others as you would have them do unto you.

    d. Give me liberty or give me death!

    e. Laugh and the world laughs with you;
        Weep and you weep alone!

7. Analyze the following selections, and decide what inflections to use in order to bring out the predominant mood and inner meaning of each. If possible, use a tape recorder and read the lines aloud. Then study the pitch of your voice and try again, concentrating particularly on inflection and modulation.

a.

[PETRUCHIO:]

    Good-morrow, Kate, for that's your name, I hear.

[KATHARINE:]

Well have you heard, but something hard of hearing:
They call me Katharine that do talk of me.

[PETRUCHIO:]

    You lie, in faith; for you are called plain Kate,
    And bonny Kate, and sometimes Kate the curst,
    But Kate, the prettiest Kate in Christendom.

The Taming of the Shrew
by William Shakespeare

b.

[The PIPER:]

    She was my mother.—And she starved and sang;
    And like the wind she wandered and was cold
    Outside your lighted windows, and fled by,
    Storm-hunted, trying to outstrip the snow.
    South, south, and homeless as a broken bird,—
    Limping and hiding!—And she fled, and laughed,
    And kept me warm; and died! To you a Nothing;
    Nothing, forever, oh, you well-housed mothers!
    As always, always for the lighted windows
    Of all the world, the Dark outside is nothing;
    And all that limps and hides there in the dark;
    Famishing,—broken,—lost!

The Piper
by Josephine Preston Peabody

c.

[PAOLO:]

    She called me into the hotel. There were other people there, rich people all in grand clothes. Psh, what did I care for that? I'll be the equal of them all soon and more, for I have a fortune in my throat. That's what she said—a fortune in my throat! Maddalena, she's going to send me to Milano—oh, she needn't fear, I'll give her back the money—I'll study there—I don't need much study, it's true—and in a few years you'll see, posted in big head-lines, "Rubini, Paolo Rubini, the greatest tenor in Italy, the greatest in the world."

Poor Maddalena
by Louise Saunders

d.

[VIOLA:]

I left no ring with her. What means this lady?
Fortune forbid my outside hath not charm'd her!
She made good view of me; indeed, so much
That sure methought her eyes had lost her tongue,
For she did speak in starts distractedly.
She loves me, sure; the cunning of her passion
Invites me in this churlish messenger.
None of my lord's ring! Why, he sent her none.
I am the man;—if it be so—as 'tis—
Poor lady, she were better love a dream. . . .
How will this fadge? My master loves her dearly,
And I, poor monster, fond as much on him;
And she, mistaken, seems to dote on me.
What will become of this? As I am man,
My state is desperate for my master's love;
As I am woman, now alas the day!
What thriftless sighs shall poor Olivia breathe!
O time, thou must untangle this, not I;
It is too hard a knot for me to untie!

Twelfth Night
by William Shakespeare

Volume

    Volume is the relative strength, force, or intensity with which sound is made. You must not confuse volume with mere loudness, for you can utter a stage whisper with great intensity, or you can call across a room with little intensity. Volume depends upon the pressure with which the air from the lungs strikes the vocal folds, and while a certain amount of tension is required to retain the increased breath pressure, this tension should be minimal. If your throat is as relaxed as possible, you will not become hoarse even when speaking with increased volume, and your words will be resonant and forceful.

To speak loudly enough to be heard in the largest auditorium without forcing the words from your throat, you must breathe deeply and centrally. Think that you are talking to a person in the back row of the theater. Such concentration will cause you to open your mouth wider, speak more slowly, and enunciate more clearly. When you use a microphone, remember that no greater volume is necessary than might be used in ordinary conversation—no matter how large the auditorium may be.

Force is of two types. A sudden, sharp breath pressure creates explosive force, which is useful in commands, shouts, loud laughter, and screams. When the breath pressure is held steady and the breath released gradually, the force is said to be expulsive. This type of force is necessary in reading long passages without loss of breath and in building to a dramatic climax.

Like the other voice characteristics, volume is closely related to the expression of ideas and emotions. Fear, excitement, anger, hate, defiance, and other strong emotions are usually accompanied by an explosive intensity. On the other hand, quiet, calm thoughts call for a minimal amount of force.

In Eugene O'Neill's A Touch of the Poet, *the language shows the lilt and inflections of Irish dialect. The actors—Kathryn Walker, Jason Robards, and Geraldine Fitzgerald—spoke realistically in dialect without sacrificing intelligibility.*

Volume is used in combination with other voice characteristics to suggest various feelings. For example, a quiet voice accompanied by a flat quality suggests dullness, indifference, and weariness. A quiet voice with a full tonal quality may express disappointment, shock, despair, bewilderment, and sometimes even great joy.

When you are on the stage, it is important to remember that you must use more energy to convey impressions of all kinds than is necessary off the stage. Thus, if you are merely chatting comfortably at home with a friend, your voice will have relatively little intensity. Put that identical scene on the stage, try to make it equally informal, and you will have to increase your vocal intensity considerably—otherwise the scene will fall flat. Keep the person farthest away from you constantly in mind and talk directly to that person, using your jaw, tongue, and lips to enunciate clearly.

Using greater force to emphasize the important words in a sentence is the most common means of clarifying a thought. You can change the meaning of a sentence by shifting the force from one word to another, thus expressing innocence, surprise, anger, and other emotions. In acting, the entire thought of a line can be clarified or obscured by emphasizing a word or phrase. Key words brought out forcibly can make a character's personality understandable to the audience.

APPLICATIONS

1. Pant like a dog. While you do so, feel the movement of your diaphragm with your hands. Then say ''ha-ha'' as you pant.

2. Repeat ''ha-ha'' many times, making the syllables by a sharp ''kick'' of the diaphragm. Gradually work from a light sound to a shout. Be careful not to allow an audible escape of breath on the *h* sound.

3. Take a full breath and call ''one'' as if you were throwing a ball against a wall at some distance. Exhale, relax, inhale, and call ''one, two'' in the same manner. Count up to ten in this way, but be careful to relax between each effort. Get your power from a quick ''kick'' of the rib cage rather than from tightening the vocal bands. In the same way, use the words *no, bell, on, never,* and *yes.*

4. Repeat the letters of the alphabet, increasing your energy whenever you come to a vowel. Then reverse the exercise, beginning with a strong, firm tone and gradually reducing the energy involved. Keep all the sounds on the same pitch.

5. Say the sentence ''I am going home'' as though you were saying it to the following people:
   a. A friend sitting next to you
   b. A person 10 feet away
   c. Someone across the room

    d.   Someone in the back row of your auditorium, when you are on the stage
Notice that if you are thinking about the person to whom you are speaking, your
voice adjusts itself naturally to the distance involved.

6.   Change the meaning of the following sentences in as many ways as you can by
using force to emphasize different words. Explain your exact meaning.

    a.   I didn't say that to her.

    b.   You don't think I stole the book, do you?

    c.   Why didn't you warn me before it happened?

7.   Read these passages aloud, making the mood and meaning clear by the amount of
force you use and the words you emphasize. Use volume sufficient for a large
auditorium by getting enough breath, keeping an open throat, and sounding the
vowels clearly. Stand correctly.

a.

[PORTIA:]

> The quality of mercy is not strained.
> It droppeth as the gentle rain from heaven
> Upon the place beneath. It is twice blest;
> It blesseth him that gives, and him that takes.
> 'Tis mightiest in the mightiest; it becomes
> The throned monarch better than his crown.
> His sceptre shows the force of temporal power,
> The attribute to awe and majesty,
> Wherein doth sit the dread and fear of kings;
> But mercy is above this sceptred sway;
> It is enthroned in the hearts of kings,
> It is an attribute to God himself;
> And earthly power doth then show likest God's
> When mercy seasons justice.

The Merchant of Venice
by William Shakespeare

b.

> The rhino is a homely beast,
> For human eyes he's not a feast,
> But you and I will never know
> Why nature chose to make him so,
> Farewell, farewell, you old rhinoceros,
> I'll stare at something less prepoceros!

''The Rhinoceros''
by Ogden Nash

c.

To make a prairie it takes a clover and one bee,
One clover, and a bee,
And revery.
The revery alone will do,
If bees are few.

"To Make a Prairie"
by Emily Dickinson

d.

When I
die
I'm sure
I will have a
Big Funeral . . .
Curiosity
seekers . . .
coming to see
if I
am really
Dead . . .
or just
trying to make
Trouble. . . .

"The Rebel"
by Mari Evans

e.

OYES! OYES!! OYES!!!
We, the holders of the oldest office in Britain, salute you good people at Hastings
by the Sea. Long before Press and Television we cried the King's commands and
brought news of the day. Still pursuing our ancient calling, we give you current
important tidings, wish you well, and cry with heart and voice:

GOD SAVE THE QUEEN!

Great Britain's Town Criers' Competition
Courtesy of Alfie Howard,
Town Crier of Lambeth

Rate

Rate, in speech, is the speed at which words are spoken. Each person has a characteristic rate of speech, which is usually more rapid in informal conversation than in public speaking or in work in dramatics. Like quality, pitch, and volume, rate is also an important means of suggesting ideas and emotional states. A steadily increasing speed creates a feeling of tension and excitement, while the deliberate delivery of important passages impresses the hearer with their significance. Light, comic, happy, and lyric passages are usually spoken rapidly. Calm, serene, reverent, tragic, and awesome passages are delivered more slowly.

Practically all our sentences in both speaking and reading are divided into groups separated by pauses of varying lengths. The breathing pause is a necessity because we must have breath in order to speak. One of the worst faults a beginner can have is gasping for breath, thus breaking the thought of a sentence. You must train yourself at once to get your breath between thought groups when reading or speaking in front of an audience. You undoubtedly manage it properly in normal conversation, unconsciously putting into groups words that belong together before you catch your breath. You will find it harder to do this on the stage. The number of words in a group necessarily varies with the thought. A single word may be important enough to stand alone, or there may be twelve or more in a group; ordinarily there are four or five. Too many breath groups tend to create choppy speech. Punctuation can be of great assistance, for it often clarifies meaning as well as grammatical relationship.

Logical grouping and pausing is a matter of making the thought clear and depends upon your knowing exactly what you are saying. The secret of great interpretative power is the ability to realize an idea—to visualize, emotionalize, and vitalize it for yourself—and then give the audience an opportunity to do the same thing. Logical and dramatic pauses demand thought and feeling on your part, or you will not have your audience thinking and feeling with you. Therefore, work out your thought groups carefully. Remember that pauses are often more effective than words. After the pattern is set, approach each group as if for the first time every time you speak or read aloud. This is one of the secrets of giving a sense of spontaneity and freshness to every performance throughout a long run.

Go back over the passages you have been reading in the exercises in this chapter, and decide where the thought groups divide. Then read the passages aloud again, watching your timing. Hold the important words longer than others, and slip rapidly over the unimportant ones. Let the idea speed you up or slow you down, and take time to feel the emotions and moods. A skillful use of phrasing and pausing is one of your most valuable tools in putting over ideas and arousing emotion, and the more you practice reading aloud, either from prepared selections or at sight, the more effective you will become.

Priscilla Lopez as Harpo Marx, David Garrison as Groucho Marx, and Frank Lazarus as Chico Marx believably recreate the vocal characteristics of the famous Marx brothers in the musical comedy A Day in Hollywood/A Night in the Ukraine.

USING THE VOICE IN INTERPRETATION

Emphasis and subordination are the light and shadow of interpretation in acting. The key words of every passage must be highlighted to be heard by everyone in the audience so that the meaning may be understood. To stress such words, you must first feel their emotional context to give them color. They can be made to stand out in the following ways: by delivering them with greater force, by holding them for a longer period, by lifting or lowering them in pitch, and by giving them a rich resonant quality. They can also be set off by pauses before or after, or sometimes both before and after. To subordinate unimportant words or phrases, ''throw them away'' by saying them rapidly at a lower pitch with less volume.

Stress also involves tone placement and projection. There are two rather different but not conflicting ideas regarding the matter of placement of tone. One is that tone should be placed in the mask of the face (the area of the face where you feel vibrations when you hum) by forming the sounds of speech with the position of the lips, lower jaw, and tongue. The other is that the voice should be thrown as far as the size of the auditorium requires. This is accomplished by breathing deeply, opening the mouth, and forming the sounds accurately, while consciously putting attention on the person farthest away. In both cases, the throat is never tightened but kept open. The term *swallowing words* is used when the sound is prevented from reaching the resonating chambers of the head. This happens when the throat is closed by tension or by carelessness in controlling the breath and the vocal folds cannot vibrate to produce sound.

Climax is another principle of great value in interpretation. A climactic passage must, of course, be well written by the author before it can be effectively spoken by the speaker. In such a passage, the emotional intensity of the lines is increased to a high point of feeling at the end. Naturally, to reach a high point it is necessary to start at a relatively low one. In a strong emotional passage, begin with a relatively slow rate, deliberate utterance, low pitch, and little or medium vocal energy. Gradually increase the energy and speed and change the pitch until you reach the highest point of interest or feeling.

A flexible, responsive voice is the most valuable asset an actor or a speaker can have. Speaking is like painting. In both arts, the main purpose is to express an idea. The painter may use dull grays or a great variety of colors, exquisitely blended and harmonized. So, too, the speaker or actor may use a lifeless voice— monotonous in tone, energy, and pitch—or may utilize all the resources of vocal technique.

In the Applications that follow, try to use all the suggestions made in this chapter, first thinking and feeling and then using the intonation, inflection, and emphasis necessary to express the ideas behind the sounds and words. Be sure to take the time you need, and be careful not to tighten your throat.

APPLICATIONS

1. Tell the story "The Three Bears," stressing the vocal characteristics of Goldilocks and the bears and getting all the contrast possible. Also read Lincoln's Gettysburg Address aloud, doing the same thing.

2. Using the letters of the alphabet instead of words, tell a funny story, a moral tale, a short tragedy, and a ghost story.

3. Say "oh" to suggest keen interest, sudden pain, deep sympathy, utter exhaustion, delight, fear, irritation, anger, sarcasm, hesitation, embarrassment, good-natured banter, polite indifference, horror, and surprise.

4. Address the following sentences first to someone 5 feet away and then to someone 25, 100, and 500 feet away. Keep an open throat, but control the breath from the diaphragm. Make full use of the vowel sounds.

   a. Run for your life!
   b. Fire! Help!
   c. Are you all right?
   d. Come here at once!

5. Read the following passages aloud. First carefully analyze their meanings. Then determine the mood, the situation, and the emotion portrayed. Finally decide what quality, energy, change of pitch, and rate will best suit your interpretation.

a.

[PIERRETTE:]

> Pierrot, don't wait for the moon,
> There's a heart-chilling cold in her rays;
> And mellow and musical June
> Will only last thirty short days.

The Maker of Dreams
by Oliphant Down

b.

> Work!
> Thank God for the might of it,
> The ardor, the urge, the delight of it—
> Work that springs from the heart's desire,
> Setting the brain and the soul on fire.

"Work"
by Angela Morgan

c.

[THE PIPER:]

> If I knew all, why should I care to live?
> No, No! The game is What-Will-Happen-Next? . . .
> It keeps me searching. 'Tis so glad and sad
> And strange to find out, What-Will-Happen-Next!

The Piper
by Josephine Preston Peabody

d.

During the whole of a dull, dark, and soundless day in the autumn of the year, when clouds hung oppressively low in the heavens, I had been passing alone, on horseback, through a singularly dreary tract of country; and at length found myself, as the shades of evening drew on, within view of the melancholy House of Usher.

"The Fall of the House of Usher"
by Edgar Allan Poe

e.

[THE PRINCE OF MOROCCO:]

> All that glisters is not gold;
> Often have you heard that told:
> Many a man his life has sold
> But my outside to behold:
> Gilded tombs do worms infold.
> Had you been as wise as bold,
> Young in limbs, in judgment old,
> Your answer had not been inscroll'd:
> Fare you well; your suit is cold.

The Merchant of Venice
by William Shakespeare

f.

> We shall walk in velvet shoes:
>   Wherever we go
> Silence will fall like dews
>   On white silence below.
>   We shall walk in the snow.

''Velvet Shoes''
by Elinor Wylie

g.

[ROMEO:]

> Night's candles are burnt out, and jocund day
> Stands tiptoe on the misty mountain tops.

Romeo and Juliet
by William Shakespeare

h.

> 'Tis not too late to seek a newer world,
> Push off, and sitting well in order, smite
> The sounding furrows; for my purpose holds
> To sail beyond the sunset, and the baths
> Of all the western stars, until I die.

''Ulysses''
by Alfred, Lord Tennyson

i.

[MACBETH:]

Ring the alarum bell! Blow, wind, come, wrack!
At least we'll die with harness on our back!

Macbeth
by William Shakespeare

6. Study the following passages. Decide what type of person is speaking, exactly what is being said, what mood that person is in, and why that person is saying these lines. Read them aloud, trying to convey the exact meaning and mood.

a.

[ANNE'S VOICE:]

I expect I should be describing what it feels like to go into hiding. But I really don't know yet myself. I only know it's funny never to be able to go outdoors . . . never to breathe fresh air . . . never to run and shout and jump. It's the silence in the nights that frightens me most. Every time I hear a creak in the house, or a step on the street outside, I'm sure they're coming for us.

The Diary of Anne Frank
by Frances Goodrich and Albert Hackett

b.

[MABEL CHILTERN:]

Well, Tommy has proposed to me again. Tommy really does nothing but propose to me. He proposed to me last night in the music room, when I was quite unprotected, as there was an elaborate trio going on. I didn't dare make the smallest repartee, I need hardly tell you. If I had it would have stopped the music at once. Musical people are so absurdly unreasonable. They always want one to be perfectly dumb when one is longing to be absolutely deaf.

An Ideal Husband
by Oscar Wilde

c.

[JULIUS CAESAR:]

Cowards die many times before their death,
The valiant never taste of death but once.

Julius Caesar
by William Shakespeare

d.

[BEATRICE:]

O that I were a man for his sake! or that I had any friend would be a man for my sake! But manhood is melted into courtesies, valour into compliment, and men are only turned into tongues, and trim ones too: he is now as valiant as Hercules that only tells a lie and swears to it.—I cannot be a man with wishing, therefore, I shall die a woman with grieving.

Much Ado About Nothing
by William Shakespeare

e.

Look to this day
For it is life—the very life of life.
In it lie all the verities and realities of existence:
The bliss of growth,
The glory of action,
The wealth of beauty.
For yesterday is but a dream,
And tomorrow is only a vision,
But today well lived
Makes every yesterday a dream of happiness
And every tomorrow a vision of hope,
Look therefore to today!

Sanskrit

IMPROVING YOUR DICTION

There are various definitions of diction, but for all practical purposes, it means the selection and pronunciation of words and their combination in speech. Technically, diction involves the correct articulation of sounds, which results in the proper formation of words; careful enunciation of syllables, which results in clear and distinct speech; and the musical rhythm that characterizes cultivated speech.

If your speech is to be an asset rather than a liability, in addition to correct and distinct utterance of sounds, you must also improve your choice of words in your normal daily usage. Your aim should be clear, correct, pleasing speech that carries well. There are some very common habits of sloppy speech you should avoid. They include mumbling, muttering, dropping words at the ends of sentences and letters at the ends of words, and indistinctness due to the lazy use of the vocal apparatus, especially the tongue. There are some less common habits that are likely to creep up on you after a little speech training. One is speech that is pedantic—too accurate and meticulous and artificial, that is, affected and unnaturally theatrical. Another is speech that is imitative—expressive of characteristics that you admire in someone else's speech but that do not suit your own personality. Practice reading aloud every day using your own best speech, and then relax and speak naturally. You will find the habitual use of your vocal apparatus improving.

Television offers an opportunity for the study of diction that no other generation has had. In the field of colloquial speech, television is especially useful. In the news reports from all sections of the country and in panels made up of people from all areas, you hear the habitual conversational expressions of people from everywhere. On both sides of the Atlantic, there are numerous dialects in the English of daily life. This colloquial or provincial speech is picturesque but confusing in communicating thought and should be avoided on the stage except when a role demands it.

For Colored Girls Who Have Considered Suicide When the Rainbow is Enuf by Ntozake Shange is classified as a choreopoem. In this contemporary verse play, the emotional intensity of the poetry comes through because the performers are masterful vocal interpreters.

The use of tape recorders is another advantage of this generation. You should get someone to set up a recorder when you are unaware of it, in order to record your ordinary diction, which you can analyze for its good and its weak points. Also, early in the term you should record your reading of some of the selections in this book. Then remake them at the end and note your improvement.

Records and tapes offer opportunities for studying the diction of professionals. Many excellent records of plays, readings of poetry and prose, examples of the dialects in various sections of the country, and even lessons in speech improvement are available for your entertainment, enlightenment, and instruction.

As suggested earlier, you should take a course in speech as well as in dramatics. Such a speech class helps you distinguish between the styles of speech appropriate for different occasions. In informal conversation, it is natural to use speech patterns that differ somewhat from those you use for formal conversation or stage performance.

Ear training is almost as important as speech training. Therefore, you should accustom yourself to the best speech used in your community. As far as possible, associate with people who speak well, for there is nothing more contagious than speech habits.

The exercises that follow are based largely on the standard sounds of vowels and consonants, which can be learned with patience and practice. They will help you use your vocal apparatus properly and without self-consciousness, making your daily speech correct and clear at all times and effective when projected from the stage.

Vowel Sounds

The vowel sounds are unobstructed tones through the mouth, given characteristic tone by the positions of the lips, tongue, jaw, and soft palate, which necessarily differ for each vowel sound.

The vowel sounds may be classified as front vowels, middle vowels, and back vowels, according to the position of the tongue as each is formed. Remember that the tip of the tongue remains at the base of the lower teeth in all vowels. In the front vowels, the front of the tongue is gradually raised until it almost touches the inner gum ridge, as with *ē* in *mē*. In the middle vowels, the front of the tongue is midway to the roof of the mouth, as with *ŭ* in *ŭp*. In the back vowels, the back of the tongue is raised, the jaw relaxed, and the lips rounded, as with *o͞o* in *fo͞od*. In all the back vowels, the lips are rounded until only a small opening is left. Diphthongs are combinations of two vowel sounds, as in *how* (*ä* + *o͞o*) or *hay* (*ā* + *ĭ*). Prolong the vowel sounds and see how the quality changes from one sound to another. Listen carefully and perhaps tape record yourself as you practice.

FRONT	MIDDLE	BACK
ē as in *ēve*	*ŭ* as in *ŭp*	*ä* as in *äh*
ĭ as in *hĭm*	*à* as in *àlone*	*ŏ* as in *ŏccur*
ĕ as in *ĕnd*	*û* as in *ûrn*	*ô* as in *lôrd*
ă as in *căt*	*ē* as in *makēr*	*ō* as in *ōld*
		o͝o as in *ho͝od*
		o͞o as in *fo͞od*

(Note: Modern dictionaries use various symbols to represent vowel sounds; these will be shown in the pronunciation key. The system used here is a simplified one.)

Practice to distinguish among the vowel sounds as you read the words in the following lists.

1. feel, fill, fell, fall, fail, file, foil, foul
2. tea, tin, ten, tan, ton, turn, tarn, torn, tune, town
3. eat, it, at, ought, ate
4. peak, pick, peck, pack, puck, perk, park, pock, pork, poke, pike

Consonant Sounds

The consonant sounds are made when the air passage is obstructed at some point by the tongue, soft palate, or lips. If there is no vibration of the vocal folds, the consonant is said to be voiceless. If there is a vibration of the vocal folds, the consonant sound is voiced. You can tell whether a consonant sound is voiced or voiceless by placing your finger lightly on your throat and feeling whether there is any vibration.

Plosive Consonants

In these sounds, the air is stopped and suddenly released.

VOICELESS	VOICED	AIR STOPPED BY
p as in *pop*	*b* as in *bob*	Lip against lip
t as in *tame*	*d* as in *dame*	Tip of tongue against upper gum ridge
c or *k* as in *came*	*g* as in *game*	Back of tongue against soft palate

Fricative Consonants

In these sounds, the air passage is narrowed at some point and a slight friction results.

VOICELESS	VOICED	AIR PASSAGE NARROWED BY
f as in *fan*	*v* as in *van*	Upper teeth on lower lip
s as in *bus*	*z* as in *buzz*	Front of tongue against upper and lower teeth, which are almost closed
sh as in *sure*	*zh* as in *azure*	Tip of tongue turned toward hard palate; teeth almost closed
th as in *breath*	*th* as in *breathe*	Tip of tongue against upper teeth
wh as in *which*	*w* as in *witch*	Rounded lips and raised tongue

Nasal Consonants

In these sounds, the mouth is completely closed at some point, and the soft palate is lowered. Thus, the air is forced to pass through the nose.

m as in *mommy*	Mouth closed by lip on lip
ng as in *sing*	Mouth closed by back of tongue on soft palate
n as in *ninny*	Mouth closed by tip of tongue on upper gums

Practice to distinguish among the consonant sounds as you read the words in these lists.

1. pen, Ben, ten, den, ken, fen, when, wen

2. have, cat, gap, quack, land, nag, tap, dash, rat, map, pat, bat, fat, vat, thank

3. than, sad, sham, chap, jam, plaid, black, flat, slack, clan, glad, snack, stand

4. smack, span, scan, trap, dram, prank, bran, frank, crab, grab, thrash, shrapnel

5. strap, sprat, scrap, splash, swam, twang, wag, yap

6. hood, could, good, look, nook, put, book, foot, soot, should, brook, crook, wood

There are a number of vowel and consonant sounds that are not formed in the standard way in the colloquial speech of various parts of the United States. The important thing to remember is how they are produced in standard English.

Difficult Consonants

The consonants that give difficulty include the following:

1. The *r* is a consonant sound when it comes before a sounded vowel, whether the vowel is in the same word or is the first letter in the next word. The tip of the tongue should be on the upper gum ridge of the hard palate in such words as *red, grumble, three,* and *breeze,* or in such expressions as *butter and bread, as far as you go,* and *there are three boys.* The *r* is silent before consonant sounds or at the ends of words. The tip of the tongue is held at the base of the lower teeth and is not permitted to turn back to form what we call the "rolled *r.*" When it is retroflex (back in the mouth), the inverted *r* is formed, which gives an incorrect value to the vowel sound which precedes it—*bird* becomes *bŭrrd, mother* becomes *mŭthŭrr,* and *art* becomes *äurrt.* In stage diction the *r* is frequently trilled when it comes between two vowels or when it is doubled as in such words as *American, marry, courage, orange.*

Patti LuPone and Robert Gutman as Juan and Eva Péron in the rock opera Evita *must use precise enunciation to portray this Argentinian couple. The voice and diction demands are particularly great in* Evita *since all dialogue is sung rather than spoken.*

2. The *l* is formed by pressing the tip of the tongue against the upper gum, with the air passing over the sides of the body of the tongue. Do not turn the tip of the tongue back in the mouth (retroflex), do not follow it with a *ŭ* in words such as *elm* and *film,* and do not put an *ĕ* before it in words such as *fool.*

3. Such combinations as ''Didn't you?'' ''Wouldn't you?'' ''Haven't you?'' ''Shouldn't you?'' and ''Why don't you?'' are often run together slightly. Practice them carefully to avoid separating them too much and yet not say ''Didncha?'' or ''Didn'tchew?''

4. Do not pronounce the *r* at the ends of the following words. Keep the tip of the tongue at the base of the lower teeth.

    a. air, bare, care, dare, fare, hair, lair, mare, pare, rare, share, stare, tare, wear

    b. bore, core, door, four, gore, hoar, lore, more, pore, roar, soar, tore, wore, yore

5. Note the distinction between the *w* and *wh* sounds in such words as *wear* and *where, weather* and *whether, wight* and *white.* The *wh* is pronounced like *hw;* if you blow on your finger, you get the correct sound.

APPLICATIONS

Read the following clearly, pronouncing the consonant sounds carefully.

a.

Dry clashed his harness in the icy caves
And barren chasms, and all to left and right
Thè bare black cliffs clanged round him, as he based
His feet on juts of slippery crag that rang
Sharp-smitten with the dint of armed heels—
And on a sudden, lo! the level lake
And the long glories of the winter moon.

''Idylls of the King''
by Alfred, Lord Tennyson

b.

In the heel of my thumb
are whorls, whirls, wheels
in a unique design:
mine alone.
What a treasure to own!
My own flesh, my own feelings.
No other, however grand or base,

can ever contain the same.
My signature,
thumbing the pages of my time.
My universe key,
my singularity.
Impress, implant,
I am myself,
of all my atom parts I am the sum.
And out of my blood and my brain
I make my own interior weather,
my own sun and rain.
Imprint my mark upon the world,
whatever I shall become.

''Thumbprint''
by Eve Merriam

c.

Over the cobbles he clatters and clangs in the dark inn-yard.
He taps with his whip on the shutters, but all is locked
   and barred.
He whistles a tune to the window, and who should be waiting
   there
But the landlord's black-eyed daughter,
   Bess, the landlord's daughter,
Plaiting a dark red love-knot into her long black hair.

''The Highwayman''
by Alfred Noyes

Difficult Vowels

The vowels that give difficulty include the following:

1. *à* as in *last, ask, after, path, dance, pass* (This sound is often confused with the short *ă*.)

2. *ô* as in *audience, lord, daughter, because, water, automobile, thought* (This sound is often confused with the short *ŏ*.)

3. *ōō* as in *root, soon, bloom, roof, soup, rude* (This sound is often confused with the short *ŭ* or the diphthong *iu*.)

4. *ŏ* as in *God, John, stop, was, yacht* (This sound is often confused with *äw* or *äh*.)

5. *ē* as in *sleek, creek, sheep, clique* (Often confused with *ĭ*.)

6. *ă* as in *have, man, began, shall, and, than, glad* (This sound is often confused with *à* or *ä* when a student is being particularly careful, or when a *ŭ* is sounded after it.

7. The vowel sound in *perfect, purple, world, girl, learn, nerve* (This sound is often confused with *ŭ* or the diphthong *oi*.)

8. The diphthong *iu* as in *assume, Tuesday, student, duty, stupid, avenue* (This sound is often confused with *ō͞o*.)

9. The indeterminate *e* in unstressed syllables is barely sounded.

10. The *ĕ* sound as in *men, experiment, engineer, sincerity* (This sound is often confused with *ĭ*.)

APPLICATIONS

Read the following clearly, pronouncing the vowel sounds carefully.

a.

Water, water, everywhere,
   And all the boards did shrink.
Water, water, everywhere,
   Nor any drop to drink.

                  ''The Rime of the Ancient Mariner''
                  by Samuel Taylor Coleridge

b.

Don't be polite.
Bite in.
Pick it up with your fingers and lick the juice that may run down your chin.
It is ready and ripe now, whenever you are.

You do not need a knife or fork or spoon
or plate or napkin or tablecloth.

For there is no core
or stem
or rind
or pit
or seed
or skin
to throw away.

                  ''How to Eat a Poem''
                  by Eve Merriam

c.

We wait in the darkness!
Come, all ye who listen,
Help in our night journey:
Now no sun is shining;
Now no star is glowing;
Come show us the pathway:
The night is not friendly;
She closes her eyelids;
The moon has forgot us,
We wait in the darkness!

"Darkness Song"
Iroquois

Pronunciation

Good pronunciation entails the use of correct vowel and consonant sounds in words and the placing of the accent on the stressed syllables.

The following commonly used words are only a very few of those that are constantly mispronounced.

1. Place the accent on the first syllable in the following words:

ex′qui site	pos′i tive ly	in′flu ence
des′pi ca ble	mis′chie vous	the′a ter
lam′en ta ble	ad′mi ra ble	in′ter est ing
ab′so lute ly	req′ui site	hos′pi ta ble

2. Place the accent on the second syllable in the following words.

ho tel′	ro mance′	en tire′
in quir′y	ad dress′	al ly′
a dult′	a dept′	man kind′

3. Drop the silent letters in the following words.

often	corps	heir
toward	subtlety	indictment
debt	forehead	business

Note the consonant and vowel sounds, as well as the accent marks, in the following list of words. Say these words according to the pronunciation spellings that are given within the parentheses following the words themselves. An italicized vowel or a vowel marked with a half-long (ŭ, ŏ) is pronounced rapidly. The first pronunciation is considered preferable, but the others are also in good usage.

hearth (härth)
na·ive' (nä·ēv')
gen'u·ine (jen'ṷ·ĭn)
I·tal'ian (ĭ·tăl'yạn)
come'ly (kŭm'lĭ)
with (wĭth; wĭŧ)
bade (băd)
her'o·ine (hĕr'ȯ·ĭn)
col'umn (kŏl'ụm)
ab·surd' (ăb·sûrd')
says (sĕz)
been (bĭn; bēn)
a'li·as (ā'lĭ·ạs)
wom'en (wĭm'ĕn; wĭm'ĭn)

Feb'ru·ar'y (fĕb'rōō·ĕr'ĭ; fĕb'ṷ·ĕr'ĭ;
  fĕb'ōō·ĕr'ĭ; fĕb'ōō·ēr·ĭ)
vau'de·ville (vô'de·vĭl; vōd'vĭl)
ir·rev'o·ca·ble (ĭ·rĕv'ȯ·ka·b'l)
har'ass (hăr'ạs; ha·răs')
bou·quet' (bōō·kā'; bō·kā')
ac·cli'mate (ă·klī'mĭt; ăk'lĭ·māt)
fin'an·cier' (fĭn'ăn·sēr'; fī'năn·sēr';
  fĭ·năn'sĭ·ēr)
sin·cer'i·ty (sĭn·sĕr'ĭ·tĭ)
am'a·teur' (ăm'a·tûr'; ăm'a·tûr; ăm'a·tụr)
chauf·feur' (shō·fûr'; shȯ'fēr)
ar'chi·tec'ture (är'kĭ·tĕk'tụr)

Read these sentences aloud very carefully.

1. The speech of the children over the radio was scarcely intelligible and entirely lacking in spirit and enthusiasm.

2. Some sparks from the largest of the rockets burned holes in her scarlet jacket.

3. The President of the United States of America delivered the dedicatory address.

4. His vocabulary is as meager as when he was in the elementary grades, and he is entirely lacking in intellectual curiosity; this is a sad commentary on his secondary education.

5. Her thought that remaining in the automobile would allow them to see over the audience placed them in an awkward position.

6. They quarreled as to whether or not to take the spotted dog on the yacht.

7. Aunt Blanche answered the demand by advancing with her passport.

8. We hope next year to hear that she has started her career as an engineer rather than as a mere cashier.

9. He was so boorish that he could endure the lonely moor and the obscure rural life.

Read the following as rapidly as you can, keeping the sounds clear.

1. The perfectly purple bird unfurled its curled wings and whirled over the world.

2. Amidst the mists and coldest frosts
　　With stoutest wrists and sternest boasts,
　He thrusts his fists against the posts
　　And still insists he sees the ghosts.

3. The weary wanderer wondered wistfully whether winsome Winifred would weep.

4. When and where will you go and why?

5. The sea ceaseth and sufficeth us.

6. To sit in solemn silence in a dull, dark dock
　In a pestilential prison with a life-long lock,
　Awaiting the sensation of a short, sharp shock
　From a cheap and chippy chopper on a big black block!

7. The queen was a coquette.

8. They know not whence, nor whither, where, nor why.

9. Judge not that ye be not judged, for with what judgment ye judge ye shall be judged.

10. The clumsy kitchen clock click-clacked.

11. Didn't you enjoy the rich shrimp salad?

12. The very merry Mary crossed the ferry in a furry coat.

Careful diction also involves discrimination in the choice and use of words. A wide and constantly increasing vocabulary, free from an overuse of slang, is a cultural asset you cannot afford to neglect. Standard usage and grammatical structure are taken for granted.

VOICE AND DICTION IN ACTING

A play comes to life by means of the voices and words of the actors. It is their ability to arouse emotion through the playwright's lines that creates the illusion of reality for the audience. Actors must make the meaning of every passage clear to all listeners by the proper projection of the key words. It is their responsibility to avoid spoiling lines by blurring pronunciation, muffling enunciation, or speaking with a nervous rhythm. The inner soul of the characters they are creating must be expressed through clear-cut patterns that are suitable to the roles but are varied with every change of mood and situation.

Legendary actress Eva Le Gallienne portrays Grandie (center) in Joanna M. Glass's play To Grandmother's House We Go. *Ms. Le Gallienne, who has been a notable theatrical personality for over 50 years, remains a vigorous performer.*

The presentation of a character through voice alone is possible only if you can visualize and empathize with that character accurately. As in daily life, each character has an individual voice quality, pitch, and tempo. However, these must all be varied in keeping with an immediate situation and mood without the loss of the character's individuality.

Remember that variety is the spice of speech and that a flexible, responsive voice is an invaluable asset to the speaker and actor. A lifeless voice—monotonous in pitch, lacking in energy, unpleasant in tone, and uniform in rate—is ruinous to an actor. Colloquial, mumbled, or inarticulate diction is equally disastrous on the stage. More actors today are not heard and understood because of poor enunciation than because of lack of vocal power. Think always of the person in the audience who is farthest from you, emphasize the important words and sounds of letters, and subordinate the unimportant ones, for only in that way can you make your role live for your audience. No matter how sensitive and responsive you are as an actor, if you are not heard and understood, your characterization will fail. Only training and experience can free your abilities. Your dramatics classwork can give you a good foundation if you make use of it by daily practice.

APPLICATIONS

1. The following play excerpts present strongly contrasted roles, worthy of careful practice. Work with the passages until you have created totally individual characterizations for each of the speakers.

a.

Will you go with him?
He will gentler to you than a father!
He would be brothers five, and dearest friend,
And sweetheart, aye and Knight and serving man.

The Piper
by Josephine Preston Peabody

b.

[ABE LINCOLN:]

   I went through something like this once before! Someone you love—standing helpless—waiting. I sat day by day reading Ma parts of the Bible she liked best. On the sixth day she called me to her bed—talked of many strange things—principalities and powers—and things present—and things to come—urged me and Sairy always to walk in paths of goodness and truth—and told us many things would come t'him that served God—an' th' best way t'serve Him was t'serve His people. *(Pause)* She was amongst the lowliest of mankind. She walked the earth with her poor feet in the dust—her head in the stars—*(Pause)* Pa took me down into the woods t' make her a coffin. Pa was sawin' and I was hammerin' the pegs in. The hammer dropped at my feet; it was like someone was drivin' 'em into my heart. It's—just goin' through all that again—now!

Prologue to Glory
by E. P. Conkle

c.

Those foolish mortals who spend their time chasing bright bubbles sure to burst. Only art my children, accomplishment, can lead them to discover riches that may be stored away one by one, until they grow to treasure indestructible. If they but knew!

Poor Maddalena
by Louise Saunders

2. Practice reading aloud any selections in this book, applying the technical principles brought out in this chapter. Use a tape recorder as you work with the selections, and check your progress. Many of the selections can be found in records of the plays from which they were chosen. Do not imitate the actors in their vocal habits or interpretations but practice expanding your own.

3. Turn to the chapter on pantomime and put words into the mouths of the characters in all the suggested situations. Practice changing your voice completely for each character and coordinating your voice and body as you present each situation.

4. Using the following play excerpts, paint voice pictures of each of the characters by employing as much beauty, variety, and effectiveness of voice and speech as you can.

a.

[G<small>WENDOLEN</small>:]

Ernest, we may never be married. From the expression on mamma's face, I fear we never shall. Few parents nowadays pay any regard to what their children say to them. The old-fashioned respect for the young is rapidly dying out. Whatever influence I ever had over mamma I lost at the age of three. But though she may prevent us from becoming man and wife, and I may marry someone else, and marry often, nothing that she can possibly do can alter my eternal devotion to you.

The Importance of Being Earnest
by Oscar Wilde

b.

[A<small>NNIE</small>:]

Cleanliness is next to nothing, she has to learn that everything has its name! That words can be her *eyes,* to everything in the world outside her, and inside too, what is she without words? With them she can think, have ideas, be reached, there's not a thought or fact in the world that can't be hers. You publish a newspaper, Captain Keller, do I have to tell you what words are? And she has them already ———
. . . .——— eighteen nouns and three verbs, they're in her fingers now, I need only time to push *one* of them into her mind! One, and everything under the sun will follow. Don't you see what she's learned here is only clearing the way for that? I can't risk her unlearning it, give me more time alone with her, another week to

———

The Miracle Worker
by William Gibson

c.

[A<small>NTONIO</small>:]

Give me your hand, Bassanio; fare you well,
Grieve not that I am fallen to this for you.

The Merchant of Venice
by William Shakespeare

BIBLIOGRAPHY

Fischer, Hilda B.: *Improving Voice and Articulation,* Houghton Mifflin, Boston, 1966.

King, R. G., and E. M. DeMichael: *Improving Articulation and Voice,* Macmillan, New York, 1966.

Mayer, Lyle V.: *Fundamentals of Voice and Diction,* Wm. C. Brown Company, Dubuque, Iowa, 1968.

Wise, Claude M.: *Applied Phonetics,* Prentice-Hall, Englewood Cliffs, New Jersey, 1957.

Woolbert, C. H., and S. E. Nelson: *Art of Interpretive Speech: Principles and Practice,* Appleton-Century-Crofts, New York, 1947.

CHAPTER FIVE

Acting

Acting brings the play to life against a scenic background that creates the proper mood and atmosphere. The play is the culmination of the ideas of the dramatist; the feeling, understanding, and techniques of the director and actors; and the aesthetic standards and practical abilities of the backstage personnel. Without the appeal of creative acting, the drama would not be the power it has been for generations. It is the acting of roles in your classroom and in public performances that will bring you the inspiration, excitement, and satisfaction of theater work.

In all forms of creative art, teachers and textbooks can only point the way to achievement. Inborn talent backed by ambition and a driving force controlled by self-discipline and perseverance must transform the amateur into the artist. Even in cases of exceptional talent, the tools of the trade must be mastered, the divine spark nourished, and the student inspired.

In your school dramatics work, you have the advantage of the trained teacher-director to stimulate your theater achievements. But your real growth depends upon your personal grasp of the fundamentals of the art. Acting is both intensely individual and intensely social. The actor must develop as an individual only to lose self-identity in a characterization that is but a part of a unified production. Therefore, analyze your own and other persons' reactions while improving your ability to create another personality. The wise director will encourage you to use your own interpretation as long as it is in harmony with the underlying spirit of the production. Learn to check your individual reactions to the internal and external phases of your role and of the other roles as they relate to the meaning of the scenes and plays of your various assignments. Also check your own improvement and powers of interpretation.

SHAKESPEARE'S ADVICE TO ACTORS

The finest lesson in dramatic art ever expressed in concrete form is Hamlet's advice to the players (*Hamlet,* Act III, Sc. 2), from the world's greatest actor-

A quiet, true-to-life moment between Eva Le Gallienne (Grandie) and Pamela Brook (Muffy, her granddaughter).

director-dramatist. The standards he set down have long been the universal rules of acting.

The fundamental principles of Hamlet's advice to the players can be modernized for you to apply.

Speak the lines of the author as written, distinctly and fluently, with understanding of their meaning.

Do not use elaborate and artificial gestures, but keep a reserve force in order to build to an emotional climax smoothly and effectively.

Do not resort to farfetched action and noise to please unintelligent and unappreciative onlookers.

Do not be apathetic or dull, either, but let your inner understanding of the role guide your movements. Suit the action to the word and the word to the action, with this special warning, that you are always natural. Overacting is not true interpretation. The purpose of true interpretation is always to present the real character so as to bring out the character's virtues and faults truthfully. The purpose of acting is to show life as it is in accordance with the time and custom of the play.

Do not either overact or underact to get a laugh from the audience. Anything you do that is not true to life will spoil the play for the intelligent few whose criticism outweighs that of all the rest of the audience.

There are actors, sometimes highly praised, who show no resemblance to the people they are portraying, or even to humanity, when they strut and bellow in their bad imitations on the stage.

Never put in extemporaneous lines, especially in humorous roles, even when these lines are clever enough to make some stupid people in the audience laugh or when the actors themselves laugh at their antics. Such methods draw the attention away from the center of interest and ensure the loss of important lines. Such action is inexcusable and shows a most pitiful ambition in the fools who use it.

Modern directors usually say the same sort of thing to beginners in the first few rehearsals: Get your lines; speak clearly; keep your hands still; do not overact; be natural and easy; do not play to the least discerning in the audience; hold back; be yourself at your best; stick to the script; use your head; act like a human being; do not steal the scene from the main business.

ACTING TERMINOLOGY

There are a number of expressions with which you must be familiar if you are to work on the stage. Those most frequently used in connection with acting are listed here. Technical terms applying to staging and lighting will be found in the sections dealing with those aspects of the theater.

ad-lib: To extemporize stage business or conversation.

back or *backstage:*   The area behind the part of the stage visible to the audience.

blocking yourself: Getting behind furniture or actors so that you cannot be seen by the audience.

building a scene: Using dramatic devices such as increased tempo, volume, or emphasis to bring a scene to a climax.

business: Any action performed on the stage.

C: The symbol used to designate the center of the stage.

countercross: A shifting of position by one or more actors to balance the stage picture.

cover: To obstruct the view of the audience.

cross: The movement by an actor from one location to another onstage.

cue: The last words or action of any one actor that immediately precedes any lines or business of another actor.

curtain: The curtain or drapery that shuts off the stage from the audience; used in a script to indicate that the curtain is lowered.

cut: To stop action or to omit.

cut in: To break into the speech of another character.

down or *downstage:*   The part of the stage toward the footlights.

dressing the stage: Keeping the stage picture balanced during the action.

exit or *exeunt:*   To leave the stage.

feeding: Giving lines and action in such a way that another actor can make a point or get a laugh.

getting up in a part: Memorizing lines or becoming letter-perfect.

hand props: Personal properties, such as notebooks, letters, or luggage, carried onstage by the individual player.

hit: To emphasize a word or line with extra force.

holding for laughs: Waiting for the audience to quiet down after a funny line or scene.

holding it: Keeping perfectly still.

left and right: Terms used to refer to the stage from the actor's point of view when facing the audience.

left center and right center: The areas to the left and right of the center stage, with reference to the actor and not the audience.

off or *offstage:*   Off the visible stage.

on or *onstage:*   On the visible stage.

overlap: To speak when someone else does.

pace: The movement or sweep of the play as it progresses.

places: The positions of the actors at the opening of an act or a scene.

plot: To plan stage business, as to ''plot'' the action; to plan a speech by working out the phrasing, emphasis, and inflections.

pointing lines: Emphasizing an idea.

properties or props: All the stage furnishings, including furniture.

ring up: To raise the curtain.

set: The scenery for an act or a scene.

set props: Properties placed onstage for the use of the actor.

showmanship: A sense of theater and feeling for effects.

sides: Half-sheets of typewritten manuscript containing the lines, cues, and business for one character.

stealing a scene: Attracting attention away from the person to whom the center of interest legitimately belongs.

tag line: The last speech in an act or a play.

taking the stage: Holding the center of interest; moving over the entire stage area.

tempo: The speed with which speech and action move a play along.

timing: The execution of a line or piece of business at a specific moment to achieve the most telling effect.

top: To build to a climax by speaking at a higher pitch, at a faster rate, or with more force than in the preceding speeches.

up or *upstage:*   The area of the stage away from the footlights, toward the rear of the stage.

Properties add dramatic interest to every type of play. The Haggadah (left) is a Hebrew parable drama. The props—the book and branch—are symbolic.

Vanities by Jack Heifner is a comedy about three high school cheerleaders growing up in the sixties. Pom-poms are perfect props for cheerleaders.

upstaging: Improperly taking attention away from an actor who is the focus of interest.

warn: To notify of an upcoming action or cue.

EMOTION AND/OR TECHNIQUE

There are two major approaches to acting. Supporters uphold each and point out the followers from among the world's artists to support their claims.

In one, the emotional or subjective approach, the actors live their parts so that they actually weep, suffer, and triumph before the audience. They become the parts they play, as far as possible, and experience all that their characters do. In the other, the technical or objective approach, absolute control based upon perfect technique is the aim. The actor analyzes the play's structure and the characters. Then technical skills in acting, movement, speech, and interpretation are used in the creation of a role. No emotional response is allowed to interfere with the conscious artistry that alone is responsible for the results obtained. The actor does not live the part but acts it so well that the illusion of living the part is maintained.

In the first case, the emphasis is placed upon the actor's emotional response because of personal inner reactions. In the other, the emphasis is placed upon an assumed personality based on a conscious technique.

There is much to be said for both points of view, but today most actors use a combination of the two approaches. You would do well, then, to identify yourself with your part so that you can interpret it naturally, simply, and spontaneously, using your technical training to achieve a clear-cut, convincing, and consistent characterization. Lose your individuality in the part you play, but never forget that you are presenting it to be seen, heard, and appreciated by your entire audience.

The most discussed acting theory today, "the Method," was formulated by the dominant actor-director of this century, Konstantin Stanislavski. His books—*My Life in Art, An Actor Prepares, Building a Character,* and *Creating a Role*—set forth his theories on the art of acting together with practical exercises in the techniques of vocal and bodily expression.

Stanislavski's theories have been interpreted and misinterpreted by earnest theater people. Too much emphasis has been put on the actor's use of self-analysis and personal emotional experiences in creating a role and not enough on Stanislavski's equal insistence on disciplined control of the techniques of vocal and bodily expressiveness. As a result, many so-called Method actors on the stage become so involved with their inner resources that they fail to communicate with the audience because of slovenly speech and action.

Sir Tyrone Guthrie

Konstantin Stanislavski

Probably Stanislavski's most valuable counsel to help you in creating a characterization is his ''magic *if*,'' which can be called the key to his method. While using the full powers of concentration and imagination, the actor should ask himself or herself what he or she would do if the events in the play were actually happening and he or she were intimately involved in those events. The answers to these questions lead to an analysis of both the actor's own and the character's inner natures, the basis for kinship with the part. Only then can the actor use the technical resources of voice and body to interpret the reactions of the character truthfully and naturally. This analysis also leads to appreciating exactly what the author had in mind and to a correct understanding of the play itself.

Today actors, directors, and teachers who use the Method have advanced their own approaches to it. The Actor's Studio, under the direction of Lee Strasberg, has been the controversial center where many well-known actors have studied and worked. You are probably familiar with many of them—Geraldine Page, Rod Steiger, Anne Bancroft, Marilyn Monroe, Marlon Brando, Paul Newman, Julie Harris, Eli Wallach, David Wayne, and Shelley Winters.

In contrast to Method acting is the theatrical style that emphasizes conscious technique rather than emotional involvement. Its outstanding exponent was the dynamic director Tyrone Guthrie. Guthrie disapproved of the intensive analysis and frequently inarticulate speech of Method actors, believing that people go to the theater to be thrilled and entertained. His influence has been very strong in this country, where he directed and lectured on many university campuses and produced in a number of repertory and regional theaters.

Most actors today believe in working seriously and imaginatively to create roles through understanding them, and in using their own abilities of interpretation to present them effectively to the audience. There is a growing enthusiasm for understanding the motivations behind an actor's physical and psychological responses. Bringing the play to life and making the author's meaning clear through careful teamwork is the aim of most director-teachers. As a student, you should try to be as flexible and spontaneous as you can, applying your technical training to making your character a living personality for your audience. Thus, you will appreciate that the best principle to employ is emotion *and* technique.

CREATING A CHARACTER

Characterization is the be-all and end-all of acting, a creative process involving an inner grasp of the fundamental personality of your role and its projection to your audience so that the character becomes a living, convincing human being.

The Background of Characterization

Your personal experiences as well as your inherent dramatic talent determine your ability to live a part. You must broaden your own interests along many lines.

The Great White Hope, *starring James Earl Jones, was made into a movie following its success on the stage. With Jones are Jane Alexander and Jimmy Pelham.*

You must also increase your knowledge of the lives and emotions of theater people in order to understand how they created their roles. You will find that a constant study of human beings in all walks of life and in all types of literature can be an unending source of material and inspiration upon which to draw.

Successful projection of character depends not only upon the skillful use of techniques but also upon your insights into your character's behavior and your ability to express your interpretation. The successful blending of technique and interpretation comes naturally only with continued rehearsing and with the acting of many parts in various types of plays. Restrained action, which, however, is still sufficiently exaggerated to be appreciated in the top row; the use of the pause, in which emotion pulsates while the body and voice are still; originality, which colors the work of every distinguished artist; versatility, which surprises and delights—these are some of the means by which a character becomes a unique individual. Look for them and other fine points in acting as you watch the work of first-class actors, not only on the stage but also in motion pictures and on television.

Studying the Play

To understand a role, you must make a careful study of the whole play. Usually the first rehearsal is the reading of the entire script, either by the director or author or by the actors assigned to the parts. This reading should bring out the author's purpose in writing the play, the chief problems of the protagonist, the locality and type of speech, and the plot structure, especially the ways it builds up to the climax and holds interest to the conclusion. Pay close attention not only to your own lines but also to those lines about your character spoken by the other characters. Note closely the shifting of moods throughout the play and how your character is affected by them.

You will want to know what kind of person you are in the play, why you behave as you do, what you want, and what stands in the way of your achieving your aims. Pay careful attention to the lines your character speaks, for characters reveal themselves in their speech and actions. Try to imagine what might have happened in your character's childhood to affect the personality. Note any changes that take place within your character during the action of the play.

If the setting is an unfamiliar one, study the place and period. Learn all you can from books, pictures, and travelers so that you may enter into the atmosphere, wear the costumes naturally, and feel a part of the life depicted by the playwright. Where dialect is involved, try to talk with people from the locality or listen to recordings of their voices and notice their inflections and pronunciation.

You will find it helpful to make an outline of the character traits brought out by your own lines and those spoken to and about your character. Use any main headings that seem appropriate, such as physical, mental, and spiritual character-

Geraldine Fitzgerald had to prepare her role as Nora in Eugene O'Neill's A Touch of the Poet *by studying the play. She had to research Nora's Irish heritage and her life as a tavern keeper's wife in Boston in 1828.*

istics; individual and social behavior; and emotional, environmental, physical, and intellectual motivations. As soon as you can, visualize your character in detail and begin working out specific ways to clarify your character for your audience.

It is wise not to see a motion picture or stage production of the play you are working on, for you are likely to find yourself copying another person's mannerisms rather than developing a sound understanding of the play and the role. A better means of getting material for building a characterization is to carefully observe a person in real life who is similar to your conception of the part. This individual is your *primary source*. You may wish to adopt that person's posture, movements, vocal inflections, and habit patterns. Ordinarily you will combine characteristics from several primary sources. The books you read are your *secondary sources*. They are helpful, but the best actor must always refer to life for materials and inspiration.

As you get better acquainted with your part, ask yourself questions: How good is the social adjustment of my character? Is my character shy or uninhibited? How intelligent is my character? Is there any suffering from major or minor maladjustments? In what way has environment influenced my character? What are particular problems? Is my character meeting or evading responsibilities? How and why? How does my character react to all the other characters in the play? Have defense mechanisms developed to evade the main issues of situations? What makes my character cynical, talkative, rowdy, tense, aggressive, shy, charming, friendly, fearful, envious, courageous, or idealistic? Altogether, you must understand both the social and personal background of your character.

Naturally the study of the play involves knowing the exact meaning and correct pronunciation of all unfamiliar words, for vocal inflections convey the speaker's inner reactions of the moment. This phase of your acting experience will carry over into all your classes and into your future enjoyment of books.

Building Up Your Part

There are two phases of building up your part. After studying the play and analyzing the playwright's characters, you work on your own conception of your part. The second phase is going into rehearsal of the play with the cast under the director's guidance. It is, of course, in rehearsing that your character becomes a living person as you react to others and incorporate the principles of acting in preparation for a performance.

After you have determined the general interpretation of your part, you must grow into it physically, intellectually, and emotionally. Your character's actions and speech are your means of making that character real to your audience. Your voice, your body, and your imagination are the tools to use to make your character come alive on the stage. If you have an understanding of the character, you will be

Your voice, your body, and your imagination are the tools that make your character come alive onstage. In Shakespeare's Corio- lanus, *Gloria Foster is one with her character.*

able to create movements that reveal the character's inner nature. You may want to develop a *master gesture*—some distinctive action that can be repeated effectively as a clue to the personality. This might be a peculiar walk, laugh, or turn of the head. Even the position of your feet while you are standing, walking, or sitting can help characterize your part truly.

Never drop out of character from the moment you assume it before you make your first entrance. Then enter, coming from a definite place for some specific reason, and when you leave, depart for some definite place, knowing why you are going there. Stay in character until you are safely in the wings.

Keeping in Character

To keep in character means that every gesture and facial expression must be in keeping with the underlying mood of both person and play. It is easy to stay in character when you are the center of interest. But it is most difficult to listen in character, without attracting attention to yourself, when you are in the background. It is always a temptation, if you are a talented actor, to work out clever bits of byplay when it is really your business to assist the character speaking by focusing your attention on that character. At all times, every unnecessary movement or gesture must be eliminated in order that you point up important words and feelings with effective gestures timed exactly right to clarify the thought. However, you must never become passive when listening and then come to life on a cue. If you are imaginatively in character every moment, you will soon learn to be alive and spontaneous, with no aimless fidgeting or stealing of scenes.

Working out details comes after setting your character in clear-cut lines by your bodily attitude and a few expressive gestures. Then plan how to use the small muscles of the face and body to point essential lines or feelings. However, in your interest in details, never forget that the coordination of the entire body is essential every moment and that the tone and inflections of your voice, the glance of your eye, the gestures of your hands, and the position of your body must create a single impression at any one instant. Doing one thing at a time and doing it effectively will keep your role clear-cut.

You and Your Role

The image of your role, which the audience will accept or reject, is determined by your identification with the character. When you have studied your character's thoughts, actions, and reactions, you must bring your powers of imagination into your interpretation. Your sensitiveness to your character's words, actions, and relationships to the other persons in the play naturally depends upon your own personality and past experiences. It is your creative imagination as an actor that permits you to feel with the character sympathetically. As you work alone with a part, you can so lose yourself in emotion that you cry or laugh and use your voice and body exactly as your character would. You must fix these intuitive responses by marking your script in some personal way so that you can repeat the responses in rehearsals and performances without losing control. You want your audience, not you yourself, to laugh and cry.

This ability to arouse your own emotions comes as you actively work aloud with many roles. That is the value of studying and reading the scenes in this book and others as a means of freeing your feelings. Every day you should read passages from plays until you find your voice and body reacting quickly to every shift in feeling because your imagination is functioning.

Acting is exceedingly personal, and methods of coordinating yourself with a role depend upon your training in techniques and your experience in rehearsing and acting before an audience. An important point to remember is that imagination, concentration, alertness, and attention to both general effects and small details are all vital. Dependence upon talent and an appealing personality will never lead you beyond the show-off stage.

Never try to think of the techniques of movement and speech when you are absorbing the emotions of a character either by yourself or in rehearsals. Follow a daily routine of bodily and vocal exercises and practice improvisational and reading applications of them, ending with interpretative passages from poems and plays. Then forget all about exercises when emotionally developing a role. If you listen to your voice and diction and watch your own movements, you will become stilted and self-conscious and will think of yourself rather than of your character.

Effective bodily and vocal responses are absolutely essential in acting, but they have to become subconscious when feeling a part. Every detail of characterization must be worked out alone and in rehearsals. Nothing should be left to the inspiration of the presence of an audience.

There are many means of bringing a character to life that involve special techniques. You can find an answer to all your problems if you browse among the theater books in any good library. The following are some elements you should familiarize yourself with.

The Keys to Characterization

The actor is called upon to create living believable characters on stage. Acting is action showing human beings engaged in those activities that demonstrate human struggles, mishaps, and aspirations. Part of the actor's characterization is *external*, which the audience immediately sees and hears. The costumes, makeup, hand props, dialect, vocal quality, and so on are part of the actor's external characterization.

The really important part of character development comes from *internal* characterization. This internalizing involves the thinking, feeling, and experiencing that must take place within the actor if the role is to have depth and uniqueness. It is too easy to put a cloak on the role and to have a walking character-skeleton with no flesh and bones.

Concentration

The first key to characterization is *concentration*. This is the ability to direct all your thoughts, energies, and skills into what you are doing at any single moment.

The first key to characterization is concentration. Phyllis Frelich (left) is totally deaf and totally without speech. In Children of a Lesser God, *she used sign language to communicate with others onstage. Only through intense concentration could communication occur between actors.*

It often helps to remember that every line comes from the middle of some larger thought. Lines are not isolated and independent from other thoughts and actions. You, as an actor, must learn how to concentrate simultaneously on character, line, and action, sustaining your concentration over each performance and over the length of the production's run.

Observation

The second key to characterization is *observation*. Observe people carefully, noting fine shades of emotions, workings of small facial muscles, distinguishing physical characteristics, and unique voice and diction patterns. Do what most professional actors do: begin an actor's notebook, where you record your observations. Also include pictures of real people that you might want to use as makeup models in the future. Jot down comments and suggestions made by your directors, other actors, or authors.

Emotional Memory

The third key to characterization is the use of *emotional memory*. Emotional memory is the recalling of specific emotions as you experienced them. You have experienced fear, joy, jealousy, timidity, anger, love, and many more emotions. As an actor, you draw upon your emotional memories to give life to your character. However, your emotions as you remember them might be adjusted to fit your character, the situation, the time, and the environment of the play.

As you well know, people experience more than one level of emotion at a time. People are sometimes happy and sad at the same time. As Romeo said, ". . . parting is such sweet sorrow. . . ." It is a real challenge to you when a part calls for multiple emotional expressions. It is at such a time that you must reach back into your emotional memory bank to determine how to play a role so that the audience will see the emotional conflicts, the tug of war between two feelings, within your character.

Externalization

The fourth key to characterization is *externalization*. This is the process by which the deep personality of a character is made visible for an audience. This is done through careful interpretation, nonverbal expression, vocal quality, pitch, rate, and physical action. For example, in *The Caine Mutiny Court Martial*, the paranoia of Captain Queeg is externalized through the ball bearings Queeg carries in his pocket. Whenever the Captain becomes nervous and panicky, he removes the ball bearings from his pocket and begins fidgeting with them in his hand. As a result, the audience can see evidence of the inner man breaking down.

Projection

Now that inner feelings have been externalized for the audience, they must be projected to the audience. *Projection* is the fifth key to characterization. Although strong volume is part of projecting, projection is more than loudness. Projection is the "reaching out" to the last person in the last row of the balcony typical of fine acting. You project your character through dialogue and action made larger than life. It is this larger-than-life exaggeration that carries the subtleties of a polished performance beyond the proscenium. This projection of character generates an electricity between actor and audience that creates the dynamics of the theater experience.

Motivation

The sixth key to characterization is *motivation,* the why of characterization. Your character's behavior, to be believable, must be driven by an inner force, which is intent. *Intent* is what the character wants to do; *motivation* is why the character wants to do it. For example, does the character want to help, heal, or hide? Motivations impelling a character to act are influenced by personal convictions, mind set, self-interest, past experience, situation, environment, friends, and loved ones.

Uniqueness

The seventh key to characterization is *uniqueness*. Every actor who plays a character should be unique in that role, not a carbon copy of someone else. Each

Julius Caesar *is a popular Shakespearean tragedy. Many players have acted in it. Here, Mary Alice and Roscoe Orman interpret two of the roles in their own unique way.*

actor and each director will have a different picture of the play and its characters. The director envisions each character as part of the total production. Within the director's image of a character, the actor must shape a personality special unto itself.

Role Scoring

Another helpful process in character analysis is *role scoring*. There are twenty-five questions that you need to answer when you score your role. If you take the time and work diligently in answering these questions, you will unlock exciting and broad dimensions of your character. This procedure was adapted by Paula Parker from Northwestern University in Illinois.

1. How does the title of the play relate to your character?

2. What special texture does your character relate to? For example, Grandma in Edward Albee's *The Sand Box* might relate to the texture of sand.

3. What is your character's main sense of urgency? There is a strong impulse that motivates every character to act. For example, Juliet's sense of urgency is shown when she becomes impatient with the Nurse for not telling her immediately about the plan for marrying Romeo.

4. What is your character's secret? Having a secret adds a sense of mystery to your character.

5. What rhythm do you associate with your character? An example is the rhythmic swinging of a pendulum.

6. What personal sound do you associate with your character—sighing, wheezing, grunting?

7. What is your character's leading gesture? A leading gesture is an abstract movement that your character unconsciously uses throughout the play. An example of a leading gesture is the brushing of imaginary dust from clothing. (Note: Combine your rhythm, sound, and leading gesture as you work with your lines. Exaggerate the sounds and movements at the beginning of your work. As they become a part of your character's natural stage behavior, they automatically become subtle and nonintrusive.)

8. What is your leading center? What is your character's leading center? Head? Heart? Stomach? Gesture from your character's leading center.

9. What color do you associate with your character? Why? For example, you might associate green with a jealous character.

10. What object do you associate with your character? Why? For example, you might associate a child's spinning top with your character.

11. What animal do you associate with your character? Why? For example, a fox may represent a sly character.

12. What are your two primary senses? Your character's?

13. If your character saw the play, what reaction would she or he have?

14. Does your character ''mask,'' or cover up, feelings and behaviors? If so, what does your character mask?

15. What ''as if'' images does your character use? An example is ''I feel as if I were an unwanted kitten.'' ''As if'' images can be bizarre, but they must have a ring of reality.

16. Does your character have a sense of humor? Is this sense of humor used in a positive or negative way?

17. Would you, in real life, be your character's friend? Why? Why not?

18. What is your character's most positive trait?

19. What is your character's status in the world? Does your character have money and power?

20. What are your character's major wants and desires?

21. What is your character's major objective for each scene in which that character plays a part?

22. How does your character go about achieving those major objectives?

23. What is your character's life objective?

24. How does your character go about achieving his or her life objective?

25. Has your character changed by the end of the play? If so, in what ways?

Script Scoring

One helpful process in character analysis is *script scoring*. This is the marking of a script to indicate pauses, pitch levels, emphases, speeding up and slowing down of lines, phrasing, pronunciation, function in context of the play, and character revelation. The term comes from a musical score with its similar dynamic markings to indicate tempo, rhythm, pauses, style, and interpretation. Script scoring may be done simply or with a great amount of detail. In its simplest form, a scored script may be marked to show only pronunciation, pauses, emphasized words and phrases, movement, and business. There are no hard-and-fast rules for script scoring and its marking symbols. As an actor, you must devise a personal marking system that will be of help to you.

A detailed script scoring of the first few lines of the famous ''nose'' speech from *Cyrano de Bergerac* by Edmund Rostand is on page 108.

Ah, no, young sir!/

You are too simple.//Why,+you might have said—/

Oh,+a great many things!//Mon dieu, why waste   *mōn dyū (My God)*

Your opportunity?//For example,/thus:—///

AGGRESSIVE://I,/sir,/if that nose were mine,/   *C—Cyrano's*

I'd have it amputated±on the spot!//   *subconscious wish*

FRIENDLY:/How do you drink with such a nose?/

You ought to have a cup made specially.//   *L—prepare for audience reaction*

DESCRIPTIVE://'Tis a rock±a crag±a cape—/

A cape?/say rather a peninsula!//   *C—Cyrano's ego concept*

INQUISITIVE://What is that receptacle±

A razor-case+or a portfolio?

KINDLY:/Ah,/do you love the little birds

So much/that when they come and sing to you,

You give them/this to perch on?   *L—prepare for audience reaction*

Symbol Key

+	slight pause	⌐	pitch level rising	
/	1-second pause	⌐	pitch level lowering	
//	2-second pause	⋎⋎⋏	speed up reading	
///	3-second pause	⋏⋏	slow down reading	
—	phrase	⟋	rising inflection	
—	simple stress	⟍	falling inflection	
=	greater stress	L	laugh line	
≡	greatest stress	C	character line	
		P	plot line	
		T	theme line	

TYPES OF ROLES

The leading roles are those through which the playwright brings out the theme. They include the protagonist, who must solve the problem, win, or go down to defeat in the conflict; the antagonist, who may be a villain; the gods, Fate, or any other force opposing the goals of the protagonist; the juvenile, a term for a young romantic male lead between the ages of 16 and 30; and the ingenue, the young romantic female lead. Most young actors are disappointed if they are not cast in leading roles. But in reality, the supporting roles are often more interesting to work with and more demanding of ability. The difference lies in function and degree, and the challenge lies in the type of person to be portrayed—no matter how long or short the part may be. Together, the leads and supporting roles are referred to as the *principals*.

Both leading and supporting roles may be straight or character parts, although most leading roles are straight parts or are called "character leads." Straight parts are usually attractive, normal people of any age. The actors chosen for straight parts usually resemble in appearance and personality the persons envisioned by the dramatist. In a sense, the actors are playing themselves and are said to be "cast by type." Character parts embody some degree of eccentricity—physical, psychological, mental, or spiritual—and demand a high degree of ability to interpret. Such roles seldom resemble their actors in either appearance or personality. Many directors and actors feel that all parts should be considered character parts.

When an actor is identified with a certain personality, such as the girl next door, the business tycoon, the addle-brained fool, or the faithful companion, and is cast over and over again in that same kind of role, it is called "typecasting." Note the difference between casting by type and typecasting. If, for example, the role calls for a man with a Santa Claus-like physique and the actor selected happens to be a portly, white-bearded gentleman in his late sixties, the director has probably cast by type. However, if a similarly built man with dark hair and beard has been cast in his last twenty roles as the heavy, this actor has very likely been typecast as a villain.

Minor roles demand as careful attention to detail as supporting roles. The difference lies only in the number of lines and scenes involved. When an actor has only a few lines, that performer has a bit part. An actor who appears briefly on stage with no lines at all has a walk-on part.

The great appeal of the old stock companies and of the present-day regional and repertory companies is that the audience has the opportunity to watch actors in many contrasting roles. A variety of roles really tests the actors' artistic powers and shows their versatility and flexibility. It is in such variety of roles that actors can receive the finest training. Most of the stars in theater history gained their fame through such training.

Character Acting

Character parts include many interesting challenges, which you should try to experience while in school. In classwork you will be wise to choose difficult roles, roles entirely different from your own self, so that you can develop as both an actor and an individual.

Character parts are usually roles dealing with interesting characteristics such as age, nationality or section of a country, race, physical differences, psychological idiosyncrasies, or erratic behavior. They are fascinating to work with. Of course, external resources are very important—makeup, hairdo, dress, posture, gestures, facial expression, and movement—but inner reactions are far more significant if you want to avoid artificiality and exaggeration. Young people especially have to work very hard to be convincing in character roles.

Old age offers an intermingling of humor and pathos, tragedy and comedy, serenity and uncertainty that is challenging emotionally and physically. Even in today's youth-oriented society, when it is fairly difficult to assess the age of older people, the character part must be intensified for the purpose of contrast with other characters. The varying success with which individuals have met the experiences of their lifetimes is reflected in old age in mellowness or grumpiness of temperament. Physically, there is a slowing down of bodily responses, with a resulting insecurity of movement, a lack of vigor, and a dependence upon others. The voice is higher or lower in pitch, slower in rate, and thinner in quality than normal speech, and there are many mannerisms and tricks of inflection that have become

Character parts usually deal with interesting characteristics such as age, nationality, or psychological idiosyncrasies. In Joseph Kesselring's comic melodrama Arsenic and Old Lace, *Abby and Martha Brewster are eccentric old ladies who murder lonely old men.*

set with the years. Old people are likely to be either spare, angular, thin-lipped, and reserved or fat, flabby, and talkative.

Middle age often affords a real problem for high school actors. Here your own physical build is of great importance, and you are really lucky to be tall or a bit overweight. Makeup and padding can more easily give you the appearance of the father, mother, uncle, aunt, or family friend. These parts are usually straight, and professional actors can often be themselves in such parts. Your best bet is to find someone like the role you are playing and imitate some of that person's mannerisms and facial expressions. In the latter case, the accenting of the slight wrinkles you may already have acquired can be of great help, with a touch of gray added over the temples. Usually poise, sophistication, and self-control are dominant traits in such roles, with slightly sharpened intonations of voice. Otherwise you have to put yourself in the place of the character and imagine what your mature reactions to the situations in the play may be when you are 40 or 50. Watching television movie films with older stars in outstanding roles can be of real value.

Children's parts are frequently of vital value in high school plays. Again you are lucky if you have a very slight build and a high-pitched voice. Teenagers are likely to overdo the childish voice and movements and thus spoil what could be utterly charming characterizations. Studying children at play, when they are not conscious of being watched, should be your main source of inspiration. Children are naturally graceful, unselfconscious, and full of delightful surprises in every way. Usually their responses are exactly right when they are allowed to be themselves.

EMOTIONAL ACTING

Emotional acting is the recapitulation of all phases of acting so far presented in this discussion of characterization, beginning even with ''Reading Scenes Aloud'' in Chapter 1, which you should review. With added work on the technique of vocal and bodily responses, you are now ready to approach an impassioned scene with understanding.

If you are seriously considering a theatrical career, now is the time to read one or two of the current books on the Stanislavski system. They are listed at the end of this chapter. Apply his ideas about recalling some emotional experience of your past life and comparing your reactions to those of the character you are creating in the situation depicted; about thinking out the problems of the scene; about seeing and analyzing the character; about feeling with the character in the initial mood and changing as she or he does; about then using your voice and body to make the character real to your audience.

All acting is emotional. The skilled actor knows how to reach the greatest emotional intensity without overacting. In this scene from FOB by David Hwang, notice the three different levels of emotional intensity revealed through facial expression, body movement, and gesture.

In passages with rising emotional intensity, strike a balance between overacting and underplaying your role. It is best to begin quietly, saving your vocal and physical resources for the most intense moment at the climax of the speech or scene. Go over your lines until you are so caught up in the spirit of the situation that you speak and move as the character would in those circumstances.

When you have satisfied yourself that you have caught the feeling that will result in the right inflections, pauses, movements, and emotional buildup, mark your script to help you retain them. Then go over the lines orally again and again. When at last you have so immersed yourself in the character and situation that it moves you deeply, you can be sure the audience will react the same way.

APPLICATIONS

In the following excerpts from plays, rise to the appropriate emotional pitch.

1.   *A young prince pleads with his jailor, who is threatening to put out his eyes.*
[PRINCE ARTHUR:]

> Alas, what need you be so boisterous-rough?
> I will not struggle, I will stand stone-still.
> For heaven's sake, Hubert, let me not be bound!
> Nay, hear me, Hubert!—Drive these men away,
> And I will sit as quiet as a lamb.

The Life and Death of King John
by William Shakespeare

2. *Cyrano, a seventeenth-century poet, swordsman, and philosopher, is charming, witty, and bold. However, his huge nose often makes him the object of ridicule. In this speech, he sadly tells a friend that he knows no woman can ever love him.*

[CYRANO:]

My old friend—look at me,
And tell me how much hope remains for me
With this protuberance! Oh I have no more
Illusions! Now and then—bah! I may grow
Tender, walking alone in the blue cool
Of evening, through some garden fresh with flowers
After the benediction of the rain;
My poor big devil of a nose inhales
April . . . and so I follow with my eyes
Where some boy, with a girl upon his arm,
Passes a patch of silver . . . and I feel
Somehow, I wish I had a woman too,
Walking with little steps under the moon,
And holding my arm so, and smiling. Then
I dream—and I forget. . . . And then I see
The shadow of my profile on the wall!

Cyrano de Bergerac
By Edmond Rostand, translated by Brian Hooker

3. *A middle-aged mother vehemently expresses her views on marriage.*

[MRS. HARDY:]

Well, James, aren't you going to say something? Aren't you a judge? You're not going to uphold these girls in this nonsense about not being happy, are you? What has happiness to do with marriage, I'd like to know? Marriage means discipline and duty and you know it. Any man and woman can get along if they're willing to sacrifice their own desires once in a while. If one won't the other must. Somebody has to yield. Generally it's the woman.—Now, Myra, you think you'd be better off if you had a more practical man to deal with and Estelle thinks she'd like a little more attention. I don't doubt you would, both of you. I don't doubt that many a woman would like to shake her own husband and get another picked to order. But husbands aren't made to order. You took George and Terrill for better or for worse and even if it's worse than you expected, you'll have to make the best of it! I've raised one family. I'm not going to start in now and raise another. I've had my problems to work out and I've stood it. You can!—Do you imagine my life's been a bed of roses? At times I have been dissatisfied, mighty dissatisfied. I'd have liked a husband who took me to parties and brought me roses and carnations and chocolate creams—but I didn't get them. You never sent me a box of flowers in your life! Sometimes when I've spent the day darning your socks and turning your cuffs and hemming flour sacks for dishcloths, and buying round steak when I wanted porterhouse, and I've seen one of my old chums drive past in her new automobile while I was hanging out the wash—I've been so dissatisfied I could have smashed the whole house down. But I didn't do it. I pitched in and beat up some batter cake and scrubbed down the back steps and worked it off. And so can they!

> *Skidding*
> by Aurania Rouverol

4. *Mercutio dies by the sword of Tybalt.*
[MERCUTIO:]

I am hurt;—'tis not so deep as a well, nor so wide as a church door; but 'tis enough, 'twill serve; ask for me tomorrow and you shall find me a grave man. I am peppered, I warrant, for this world. A plague o' both your houses! Zounds, a dog, a rat, a mouse, a cat, to scratch a man to death!—Why the devil came you between us? I was hurt under your arm.

> *Romeo and Juliet*
> by William Shakespeare

5. *Brutus rebukes Cassius for taking bribes.*
[BRUTUS:]

Remember March, the ides of March, remember!
Did not great Julius bleed for justice' sake?
What villain touch'd his body, that did stab,
And not for justice? What, shall one of us,
That struck the foremost man of all this world
But for supporting robbers, shall we now
Contaminate our fingers with base bribes,
And sell the mighty space of our large honors
For so much trash as may be grasped thus?—
I'd rather be a dog and bay the moon
Than such a Roman!

> *Julius Caesar*
> by William Shakespeare

6. *Fanny, an elderly actress, is answering her granddaughter, who has just said "Acting isn't everything."*
[FANNY:]

It's everything! They'll tell you it isn't—your fancy friends—but it's a lie! And they know it's a lie! They'd give their ears to be in your place! Don't make any mistake about that! . . . You've got to leave, and go down to a stuffy dressing room and smear paint on your face and go out on the stage and speak a lot of fool lines, and you love it! You couldn't live without it! Do you suppose I could have stood these two years, hobbling around with this thing *(brandishing her cane)* if I hadn't known I was going back to it? . . . Every night when I've been sitting here alone I'm really down at the theater! Seven-thirty, and they're going in at the stage door! Good evening to the doorman. Taking down their keys and looking in the mail rack. Eight o'clock! The stage hands are setting up.

   Half hour, Miss Cavendish! Grease paint, rouge, mascara! Fifteen minutes, Miss Cavendish! My costume! More rouge! Where's the rabbit's foot? Overture! How's the house tonight? The curtain's up! Props! Cue! Enter! That's all that's kept me alive these two years. If you weren't down there for me, I wouldn't want to live. . . . I couldn't live. You . . . down there . . . for me . . . going on . . . going on . . . going on. *(She goes limp, topples over, and crumples.)*

The Royal Family
by George S. Kaufman and Edna Ferber

Laughing

Laughing is difficult on the stage, for laughter demands a sense of relaxation seldom felt under the strain of a performance. You must become interested in laughs all the time, both in real life and on the stage and television. Listen constantly for unusual ones and form the habit of catching the vowel sounds and inflections employed by people.

There are uproarious guffaws, artificial simperings, musical ripples, hysterical gurgles, and sinister snorts. For stage work, all types of laughter must have a definite vocal sound. Beginners usually manage merely to grimace and gasp without making a sound.

A laugh is produced by a sudden contraction of the abdominal muscles, which forces the breath out in sharp gasps. These gasps must be given sound as they pass through the larynx. The first step in learning to laugh is to pant like a dog, tightening your abdominal muscles as you exhale and relaxing them as you breathe in. You will probably only make faces without sound when you first try, because you will undoubtedly try to say "ha" when you are drawing in the breath instead of when you are expelling it in sharp, quick spurts. As you practice, you will literally "laugh until your sides ache." It is the continuous, rapid movement of the abdominal muscles that causes this perfectly harmless ache.

In order to master the laugh, you must relax first and then let yourself go. Take such vowel combinations heard in laughter as "ha-ha-ha, ho-ho-ho, he-he-he, hoo-hoo-hoo," and say them in rapid succession with sharp contractions of the abdominal area. Do not stop or become self-conscious. Begin at a high pitch and run down the scale. Begin at a low level and go up the scale. Then select any combination of vowel sounds and go both up and down, prolonging some sounds and shortening others in various combinations. Be sure to spread the laughter throughout a whole sentence or speech in your part; let it die off as you speak, ''Ha-ha-ha, you don't say so! Ha-ha-ho-ho, that's the funniest thing, ha-ha-ha-ha, I ever heard, ho-ho-huh-huh.''

APPLICATIONS

1. Practice laughing like the following people: a giggling schoolgirl on the telephone, a fat man at a comic television show, a polite lady listening to a joke she has heard many times, a villain who has at last captured the hero, a miser gloating over his gold, a boy seeing his pal trip over a brick, a member of the clergy at a ladies' guild meeting, a farmer seeing a motorist whose car is stalled, and a charming girl much thrilled over her date.

2. Read the following passages from Shakespeare, accompanying the lines with appropriate laughing.

a.

[PORTIA:]

God made him, therefore, let him pass for a man.

The Merchant of Venice

b.

[JAQUES:]

A fool, a fool!—I met a fool i' the forest
A motley fool;—a miserable world!

As You Like It

c.

[CELIA:]

O wonderful, wonderful, and most wonderful, wonderful, and yet again wonderful!

As You Like It

d.

[MARIA;]

Get ye all three into the box-tree: Malvolio is coming down this walk: he has been yonder i' the sun practicing behavior to his own shadow this half-hour: observe him for the love of mockery; for I know this letter will make a contemplative idiot of him. Close, in the name of jesting.

Twelfth Night

e.

[GRATIANO:]

Let me play the fool;
With mirth and laughter let old wrinkles come.

The Merchant of Venice

Crying

Crying is much easier on the stage than laughing, although the technique is much the same. Gasp for breath, using the abdominal muscles in short, sharp movements. Words are spoken on the gasping breath, but you must be very careful to keep the thought clear by not obscuring the key words. In sobbing without words, sound the syllable ''oh'' through the gasps, intensifying and prolonging the sound to avoid monotony. Occasional indrawn and audible breaths for the ''catch in the throat'' are effective, and ''swallowing tears'' is achieved by tightening the throat muscles and really swallowing. In uncontrolled or hysterical weeping, your ''oh'' will be stronger, and if words are needed, they will be greatly intensified. Your entire body should react in crying. Facial expression is most important and can be created by puckering the eyebrows, biting the lips, and twisting the features to obtain the necessary effect.

APPLICATIONS

1. Practice sobbing like a young child put in the corner for punishment; a husband at the bedside of his sick wife who is asleep; a spoiled child putting on an act; a hysterical woman after a serious automobile accident; an old woman alone on Christmas.

2. Read the following passages, crying through the words but being careful to keep the meaning clear.

a.

A young girl has just heard that her brother is a thief.

[POLLY:]

I can't believe it. I can't—I can't—He's only a little boy—just a kid.

Pearls
by Dan Totheroh

b.

An American tourist in her thirties has had an unfortunate flirtation with a charming Italian.

[LEONA:]

I'm Leona Samish. I *am* attractive. I'm bright and I'm warm and I'm nice! So *want me!* Want me!—Oh, why couldn't you love me, Renato? Why couldn't you just *say* you loved me?

The Time of the Cuckoo
by Arthur Laurents

DIALECT

Dialect presents interesting problems in many roles. National and regional speech differences show themselves in the pronunciation and selection of words and in the inflections of sentences. You should train your ears to catch the changes in quality, pitch, timing, stress, and rhythm and the occasional substitutions and omissions of sounds.

When you are beginning work with a role involving a dialectal shift in English, you might find records most valuable because you can play them again and again. Television is also becoming a growing source for the study of dialectical variances in speech. Books presenting patterns of dialects, idioms, and many types of colloquial speech are being published all the time. Actors with a natural gift for dialects are never without opportunities to act on stage, screen, and television. However, a dialect that is too precise can be very distracting to an audience.

A few suggestions may help you interpret the most commonly used dialects, but nothing can take the place of speaking with people who use the dialects until you catch the inflections, omissions, and elisions of sounds. Having a tape recorder with you on interviews will be of great value for later practice. Dialects can be imitated orally until they become more or less natural to an actor, but the audience must never be forgotten. Communication is the first consideration.

British

At its best, British speech is the basis for so-called stage diction. It can be heard in the BBC dramas on television or on records made by such players as Laurence Olivier, John Gielgud, or Edith Evans, especially in Shakespearean plays.

The *ä* is emphasized in such words as *bäsket, äunt, bänänä, läugh;* in American speech these are usually *ă*. However, the British do say *ă* in *chăp, făncy, ăn, mădam, hănd*. The *ä* appears in unexpected words like *rahly* for *really*, in *Derby* and *Berkeley,* and in the sound at the end of words like *fathäh, neväh, remembäh*.

The short *ĭ* is used in the words *Tuesday* and *nobody* and in the *ly* in *certainly* and other adverbs. Long *ee* is used in *been;* long *ā,* in *agāin.* Long *ī* is used in *eīther* and *neīther. Leisure* is *lĕshȧ.* The *ŏ* is made with the rounded lips and is never *aw* or *äh.*

In words like *dictionary* and *necessary,* the accent is on the first syllable, the *ary* is slurred, and the *y* is *ĭ.*

The *r* between vowels or the doubled *r* is definitely trilled in such words as *very, America, orange, courage, marry,* and *spirit.* The *r* is silent before consonants and is almost an *äh* in words ending in *er.* The authority that actors follow most carefully in British roles is Daniel Jones's *An English Pronouncing Dictionary.*

Cockney

This is British speech at its worst. A record of *My Fair Lady* gives excellent examples in the speech of Eliza and her father. The outstanding vowel changes include the long *ī* for the long *ā,* as in *plīce* for *plāce;* the *äh* for long *ī,* as in *räht* for *right; ow* for *ō* as in *now* for *knōw.* The sounded *h* at the beginning of words is dropped—*'abit, 'ome*—and added to words beginning with vowels—*hit* for *it.* A

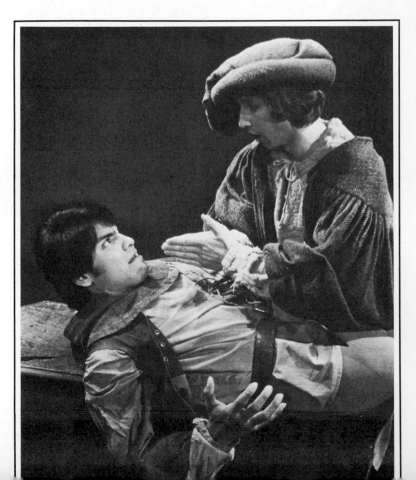

Dialect is often important in creating a realistic characterization. A Cockney dialect is used in the musical The Canterbury Tales *by Martin Starkie and Neil Coahill.*

peculiar *l* sound is confusing, and the rhythms and phrasing are very difficult to acquire. Below is an example of Cockney speech.

Thärt's ärl räht. The bĕttäh the plīce the bĕttäh the seat. Hit īnte a featha bed in the howld 'ous at 'ōm, but h'I've sorta lorst the featha bed 'abit lītelĭ.

> *Maid of France*
> by Harold Brighouse

Irish

The Irish dialect is a lilting one, marked by much variety in pitch and inflection. The natural speech of the cultivated Irish and their fine actors is very beautiful. The provincial accents of Southern Ireland are charming and are used in most characterizations on the stage.

Vowel changes include notably *oi* for *ī*, *ĭ* for *ĕ*, *ă* for *ŭ*, *ä* for *ŭ*, and *ā* for *ē*. Thus we have *foine* for *fine*, *whĭn* for *when*, *wăn* for *one*, *äv* for *of*, and *dāle* for *deal*. The pronouns *my* and *you* become *mĭ* and *yĕ*.

Consonant changes are more difficult to explain. The sound of *s* before another consonant is almost a *sh;* thus we have *shlāpe* for *sleep* and *shmile* for *smile*. The final *ing* is usually shorted to *in'*, and sometimes a *t* is substituted for *g*, resulting in *darlint* for *darling*.

American

Dialects vary in practically every state in the United States, but there are a few distinguishing characteristics used in whole areas. Broad colloquial accents are noticeable in news reports on television, and there are records available of regional speech from many isolated places.

A few general suggestions should be considered in regional roles. The Western accent is very nasal and noticeably rolls the *r*, especially at the ends of words, and replaces the trilled *r* always. The short *ă* always takes the place of the *ä* or *ȧ*. The short *ĭ* frequently takes the place of long *ē*, and *ŏŏ* is practically always used for *ū* and *o͞o*. The *ē*, *ō*, *ī*, and *ū* are seldom heard.

The Southern accent is unusually pure and pleasing because of relaxation of the vocal apparatus and general lack of nervous tension. This probably is because of the warmer climate. There are numerous dialects in all the Southern states.

In general, the vowels are rich and round, but there is a good deal of substitution of one vowel for another in different sections. Frequently the *ī* becomes *äh*, as in *I*, *my*, and *like*. The final *er* is practically always *äh* because of the dropping of *r* at the ends of words; thus you might hear "Ah lähk that view oväh yondäh."

Many consonants are dropped because of the lazy use of the tongue, as in *lemme* for *let me, fac'* for *fact;* almost all final *g's* in *ing* words are also dropped. In some places *haid* takes the place of *head;* a *y* is added, as in *hyeah* for *hear;* and *ĕ* becomes *ä,* as in *yäs* for *yes.*

There is a great deal of vocal inflection and sustained, drawled, slow sounds. Andy Griffith's early monologue records are great fun to imitate if you want the colloquial expressions and inflections of isolated regions. The attractive cultivated speech of the leading roles of Tennessee Williams's plays centering around Southern women can be followed in recordings.

The Eastern and Northern speech has a decided nasal quality, possibly because of the cold climate and consequent tightening of the vocal apparatus. Bostonians speak more nearly like the British than do other Americans. But they frequently add an *r* to words like *idea.* Their use of the *ä* is correct for the stage, as is the dropping of the final *r* in words and sentences and before consonants. Their vowel sounds are accurate and pleasing.

The Yankee accent is used in many plays. Spoken with tight lips and tense muscles, it is nasal and not inflected. Final consonants are dropped, the short *ĭ* and long *ē* are interchanged, and the short *ă* is used for the *ä* and *à.*

European

European accents are too difficult to imitate without listening to people who use them habitually. A few suggestions may be helpful.

Italian is exceedingly musical and pleasant to hear, with many attractive inflections. The vowels are open and pure, but the short *ĭ* becomes *ē,* the *ä* is marked, and the short *ă* is seldom heard. The occasional *ä* sound added to consonant sounds is most pleasing, as in *soft-ä-ting* (soft thing) or *fruit-ä-stand,* and ''I gottä'' as in T. A. Daly's delightful poem ''I gotta love for Angela, I love Carlotta, too.'' All of Daly's poems offer excellent phrasing and pronunciations; he uses *dä* for *the, āy* for *ē,* and adds *ä*'s between words.

The German dialect is definitely gutteral; many of the sounds are made with the back of the tongue. *V* takes the place of *w;* and *t* is used for *d, p* for *b,* and *ē* for *ī.*

The Scottish dialect is somewhat gutteral and uses heavily rolled *r*'s. However, there is a lilting rhythm similar to that of the Irish dialect.

Swedish is inclined to be high in pitch, with recurring rising inflections and a flat tone, which is not nasal. The *oo* is *ū,* so *good* becomes *gude; w* is *v;* and *j* is *y,* as in *yūst* for *jŭst.*

All the European dialects depend upon the original inflections and rhythms of their speech and the position of the parts of the sentence, which frequently differ very much from those of the English language. Authors can give some help in writing passages, but listening to people and recordings is essential to an actor using the dialects.

APPLICATIONS

1. The following are selections for practice in dialect.

a.

A very old lady in a small town in Wisconsin has been pushed aside by the energetic younger members of her family and talks to herself by the fireplace.

[GRANDMA:]
Dum 'em. They've gone off to do things. And I'm so old, so fool old. Oh, God! Can't you make us hurry? Can't you make us hurry? Get us to the time when we don't have to dry up like a pippin before we're ready to be took off? Our heads an' our hearts an' our legs an' our backs—oh, make 'em last busy, busy, right up to the time the hearse backs up to the door!

Neighbours
by Zona Gale

b.

A middle-aged Irish woman quarrels with another woman.

[MRS. FALLON:]
Is that what you are saying, Bridget Tully, and is that what you think? I tell you it's too much talk you have, making yourself out to be such a great one, and to be running down every respectable person!

Spreading the News
by Lady Gregory

c.

An old Irish woman muses to herself after her last son has been drowned at sea.

[MAURYA:]
They're all gone now, and there isn't anything more the sea can do to me. I'll have no call to be up crying and praying when the wind breaks from the south, and you can hear the surf is in the east, and the surf is in the west, making a great stir with the two noises, and they hitting one on the other.

Riders to the Sea
by John Millington Synge

d.

A young Englishman of twenty tries to propose.

[BRYAN ROPES:]

I say, look here, I'm not a bit mad, you know. There never has been any madness in my family. I mean that might be important, you know.—Look here, I'm awfully sorry but I love you.—I was awake all night about it. It's frightfully short notice, I know.

The Lilies of the Field
by John Hastings Turner

e.

Mr. Doolittle, a Cockney dustman, has become a gentleman in London society because a benefactor left him money. He objects violently to his new position.

[MR. DOOLITTLE:]

It's making a gentleman of me that I object to. Who asked him to make a gentleman of me? I was happy. I was free. I touched pretty nigh everybody for money when I wanted it, same as I touched you, 'Enry 'Iggins. Now I am worrited; tied neck and heels; and everybody touches me for money. It's a fine thing for you, says my solicitor. Is it? says I. You mean it's a good thing for you, I says. A year ago I hadn't a relative in the world except two or three that wouldn't speak to me. Now I've fifty, and not a decent weeks's wages among the lot of them.—And the next one to touch me will be you, 'Enry 'Iggins. I'll have to learn to speak middle class language from you, instead of speaking proper English. . . .

Pygmalion
by George Bernard Shaw

f.

A very domineering Southern woman talks condescendingly to her seventeen-year-old son about his girl, who has just jilted him.

[ELIZA:]

Gene. You know what I'd do if I were you? I'd just show her I was a good sport, that's what! I wouldn't let on to her that it affected me one bit. I'd write her just as big as you please and laugh about the whole thing.—Why, I'd be ashamed to let any girl get my goat like that. When you're older, you'll just look back on this and laugh. You'll see. You'll be going to college next year, and you won't remember a thing about it. . . .

Look Homeward, Angel
adapted by Ketti Frings from the novel by Thomas Wolfe

g.

A kindly, old Italian discusses life and its beauties with his friend, Mr. Carp.

[MR. BONAPARTE:]
  You make-a me laugh, Mr. Carp. You say life'sa bad. No, life'sa good.—You say life'sa bad—well, is pleasure for you to say so. No? The streets, winter a' summer—trees, cats—I love-a them all. The gooda boys and girls, they who sing and whistle—very good! The eating and sleeping, drinking wine—very good! I gone around on my wagon and talk to many people—nice! Howa you like the big buildings of the city?

Golden Boy
by Clifford Odets

2. Select one of the following plays and work up several speeches in it for further practice in dialect.
  Anna Christie by Eugene O'Neill
  Brigadoon by Alan Jay Lerner and Frederick Loewe
  The Emperor Jones by Eugene O'Neill
  Fiddler on the Roof by Joseph Stern, Jerry Bach, and Sheldon Harmich
  The Glass Menagerie by Tennessee Williams
  My Fair Lady by Alan Jay Lerner and Frederick Loewe
  Neighbours by Zona Gale
  No Time for Sergeants by Ira Levin and Mac Hyman
  Playboy of the Western World by John Millington Synge
  Pygmalion by George Bernard Shaw
  Riders to the Sea by John Millington Synge
  Sunup by Lula Vollmer
  The Teahouse of the August Moon by John Patrick
  Tovarich by Jacques Deval, translated by Robert E. Sherwood
  Trifles by Susan Glaspell
  West Side Story by Arthur Laurent and Leonard Bernstein

PRESENTING ONE-PERSON SCENES

The presentation of poetic or prose selections with only one person speaking is an excellent first step to acting a part, for it demands the same analysis of character, visualization of situation, and understanding of meaning. In a sense, one-person scenes afford an even greater opportunity for characterization, for the interpreter alone must reveal the soul of a human being caught at a crucial moment and present it sympathetically to an audience.

One-person performances for full-evening programs are becoming more and more popular. In them an actor or actress, made up in detail and costumed correctly, presents a first-person sketch based on selections from an author's works. The actor brings out the character as well as the leading incidents in the life of the person portrayed. Hal Holbrook as Mark Twain and Julie Harris as Emily Dickinson are among the most distinguished successes in this field.

In the dramatics class, you may make your choice of a role, with the advice of your teacher. Either choose for a public performance a role for which you are well-suited in type, or select one that will develop you as an individual seeking improvement in emotional or mental attitudes, vocal power, or clarity in speech and movement. Since you will spend a great deal of time and effort in perfecting this assignment, your choice is important. There are four steps to take as you work out the character you have chosen.

Preparation

The first step is to study the selection carefully. Look up the meanings of words and expressions, and study any dialects employed. Determine the author's purpose, and then divide the selection into logical units leading to the climax and an effective conclusion. Plan your general outline of actions, centered upon the person or persons whom you are addressing. Most short selections have only one imaginary individual with whom you are talking. But sometimes people come and go, and you must plan definitely when they enter, where they are placed, and when they leave. In many cases, the audience is to be addressed as a person.

The second step is to analyze the character speaking. Who is he or she? How old is she or he? What are the predominating physical and spiritual characteristics? How did your character get into the situation reflected in the scene? What is your character's present state of mind? How is she or he dressed? How does he or she move and speak? To give validity to your analysis, use a primary source—a real person who resembles the character you are portraying. Study the speech, gestures, and movements of the person you are using as a model.

The third step is to imagine the stage setting for the character. It is especially important to visualize the person whom you are addressing and talk to that person throughout the selection. Place your imaginary character on a diagonal line downstage, so that you may face your audience. The angle or direction of your glance is a vital consideration; it tells the audience where the other characters are and helps identify them. For example, a child speaking to an adult looks up, a woman speaking to someone in a chair looks down, a man talking with friends around a table looks first at one and then another of them. Visualize, too, the imaginary stage setting with the essential furniture, doors, and windows in set places. Once places are established, you may not move the person to whom you are speaking or the furniture without losing the illusion—unless, of course, such action is necessary in the story. If new imaginary characters enter during the scene, they should receive your attention as you turn to address them. It is not easy to make clear-cut turns toward imaginary characters and still keep the entire audience in view.

The fourth step is to memorize and rehearse the selection. Memorizing is the final, not the first, step. You will naturally memorize in any manner you prefer, but the "whole part" method is recommended. Repeat the entire selection orally over and over again until it is fixed in your mind as a complete unit. Then polish it paragraph by paragraph, stanza by stanza, and at last, sentence by sentence and word by word. Combine the memorizing with rehearsing in order to avoid falling into errors of emphasis, phrasing, and pronunciation. These errors are almost impossible to eradicate after they are fixed in your mind.

Rehearse out loud and constantly imagine the person to whom you are speaking, the setting, and the audience. It is usually better to memorize while moving about, for when the body is active, the brain is alert. Fixing the entire selection by several repetitions immediately before going to sleep is also helpful.

Presenting Your Monologue

When you present the selection, step to the front of the stage in your own person and include the entire audience in a friendly and confident glance. Give any introductory remarks in a clear voice, using good articulation and speaking unaffectedly and graciously. Then pause for a moment as you assume the bodily attitude of your character. The opening words should suggest to the audience the age, sex, personality, strength, and mood of the character. During the performance, keep your character consistent in voice, gesture, and movement. Hold the person to whom you are speaking and the properties clearly before the audience by the position of your body and the direction of your glance. Complete the closing sentence in character. Then pause and, in your own person, depart.

INTERPRETING MEMORIZED SCENES

Interpreting scenes, which serves two purposes, has become the most vital part of high school dramatic work. First, it gives you a chance to create a number of brief but contrasting roles in varying moods. Second, it brings you in contact with sections of plays in different classifications and of historical interest and lets you become acquainted with the styles of many dramatists. Interpreting scenes is the most important step in acting.

Selecting Scenes

The selection of scenes to be memorized and produced as classwork involves both the teacher and the student. Psychologically it is often wise to find roles that tend to bring out acting abilities or that give experience in needed emotional and physical responses rather than to cast to type. However, playing a part you really know you can do well is important to building self-confidence and if you are appearing before an audience, is a requirement.

Depending upon the teacher's wishes, you and the members of the group should select a scene that you are enthusiastic about and that will give each of you a real opportunity to create a good part. Small casts are preferable, for they give greater opportunities for characterization in depth. Two-character scenes are especially valuable, since close interaction of interpretation is more easily worked out in them.

Producing memorized scenes will give you a greater sense of accomplishment than either reading or improvising them. You will be able to create a role and give an accurate interpretation of what a distinguished playwright has written. If you take time to produce a scene carefully, you have the satisfied feeling of having presented a finished performance. In rehearsing such scenes throughout the course, you will put into use the fundamentals of acting. This will help you greatly when you take part in public performances.

The scenes presented in Part Four, "A Treasury of Scenes and Monologues," have been chosen with care to give you special insights into theater experience. In addition, you will find other scenes in the plays you read and see during the course that you will enjoy working on by yourself or with groups. If possible, you should read the entire play from which the scene to be produced has been selected.

Rehearsing

You are now ready to put into practice what you have learned in creating a role and responding to the other characters. Read the scene with the rest of the cast conversationally, and discuss what the emotional high point of the scene is and how best to work up to it. Then make plans for rehearsing outside of class as well as in it, when probably all students will be working in groups. Rehearsing in class is excellent training for complete concentration on everyone's part, but if you want to do the play really well, you will need to work outside also. At this time, decide what period the scene is in and what style of acting is appropriate and what essential pieces of furniture you will need. Plan an effective stage arrangement that can function easily and simply.

Rehearsing scenes demands a sacrifice of time and effort, but you will acquire working knowledge of the following essentials of acting.

Memorization of lines should be letter-perfect. You cannot create a part if your mind is thinking "What do I say next?" Apply the whole part method to the entire scene so that you are fixing ideas and not words, not only in your own lines but in those of other characters as well. Do not begin memorizing until you have worked out the movements and stage business, with the group holding scripts in hands. Mark the directions and then memorize your lines, beginning with paragraphs and finishing with sentences and words. Be sure of your pronunciation, phrasing, and emphasis so that false inflections do not become fixed.

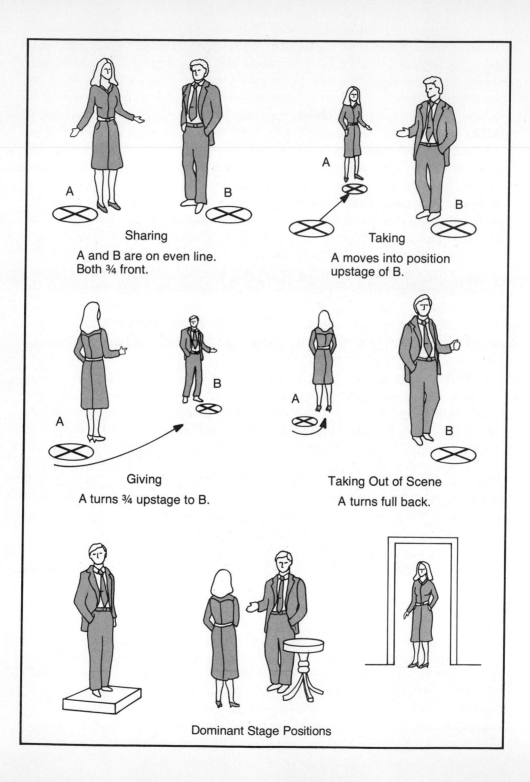

Sharing

A and B are on even line.
Both ¾ front.

Taking

A moves into position
upstage of B.

Giving

A turns ¾ upstage to B.

Taking Out of Scene

A turns full back.

Dominant Stage Positions

Rapidly picking up cues determines the timing of the scene. Most amateurs slow up the action of a play by pausing slightly between speeches. The cue is the last phrase of the line before you speak, so be prepared to come in right on its final word without a break.

Listening in character without moving allows your facial reaction to follow the meaning of the words you are hearing and permits you to hold a strong, not a weak, stage position. Then when your cue is coming up, your face, body, and voice will respond on time together, so that you will avoid beginning to act only when you hear your cue, thus causing the scene to drag.

Keep the stage picture constantly in mind in order to permit all action to be clear to the entire audience all the time. In other words, do not cover other actors, huddle in tight groups, or stand in straight lines.

Emphasize the center of interest at all times—whether it is the person speaking, an object, or a sound offstage—by giving it your alert attention. The attention of the audience should always be focused where it should be: on a line, an action, or a character.

Focus can be achieved through the playwright's writing, the director's staging, or the actor's delivery of lines. The author may focus a scene on certain characters (their internal and external conflicts, their emotional stresses, their relationships) or on the situation in which these characters are involved. The director may focus attention on a key actor by placing that actor in a doorway, on an elevation, or upstage of all the other actors. However, the main responsibility for focusing attention falls upon the actor. By stressing particular lines, gestures, mannerisms, facial expressions, or behaviors, the actor focuses audience attention on key ideas of theme, plot, or characterization.

When you play in a scene, there are certain techniques of stage movement that you should recognize and follow. *Sharing the scene* is one. You share a scene with another actor when you stand or sit parallel to each other. A shared scene should be played three-quarter front or in profile. However, a profile scene does not allow the audience to see your face. Also, a profile scene is a confrontation-type scene and can be played for only a short time before a strong emotional reaction, such as a fight or an embrace, will result. A second staging technique is *giving the scene*. When the audience's attention is shifted from one actor to another by a cross downstage followed by a slight turn upstage toward another actor, the scene has been given to the upstage actor, who now holds the dominant stage position. *Turning the scene in* is a third staging technique. This type of staging is important in scenes of more than two characters because audience attention must be focused on the real center of the dramatic action. This focus is achieved when the actors who are not the key characters in a particular scene shift the angle of their bodies more upstage and look directly at the key character. A fourth staging technique is

This young actress effectively uses a pigeon as a bit of stage business during a song from Runaways, *written and directed by Elizabeth Swados.*

taking yourself out of the scene. This is done by turning away in three-quarter or full back position. You may look out a window, leaf through books in a bookcase, or engage in some other stage business, such as reading a magazine.

Stage business is an essential part of acting. Stage business involves the use of hand props, costume props, stage props, other actors, and parts of the set itself (doors, windows, lighting fixtures). Handling a cup and saucer, a cigarette holder, or a handkerchief will vary from characterization to characterization. It takes training and practice to use props well, especially historical props such as swords, fans, parasols, canes, and swagger sticks. If not handled properly, their use may seem awkward and distracting, calling more attention to the hand props than to the actor. Such stage business as writing a letter, drinking from a cup, or stirring a fire requires concentration, imagination, and much practice to make these actions seem natural. Good stage business enhances a characterization and a production. Too much business, especially nonmotivated or out-of-character business, is meaningless and harmful.

Make no movement or gesture without a definite reason inherent in the script or action of the scene. This means to keep still without being rigid or disinterested and to be intelligently alert and in character without distracting the attention of the audience. Avoid aimless little gestures or fidgeting in position. When you move, walk in an S or curved pattern but go directly to the chair, person, or entrance without ambling about uncertainly. Stage crosses should always have a purpose.

Keep the action in view of the audience without appearing to do so. This is not easy. The person speaking for any length of time should be upstage center so that other characters are looking at him or her and so that the person's voice can more easily reach the audience. Usually gestures should be made with the upstage arm and turns made toward the front. Move forward on the upstage foot and kneel on the downstage knee. Do not, when speaking, cover your face with your hands or with an object like a fan or a telephone. A two-character scene has to be carefully worked out to avoid actors' covering each other or holding the same positions too long, or using similar gestures (like folded arms or clasped hands in lap) at the same time. Find reasons for avoiding these situations.

Your eyes are your most expressive feature. The speed and direction of a single glance can tell volumes. Always know exactly where you are focusing your attention, but do not make the mistake of keeping your eyes glued to the eyes of the person to whom you are speaking. Remember to include the entire audience in your conversation, and avoid looking at the ground or at objects that will throw your voice to the floor.

After establishing your character in clear-cut lines by your bodily attitude and a few striking gestures, use your small muscles in delicate movements to point essential lines, but never fidget, wave your arms, or make faces. Coordination of the entire body is essential every moment, and the tone and inflections of your voice, the expression and direction of your eyes, the gestures of your hands, and the position of your body must always create a single impression.

Doing one thing at a time and doing it effectively will help you keep your role clear-cut. Never anticipate what the next line or move is to be by either an uncertain inflection of the voice or the slightest gesture. Inexperienced actors often signal who will deliver the next line or where an entrance will be made by looking in that direction before the action occurs. Another form of anticipation is emotional. Young actors may tend to shift emotions before the onstage action motivates any emotional change. Only through concentration can spontaneity and the illusion of the first time be maintained with every performance.

It pays to wear clothes that relate to your character in their general impression. Avoid ultra-modern styles entirely out of keeping with your character and extreme hair styles and arrangement. Wear colors your character might select; they help put you in the mood of the scene. Your shoes are very important and should not have extremely high heels unless the character would be wearing them. Neither should your shoes be particularly casual except for the same reason. Your movements are greatly affected by footwear. Boys should wear coats in order to have pockets to use in showing feeling and mannerisms. Girls should avoid showy costume jewelry. It may be tempting, for example, to fidget with a long necklace. Skirts should always be long enough to suggest the age of feminine roles without being so out of style as to be conspicuous.

If all of you work together, you will achieve the joy of the rapid give-and-take of real conversation as you toss the lines back and forth. You will feel the different personalities reacting to each other and realize that acting is a cooperative experience. Discovering how personality plays upon personality in a scene is what makes rehearsing so exciting. It is in rehearsals that you will sense phases of your character you had not fully realized when practicing alone. You will note prejudices as your character reacts to other people, and you will recognize ideals as they

1. Sharing the scene

3. Turning the scene in

4. Taking yourself out of the scene

2. Giving the scene

The attention of the audience must be focused where it should be. Stage movement techniques help focus audience attention.

are clarified by a reaction to some remark by another character. In response to a cue, you will suddenly find yourself saying a line exactly as you know it should be said. When this happens, mark the exact inflection and phrasing, for you may forget them. After an especially good rehearsal, go home and restudy your lines at once while you remember what changes you made and what worked well.

Giving a Program of Scenes

Arranging a program of scenes can be a fascinating class or club project. In arranging such a program, you should always have a unifying idea behind your choices. For example; you may select scenes showing different countries or periods, scenes from different plays by the same author, or a group of contrasting quarrels, fare-wells, or love scenes.

There should be a stage manager for the whole program who is responsible for changing the furniture, props, and lights for each scene. The stage manager should have a summary of the plot; a list of the furniture, props, and effects wanted; and all cues for the curtain and lights.

Your teacher will decide whether or not to have student directors for your scenes, since problems of class procedure must be considered. Someone outside the cast should be the announcer, giving the names of the plays, the writers, and the student actors. The announcer should also give a brief summary of the action leading up to each scene presented.

At the end of the program, if it is presented in class, there should be an evaluation, either oral or written, of each scene. The strong and weak points in each characterization and the general effect of the scene as a whole should be analyzed. Suggestions should be constructive, with the aim of improving the acting ability of the performers.

ACTING IN PLAYS

Acting a part is the culmination of your work in dramatics. There are two distinct phases of dramatic activity in high school: the work done in the classroom and the public performance. Acting a part gives you the opportunity to assess your achievements in characterization through an understanding of the dramatist's goals and the development of your communication techniques. Therefore, in both phases, the acting experience is the same. Logically, public appearances should be preceded by classroom performances. The differences lie in production methods, which include detailed direction by an experienced teacher-director, performing on a stage with full equipment before an audience of all ages, and, most important, far longer in-depth rehearsals. Today the standards of high school theater are very high, and polished public performances of first-class plays are expected.

One-act plays performed in the classroom will give you excellent experience in creating roles in relation to a full cast. You will have the advice and the overall direction of the teacher, but the group is largely on its own. You may have a director, preferably one who has been in another class play, or you may work as a group. Your staging will be simple, but it should be as complete as the facilities of the classroom permit. In large, new buildings, such facilities are almost like a little theater, but equally high-grade class performances can be given without such facilities if creative imagination and real effort are put to use by everyone involved. In fact, ingenuity and skill utilized with very limited equipment often encourage far higher accomplishment in acting.

In classroom acting, you are afforded an opportunity for character development. The emphasis is on personal growth, not personal exploitation. With a number of groups putting on different plays, the casts become cooperative teams. In the friendly atmosphere of a classroom, without the strain of public acclaim to worry you, you gain a proper perspective on acting. You develop good sportsmanship, dependability in gathering props, punctuality in attending rehearsals, and ingenuity in working out productions with limited equipment. You may discover that you can do well as an actor, a scenic artist, a technician, or a director. In every case, your life may become richer and fuller in experience and artistic achievements, and you may gain an added assurance, which carries over into all your school activities. You may even be inspired to stage plays in your church or with a community group.

Stage Techniques

There are some technical suggestions relating to acting on a stage that should be put to use in your class plays. They should become subconscious so that you will use them easily before you undertake a public performance, when the director will not have time to train you.

Movement and Grouping

Movement and grouping are important because the audience sees the actors before they speak and thus catches the spirit of the situation upon their appearance.

Entrances set the key to your role, so you must get into character long before you come onstage. Plan exactly how you wish to appear, especially in regard to your posture, which will be affected by your character's age, mood, and attitude toward the people on the stage. Be sure that every detail of your makeup, costume, and hand props is exactly right so that you will not be worrying about them onstage. As you wait for your entrance, be careful not to cast a shadow onstage by getting in front of a backstage light; also, do not block the exit.

You must always plan your entrance so that you have time to come onstage and speak exactly on cue. If the set has steps for you to come down when making your appearance, negotiate them, deliberately or rapidly, in a direct or curved line,

The center of interest depends upon how the characters are grouped.

In this scene from Morning's at Seven, *the focus is on the down front character.*

In this scene from For Colored Girls Who Have Considered Suicide When the Rainbow Is Enuf, *the focus is center stage.*

In this scene from Death of a Salesman, *the focus is on the seated character.*

depending upon the mood you are trying to establish. Do not look down at the steps. Suit your rate of motion to your character. If you enter through a door, open it with the hand nearest the hinges and close it with the other as you step in. A pause in the doorway is effective if the action of the play permits it or if you have a line to say.

In every entrance you should keep the audience in mind without appearing to do so. Enter on the upstage foot, so that your body is turned downstage. If several characters enter together, one of them speaking, the speaker should come last to avoid turning his or her head to address the others.

Adjust yourself at all times to the stage space, keeping the stage picture in mind. Plan your turns and moves on definite cues that point the lines. If you find yourself blocked, get yourself to the right position as inconspicuously as possible—unless you are the center of interest. If you are the center of interest, do not hesitate to take the stage and let the other actors adjust to you.

Grouping characters depends upon maintaining the center of interest. Using a triangular arrangement with the important character of the moment at the apex works out well, as does placing that character on a higher level for an important speech. When the interest changes, crossing to new positions becomes necessary. Such crossing and countercrossing is an important part of rehearsing and must be worked out to be meaningful and well motivated. It is best not to move on vital lines, either of your own or of another character, because movement distracts from the words themselves. Try to cross between speeches on a definite piece of business, and manage to countercross easily and naturally when giving way to someone else. In public performances, the director plans such action carefully, but in your class plays, it is good experience to work it out for yourselves. Be careful to keep all action clear-cut and uncrowded unless the scene demands unusual rapidity and intensity.

Sitting and rising must be a part of strictly motivated action. Practice crossing to a chair or sofa and sitting down in character until it becomes natural for you to do so easily. Avoid looking behind you for the chair or sofa before you sit. Locate the edge of the chair or sofa with the back of the calf of your leg. Then sit down, remembering to stay in character. Sit with your feet and knees together. Never cross your knees or feet and never spread your feet apart with the knees together unless your character would do so. When rising, put one foot slightly in front of the other and push yourself up with the back foot, letting the chest lead. Unless in character, do not grasp the arms of a chair to push yourself up.

In conversations, avoid staring steadily at another actor by standing at angles to the footlights so that your faces can be seen. Occasionally glance directly at each other to give the illusion of real conversation.

Exits are as important as entrances. Plan ahead for them and leave in a definite state of mind, with a definite purpose, to a definite place. Keep in character until you are completely out of sight. If you go through a door, use the hand nearest the hinges to open it. If you are lucky enough to have a good exit line or a reason to look back, turn on the balls of your feet, still holding the doorknob, and deliver the line or glance pointedly. Otherwise, go right off, closing the door with the hand farthest from the hinges.

Speaking Lines

Speaking lines conveys the playwright's meaning and style as well as revealing the characters and their emotions in each situation. Of course, lines are closely involved with action and must not be blurred or lost by movements. Significant words must be heard by each person in the audience no matter where that person is seated. You should mark the important words plainly on your script as soon as you have studied every situation carefully. Recheck them after the first rehearsals, in which movements are determined. Review the techniques of using the voice in interpretation, and apply them in both memorizing and rehearsing. Be very careful to avoid fixing imperfect inflections until action is set, for when they become automatic, you can seldom change them.

A rapid picking up of cues must be established as early in rehearsals as possible. Therefore, cues should be memorized along with the lines. Many amateurs wait until their cue has been given before they show any facial or bodily reaction. Let your face respond during the other person's lines, and then you will be ready to speak on cue. One secret is to take a breath during the cue; then speak on the last word of the cue. Failure to pick up cues swiftly causes many amateur performances to drag in spite of painstaking rehearsals, for this loss of a fraction of a second before each speech slows the action.

Ad-libbing is used in emergencies to avoid a dead silence, and such lines should be spoken as though they were part of the script, without any cutting down in volume and inflection. When one actor forgets the lines or gets into a speech ahead of the appropriate point in the action and skips important information, the other actors have to ad-lib the missing facts while carrying on the conversation naturally. Whole conversations are ad-libbed in crowd or social scenes, but they must be subdued to avoid drowning out the lines of the speaker carrying the scene. Frequently, reciting the alphabet with appropriate inflections can be used in background groupings to simulate conversation.

Pointing lines means placing the emphasis on exactly the right word and timing the rate and pauses to enable the audience to get the emotional impact. Stage conversation must be kept fluent, with the give and take of ideal normal conversation. The difference lies in sharing it with the silent partners in the audience, who should become so engrossed that their reactions of laughter or tears are involuntary. Pointing lines is essential in comedy, for getting laughs in the right places makes or breaks a scene. Actors must work together to build up to the laugh

In this scene from the comedy Sly Fox *by Larry Gelbart, based on* Volpone *by Ben Jonson, the actors' positions clearly focus attention on the actress, who is obviously pointing her lines.*

line, so feeding cues properly becomes vital. Unless the preceding line or word leads to the point of the joke, the joke will fall flat. You can watch people in comic sketches on television getting laughs by leading into them. Note how they combine pausing in the right place and using their faces to help get laughs without stealing the scene from the actor who should have it. In a play on the stage, it is inexcusable for the actor feeding the line or the one making the point to laugh; this is often done on television.

Holding for laughs is difficult without dropping the scene. The actors must wait to say the next line, keeping the sparkle and action intact without slowing the tempo. After the laughter or applause has begun to die down, the actor can give the first words of the next line at a slower tempo, speeding up when the sound of the voice has silenced the noise. Amateurs can seldom adapt their words and action to the response of the audience with ease. Thus the presentation of rapid-fire comedies by amateurs is far more difficult than the playing of serious drama.

Sentences broken in the middle for some reason can also slow a scene, for they leave no sensible cue for a new sentence. In order to avoid abrupt breaks, have a complete thought worded for every sentence that is to be interrupted and go right on speaking until you are stopped by the other person. Be sure to use as full a voice for these extended lines as you do for those that are a part of the script. In a telephone conversation, write out what the other person is supposed to be saying. Count how many beats it would take that person to say it, and listen with a responsive face while you count.

Playing Comedy

Playing comedy requires special techniques depending largely upon pointing both lines and action to bring out the humor. Much of the success of comedy rests in the comic mood established by the cast. A cast should always appear to enjoy what it is doing, particularly when maintaining the fast pace necessary for comedy. Actors need to keep in mind a few techniques for playing comedy. Lift the end of the punch line and leave it hanging, or play it ''flat,'' or deadpan, in order to say ''laugh now.'' Clinch the line with a facial or body reaction. Develop an air of innocence—comic characters are often quite unknowledgeable. Learn to ''feed'' a line to a fellow performer so that that actor can catch it in midair and clinch the laugh on the following line. Laugh lines are usually short—the length determined by sounds rather than words. A line too long or too short will kill a laugh. This is one reason why actors are admonished to deliver comic lines exactly as written. Adding or omitting even one word may affect the line as far as laughs are concerned.

Topping also becomes an important factor. As in any scene that is building to a climax, the actors top one another by increased volume, higher pitch, faster tempo, or greater emphasis. However, when the comedian breaks a topping sequence, the comedian may get a laugh by a sudden change of pitch, by saying the line in an almost expressionless manner, or by a look or gesture that seems incongruous to the character or situation. Remember: Timing must be perfect or the laugh may easily be killed. Comedians even learn how to ''milk'' audiences for laughs by adding some exaggerated bit of business to their punch line.

The comic actor needs to play to the audience, using them as a comic barometer. The saying ''no two audiences are alike'' is applicable principally to comedy. One night the response to a line or an action may be a trickle of barely discernable chuckles; the next night a roar of laughter may shake the walls. Some audiences will laugh at almost anything, some will laugh in outbursts of guffaws, and some never stop laughing from the opening curtain to the end.

In this scene from The Canterbury Tales, *the actors clearly enjoy what they are doing and communicate the fun to the audience.*

One thing the beginning actor often fails to do is hold for laughs. After weeks of rehearsal to pick up cues, the performers often rush on from line to line without giving the audience an opportunity to react by laughing. An audience will always silence itself in order to hear lines. Therefore, the actor must have some idea where the audience can be expected to laugh and be prepared to freeze until the laughter begins to die. The actor must listen to the "laugh curve," which begins with the laughs of the members of the audience who catch on quickly. This laughter swells rapidly as others join in, for laughter is contagious, until a peak is reached.

Just after the peak, the laughter will start to fade and then will seem to quaver. It is at this instant that the actor having the "cut in" line must kill the laugh. Usually the line is not essential to the play; its function is to silence the audience. It is very important that an audience not be allowed to "laugh itself out," because they would then sit back relaxed and satisfied, willing to wait awhile before getting so aroused again.

Climax is another form of pointing lines in which emotion in a scene rises rapidly. In a well-written play, all the scenes rise to the climax of the play, each topping the last one. Climax is a matter of accurate pacing and increasing tempo working up to a high emotional pitch.

Daily Practice

Stage techniques must become automatic and subconscious during rehearsals and performances. A daily practice schedule the rest of your life will establish these techniques and keep your body and voice at their best. The following outline is a good plan to follow. It is based on Chapters 3 and 4.

Daily Practice Schedule

Deep Breathing: at least twenty full breaths
Loosening-up Exercises: stretching, bending, twisting
Pantomime Exercises:
  Shaking hands vigorously
  Opening and closing fists
  Moving fingers as in five-finger exercises
  Turning hands from wrists in circles
  Moving entire arms in circles
  Moving arms from elbows in circles
  Moving hands from wrists in circles, making formal gestures of giving, refusing, and pointing
  Using body and arms, with gestures flowing from shoulder to finger tips, to show emotions, such as pleading, fear, and commanding

Vocal Exercises:
   Relaxation of entire body; yawning to relax throat
   Posture exercise
   Jaw exercises
   Lip exercises
   Babbling
   Humming
   Breathing and counting
   Tongue twisters
   Chanting lines and stanzas of poetry
   Reading poems
   Reading stories aloud

Rehearsing a One-Act Play

Rehearsing a one-act play, especially as classwork, does not demand the intensive effort that rehearsing a long play for public production does. But the techniques are the same. Since the relation between an experienced adult director and a student cast are taken up in Chapter 10 in connection with play production, they need not be gone into here. The following suggestions can be adapted to your immediate needs.

A one-act play allows you to produce a complete dramatic experience, demanding a sustained and consistent characterization, without the strain a long play places on the memory and ability of all performers. In a class period, both the actors and audience can appreciate the type of play and the author's style sufficiently to discuss it intelligently and to write a dramatic criticism about it. You can prove technical efficiency and talent adequately in a one-act play.

Rehearsing is like practicing for an athletic event. It determines the success or failure of performance before an audience. Each rehearsal should show a decided improvement over the former one, especially in the emotional and technical development of the roles. Work out the stage business as soon as possible, keeping it simple and clear-cut. Stage pictures should be good all the time, and there should be as little distracting movement as possible. All members of the cast must write down on their scripts what the action is, where the pauses come, and where the emphasis should be placed on words of importance.

Apply the technical phases of everything you have studied concerning the interpretation of your lines. The quality, rate, emphasis, and pitch suitable for meaning and characterization must be checked all the time. Dropping the voice at the end of sentences regardless of the importance of words is a fatal error. Keep asking yourself "What am I saying?" until you get an intelligent interpretation of the meaning.

Runaways, *a musical directed and written by Elizabeth Swados, is a play about children from various ethnic and racial backgrounds who have one thing in common—they are all runaways. The use of childhood props creates an ironic atmosphere in this play about children confronted by overwhelming adult problems.*

The structure of the play must be considered at all times. Be sure the exposition is made perfectly clear and the initial incident pointed to arouse interest in what is happening. Each situation builds up the emotion to the climax. Lines should top each other with rising pitch, increased speed, and greater emphasis, but they should never rise above the one climax of the play. Tempos of contrasted situations must be watched for variety, but in a one-act play the shortness of the action does not permit distracting changes. Because the conclusion is usually brief, there is a danger of anticipating it and dropping the intensity before the very end.

The structure of your acting area is equally important. In a classroom, you may not have a stage curtain. Therefore, you must plan how to get your characters on the stage at the beginning and off at the end as a part of the action. Be careful to put as much importance on this as on the rest of the play. If you do have a small stage, a schedule must be worked out by the class as a whole and each group given an equal chance to use the stage.

Because this is the opportunity for each of you in the class to play a part before an audience, this one-act play should be an exciting and delightful experience.

Avoid getting tense and nervous as details pile up. Putting on any production is hard, demanding work, but it is fun!

Producing Plays in Class

Procedure in producing class plays can follow this order so that all concerned will gain the major values from the total experience.

1. Divide the class into groups, and make each group responsible for the production of a one-act play. The teacher should select and cast the plays so that each member of the class has a part that suits her or his individual needs. The entire series of plays should include the various types discussed in Chapter 7. A definite production schedule should be posted. If a member of the cast is absent on the day of performance, someone should read the part from a script.

2. Each group should select a student director (preferably an advanced student who is not a member of the cast) to be responsible for calling outside rehearsals, checking on props and costumes, and generally managing the show.

3. Permission to perform in public any play held under copyright must be obtained from the copyright holder before any definite production plans are made. The copyright holder or play publisher will either provide you with copies of the scripts or tell you how to obtain them. Copying parts and cues from plays in the library is expressly forbidden by copyright laws.

4. Rehearsing is not merely going over lines; it is continually planning how to make the most of the allotted time. Every moment of class time must be used to advantage, with the teacher passing from group to group to direct the action and answer questions. Every group should be allowed sufficient use of the stage or platform to plan the action and setting. It is best to take up the action each day from where it was dropped the day before, rather than to begin at the opening every day. Separate scenes between different characters can be rehearsed at the same time, so that no one has to sit around with nothing to do. Several intensive rehearsals at the homes of the cast members provide an opportunity to go through the entire play without interruption. These meetings help build the friendliness that is one of the greatest joys of amateur work in dramatics. All rehearsals should be handled in a businesslike manner, without waste of time and with every effort made to attain a satisfactory result. A prompter should keep a record of directions.

5. The setting cannot be elaborate, but it should be in keeping with the mood, atmosphere, and period of the play. Simple lighting effects, costumes, makeup, and all the necessary props should make the action live for the audience. Originality and ingenuity in working out the background should be considered in evaluating the final production.

6. The presentation should be as polished as possible, with lines and cues memorized and the action and tempo developed to create definite emotional reactions. The prompter should be on the job every moment.

7. After each presentation, the group responsible must move all props and leave the stage clear for the next group to take over. Anything brought from home should be returned at once, and scripts should be collected and filed for use by other classes in the future.

8. Invite guests to see the plays, but make it clear to them that the productions are regular classwork and educational in purpose. At the close of each performance, ask the audience to discuss the play and its interpretation in detail. The audience should offer constructive criticism of the acting and point out the strong and weak points of the production. A skillful teacher can direct this discussion and bring out the structure of the play and the methods of judging it.

9. If some of the plays are sufficiently well produced and likely to appeal to a large audience, they can be repeated in the school auditorium at assembly periods, or for school and community groups. A public production, however, should never be the goal of the classwork, for then the matters of individual development and educational value may be lost in the effort to put the best students into an exhibition of dramatic art. The dramatics club should be the group to present public productions, not the class in dramatics.

10. When the entire series has been presented, a careful discussion should be held, stressing the best characterizations, settings, and emotional appeals. Reasons for any poor productions should be discussed without too much emphasis upon the shortcomings of individual members of the class. Private conferences between the teacher and students concerning their success or failure and their overall dramatic ability can be very valuable after so important a class activity.

Short Plays for Production and Study
Aria da Capo by Edna St. Vincent Millay
At the Hawk's Well by William Butler Yeats
The Bald Soprano by Eugene Ionesco
Black Comedy by Peter Shaffer
The Case of the Crushed Petunias by Tennessee Williams
The Devil and Daniel Webster by Stephen Vincent Benét
Early Frost by Douglas Parkhirst

Feathertop by Maurice Valency
Fumed Oak by Noel Coward
The Happy Journey to Camden and Trenton by Thornton Wilder
Hello, Out There by William Saroyan
Ile by Eugene O'Neill
Impromptu by Tad Mosel
In the Zone by Eugene O'Neill
The Lesson by Eugene Ionesco
The Lottery adapted by Brainerd Duffield from Shirley Jackson
The Maker of Dreams by Oliphant Down
The Marriage Proposal by Anton Chekhov
Mr. Flannery's Ocean by Louis John Carlino
The Monkey's Paw by W. W. Jacobs and Louis Parlar
Neighbours by Zona Gale
A Night at an Inn by Lord Dunsany
Objective Case by Louis John Carlino
The Old Lady Shows Her Medals by James M. Barrie
Pearls by Dan Totheroh
Riders to the Sea by John Millington Synge
The Rising of the Moon by Lady Gregory
The Sandbox by Edward Albee
Sorry, Wrong Number by Lucille Fletcher
Spreading the News by Lady Gregory
Trifles by Susan Glaspell
The Twelve-Pound Look by James M. Barrie
The Ugly Duckling by A. A. Milne
The Valiant by Holworthy Hall and Robert Middlemass
Where the Cross Is Made by Eugene O'Neill
The Zoo Story by Edward Albee

Acting in the Round

Learning to act in the round is now becoming a necessary part of dramatic training. The arena and thrust stages are being built into modern theaters and auditoriums, and platforms are set up in large rooms and out-of-doors. The open stage, completely or partially surrounded by seats, is somewhat similar to the theaters of the Greeks and Elizabethans and creates a close contact between the actors and spectators. If you do not have a stage, you can make an open stage in your classroom by placing chairs around a space and leaving one or two aisles for entrances.

Staging plays in the round demands careful planning and rehearsing. The director cannot depend upon a set for effects, and the audience is so close that every detail of costumes, furniture, and lighting must be right. The acting area must be lighted by spots that do not hit any member of the audience in the eyes. Acts can be ended by blacking out the lights or by incorporating exits into the play's action. Either will take the place of the usual stage curtain. The furniture must not block the action from any side, and scenes must be arranged so that they can be seen from all angles. The director also must plan to keep the actors moving and speaking as they cross and countercross rather than have them seated for too long a time. Keeping the actors in motion allows their faces and voices to carry the meaning of the play to everyone. If possible, the director must plan the action to be seen from all sides at once.

The demands on the actors are much greater in arena staging than on an orthodox stage. Each actor must be conscious all the time of being surrounded by spectators who must see and hear everything. The actor must speak very clearly, projecting the voice so that everyone can hear even when the actor turns away from part of the audience. Very accurate pointing of lines and accenting of key words must be combined with a few clear-cut gestures that are effective from every angle. With the audience so close, any artificiality or exaggeration becomes so apparent that all sense of reality is lost. Also, fidgeting and aimless gestures are far more irritating at close range.

The actors must move in curves and S patterns. This not only uses all the acting areas efficiently but also gives the audience a continually changing and interesting view. Since there are no upstage/downstage or right/left directions in arena staging, the acting areas must be identified in a different way from UR (up right), DL (down left), or DRC (down right center). Some directors simply use clock directions for stage movements. Starting at the middle of the arena's one side, the twelve o'clock position is assigned. From there, all the other directions can be worked out according to the positions of the numbers on a clock's face. Another system frequently used is that of dividing the arena stage into quadrants. These quadrants may be named according to compass locations, such as NE, SE, SW, NW; or by numbers, such as 1, 2, 3, 4; or by letters, such as A, B, C, D.

Plays must be selected rather carefully for an arena production. Entrances and exits are sometimes difficult in arena staging because the actor can be seen long before the acting area is reached and for some time after having left the stage. Entrances must permit effective approaches for actors before they speak, and exits must allow for convenient departures. Actions and lines must be suitable for the close attention of the audience. Sofas, benches, and low-backed chairs must be appropriate as a background for the actors, since there is no setting. When done well in the round, a suitable play can move the spectators deeply. If it is poorly selected or acted, every fault is enlarged and a production that may be good enough for a regular stage is spoiled.

BIBLIOGRAPHY

Albright, H. D.: *Working Up a Part,* Houghton Mifflin, Boston, 1959.

Blunt, Jerry: *The Composite Art of Acting,* Macmillan, New York, 1966.

Boleslavsky, Richard: *Acting, the First Six Lessons,* Theater Arts Books, New York, 1975.

Chilver, Peter: *Staging a School Play,* Harper & Row, New York, 1968.

Cole, Toby, and Helen Krich: *Actors on Acting,* Crown, New York, 1949.

Dolman, John, Jr.: *The Art of Acting,* Harper & Row, New York, 1949.

Easty, Edward Dwight: *On Method Acting,* House of Collectibles, Orlando, Florida, 1978.

Hagen, Uta: *Respect for Acting,* Macmillan, New York, 1973.

McGaw, Charles: *Acting Is Believing,* 4th Edition, Holt, New York, 1979.

Mackenzie, Frances: *The Amateur Actor,* Theater Arts Books, New York, 1966.

Munk, Erika: *Stanislavski and America,* Fawcett, Greenwich, Connecticut, 1967.

Nahas, Rebecca: *Your Acting Career,* Crown, New York, 1976.

Stanislavski, Konstantin: *My Life in Art,* Theater Arts Books, New York, 1924.

————: *Building a Character,* Theater Arts Books, New York, 1949.

————: *Creating a Role,* Theater Arts Books, New York, 1961.

Overleaf: *Evita addresses her adoring people, from the award-winning musical* Evita.

PART TWO

Appreciating the Drama

CHAPTER SIX

The Structure of Drama

In the historic world of Western drama, "the play's the thing." Brought to life by the actors; expressed through the mediums of color, light, and movement against the background of stage and scenery; and unified by the creative genius of the director, the play itself is the nucleus about which the art of the theater is centered.

The only true test of the success of a production is the emotional response it arouses in the audience. A good play can fail to arouse that response because it is inadequately produced. A poor play may be so effectively acted and staged that it is reasonably successful. The great dramas of the world have survived, however, because the plays themselves are fine enough to rise above inadequate production or can be effectively adapted to changing tastes.

Drama is the most thrilling form of literature because through it we lose ourselves in the experience of others. We sorrow or rejoice in their defeats or triumphs because the characters have become living human beings to us. The dramatist is dependent for both character portrayal and plot development solely upon dialogue that must be concise and can build action swiftly. The play's action unfolds before our eyes in a closely related series of events that reach a dramatic climax, work out to a logical conclusion, and bring out a definite idea. In other words, a play has the four narrative essentials—exposition, plot, character, and theme—presented by means of dialogue and action, in which the elements of conflict and suspense arouse a definite emotional response on the part of the spectators. To build a drama, then, the dramatist must arrange the presentation of these four narrative essentials. This "arrangement" is the *structure* of the play.

TRADITION AND THE CHANGING SCENE

Since the middle of the twentieth century, playwrights have broken away from traditional rules, and many of them have modified play structure to a lesser or greater degree. For example, there was a tradition for many years that divided a play into three or five acts. The climax came at the end of the second act in three-act plays and at the end of the third act in five-act plays. Minor plots were frequently introduced and the resolution of the plot lengthened. Now plays are more often separated into two parts or several scenes with a single intermission or, on occasion, no intermission at all. The assumption is that fewer breaks in the action encourage more concentrated attention. This change affected plot structure.

Today the dramatist must adapt the play's structure to fit the theater structure, for the open stage has come into increasing use. These stages—the arena, the theater-in-the-round, the thrust stage, and the raised platform—eliminate the principle of aesthetic distance, that reminder that a play is a play and not reality, maintained by the proscenium arch, which physically and psychologically separates the spectators from the actors. The resulting intimacy and lack of realistic sets and stage curtains naturally affect the playwright's style. Improvisation and action are more and more taking the place of written dialogue. From the standpoint of structure, modern tendencies have based the play on an emotional state rather than on the development of plot, character, and theme. Clear-cut dialogue and the play of wit are frequently eliminated, and ideas are obscured to produce shock and excitement.

However, since you are now studying the art of the theater, it is necessary for you to appreciate the traditional drama, which has charmed millions the world over.

In a well-written play or movie, one of the satisfactions is seeing how the actions of people we are deeply interested in are carried to a logical conclusion. We seldom see such results in life itself, where even intimate friends drift out of our lives and we never find out what happened to them. In a well-constructed play, we see how the lives of human beings end in success or failure as the result of their own reactions during crucial events. Out of their experiences, we are shown a fundamental truth that inspires and uplifts us or deepens our insights into the human experience.

The traditions that established these principles were originally expressed by the world's first literary critic, the great Greek philosopher Aristotle (384–322 B.C.). His principles have usually been applied in the great dramas of most periods.

When Aristotle discussed tragedy in his *Poetics,* he stressed the theory that drama is an imitation of life, that humankind learns through imitation, and that learning something is the greatest pleasure of life. He pointed out that all human happiness or misery takes the form of action. Therefore, he places plot first in his list of the parts of a play; which include plot, characters, diction (language), thought, spectacle, and melody.

In Aristotle's discussion of plot, he maintains that the action must be complete in itself, with a beginning, a middle, and an end. The incidents must follow each other in logical order and reach a plausible conclusion. Out of the complications of the plot the main character, called the protagonist, does and says the things that are consistent with the protagonist's personality. Therefore, failure or success is the result of the protagonist's inherent nature. The characters must imitate reality in that they are true to life. And they must experience happiness or misery as the result of their reactions to the situations of the plot. The resulting impact of the action in a serious play should purge the emotions through pity and fear and bring out a universal truth.

Aristotle did not formulate the three unities of time, place, and action, but he did emphasize that the drama be restricted to one basic idea dependent upon a single incident taking place within "a single circuit of the sun." Many Greek plays do keep the action in one place, but it was the French and Italian neoclassicists of the sixteenth century who misinterpreted Aristotle and set up definite rules. These rules, which they felt followed the ancient dramatic traditions, are used in the many productions of their plays such as *Tartuffe* and *Volpone,* being given today. These rules in turn have been applied down through the years by

Caesar, played by Robert Christie, is stopped by a soothsayer who warns him to "beware the Ides of March" (initial incident in Julius Caesar). *This was a 1955 production at the Stratford, Ontario, Festival Theatre.*

many leading dramatists in famous plays. They require the use of the three unities, verse forms in five acts, one series of events without subplots, characters of nobility and power, and exalted themes. The rules also prohibit the showing of scenes of violence on the stage. The audience learns about such events in great detail from long speeches by some person who has witnessed them.

The traditions and principles, then, that have most affected playwrights down to our time have come to us from ancient Greek drama, from Aristotle's *Poetics*, and from the refinements and misinterpretations of Aristotle by the French and Italian neoclassicists. If contemporary playwrights are departing from a tradition, it is this tradition, or elements of it, that they are reacting against. Now let us look more closely at the four essential narrative elements as they have been employed traditionally in Western drama.

THE EXPOSITION

As soon as possible after the play begins, the audience must know what kind of play is being presented, where and when it is taking place, who the leading characters are, and in what situation and conflicts they find themselves. These facts constitute the literary setting. The process of putting them before the audience is called the exposition. A skillfully written exposition is brief and unobtrusive. It tells us the *where, when, why,* and *who* without us realizing we have been told anything.

Exposition of the Setting

Today the time and place are usually printed clearly on the program, but the script should describe the complete setting in detail. Sometimes the author merely states the facts. Shakespeare did this many times because he had no scenery to show the place and no programs to supply the information. For example, in *Twelfth Night*, the captain says to Viola, ''This is Illyria, lady,'' and the entire scene that follows (Act 1, Scene 2) is the statement of what has happened to the leading characters.

Mood and Atmosphere

Mood and atmosphere are also established in the exposition. The spirit, or mood, of the play is brought out by the opening characters, not only through their costumes and manner of speaking and moving but also through their attitudes toward each other and their present feelings.

The atmosphere is created largely by the staging and lighting. But it is also created by the tempo of speech and movement and by the choice of language, which show what country and class of society are the background. The type of play determines the author's style, and it is at the start of the play that the audience will identify with the mood of the play.

Preliminary Situation

The most important part of the exposition is the preliminary situation, sometimes referred to as the antecedent action. This is a clearly defined explanation of the events that have occurred in the lives of the leading characters before the action of the play itself begins and the events that place them in the situation in which we find them.

Playwrights use all sorts of devices to handle the exposition of the preliminary situation. The most common is to have minor characters discuss the leading characters and gossip about their pasts. More original means are the use of prologues, telephone conversations, narrators, and ingenious scenic effects. In *The Caine Mutiny Court Martial,* a drama about a court trial, front curtains are not used. So the audience becomes a part of the courtroom action while the clerks, attorneys, and attendants casually explain the case. In *The Diary of Anne Frank* and *I Remember Mama,* the young heroines, at the opening of the play and between the scenes, are shown or heard writing about themselves and their lives in their journals.

THE PLOT

The plot is the series of related events that take place before the audience. It is the working out in action of the major conflict. A well-constructed play can be diagrammed by steps of varying heights going up to a turning point, which is then followed by steps going down. These steps are the situations involved in the problem facing the protagonist and in the conflict between the protagonist and the antagonist arising from the problem. The conflict need not be physical as in many plays of violence, particularly in motion pictures and television. It can be a clash of wills or wits. It can be a psychological struggle between phases of the protagonist's personality and the environment. It can be a battle between a group and ideological antagonisms. Whether physical, mental, or emotional, the conflicting elements must be evenly balanced so that the outcome of the struggle is in doubt—thus giving rise to suspense.

The Initial Incident

The initial incident opens the plot. It is the first important event to take place on the stage after the preliminary situation and the point from which the rest of the plot develops. All the action of the play itself starts with the initial incident, which makes the audience want to know what will happen next. For example, the first scene of *Julius Caesar,* in which the people and the patricians are discussing the

On the steps of the Senate House, the conspirators stab Caesar to death (rising action in Julius Caesar*). The actors are Max Helpmann, Joseph Shaw as Caesar, Dan MacDonald, and Peter Donat at the Stratford, Ontario, Festival Theatre.*

war between Caesar and Pompey, presents the situation in Rome. The initial incident comes when the soothsayer cries out to Caesar, "Beware the Ides of March." At that point the future danger to Caesar is foreshadowed.

The Rising Action

The rising action is the series of events following the initial incident. These events take place on the stage; they are not talked about. Each situation developing out of the conflict between the protagonist and antagonist lifts the action to a higher level of interest and suspense.

In *Julius Caesar,* the rising action moves from Caesar's refusal to listen to the soothsayer into the scenes in which Cassius works upon Brutus to join a conspiracy to assassinate Caesar. Cassius plays upon Brutus's democratic ideals and loyalty to the citizens of Rome. Then Cassius stirs others to join the conspiracy. Important steps include Brutus's decision to join the conspiracy; his resolution not to kill Antony; his wife, Portia's, plea to share in whatever he is undertaking; the effort Calpurnia, the wife of Caesar, makes to prevent Caesar's going to the Senate and the conspirators' persuading him to go; the assassination; the permission to Antony to deliver the funeral address; the brief remarks of Brutus calming the citizens; and the beginning of the address by Mark Antony.

The Climax

The climax is the turning point of the play toward which the rising action leads. It is the moment that determines what the outcome of the conflict will be. The dramatist often makes this event a thrilling one, and the director must arrange the action to arouse the most intense interest in the audience.

There must be several important events before and after the climax to sustain the suspense and keep the interest of the audience to the end. However, the climax must be the crucial event of the play as a whole. The dramatist must build up to it in the lines and situations, and the director must use every appropriate stage technique to emphasize it. In *Julius Caesar,* the climax comes at the close of Mark Antony's funeral address, when the citizens rush away to burn the houses of the conspirators with the brands from Caesar's pyre.

The Falling Action

The falling action is the series of events following the climax. It is usually shorter than the rising action, but the incidents must be of real significance and of keen interest. In five-act plays, there are two acts to be filled, so there are usually entertaining or exciting subplots to be completed. In *Julius Caesar,* the mob murder of Cinna the poet and the meeting of the Triumvirate precede the final events: the quarrel between Brutus and Cassius and the decision to face battle at Philippi. The appearance of the ghost of Caesar to Brutus in his tent on the night before the battle leads into the fighting and the suicides of Cassius and of Brutus.

The Conclusion

The end of the play must be the logical outcome of all that has gone before. All the characters should receive their just deserts to satisfy the audience's demand for ''poetic justice.'' The success or failure, happiness or sorrow of the characters must be the result of their inherent natures or their actual deeds. It must never be the result of an outside force previously unrelated to them nor a matter of luck, chance, or happy accident. In *Julius Caesar,* the famous tribute of Antony above the body of Brutus is a fitting conclusion.

When the plot of a play consists of a mystery to be solved or a complicated series of interrelated events involving the leading characters, another step in the plot—the denouement—may be added in the falling action or in the actual conclusion. The denouement provides a solution of the mystery and/or the explanation of the outcome. It frequently involves an ingenious incident or exposure that leads not only to a satisfactory outcome of the plot but also to an explanation of all the secrets and puzzles connected with the complications.

CHARACTERS

Nothing in the world is as interesting as people. Since a play represents life as we know it, as it has been, or as we might like it to be, the characters, inextricably related to the plot, must be interesting people who determine the center of interest in every event. The main characters naturally hold our attention. In a well-written play, however, the minor ones who assist in working out the main issues—and even characters in the background—are also living, individual people. Occasionally a dramatist may resort to stage "types" every audience will accept without question. Shakespeare holds his position as the world's finest dramatist because even his minor characters are individually developed and live on from generation to generation.

Characters in a play must be vivid and varied in personality, with their dominant traits clearly brought out in their speeches and actions. Their success or failure must be the logical result of their own actions or the situations in which they are placed.

Methods of Characterization

In creating characters, the playwright reveals them chiefly by what they themselves say and do. They must behave not only as persons of their social group would but also as their past experience would cause them to act and speak.

The playwright also reveals characters by what they say about each other. This is especially true of the leads. If, indeed, drama is an imitation of life, friends and enemies alike know a great deal about each other. The writer's problem is to make a character's personal revelations consistent with what other characters reveal about that character in their speeches.

After a funeral oration, Robert Stephens as Mark Antony shows the crowd the body of the murdered Caesar. He turns the people of Rome against Brutus and the other conspirators (climax in Julius Caesar).

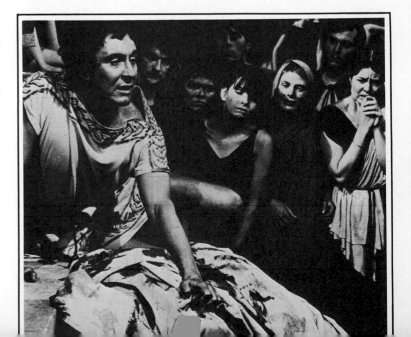

Sometimes playwrights use soliloquies to reveal character. Soliloquies are speeches in which actors talk alone—think out loud—about themselves and their motives or describe other people and situations. Soliloquies were accepted as a vital part of drama until the realistic play became prevalent. In real life, people do not talk aloud to themselves very often. However, the soliloquy is such a simple way to reveal inner reactions and character that modern playwrights still use it effectively. Thornton Wilder does this in *Our Town,* and Tennessee Williams does it in *The Glass Menagerie.* Usually today's tendency is for dramatists to avoid direct descriptions as much as possible and have their characters reveal themselves rather unconsciously through action and speech.

Motivation of Action

The most important phase of characterization is the motivation of action. Every action of a character must have a reason behind it, which in turn must be the result of both the character's personality and the situation of the moment. As you read or see a play, you must be able to ask why a character did something and find a logical answer in the nature of the person as brought out by what happened in the play. Lack of proper motivation is a fatal flaw in a play or motion picture. That fact is why so many impromptu happenings in improvised productions are boring and irritating. It is also the constructive demand of psychologically inclined actors to ask, "Why should I do that?"

Therefore, the playwright should have asked constantly such questions as the following regarding all the characters: Where did they come from and why (on

Brutus meditates on the coming battle with the forces of Mark Antony and Octavius (falling action in Julius Caesar*). Lorne Greene is Brutus and William Shatner is Lucius at the Stratford, Ontario, Festival Theatre.*

their entrances)? Where are they going and why (on their exits)? Why did they make certain key statements? Are such statements in keeping with these persons in this situation? Is the fact brought out here in keeping with the characters involved in this particular situation? Are these people saying exactly what I want the audience to get from their statements?

In modern drama, the terms *protagonist* and *antagonist* do not always apply to an individual hero and villain. The protagonist may be a racial group, an age category, or an economic classification; the antagonist may be another racial group, a social class like the Establishment, an ideology, or a conflict within the protagonist. Sometimes a situation exists against which humanity is pitted in a hopeless floundering. Sometimes the members of the audience are invited and expected to take an active part in the action among uncharacterized performers.

THEME

The theme is the basic idea of a play, which the author dramatizes through the conflicts of characters with one another or with life events. Sometimes the playwright states the theme in a sentence spoken by a character, but often it is left to the interpretation of the audience. The discussion of the playwright's purpose in writing the play furnishes one of the chief points of interest in a worthwhile production.

You may find it difficult to determine the theme of a play as you read or see it, but you should enjoy analyzing the plot and characters and finding what the author has expressed through them. Remember that there may be many good ideas presented in a play, but do not be misled into mistaking a minor truth for the theme of the play as a whole. The theme is the specific idea that gives unity and purpose to everything that happens. It should be an interesting phase of the particular problem, rather than a general principle that could apply to dozens of plays.

Do not confuse the theme with a moral. Many plays have no moral. They are written to show how a certain type of individual would react under certain circumstances or to portray an interesting phase of life. While it may or may not be a profound truth or teach a lesson, the theme should be an interesting idea that has wide appeal and that is clearly set forth by the characterization and plot development.

One of the difficulties facing modern audiences is that in many performances the theme of the play is either too complicated to get or does not exist. Avant-garde writers frequently state that they do not care what the audience thinks is the meaning of a play as long as it is emotionally affected by the action—shocked, depressed, disturbed.

Most theatergoers like a definite statement of the theme to help them arrive at the dramatist's reason for writing the play. Sometimes, therefore, the theme is put into the title, as in *The Taming of the Shrew, You Can't Take It with You, Beyond the Horizon, The Miracle Worker, Waiting for Godot, She Stoops to Conquer, The School for Scandal,* and *The Imaginary Invalid.* At other times, the theme is actually stated in a key line, definitely emphasized or expressed by the leading character as a personal philosophy of life, and then carried out in the situations resulting from this philosophy. For example, in *The Man of LaMancha,* Cervantes says, "Too much sanity may be madness, but the maddest of all is to see life as it is and not as it should be."

DIALOGUE, ACTION, AND SITUATION

The success of a play depends upon the writer's skillful use of dialogue and action, since they are the sole means by which the playwright can portray character, set forth theme, and develop plot.

In writing the dialogue or lines of the play, the dramatist must be sure that the characters speak as the women and men of the class, community, and experience they represent would speak in real life. At the same time, the playwright must advance the plot, motivate the actions of the characters, and place the characters in exciting or amusing situations. Of course, a great writer is bound to inject an individual style into the dialogue, but a dramatist cannot always instill personal brilliance into every sentence as other authors may do. The playwright must often sacrifice beauty of language to naturalness of speech, yet the characters cannot talk aimlessly as people do in real life, for every word must develop the play.

Clever lines in themselves are valuable in a comedy, but they should be consistent with the character of the person speaking them. Sparkling dialogue may actually be injurious to the play if it is not in harmony with the overall aim of the playwright. Words, figures of speech, and epigrams, although witty in themselves, may be completely unsuited to the play. We can hardly speak of dialogue apart from action and situation. When we refer to a playwright's style, then, we mean the cleverness or beauty of the lines in relation to the mood and characterizations in the play.

Action is the lifeblood of drama; something must happen constantly to hold the undivided interest of the onlookers. Events must not only be talked about, they must also occur on the stage. Action is the natural result of conflict.

As you attend films and plays, note how the situations are always presented in dialogue and action. The characters may be placed in embarrassing predicaments, melodramatic moments of great danger, tense emotional upheavals, or other combinations of circumstances. We must see the characters solve one difficult situation after another. Plays are built upon such situations as a man's wife disappearing while on their honeymoon; two little old ladies poisoning elderly gentlemen; a stubborn, nearly blind Irish girl being hired to teach a blind and deaf child.

The ability to place characters in exciting, tragic, comic, or pathetic situations is what makes a playwright successful. Occasionally one situation alone can be so striking that it helps make the play a hit. The next time you are at the theater, watch especially for the opening situation, the climax, and the closing event.

Whatever the future structure of drama may be, plays must maintain the universal appeal they have had through the centuries. In the long run, dramatists whose plays will survive will continue to reveal the heights and depths of human experience and be an uplifting and creative force in civilization. Those playwrights whose plays are carelessly constructed and tasteless will not exert an influence beyond their own generation.

In order to keep a simple record of the plays you see and read, you can outline them briefly and use the outlines to compare plays as theatrical seasons go by. The following form may be useful for this purpose.

Title and Author

  I. Exposition
    A. Time
    B. Place
    C. Mood and atmosphere
    D. Preliminary situation

 II. Plot (following preliminary situation)
    A. Initial incident
    B. Rising action (summarized briefly)
    C. Climax
    D. Falling action (summarized briefly)
    E. Conclusion (final outcome for each major character)

III. Characters (described in one sentence)
    A. Protagonist
    B. Antagonist
    C. Secondary
    D. Minor (listed)

 IV. Theme (stated in one sentence)

  V. Personal reaction (a brief paragraph stating honestly what you think about the play)

 VI. Quotations (lines, passages, or phrases that clearly illustrate the author's style or express ideas you wish to remember)

Mark Antony pays tribute to the dead Brutus: "This was the noblest Roman of them all" (conclusion in Julius Caesar). *Actors in this New York Shakespeare Festival production are Garnett Smith, Richard Roat, Jack Granino, and Leonard Hicks.*

THE ONE-ACT PLAY

The current short play, programmed alone or in connection with one or more others in an evening's performance, has aroused renewed interest for the one-act play. Dramatists today feel that the play should be as long as the central idea demands for full expression. As a result, many write both long plays and short ones not restricted by traditional standards.

One-act plays offer an ideal medium in the dramatics classroom to study the structure of drama, to see plays in class, and to give all members an opportunity to appear in a good part and to share in the actual production of a play. They also serve as a means of interesting young people seldom or never exposed to live plays. Students in other classes can be invited to class presentations and the whole school to assembly presentations. Such productions illustrate the techniques of writing and acting in one class period.

The one-act play is a major structural form, and justifiably so. It demands careful writing of a compact plot centered about one dramatic incident with vividly presented characters and condensed, rapidly moving dialogue. The one main idea is today considered of paramount value, so it must be brought out without confusing sidelights. Usually the exposition is brief and the rising action short, with the climax becoming the focus of the play very near the end.

DISCUSSION

1. Select for analysis a motion picture or television play that the majority of the class has seen. What was the initial incident? What was the climax? How were suspense and interest maintained during the rising and falling action? Did the drama end as

you expected it would? What was the problem presented? Did it entail mental or physical conflict? State the theme in one sentence, and then tell how the actions of the protagonist emphasized the theme.

2. Summarize, in not more than four sentences, the plot of a play or film with which the rest of the class is not familiar.

3. What plays or films have caused you to think deeply about their purpose? Do you like dramas that make you do this? Why?

4. Do you prefer plays emphasizing plot, character, or situation? Why? Give at least one example of each kind.

5. Among the earliest plays to break away from the traditional structure were Samuel Beckett's *Waiting for Godot* and Eugene Ionesco's *The Bald Soprano* and *The Chairs*. Read them and discuss them in relation to their lack of conventional plot, theme, and characters.

BIBLIOGRAPHY

Archer, William: *Playmaking: A Manual of Craftsmanship,* Dover, New York, 1959.
Bentley, Eric: *The Playwright as Thinker,* Harcourt Brace & World, New York, 1958.
————: *What Is Theatre?,* Atheneum, New York, 1967.
Brockett, Oscar G.: *The Theatre: An Introduction,* Holt, New York 1964.
Gassner, John: *Form and Idea in Modern Theatre,* Holt, New York, 1956.
————: *Directions in Modern Theatre and Drama,* Holt, New York, 1965.
Styan, J. L.: *The Elements of Drama,* Cambridge, London, 1960.
Whiting, Frank M.: *An Introduction to the Theatre,* Harper & Row, New York, 1969.

CHAPTER SEVEN

Varieties of Drama

The more plays you see and read, the more you will find yourself reacting differently to each writer's style, basic themes, characters, and dialogue. You will also soon recognize that plays fall into types or categories and that your response to each kind will vary accordingly.

Tragedy and comedy are the two chief divisions. In the broad sense, all plays may arbitrarily be placed within the definitions of *tragedy* and *comedy*. Although tragedies are among the earliest of recorded dramas, most plays—fantasy, melodrama, farce, comedy of manners, sentimental comedy, and social drama—fall within the definition of comedy. None of these divisions is absolute or entirely separate, and overlapping is quite common. Some plays that have the qualities of both tragedy and comedy are called *tragicomedies*. Some serious plays that do not fit the qualifications of tragedy but are serious in nature are simply called *dramas*.

Classification is further complicated by a consideration of the styles in which a play may be written. The most commonly recognized literary styles are classicism, romanticism, realism, naturalism, symbolism, expressionism, and impressionism. In addition, there are period styles determined by theater conventions of historical eras, such as the ritualistic formalism of the Greek theater, the madcap antics of the commedia dell'arte, and the powdered wigs, fans, and coquetry of the Restoration period.

Remember that the classification of plays is rather arbitrary. Still, the following introduction to types should challenge your critical faculties and imagination and give you some knowledge of the terms used to describe plays.

TRAGEDY

The greatest plays of all time have been tragedies. In fact, tragedy has been considered by many critics as humanity's highest literary achievement because only through suffering and sacrifice can human beings achieve true nobility. A tragedy is a play in which the protagonist fails to achieve desired goals or is overcome by opposing forces. The action usually ends with the protagonist's death, but in some plays this main character lives on, crushed in spirit and will.

Tragedies are based on profound emotions that, in their universal appeal, transcend time and place. It is through such strong emotions as love, hate, ambition, jealousy, and revenge that you are moved to identify empathetically with tragic

According to Aristotle, the tragic protagonist is a "better than average person" guilty of hamartia. Shakespeare's Othello is one of the most famous tragic characters.

figures. Since emotions are the true expressions of humanness, it is neither necessary nor desirable to intellectualize tragedy. Instead, you should be struck by an emotional bolt of lightning that leaps through the storm of conflict. Comedies, on the other hand, often depend upon local, regional, or topical situations. They seem entertaining when the audience's cultural background, temperament, and past experience relate to the comic events or when the characters go beyond their particular situations and can be related to something or someone familiar to an audience.

The most important basis for judgment of tragedy is found in a critical essay, the *Poetics,* by the Greek critic-philosopher Aristotle. According to Aristotle, the tragic protagonist is a "better than average person" guilty of hamartia. *Hamartia* is interpreted by some as an error in judgment or a shortcoming. It is interpreted by others as a tragic flaw. The most common form of hamartia is hubris, an act of excessive pride. However, it is quite wrong to look for a "flaw" in every tragic hero, for the greatest tragic characters do not possess a real flaw. They more frequently fail because of costly errors in judgment, or even because of their own almost too-virtuous nature. Through suffering, the tragic protagonist usually acquires a sense of awareness—of truth, of self, or of others. During this time of struggle, the protagonist becomes alienated and isolated from society. Human beings seem capable of seeing clearly only when under great stress.

When a person of stature, struggling mightily against dynamic forces, finally falls, the audience experiences what Aristotle termed *catharsis,* a purging or cleansing that comes as a result of emotional release. The most forceful catharsis is experienced when an audience realizes that the doomed protagonist has seen life more perceptively than most humans could ever hope to. Aristotle said that the catharsis comes through pity and terror—pity for the protagonist that such a great person should fall, and terror aroused by the fear that we could easily have made the same error in judgment and paid the same price.

To heighten the impact, Aristotle said writers of tragedy would use scenes of recognition and of reversal (peripeteia). There are usually two kinds of scenes of recognition. In one, the protagonist achieves an inner awareness as a result of great personal suffering. In the second kind, the protagonist identifies a loved one, kinfolk, or friend from a birthmark, scar, or some other means. In a scene of reversal, there is an ironic twist in which an action produces an effect opposite to what would at first seem probable.

The student of drama will observe certain other characteristics in tragedy apart from Aristotle's theories. The essential quality of a tragic character is suffering. This suffering occurs in most instances because of a rebellion against some divine or human authority or against society. Most tragedies have a ritualistic nature, and the protagonist assumes the role of a sacrifice or scapegoat. Oedipus died for

Thebes; Hamlet, for Denmark; John Proctor and Thomas More, for the honor of being true to oneself; and Willie Loman, for his dreams and for his son Biff.

Another characteristic of tragedy is inevitability. What is going to happen will happen. There is no way to prevent the protagonist's tragic fall. For example, in Romeo and Juliet the chorus informs us that Romeo and Juliet are "star-crossed lovers." From this point, their fate is sealed.

Pathos is another characteristic of tragedy. *Pathos* is the power to arouse feelings of pity and compassion in an audience. It is through these feelings that the tragic impact of events is intensified.

Tragedies are sober, thoughtful examinations of life dealing quite often with laws of the gods and laws of humanity, social conflict, or the identity and sanctity of self. In all cases, a struggle exists—a struggle of dignity and value. The higher the goals toward which the protagonist reaches, the greater may be the fall and the greater the catharsis for the audience. If the character is not noble in rank or stature, there must be something that elevates that character above the average. Willie Loman in *Death of a Salesman* has his dreams; the weavers in Hauptmann's play *The Weavers* have a hope for a better life.

It has been said that great tragic characters all have five characteristics in common: (1) they are dogmatic or unyielding, that is, they know what they stand for and do not swerve from that stand; (2) they make no apology for their actions; (3) they set goals based on their dogmatism; (4) they know the value of sacrifice and that almost everything worth having, obtaining, or keeping demands some sacrifice; and (5) they are willing to make the sacrifice themselves, never asking another to do what they alone can do. Probably one of the finest descriptions of tragedy since Aristotle's is found in a speech by the Chorus in Jean Anouilh's *Antigone*.

Antigone

by Jean Anouilh

[CHORUS:]

The spring is wound up tight. It will uncoil of itself. That is what is so convenient in tragedy. The least little turn of the wrist will do the job. Anything will set it going: a glance at a girl who happens to be lifting her arms to her hair as you go by; a feeling when you wake up on a fine morning that you'd like a little respect paid to you today, as if it were as easy to order as a second cup of coffee; one question too many, idly thrown out over a friendly drink—and the tragedy is on.

The rest is automatic. You don't need to lift a finger. The machine is in perfect order; it has been oiled ever since time began, and it runs without friction. Death, treason, and sorrow are on the march; and they move in the wake of storm, of tears, of stillness. Every kind of stillness. The hush when the executioner's ax goes up at the end of the last act. The unbreathable silence when, at the beginning of the play, the two lovers, their hearts bared, their bodies naked, stand for the first time face to face in the darkened room, afraid to stir. The silence inside you when the roaring crowd acclaims the winner—so that you think of a film without a sound track, mouths agape and no sound coming out of them, a clamor that is no more than a picture; and you, the victor, already vanquished, alone in the desert of your silence. That is tragedy.

Tragedy is clean, it is restful, it is flawless. It has nothing to do with melodrama— with wicked villains, persecuted maidens, avengers, sudden revelations, and eleventh-hour repentances. Death, in a melodrama, is really horrible because it is never inevitable. The dear old father might so easily have been saved; the honest young man might so easily have brought in the police five minutes earlier.

In a tragedy, nothing is in doubt and everyone's destiny is known. That makes for tranquility. There is a sort of fellow-feeling among characters in a tragedy: he who kills is as innocent as he who gets killed: it's all a matter of what part you are playing. Tragedy is restful; and the reason is that hope, that foul, deceitful thing, has no part in it. There isn't any hope. You're trapped. The whole sky has fallen on you, and all you can do about it is to shout.

Don't mistake me: I said "shout": I did not say groan, whimper, complain. That, you cannot do. But you can shout aloud; you can get all those things said that you never thought you'd be able to say—or never even knew you had it in you to say. And you don't say these things because it will do any good to say them: you know better than that. You say them for their own sake; you say them because you learn a lot from them.

In melodrama you argue and struggle in the hope of escape. That is vulgar; it's practical. But in tragedy, where there is no temptation to try to escape, argument is gratuitous: it's kingly.

COMEDY

The word *comedy* is derived from a Greek word, *komos,* meaning "festival or revelry." Comedies are usually light, written with clever dialogue and peopled with amusing characters who are involved in funny situations that they solve by their wit, their charm, and sometimes by sheer good fortune. Comedies are usually "societal," meaning that all the characters come together at the end of the play. These happily-ever-after endings even have the villains accepted back into the group.

Throughout the history of the theater, the greatest and most enduring comedies have taken situations and characters from life. They therefore contain certain timeless human truths. Molière, Shakespeare, and Shaw are considered three of the world's great comedy writers. Their comedies have had lasting appeal because they are based on universal human experience.

When you think of comedy, you probably think of something that will make you laugh. Although comedy does not always make you laugh, most comedy will amuse, delight, or please you. Regardless, laughter is fickle and time-place oriented. What is funny today may not be funny tomorrow. What is humorous in New York City might not be amusing in London or Paris. In any case, the protagonist in a comedy overcomes the opposing forces, achieves desired goals, or both. This character is most often "less than an average person" in some way. The comic protagonist may be an idealist, a romanticist, or an extreme pragmatist, or a blunderer, a dreamer, or a rogue.

Comedy is built around character, situations, or dialogue. A strange character bumbling along through life like a Don Quixote provokes laughter. The pleasure-loving but cowardly Falstaff, the linguistically confused Mrs. Malaprop, and the female-masquerading Fancourt Babberly become natural causes for mirth. Involved predicaments that seem insurmountable or improbable provide a "situation." Mistaken identities, rash promises, or a series of events where everything seems to go wrong focus audience attention on the solving of the problem. Trying to live one life in town and another in the country makes the situation in *The Importance of Being Earnest* ripe for amusing farce. In Noel Coward's *Blithe Spirit,* the ghost of Charles's first wife tries to murder her former husband in order that he might join her "on the other side," but by accident it is the second wife who drives off in the sabotaged car, and the hapless Charles finds himself plagued by two spirit-spouses.

It seems strange to many students of the drama that almost all comedy has its basic appeal to the intellect rather than to the emotions. However, this is the reason for the question "Did the audience 'catch on'?" There are several types of comedy, some causing great belly laughs, some bringing laughter to the point of tears, and some causing only inner smiles or chuckles.

THE CAUSES OF LAUGHTER

It is difficult to determine what makes people laugh. Some laugh at very strange things—the exaggerated, the grotesque, even the horrifying. Others laugh out of embarrassment, sometimes to save themselves from tears and sometimes, it seems, for no reason at all. Partly because of this unpredictable audience response, comic plays are more difficult to perform successfully than serious plays.

Exaggeration

Exaggeration is probably the first thing noticed when anything is comic. Almost every character, line, or situation must be at least slightly exaggerated in order to

A Day in Hollywood/A Night in the Ukraine *is a parody of the old Marx brothers' films. Exaggerations in physical traits, mannerisms, speech, and personality characteristics create the humor and cause the laughter.*

be funny. One form of exaggeration is the overstatement, or hyperbole. ''I can lick you with both hands tied behind my back'' or ''I always tell the truth'' are examples of hyperbole. The opposite of the overstatement is the understatement, which depends upon a negative approach: ''I ain't exactly the purtiest gal in the country.''

Exaggeration may also be applied to physical characteristics, such as a bulbous nose or buck teeth; to mannerisms, such as a strange walk or a twitching eye; to mental characteristics, such as the almost-too-brilliant child prodigy, or the incredibly-too-stupid servant; or to personality characteristics, such as miserliness, prissiness, or fanciful romanticism.

Another form of exaggeration stems from the ''humours'' of Shakespeare's time. The humours are personality determiners that make people giggly, carefree, happy-go-lucky (air); moody, philosophical, love-sick (earth); impatient, hotheaded, passionate (fire); and dull, lazy, sluggish (water). Each of these personality types is such an exaggeration from the normal that people cannot help responding with laughter or tears.

Incongruity

Anything that seems out of place, out of time, or out of character is called incongruous. Human beings have a built-in system of order, and if what is expected does not occur, laughter results. Someone waltzing to a rumba beat, the hulking fullback who quotes Shelley and Keats, and the "harmless little fellow" who is as brave as an army are examples of incongruities audiences find amusing. Grotesqueness is another incongruity. The grotesque can become a subject for pathos or comedy depending upon the point of view. Cyrano de Bergerac's nose speech is humorous because he jests at his own ugliness. However, we are compassionate when we realize how painful his physical features are to him. Missing teeth, an exaggerated limp that becomes a hippety-hop, or drooping eyelids may produce laughter mainly because we do not wish to cry.

Incongruity is also found in action that is unnatural or nonhuman. This is often accomplished by machinelike or puppetlike behavior. Eliza Doolittle is often pictured as a marionette-character whose strings are pulled by Henry Higgins. A person who moves about like a windup toy makes us laugh. We find it amusing to see people behave like animals or animal characters behave like people. Ben Jonson's *Volpone* has human beings with animal personalities—a fox, a fly, a parrot, a vulture, a crow, and a raven. The cowardly lion of *The Wizard of Oz* seems hilariously like his faint-hearted human counterpart. Long sweeps about the stage, seven-league strides, grandiose gestures, almost too-flowing movements, or a walk with some part of the body seeming to advance or trail unnaturally have always been good for a laugh.

Unnatural sounds—such as a brayish laugh as piercing as that of a hyena, severely trilled *r*'s that pound like a jackhammer, or an undulating pitch that soars up and down like a slide trombone—are sure to draw laughter from the audience. We will even discover that certain words are comic, not merely because they seem odd, but because the sound is incongruously funny to the ears—we laugh at "Piscataway," but not at "Schenectady."

The twist or the unexpected provides another form of incongruity, since the logical completion of a pattern is turned inside out or upside down by a strange turn of events. One kind of twist is based on what the audience knows the character is really like as opposed to what he or she pretends to be. Abby and Martha, the sweet old ladies of *Arsenic and Old Lace,* have convinced the community that they are the epitome of kindness and generosity. But the audience discovers they have poisoned twelve old gentlemen, eleven of whom are buried in the cellar.

Reversal is a kind of incongruity that enables the audience to enjoy seeing the tables turned. Reversal often involves the weak overcoming the strong, the servant overpowering the master, and the underdog beating the favorite, as well as a change from unhappiness to happiness, poverty to prosperity, or lowliness or prestige.

The irrelevant or unimportant is a final form of incongruity. This is especially true when the treatment of a lofty subject is involved. All forms of burlesque humor—the travesty, the mock heroic, and the parody—exaggerate the unimportant. A travesty involves a situation in which a subject of noble nature is treated in a lowly fashion, as in *The Man of La Mancha,* which features a hero who loses a battle with a windmill and then in his dreamworld mistakes an inn for a castle.

Anticipation

The key to many laughs is anticipation, or the looking forward to a potential laugh. The strength of the laugh is determined by how much the audience is ''in the know.'' We wait for the characters of mistaken identity to meet, the ''plotter'' to become a victim of the plot, and booby traps to ensnare innocent victims. After Teddy's initial charge up ''San Juan Hill,'' the audience watching *Arsenic and Old Lace* anticipates his next exit upstairs, holds its breath as he stops on the landing to draw his imaginary sword, and convulses in laughter as he roars ''CHARGE! Charge the blockhouse!''

The old gag of the banana peel on the sidewalk is an excellent example of anticipation. The observer will start to laugh even before the clown takes that disastrous step.

Many times anticipation is created by the *plant*—an idea, a line, or an action emphasized early in the play that is used later for a laugh. It must be remembered that it usually takes at least three exposures to an idea to provoke a laugh: one to plant, a second to establish, and the third to clinch, or bring out a response. From then on, the gag should be good for a laugh until it is milked dry.

Incompletion is another form of anticipation. Here people's sense of order is appealed to. A line or a bit of action is started but never finished. The audience completes the thought with laughter. In fact, the ability of the actor to leave a comic line hanging is a cue to the audience that something funny has been said and their laughter is required to finish it off.

A third type of anticipation is what is called the anticlimax or letdown. The excitement over something is built up to great proportions, and then, like a bursting bubble, there is nothing. The follow-through is never equal to the preparation. An example of this is what is called the *flat line,* a line delivered with either a drop in pitch or with little or no expression in the voice.

Ambiguity

Ambiguity, or double meaning, is the heart of many humorous lines. Puns and word play depend upon the audience's recognizing the possible interpretations and, almost always, selecting the one least likely. Even names like Lydia Languish, Lady Teazle, or Sir Fopling Flutter provide comic clues to personality as well as identification of characters. Mistaken identities, lines meant for one person but ''accepted'' by another, and ruses and disguises are other ways to create double meaning. Shakespeare's audiences must have been delighted when watching a boy play the part of a girl who was, in turn, disguised as a boy acting as a girl while the man she loved rehearsed a proposal intended for another woman. As a comic strip character would put it: "Confusing, but amusing."

Recognition

Recognition is discovering hidden or obscure meanings. "Solving the puzzle," especially in a line or passage of wit where the audience must think twice, is the basis of high comedy and satire. We find it humorous when we recognize the inner motivation of a character. The motivation may be implied by a subtle act, such as the sly wink of a coquette as she hides behind her fan and asks, "Why, Sir, were you addressing me?" We are also amused when we discover what is going to happen just before it does. The *take*—the "mouth-agape freeze" of farce—has always brought down the house. The character sees or hears something that apparently does not sink in, takes a step or two, and then "Pow!" the meaning hits.

Protection

One of the most important elements of comedy is called the *protection factor*. Cruel, violent, grotesque, and abusive actions and events often cause laughter when the audience is under the protection of knowing those things are not really happening. The secret of the cartoon in which a character runs off a cliff is this protection factor. The character falls 100 feet to apparent "doom," but amazingly reappears heavily bandaged in the next frame, and then, within 15 seconds of the horrible catastrophe, is completely restored. The old slapstick of pies in the face and beatings with water-filled rubber bags is another example; it made considerable noise but hurt no one. We are truly amused when we are certain that no one is really being injured and we can accept the illusion as being real, for then we laugh because it is not happening to us.

Relief

Relief of pressure, such as comic relief in a tragedy or in a situation that builds up to a point where the audience feels it can take no more, is humorous when the pent-up emotions are allowed to explode in a laugh. When your emotions suddenly erupt, you often explain: "I couldn't hold it in any longer." Good comedies built up pressures and release them, as you can see in the following example, which shows how some of these causes of laughter work together.

Good comedy is like a powder keg (plant) with a lighted fuse (anticipation). When the fuse fizzles (unexpected) at just the moment of expected explosion (anticlimax), the audience may laugh. They will probably snicker when the too-curious buffoon approaches the keg to see why it did not go off. But, as the audience could have predicted (recognition), the keg then blows up in the buffoon's face (protection). When the victim emerges ragged and soot-covered (incongruity), the audience roars even louder (relief).

TYPES OF COMEDY

The traditional classification of comedies is important, for each kind demands a special kind of staging. There are three levels of comedy: low, middle, and high.

Low Comedy

Low comedy is quite physical, is sometimes vulgar, and produces a knee-slapping guffaw or belly laugh. Low comedy is highly exaggerated in style and performance. The situation is outlandish, if not ridiculous, and the characters are not at all like anyone you might meet on the street. Low comedy includes farce and burlesque.

Farce

This kind of comedy involves almost everything done strictly for laughs—clowning, practical jokes, and improbable characters and situations. Farce frequently features a considerable amount of assault and battery: ears are pulled, shins are kicked, and pies are shoved into faces. Many of these actions come within the term *slapstick,* which is derived from an old stage prop consisting of two thin boards hinged together. The slapstick made a loud but harmless crack when applied to the backside of a performer.

The more unbelievable the situation, the riper it is for farce. A young man from Oxford University tries to pass himself off as a wealthy woman of charm from Brazil *(Charley's Aunt).* An unusual family encourages its members to do whatever they please, whenever they please: take ballet lessons, play the xylophone, write novels, make fireworks in the basement, refuse to pay income tax *(You Can't Take It with You).* Two sweet old ladies poison elderly gentlemen by putting arsenic in elderberry wine *(Arsenic and Old Lace).*

Farces usually have *chase scenes*—through gardens or houses, around furniture, or in and out of doors. *See How They Run* has a hilarious chase through the parlour; *Charley's Aunt,* through the Oxford gardens.

Farces may also have *screen scenes*. In a screen scene, some of the characters are hidden from the others onstage—behind doors, inside closets and cupboards, or behind bushes and folding screens. The concealed characters always overhear the onstage dialogue and may pop out to utter comic lines, talk to each other, or say *asides*—all unheard by the characters onstage. An aside is a line spoken to the audience. The hidden characters may change stage positions from one hiding place to another unobserved by the visible characters. An unusual screen scene is

The Canterbury Tales *is an example of a bawdy farce filled with ribald jokes and outlandish situations.*

found in *Blithe Spirit*. The ghost of Charles Condomine's first wife is onstage, but visible and audible only to Charles. Therefore, she may move about and make witty comments hidden to Ruth, Charles's second wife.

Chases and screen scenes are sometimes combined. The sidesplitting hat shop scene from *Hello, Dolly!* has Barnaby and Cornelius popping in and out of closets, hiding under tables, even marching onstage, right behind Horace Vandergelder.

Burlesque

Burlesque is a common form of low comedy that is seen most frequently in skits on television and in performances by stand-up comedians. It is a broad kind of comedy that pokes fun at people, at society's foibles, and even at other forms of theater.

One kind of burlesque is *travesty,* which pokes fun at revered and lofty subjects. A noble thought, a noble individual, or a dream is made to appear ludicrous. For example, in *The Man of La Mancha* a scarecrowlike old man sets out on a noble quest as a knight-errant 300 years too late. He fights his first battle with a windmill. The incongruous mixture of the nobility of the knight-errant tradition and a feeble old man's dream makes us laugh.

A second kind of burlesque is the *mock heroic* or *mock epic*. In this form of low comedy, a person or subject that is not of heroic proportions is humorously elevated. Shaw's *Androcles and the Lion* does just that: Androcles, the timid Greek

Travesty pokes fun at revered and lofty subjects. The Man of La Mancha *is an example of this kind of burlesque.*

tailor, survived the lion-feeding time in the Roman arena. Androcles became a folk hero that day. The lion, instead of eating Androcles, nuzzled up against him, wanting to be petted. Earlier that day, before the lion was captured in the woods, Androcles had removed a thorn from the lion's foot.

A third kind of burlesque is *parody*. A parody is an imitation of a work of literature. One kind of parody is the parody of form, in which words of the original are readily identified by the audience. Another kind of parody is the parody of idea, in which an entire subject is held up to ridicule. Soap operas, western movies, and musicals are frequent sources of parody. In *How to Succeed in Business without Really Trying,* a college song and cheer are parodied. In *No Time for Sergeants,* psychological examinations are parodied. *The Frogs* by Aristophanes is a parody of the styles of two Greek writers of tragedy, Aeschylus and Euripides.

Caricature is a fourth kind of burlesque. A caricature is like a political cartoon that overdraws a physical feature or personality trait. A caricature does not try to show a real personality but exaggerates an unusual manner of speaking, a strange posture, or a peculiar walk. This is the type of thing done by impressionists who do imitations of famous people. Children's plays often feature caricatures, such as the wicked witch, the evil adviser to the king, and so on.

The most common forms of burlesque in full-length stage productions are *spoofs* or *takeoffs*. These are burlesqued imitations of types of stage presentations. For example, *Little Mary Sunshine* is a takeoff on old movie musicals that starred a well-known musical pair, *The Boy Friend* is a spoof on the 1920s, *Dames at Sea* is a spoof of musical comedies of the 1930s and 1940s, and *Once Upon a Mattress* pokes fun at fairy-tale musicals done in the romantic style.

Middle Comedy

Middle comedy includes what we call humor. Humor involves an appeal to the heart, where the audience can gently feel love, tenderness, pity, or compassion. Humor is tied firmly to an emotional empathy, although the laughter itself comes from the thinking process. No one has to tell an actor who has studied people carefully how closely related laughter and tears may be. The closeness of happiness to sorrow, bitterness to sweetness, and hopefulness to futility increases comic effect because the leap from one extreme to the other prompts an emotional response. Some types of middle comedy are romantic comedy, sentimental comedy, melodrama, and social drama.

Romantic Comedy

Romantic comedies are those that present life as we would like it to be. They usually are set in some far-off locale with an exotic name. Romantic comedies do not necessarily involve romance, but the ''good'' characters are recognizably *good,* and the ''evil'' characters are obviously *evil*. Romantic comedies are some-

In Shakespeare's romantic comedy Much Ado About Nothing, *Alfred Drake plays the bachelor, Benedick, and Katherine Hepburn takes the part of the merry and independent Beatrice.*

times referred to as costume dramas because they so often take place in a time and location requiring the actors to wear lavish costumes.

Most of Shakespeare's comedies are of this type. Among them are *Twelfth Night, As You Like It, The Tempest,* and *A Midsummer Night's Dream.* Another classic romantic comedy is *Cyrano de Bergerac.* Cyrano stands out as one of the great protagonists of romantic comedy.

Sentimental Comedy

This kind of comedy is one of the most popular forms of drama. It tugs at our hearts as it makes us smile and laugh. Based on themes of personal relationships, self-sacrifice, patriotism, lost affection, mother love, and youthful romance, these plays at their best meet the universal need of average people to have faith in others and to lose themselves in the lives of others like themselves.

You should not overlook the superior dramas of this type, especially when selecting plays for high school production. Among the most appealing are Mary Chase's *Harvey,* John Van Druten's *I Remember Mama,* Guy Bolton's *Anastasia,* Rudolf Besier's *The Barretts of Wimpole Street,* John Patrick's *The Teahouse of the August Moon,* and the many plays of Neil Simon, including *Barefoot in the Park* and *The Odd Couple.*

At their worst, sentimental comedies were the soap operas of radio and the tearjerkers of stage and screen, which continue in television. At their best, as in the tremendously popular *The Forsyte Saga* based on Galsworthy's trilogy, they meet a deep theatrical need.

Melodrama

A melodrama is a serious play written to arouse intense emotion by bloodcurdling events, terrific suspense, and horrifying details centering around plotted murders, thwarted love and greed, and revenge. Motivation and logical explanations are not so important in melodrama. Therefore, we do not question why things turn out as they do. Some melodramas you might enjoy are *Arsenic and Old Lace, Night Must Fall, Ten Little Indians, Angel Street* (Gaslight), *Witness for the Prosecution, Dial M for Murder, The Night of January 16th, Dracula, Deathtrap,* and *Sleuth.*

A mystery play is a melodrama of the ''whodunit'' class. The plot centers on tracking down a criminal and saving the falsely accused protagonist. Dame Agatha Christie's *The Mousetrap* holds the all-time record for continuous run of a mystery play. Movie and television melodramas include the western, horror films, and courtroom, law-enforcement, and hospital dramas.

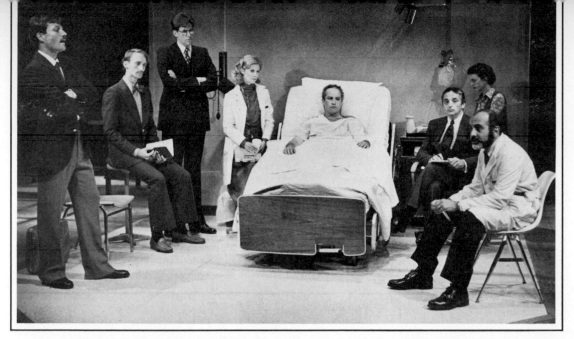

Whose Life Is It Anyway? by Brian Clark is a social drama of the 1980s. Richard Dreyfuss plays Ken Harrison, who is paralyzed from the neck down as the result of an automobile accident. How does the title reflect the play's theme?

Social Drama

Sometimes called the problem play, social drama will always be produced in one form or another as dramatists seek to right the wrongs of society. These plays are frequently comedies in the sense that they offer a solution for the problems they present. But of course many are tragedies because the protagonist's life is lost in the battle against evil. Social dramas differ from *plays of protest* because social dramas have a constructive rather than destructive point of view.

Some famous social dramas are Ibsen's *An Enemy of the People,* which shows how a man in a small town stands for civic integrity against all the citizens of his community; Bertolt Brecht's *The Caucasian Chalk Circle,* which attacks the selfishness of the elite and the plight of the poor; Anthony Newley's *The Roar of the Greasepaint, the Smell of the Crowd,* which shows life as a game in which someone is always changing the rules; Lorraine Hansberry's *A Raisin in the Sun,* which shows a black family struggling to escape the ghetto, the hypocrisy of neighborhood associations, and the limits to which blacks are pushed by society to be a success; and John Masteroff's *Cabaret,* which shows people trying to escape the realities of their lives by going to a cabaret.

High Comedy

High comedy appeals to the head. The audience must be on its toes in order to catch the clever lines, word play, and obscure allusions. High comedy often appeals only to well-educated theater-experienced audiences. An extensive vocabulary, a knowledge of historical periods and styles, and an appreciation of the subtle are requisites for both actor and audience. High comedy includes comedy of manners and comedy of satire.

Comedy of Manners

The comedy of manners has always been the delight of sophisticated actors and audiences. Built on clever use of language, its wit includes puns, paradoxes, epigrams, and ironies. The dialogue is brilliant conversation between amusing people, often razor-sharp in attacking the socially accepted standards of the day. The plays are as entertaining to read as they are to see.

Restoration drama, in almost continual production somewhere these days, represents the masterpieces of comedy of manners. Such plays as Wycherley's *The Country Wife* and Congreve's *The Way of the World* were later followed by Goldsmith's *She Stoops to Conquer* and Sheridan's *The School for Scandal* and *The Rivals*.

Comedy of Satire

Satire holds human frailty up to ridicule. The comedy of satire is a humorous attack on accepted conventions of society, or it may be only a humorous observation of the foibles and follies of humanity.

Oscar Wilde and George Bernard Shaw will probably remain unsurpassed in the field of satire. Twentieth-century dramatists of expert comedies of this kind include Noel Coward, Tom Stoppard, Peter Shaffer, and Alan Ayckbourn.

STYLES

The term *style* refers to the way in which a play is written, acted, and produced. Dramatists adopt the language and action they feel best express their ideas. Directors and scenic artists present the plays in the form most suited to the spirit of the script.

Classification of plays today is complicated by the fact that many modern playwrights are breaking away from the definite styles that have proved popular or of special value in the past. They ignore or combine these styles to suit themselves. Seeking primarily emotional responses, modern playwrights disregard conventional structure and standards.

Fortunately for you, plays of all eras are now being made available to you as the number of theaters across the country increases. Therefore, you can become familiar with all styles of drama of the past and present. You can discover those that appeal to you most by actually seeing them performed.

Classicism

Classicism is a style based on the Greek and Roman theater. Classic plays were usually written in poetic form. The stories are traditional, involving queens and kings and mythological characters. A unique feature of the classic play is the chorus. The chorus is a character in the play and is represented by either an individual or a group. Unlike in the modern theater, no sets were used. Plays were set against simple backgrounds of columns and draperies.

Fantasy

Largely a form of romantic drama but frequently introduced into sequences in realistic plays, fantasy deals with unreal characters in dreams and scenes imaginary in time and place. The land of make-believe forms the background—inhabited by spirits with supernatural powers, gods from another world, and the eternal personalities of Pierrot and Pierrette, witches, and will-o-the-wisps. Some of the most popular adult productions are Shakespeare's *A Midsummer Night's Dream* and *The Tempest,* and such modern plays as Maxwell Anderson's *High Tor* and *Star-Wagon,* Paul Osborn's *On Borrowed Time,* and J. M. Barrie's *Peter Pan.* Such musicals as *Brigadoon* and *Finian's Rainbow* have strong elements of fantasy in them.

Romanticism

In romantic drama, life is shown as people dream it should be. The setting is an ideal spot of great beauty; the language is polished, frequently poetry at its best;

Brigadoon *by Alan Jay Lerner and Frederick Loewe is a romantic fantasy.*

the characters belong to the aristocracy and live magnificently; the protagonist is a great person facing meaningful problems and conflicts in which success or failure will be met nobly; and the antagonist is worthy in many ways, perhaps possessing courage and intellectual power, but is evil on a big scale. Comic relief is usually afforded by richly humorous members of the "working or servant classes."

At its best, romantic drama reaches the heights of Shakespeare, Goethe, Schiller, Rostand, and, among our contemporaries, Maxwell Anderson, Christopher Fry, Jean Giraudoux, and Robert Bolt. At its poorest, romantic drama becomes overly sentimental, flowery, exaggerated, and theatrical. However, it did produce the "grand" style of acting, with renowned stars playing famous roles, in the brilliant sets and costumes of the days of Edwin Booth, Henry Irving, Ellen Terry, Sarah Bernhardt, and many other famous stars.

Realism

In protest against the artificiality and impossibility of too much romanticism, dramatists developed realism in the late nineteenth century. Realistic plays depict life as it actually is—often sordid, ugly, and unhappy, although not necessarily so. The characters talk and act as people in ordinary life do in whatever social group they belong. The outcome of the characters' problems is what it would logically be in the world today under ordinary conditions. Selective realism—using selected scenes to typify reality—is now the usual style of plays dominating almost all forms of theater, both of stage and of screen.

Henrik Ibsen was the father of realism. His frankness in his significant dramas shocked the romantically indoctrinated audiences of the Victorian era. You have probably seen some of his great plays—*An Enemy of the People, Ghosts, The Master Builder,* and *A Doll's House.*

George Bernard Shaw followed the realistic style and introduced philosophical discussion between voluble people so successfully that he became the outstanding dramatist of his era. The brilliant humor and extraordinary situations in which he placed his stimulating characters account for his continued popularity. This is exemplified in his *Pygmalion,* so exquisitely revamped in its musical version, *My Fair Lady.* Shaw's *Saint Joan* is considered by many theater lovers to be the greatest play of the twentieth century. In it, the romanticized historical figure becomes a real person of common sense and courage, stubbornness, and idealism who is capable of spiritual leadership in a time of national crisis.

Naturalism

The style called naturalism grew out of realism but became exaggerated in the early years of this century, culminating in photographic perfection of detail under its exponent David Belasco. Naturalism is often sordid and shocking. "Life as it is

The Haggadah *is a symbolic allegory. In Hebrew tradition, a* Haggadah *is a legend or a parable introduced in the Talmud to explain a point of law.*

with no holds barred'' is its central topic. The famous director-actor Konstantin Stanislavski brought the naturalism of acting to its finest level in the realistic plays of Anton Chekhov, produced in the Moscow Art Theater.

Symbolism

In the symbolic play, the dramatist emphasizes the theme by having characters and props, even sets, actually exemplify ideas. In Maeterlinck's *The Blue Bird,* Mytyl and Tyltyl are woman and man seeking to find happiness by learning life's secrets. The diamond in Tyltyl's cap is truth, which shows inner realities when turned; and happiness is the blue bird in their home, which they recognize after their dream is presented in ten symbolic scenes.

Many of our finest modern plays have symbolic overtones. In *Death of a Salesman,* Arthur Miller uses his protagonist as the symbol of the ordinary, blundering man caught in the incomprehensible problems of earning a living for his family and meeting the spiritual obligations of fatherhood. Eugene O'Neill uses masks in *The Great God Brown* to show the phases of his protagonist's personality in relation to other people; he shows the personification of jungle fears in *The Emperor Jones,* and in *Anna Christie,* of the ''debil sea.'' Tennessee Williams in *The Night of the Iguana* uses the captive Mexican lizard as a symbol for the people, who are literally ''at the end of their rope'' but who are freed from their particular obsessions.

Allegory

Closely related to symbolism, the allegory definitely represents abstract qualities like Truth, Justice, and Love or personalities like Death, God, and Man as characters in a play that has as its goal the teaching of moral concepts. It has been a popular form of storytelling throughout the history of humanity.

The greatest allegory of them all is *Everyman.* Everyman is suddenly summoned to meet Death. He must appear before God and seek salvation. In his desperate need, all his friends—Five Wits, Fellowship, Kindred, Discretion, Beauty, Strength, and Knowledge—fail him. Only his Good Deeds, enchained and feeble, will go with him. *J.B.* by Archibald MacLeish, the modern version of the Book of Job, is a fine contemporary allegory. Thornton Wilder's *Our Town*, which shows how typical human beings in a modern small town are failing to realize the beauty of daily life, has many characteristics of the allegorical play.

Stylization

A blending of script and production is achieved in stylized drama. Stylized productions bear the stamp of the personality and individual point of view of the director-designer. Orson Welles staged a modern-dress version of *Julius Caesar* on a barren stage without scenery. He also staged a most original voodoo *Macbeth*, with an all-black cast in a West Indian jungle. In 1968 in the "mod" presentation of *Love's Labour's Lost* at the Stratford, Connecticut, Shakespeare Festival Theatre, King Ferdinand was a bearded guru and his young lords were robed pilgrims, the princess arrived on a motorcycle in a silver sports outfit, and the tempo and feverish type of entertainment was typical of rock and roll. The stylized versions of *Hamlet* are apparently limitless.

Other stylized productions have included current presentations of Ben Jonson's *Volpone*, with the characters masked like the animals they resemble in spirit; *R. U. R.*, in which robots take over a factory from human inventors, and *The Insect Comedy*, in which insects experience events similar to those of human beings (both of these plays are by the Capek brothers of Czechoslovakia); and *Dynamo* by Eugene O'Neill, in which the stage is a huge machine. Rostand's *Chantecler* was a most successful play. It is set in a barnyard and in a forest; the trees and props are magnified in keeping with actors dressed like animals, especially fowls and birds.

The constructivistic sets, consisting of platforms and ladders and ramps, which were introduced by Meyerhold in Moscow, have been imitated in various ingenious ways everywhere today. Such sets form the background for many stylized dramas.

Period plays are considered stylized when they are presented with exactness in staging and costuming in the same way they were produced and acted in historical eras and geographical areas. The frequent revivals of Sheridan's Restoration comedies are typical period plays.

Some of television's finest productions, such as Galsworthy's *The Forsyte Saga* and Chekhov's splendid dramas, are highly stylized period productions.

TWENTIETH-CENTURY EXPERIMENTAL DRAMA

This century has seen many changes in theatrical trends. These changes continue every season. How much they will affect the drama of the future cannot be estimated at the present time, but they will undoubtedly be exciting for theater-goers.

The abstract theories of dramatic presentation, expressionism and impressionism, came into being in Germany after the First World War and are still exerting a strong influence on the relation between the script and its interpretation by simplified, nonrealistic sets and emotionally effective use of lights. Closely related to symbolism, expressionism and impressionism are similar but not synonymous.

Expressionism

In expressionism the dramatist has a theme, usually centered about ideas of justice, social relationships, and the evils of the machine age. The qualities and thoughts of the characters are expressed against highly imaginative symbolic sets.

The first such play to become a hit in the United States was *Beggar on Horseback,* produced in the twenties and revived in 1970. The hero, a young musician, is on the verge of marrying the daughter of a big businessman. In a dream, the hero experiences the horrors of an industrial career, an unhappy marriage, and in-law troubles in an exaggerated and amusing nightmare. Incidents are all accompanied by jazz rhythms from a nearby orchestra, the last thing he heard before going to sleep. Georg Kaiser's *From Morn to Midnight* and O'Neill's *The Hairy Ape* are expressionistic plays.

Impressionism

The impressionistic play gives the audience the inner reactions of characters under great stress. The trial scene from *The Adding Machine,* Elmer Rice's symbolic drama, is impressionistic. Red lights flash over the stage and the witness box revolves, making the audience feel as Mr. Zero did when he was declared guilty. The drumbeat heard in Eugene O'Neill's *The Emperor Jones* is an excellent example of impressionism. The drums begin beating at 70 beats a minute, the normal rate at which the human heart beats. By the end of the play, the drumbeats may increase to 200 beats a minute, reflecting the growing fear of Emperor Jones.

Constructivism

Constructivism is having stronger and stronger repercussions in current theater. Originated in the first quarter of the century by Vsevolod Meyerhold in Moscow, it was in direct contrast with the far more widely renowned realism of Stanislavski. Meyerhold did not present productions based on real life on a picture-frame stage. Instead, he constructed backgrounds of mechanical skeletons on various levels connected by arches, ramps, ladders, and platforms. On these, actors dressed in nondescript coveralls were trained to move with precise symbolic movements at various speeds, representing different states of mind and classes of society. He used movement to take the place of language in his desire to bring the audience into direct participation in the action. He developed the space stage idea and eliminated footlights, bringing the actors into the auditorium, thus foreshadowing the thrust and arena stages of today. The ''skeleton'' scenery you see so often is the current form of constructivism.

You have probably seen similar sets in productions like *Oliver Twist, The Threepenny Opera,* and numerous modern plays. The acting style is far more rare, however, appearing in episodes rather than in entire plays.

The Epic Theater

This provocative style also originated in Germany between the two world wars. It is strongly influencing the so-called modern drama. You can see many productions based upon its principles. Bertolt Brecht's plays are frequently produced in repertory theaters. These include *Mother Courage and Her Children, The Good Woman of Setzuan, The Caucasian Chalk Circle,* and Brecht's popular opera, *The Threepenny Opera.* Associated with Brecht was Erwin Piscator, who introduced

Gloria Foster plays Mother Courage in the Bertolt Brecht epic drama Mother Courage and Her Children.

the use of mixed media. Such devices as lantern slides, motion pictures, loud-speakers, radio, and new forms of functional lighting are used instead of conventional scenery. He invented all sorts of heavy, as well as mobile, stage machinery for experimental effects. There was no realistic setting, for illusion lighting was used only to illuminate, never to arouse moods. Only functional and necessary pieces of scenery or furniture were employed.

Mordecai Gorelik, the eminent scenic artist-director, first analyzed the epic theater for the American public in his stimulating book *New Theatres for Old*. In it he explains that epic theater is essentially a "learning theater," whose purpose is to cause viewers to think deeply about important social problems in order to correct them. The epic theater is a reaction against emotionalism, naturalism, and the "well-made play." Brecht's plays do not involve the spectators in the problems and feelings of the characters as most plays do, and entertainment is a secondary goal. The plays objectively set forth events in episodic form, using broad phases of human experience rather than individual relationships. These plays are therefore easily adapted to the thrust stage and nonrealistic backgrounds.

The Avant-Garde Theater

The term *avant-garde* has been used loosely to cover all the experimental styles of theater when they first appear. Many techniques accepted today as general theater practices were considered avant-garde at their beginning—expressionism, the symbolist plays, epic theater, playing in the round, and thrust staging.

In the United States, much of the new experimentation originates in off-Broadway and off-off-Broadway small, obscure buildings. To avoid complications of censorship and the problems of conventional play production, some groups established themselves in cafés and coffee houses to try out offbeat plays by unknown playwrights. It is important to note that many of these avant-garde movements die in their infancy, some linger awhile, and a few become a part of the living, continuing theater. However, once a style is accepted, it is no longer avant-garde.

Theater of the Absurd

The theater of the absurd introduced American audiences to a style of "anti-play" that went nowhere from the standpoint of theme, plot, or characterization. The authors of the theater of the absurd believe that human beings are absurd creatures living in an absurd world and absurdly attempting to find meaning, which is totally absurd. *Waiting for Godot* by Samuel Beckett was the first example to reach Broadway. Eugene Ionesco and Jean Genêt introduced their revolutionary ideas for backgrounds and situations that produce an emotional reaction, not suspense or motivation. The use of gesture and movement instead of expressive dialogue and characters without a personality that attracts or repels is also a part of their style.

The absurdists seem to fear that language is deteriorating. In a mechanized society, there is little need to think and, consequently, little need to communicate. In *The Bald Soprano,* Ionesco uses worn-out phrases and idioms to show language breaking down into nothingness. In *The Lesson,* he lashes out at stifling educational systems that tend to kill off what imagination and spark may be left in the children of a society intellectualized by worthless knowledge. He taunts the audience with a lesson in murder that parallels the potential destruction of humanity's intellectual pursuits because of the emphasis that is placed on superfluous and purposeless knowledge.

One of the major difficulties encountered in a study of the theater of the absurd is its frequent obscurity in meaning. Audiences have often shaken their heads in confusion at what seemed to be meaningless attacks on the meaningless. Though sometimes difficult to follow, well-written plays such as Carlino's *Objective Case,* Albee's *The Sand Box,* and Beckett's *Endgame* provide a challenge to both the actor and the audience that, it is hoped, would accomplish the goal of the absurdists—to make people feel and react before complete absurdity destroys them.

Existential Theater

Basically, the existential theater supports the philosophy of tne existentialists. They believe that human beings do not really begin to live until they define their existence. Only after existence is defined can humanity discover the true meaning of life.

Jean Paul Sartre's *No Exit* has three characters who find themselves in a room without doors or windows. As the play develops, one character discovers her real identity, only to find that she and her companions are in hell.

Tom Stoppard's *Rosencrantz and Guildenstern Are Dead* is another existential play. It is a lesson in existential frustration. All that Rosencrantz and Guildenstern know is that "they were sent for." They spend the entire play trying to find out what they are supposed to do. But before they discover the answer to what they were sent for, their time onstage is over.

Total Theater

The concept of total theater attempts to fuse all the performing arts into one presentation. At its best, it combines a strong plot with impassioned characters, well-written dialogue, and first-class acting. These are enhanced by delineative dancing and mime, atmospheric music with inspirational lyrics, and creative costuming and staging, capitalizing on the wonders of today's audiovisual special effects.

Theater of Involvement

The participation of the members of the audience in the action of the performance is the keynote of this controversial style. *Paradise Now* was one of the first productions staged by the Living Theater. It has become well known here and abroad and has been accepted and rejected with equal fervor. Theatergoers have declared themselves bored, annoyed, intrigued, flattered, and disgusted when they found themselves involved with members of the cast in arguments, physical attacks, and invitations to actually take part in the proceedings. Critics wrote cynical and amusing reviews of the episodes of "liberation, mysteries, and rites" that made up the evening's activities.

Numerous productions have appeared with the obvious objective of producing shock values in episodes and ceremonies. Whole auditoriums become the stage, without sets or scenery but completely surrounding the spectators with light and sound, while actors appear from all directions to intermingle with the audience.

SPECIAL STYLES

There are three special styles that have an important place in contemporary theater: one-person shows, children's theater, and puppet theater.

One-Person Shows

At one time, the monodrama was a favorite vehicle for personal appearances. The supreme example was *Before Breakfast,* the Eugene O'Neill tragedy in which a nagging wife drives her husband into committing suicide offstage. Today the one-person show has taken its place in the theater, and a number of actors and actresses have become famous with their arrangements of the life stories and literary works of well-known authors. Witness Hal Holbrook's presentations of Mark Twain and Charles Dickens.

Cornelia Otis Skinner's programs—two centering around the wives of Henry the Eighth and a modern solo drama in which she plays the three women dominating a man's life—are very popular.

In recent years, several actors and actresses have presented one-person shows. Among the most highly acclaimed productions are James Whitmore as Harry Truman, Julie Harris as Emily Dickinson, Henry Fonda as Clarence Darrow, and Vincent Price as Oscar Wilde.

You will be seeing more and more of these one-person shows. You may want to work some up for yourself, for they are a most appealing form of easily produced theater. The structure is loose, but the presentation should have interesting incidents, with natural conversation, depicting events in the life story of a well-known personality.

Children's Theater

A large part of contemporary theater is devoted to what is called children's theater—theater written, designed, and performed for children. Most high school drama groups produce at least one children's play each season. Regional, civic, and professional theater groups often include children's theater as part of their seasons. Some even run a separate children's theater schedule. Many original scripts and new adaptations are available for production. No longer are producing groups limited to a handful of the old fairy-tale adaptations.

Puppet Theater

Puppets have long been a part of theater the world over. However, in recent years, a new interest has developed in puppetry. This has been due partly to the television programs that have featured puppets in regular weekly shows and seasonal specials.

There are several types of puppets that have been used in theater: (1) the marionette, a puppet operated by strings from above the puppet; (2) the stick puppet, operated by sticks from below the puppet; (3) shadow puppets, silhouette puppets operated by sticks from behind the puppet; (4) hand puppets, operated by the fingers and hand; (5) "life-size" puppets, operated from inside, behind, or below; and (6) mechanized puppets, operated by motors, electronic controls, or other mechanical means.

Hand puppets have become the most popular. Three-finger hand puppets allow the operation of a head and two hands. Two-finger puppets, as they are called, usually operate only the mouth of a glove or sock puppet. This type of puppet evolved into the Muppet so well known today.

DISCUSSION

1. Which theatrical trends of today are interesting you most?
2. What directions do you think the dramatic forms of the future will take?
3. Do you think the traditions of plays from the past should be ignored, adapted, or followed in contemporary theater?
4. Discuss the various styles of stage, screen, and television that you are seeing this season. What general patterns are they following? Which styles do you think may become lasting successes?
5. What current dramatists do you think are writing enduring plays?

BIBLIOGRAPHY

Brustein, Robert: *Seasons of Discontent,* Simon and Schuster, New York, 1967.

Corrigan, Robert: *Theatre in the Twentieth Century,* Grove Press, New York, 1965.

Esslin, Martin: *The Theatre of the Absurd,* Doubleday, Garden City, New York, 1961.

Gorelik, Mordecai: *New Theatres for Old,* Dutton, New York, 1962.

Jones, Robert Edmond: *The Dramatic Imagination,* Theatre Arts, New York, 1956.

Priestley, John B.: *The Wonderful World of the Theatre,* Doubleday, Garden City, New York, 1969.

CHAPTER EIGHT

Evaluation of Drama

Watching plays has provided universal entertainment since the days of ancient Greece, but never before have so many people watched so many plays of so many varieties. You can see the best contemporary plays in the increasing number of performing arts centers or local theaters converted from motion-picture houses. You can see the famous dramas of the past in the repertory theaters. And ultra-modern productions can be seen in experimental playhouses. The fine films of the past are available on television in your own home. And satellite television presentations of actual performances in the best theaters of England and America will probably be coming to you regularly in the near future.

Many television specials sponsored by large corporations let you see great stars in great dramas you cannot afford to miss. Current Broadway commercial hits are probably reaching you in road shows and summer stock. Theater festivals on practically every university campus are available every summer and make delightful holiday trips. In motion-picture houses, you have the choice of every form of film. What plays you watch depends entirely upon your own judgment as to how you wish to use your leisure hours.

YOU AND THE DRAMA

Perhaps the biggest bonus of the dramatics class is gaining a real appreciation of theatrical values in order to watch plays, not only with intelligence but also with aesthetic and emotional sensitivity. As the work of the dramatics class advances, you will gain a deeper satisfaction in watching the talent and training of fine actors bear fruit in the roles they play. The study of plays and their production will help you evaluate dramatic literature and its interpretation. Therefore, you should see every professional performance possible and then discuss it in class.

In addition, there are deeper values. In real life you can seldom follow through the complexities of real people's lives. In the theater, because of the art of the playwright, you can see exactly what line of conduct leads to what result. Thus, your interest in humanity and the problems common to all people can be intensified and clarified.

You should learn to judge what good theater is, not to become hypercritical by going to a play to tear it to pieces, but to enjoy what it has to offer you. Usually the most highly trained theatergoers are the most enthusiastic, because they appreciate the art behind the combined labors of the playwright, the director, and the actor. They find little enjoyment in a poor play badly acted and directed. But they find deep satisfaction in a good play well directed and acted. When you have enthusiastically studied all phases of the drama and then have lost yourself in a fine production of a fine play, you will experience the same satisfaction that comes to an artist standing before a superb masterpiece or to a musician at a splendid concert. Also, when you read a drama, your imagination will set the stage for you and breathe life into the lines of the play. Thus your leisure hours can afford you a joy many people never experience, and your inner life will be enriched.

GOING TO THE THEATER

No matter what degree of mechanical perfection and electronic effects television and screen drama may achieve, they can never create that intangible, magnetic quality that passes from actor to audience. They can never become the unity of light and color, voice and movement, mass and perspective, imagination and reality that is a play produced by living actors before a living audience.

To fully appreciate any type of drama and to judge it fairly, you must consider the play itself, its interpretation by the actors, its staging by the director, and its reception by the audience. Your judgment is naturally colored by your personal

Children of a Lesser God *by Mark Medoff was the outstanding Tony Award–winning play in the 1980 New York City theater season. Phyllis Frelich and John Rubinstein won Best Actress and Best Actor awards. Mark Medoff, the playwright, won the award for best play.*

preference, your immediate state of mind, your social background, and your technical theatrical knowledge. Often the company you are in can make or mar your enjoyment of a performance.

Judging the Play

The type of play must color your attitude toward it. A light social satire cannot be judged by the same standards as a romantic drama in blank verse. A heavy tragedy cannot be judged by the standards of a farce, nor can an avant-garde vehicle be judged by those of a traditional production.

The theme of the play should receive your first consideration if you are a judicious playgoer. It is the theme that is discussed following a "first night" of a new play. And it is the themes that hold the attention of the theatrical world on great dramatists. Determine for yourself what the playwright's purpose is, and be prepared to justify your belief with adequate reasons. You might follow Goethe's example and ask: "What did the author try to do? Did the author do it? Was it worth doing?"

The plot should hold your intense interest. If the play is any good at all, you will be wondering most of the time "what is going to happen next." If you do not care, focus on whether the events are plausible and the situations interesting in themselves. Decide whether there is a convincing climax, which stirs you emotionally, and a logical conclusion, which satisfies you intellectually.

The dialogue and characterization should hold your attention more and more as you see many plays. It is through the dialogue that the dramatist's style is revealed. And it is the style that colors all the dramatist's plays, no matter how naturally the characters may seem to speak and act. Clever repartee (the swift give and take of sparkling conversation), apt figures of speech that are natural to the characters, and the turn of phrase that only the person speaking would use are all aspects of dialogue to be enjoyed.

Characterization is brought out by the dialogue and gives the actors the incentive to interpret their roles correctly. The individual characterizations you see in performances are frequently the result of careful analysis and discussion between the director and the actors. As you view the completed production, closely watch the characters of the play meet and solve their problems.

Part of the fun of going to a play comes during the intermissions, when you can discuss the theme, the plot, the dialogue, and the characters and also listen to the opinions of people about you. It is then that you can consider the playwright's skill in giving the actors worthwhile things to say and interesting things to do.

Judging the Acting

It is the acting of the play that arouses the keenest response from the onlookers. Fair appraisal of the work of the artists is to be expected as the result of theatrical training. After even a short time in a dramatics class, you should appreciate the discipline and skill responsible for a fine piece of acting. If an actor created a living person for you, you should recognize the physical, emotional, and intellectual skills that worked together to allow the actor to assume another individuality. The projection of a role to the farthest seat in the theater is something you have a right to expect. Failure to do this is a weakness of some modern actors, who frequently seem to become so involved with their own reactions to a role that they forget they have an audience.

A good actor creates a role that is convincing all the time because it is always an integral part of the action. Good actors avoid attracting attention to themselves. By speaking and listening in character, an actor builds up a personality in which you can believe. The actor does this by being natural and spontaneous and by remaining true to the period and spirit of the play. You should think of an actor not as an actor but as a person really involved in the action taking place.

Appreciating the Production

Never before have audiences been as knowledgeable concerning the actual putting on of a play as they are now. This is largely because today so many theatergoers have specialized in drama in high school and college and have had actual experience backstage. Formerly the average theatergoer knew nothing about the problems of designing and staging a play and wanted only to enjoy the show without analyzing how it was put together. You will have the advantage of understanding the drama in all its phases and of scrutinizing the methods of its presentation with an intelligent appreciation. You will naturally be more interested in some phases than in others and may even want to take up some of them as a profession.

The director is the most important factor in the ultimate success of a production and is today being recognized as such. In the past, the director was the last person involved to receive deserved praise or blame from the public and press. The director is personally responsible for every phase of the production: the selection and adaptation of the play, the casting of the parts, the interpretation of the characters, the effectiveness of the staging, the length of the rehearsal period, and the total effect of the production.

You will get real enjoyment from noting how the director has developed contrast in casting, costuming, and interpretation; how interesting stage pictures that emphasize the center of interest at all times have been worked out; and how the proper atmosphere has been created to bring out the dramatist's meaning through actors, lights, setting, and costumes. You will soon know the names of the best directors as well as those of your favorite actors.

The setting determines the atmosphere of the play. The scenic artist works closely with the director in designing the sets and is in many ways responsible for

This is a relaxed and soft grouping appropriate for Morning's at Seven, *Paul Osborn's comedy about the elderly in a small midwestern town in 1922.*

the play's success. Working with the stage manager and backstage crew, the set designer creates the proper effects with sets and lighting.

The goals of scenic art are to create the proper atmosphere, establish a center of interest, and keep the balance of the stage pictures in such a manner that the setting itself contributes in carrying out the fundamental purpose of the play. The magic of modern lighting and mechanical and electronic effects plays a vital part in this. Simplicity, naturalness, and effectiveness are the principles behind modern staging. More and more, for many reasons—the expense of labor in handling sets, the kind of stage being used, the available lighting equipment and mechanical devices—elaborate scenery is givng way to bare stages or screen projections or to scenic units that can be easily rearranged. The disappearance of the proscenium arch and its traditional curtain opens up the stage for the use of flexible set pieces, lighting, and audiovisual aids to bring out the mood and meaning of a play. Fortunately you can still see many dramas produced in the style of their own eras, with the naturalistic, period, or elaborately artificial sets of the past.

The reaction of the audience may or may not be a fair criterion in judging the ultimate success of a performance. However, a play is written to be presented before spectators, and if it does not hold the attention of playgoers, something must be wrong somewhere. Usually the fault lies in the play or its production, for the average audience is eager to be pleased.

Of course, all plays are not suitable for presentation before all audiences. Off-Broadway and off-off-Broadway shows are certainly out of place in conservative towns across the country. Often a play that succeeds on Broadway fails on the road, or vice versa. Local audiences may be affected by religious views or political situations. The degree of culture and sophistication of a community strongly influences the reception of a play. Nevertheless, if a drama deals with fundamental human reactions, presents a definite phase of a universal theme, and is produced in an adequate manner, it is certain to hold the interest of the playgoer.

Judging the Avant-Garde Theater

In every era the arts have introduced experimental innovations in attempts to express ideas through fresh techniques. The theater is no exception. Until an innovation is widely accepted, it is often referred to as avant-garde.

For Colored Girls Who Have Considered Suicide When the Rainbow Is Enuf *by Ntozake Shange is basically a verse play. Ms. Shange's choreopoem is a rejoicing at being black and a woman.*

It is difficult to judge avant-garde theater because the novelty often impresses audiences more than the lasting contribution the new approach might be making to the dramatic arts. Human beings like to experiment, yet at the same time they want to hold on to the traditional and familiar. Especially when the innovation seems too extreme, too unnatural, or too ''new,'' the observers demand a return to the kind of theater they are used to. Changes in form away from the traditional well-made play; use of shock treatment in language, theme, or physical behavior; bizarre makeup or costumes; and extreme naturalism in photographic portrayal have all been tried in recent years. These departures from the ''old theater'' familiar to Broadway have been initiated in the hope of keeping the legitimate theater from being killed by motion pictures and television and by a society straining to break away from tradition and convention.

As a student of the drama, you should want to evaluate the merits of experimental theater. A critic must evaluate these experiments from certain ''traditional'' criteria. First of all, theater is illusion, and illusion, not reality, is one of its major strengths. Shakespeare said the role of theater is ''to hold, as 'twere the mirror up to nature; to show virtue her own feature, scorn her own image, and the very age and body of the time its form and pressure.'' A mirror shows a reflection of life, never life itself. Therefore, if the events presented in a play appear to be a newscast, the audience is not really observing ''theater.''

Second, whenever you judge a work of literature, all shock, all spectacle, all obscenity in language and action should be stripped away. If what remains has something to say, provides a clever or entertaining situation, or affords insight into interesting characters, the play may stand as ''good'' drama. But if the work has no theme, no plot, no situation, no characterization, no effective use of meaningful language, it must be rejected as a poor work of art and unworthy of the term *theater*.

Third, the ability of such a play to survive time, socioeconomic changes, people, and nations is very important. Universality is a prime requisite of great works of literature and art.

Theater cannot stand still, for people and their arts cannot stand still. However, change in the theater must be judged carefully in order that drama, the most forceful of artistic expressions, does not become self-destructive. Past experience has shown that when the appeal of theater was to human weaknesses rather than to strivings upwards and outwards, both the theater and society deteriorated.

EVALUATING A PLAY

Real theater enthusiasts free their imagination and emotions while watching a play. At the same time, they use their intelligence and discrimination to heighten their appreciation of what they are seeing. The following questions may help you evaluate the plays you attend, the television dramas you watch, and the movies you see.

Theme

1. Is the fundamental idea underlying the play true or false in its concept of life?

2. Is the theme warped by a distorted or limited experience of life on the part of the author?

3. Does seeing the play add something positive to your understanding and experience?

4. Is the theme consistent with the setting, plot, and characters presented in the play?

5. Do you agree with the author's philosophy?

6. In your opinion, should the general public be encouraged to see the play? Should it have been produced at all, or even written in the first place?

Plot

1. Does the play have a clear-cut sequence of events?

2. Does it rise to a strong climax?

3. Does the suspense hold until the end?

4. Was the play emotionally stirring?

5. Are you satisfied by the final outcome?

6. If not, what outcome would you consider more satisfactory?

7. Which are most interesting: the events, the people, the style of presentation, or the shock value?

Characterization

1. Are the characters true to life?

2. Do the characters seem to fit into the social and geographical background of the play?

3. Do they definitely arouse such feelings as sympathy, affection, amusement, disgust, admiration, or hatred on the part of the audience?

4. Are the characters' actions in keeping with their motives?

5. Are the situations at the climax and conclusion the result of their inherent natures?

The Hofstra University Drama Department's Rashomon *was selected as one of the ten best collegiate theater productions of 1968–69. It opened the first National Festival in Washington, D.C., the following spring. Washington critics praised the professional quality of the production.*

Style

1.   Is the dialogue brilliant and entertaining in itself?

2.   Is the dialogue consistent with the characters and setting?

3.   Is the dialogue an end in itself, or is it an adequate means of plot advancement and characterization?

4.   Does the dialogue make you think about the playwright or about the characters themselves?

5.   After seeing the play, do you remember lines because of their significance or beauty?

6.   Would people of the social class represented talk in real life as they do in the play?

7.   Is the power of expression worthy of the ideas expressed?

8.   Do sound, electronic effects, and staging take the place of words?

Acting

1.   Is the interpretation of any given role correct from the standpoint of the play itself?

2.   Does the actor make the character a living individual?

3.   Is the actor artificial or natural in technique?

4.   Are you conscious of the methods of getting effects?

5.   Does the actor grip you emotionally? Do you weep, laugh, suffer, and exult?

6.   Is the actor's voice pleasing?

7.   Does the actor have a magnetic charm?

8.   Is use of dialect correct in every detail?

9.   Does the actor keep in character every moment?

10.   Do you think of the actor as the character depicted or as himself or herself?

11.   Does the actor use the play as a means of self-glorification, or is the actor an intrinsic part of the action at all times?

12.   Does the actor apparently cooperate with the other actors, the director, and the author in interpreting the play by knowing lines, helping to focus the attention on the center of interest, and becoming one with the role?

13.   Does the actor become an acceptable part of the style of the production?

Staging

1. Is the setting in keeping with the play itself?

2. Is it appropriate in its design to the locality and social strata represented?

3. Is it beautiful and artistic in itself?

4. Is the setting conducive to the proper emotional reaction to the play?

5. Are the costumes and properties in harmony with the background?

6. Does the setting add to or detract from enjoyment of the play?

7. Is the interest centered on the total effect or on the details?

8. Has the expenditure of money on the production been justified by the total value of the effects obtained?

9. Do you enjoy the style of the staging and special effects utilized?

Audience Reaction

1. Is the audience attentive, involved, or restless during the performance?

2. Is there a definite response of tears, laughter, or applause?

3. Is there an immediate appreciation of clever lines, dramatic situations, and skillful acting?

4. Is the applause spontaneous and wholehearted, or is it merely polite?

5. After the performance are people hurrying away, or do they linger to discuss the play? Have any or many people left before the performance ends?

6. Is the audience apathetic or animated, bored or buoyant, serious or scoffing?

7. To what types of people does the play seem to appeal?

BIBLIOGRAPHY

Allen, John: *Going to the Theatre,* Phoenix House, London, 1962.

Atkinson, Brooks: *Tuesdays and Fridays,* Random House, New York, 1963.

Blau, Herbert: *Impossible Theatre,* Macmillan, New York, 1964.

Cole, Toby: *Playwrights on Playwriting: The Meaning and Making of Modern Drama,* Hill and Wang, New York, 1960.

Dietrich, R. F.: *Art of Drama,* Holt, New York, 1969.

Kerr, Walter: *Theater in Spite of Itself,* Simon and Schuster, New York, 1963.

Nathan, Geroge Jean: *The Magic Mirror,* Knopf, New York, 1960.

Priestley, John B.: *The Art of the Dramatist,* The Writer, New York, 1955.

Whiting, John: *On Theatre,* Dufour, New York, 1966.

Wright, Edward A., and Lenthiel H. Downs: *A Primer for Playgoers,* Prentice-Hall, Englewood Cliffs, New Jersey, 1958.

CHAPTER NINE

History of the Drama

The history of the drama is closely related to the history of humanity. When the first hunters recounted their adventures by means of vivid pantomime, when the first storytellers told their tales in rhythmic chants, and when the first organized groups of people found expression in the pantomimic intricacies of hunting, war, and love dances, the dramatic impulse was showing itself. Later the primitive actor hid behind a mask to become a god or an animal. The key to people's dramatic action seems to be a desire to imitate. As civilization developed, drama took definite form in the worship of heavenly gods and the glorification of earthly rulers. The mighty Book of Job and the allegorical Song of Songs (Solomon) of the Old Testament are written in dramatic form. Then tales were told of noble types engaged in mighty conflicts and humorous types bumbling along through their comic paces. And, at last, the tales produced dramatic presentations, ultimately to be written and acted in concrete form.

THE ORIGINS OF WESTERN DRAMA

The earliest record of a theatrical performance comes from Egypt, the birth-place of much of the world's art. Carved on a stone tablet some 4,000 years ago, this account tells how I-Kher-Wofret of Abydos arranged and played the leading role in a 3-day pageant made up of actual battles, boat processions, and elaborate ceremonies that told the story of the murder, dismemberment, and resurrection of the great god Osiris. Also, carvings and murals on the walls of ancient temples and tombs show highly theatrical pictures of dancing girls and triumphal processions.

The Hymns to the Sun-god Aton, written and sung by Ikhnaton, the spiritual-minded Pharaoh, rank even today among the finest examples of dramatic religious poetry.

Greek Drama

Drama as we know it came into being in Greece in the sixth century B.C. as part of the worship of Dionysus, god of wine and fertility. To commemorate the god's death, a group of chanters, called the chorus, danced around an altar upon which a goat was sacrified. This chorus was called the "goat-singers," and their ritualistic chant was called the *tragos,* or goat-song. From this term the word *tragedy* came. These ceremonies in honor of Dionysus evolved into dramatic contests, the first of which was won by Thespis. In 534 B.C., he stepped from the chorus and engaged in a dialogue between the chorus and himself, thus becoming the first actor. The term *thespian* has been given to actors ever since. This actor-playwright is also credited with introducing masks into the Greek plays.

These dramatic contests were part of a festival that lasted 5 or 6 days. The most famous of these festivals was the City Dionysia. The first day was devoted to a grand procession, games, and general celebration. The second, and possibly third, day was reserved for dithyrambic poetry contests. On each of the last three days a different playwright would present four plays. The first three plays were tragedies, often a trilogy—three plays related in theme, myth, or characters. The fourth play was called a satyr play, what we might call a tragicomedy. It was considered a great honor to win the ivy wreath of victory in the play contests.

Production in the Greek theater was a highly complex art that made use of clever mechanical devices. The theater existed originally for men, both as performers and audience. Women were not permitted to attend performances until the fourth century B.C. The performances were at first held in the open hillsides surrounding a circular area called the *orchestra,* where the dancing of the chorus took place. Wooden and then stone seats were added to form the theater. At the same time, the dancing circle was paved with stone. In the front row facing the orchestra were special seats for the priests of Dionysus. The altar of Dionysus, located in the center of the orchestra, was sometimes used as a stage prop.

Originally, at the rear of the acting area, was a small hut called the *skene,* where the actors changed masks and costumes. After a time, the skene was enlarged into a stone building. A second story and wings (*parascenia)* were added, and scenery was painted on the front. On the roof was the god-walk, from which the gods delivered their monologues. Also, at a later date, *periaktoi,* three-sided revolving pieces of scenery, were placed on both sides of the stage. Violence was not permitted on the Greek stage, but a movable platform called the *eccyclema* could be rolled out to reveal a tableau of the results of violent acts.

The Theatre of Dionysus is shown as it appears today, after approximately twenty-four centuries of use. Productions of the Greek classics are given here each summer.

Another device used in Greek plays was the *machina,* a cranelike hoist that permitted actors to appear above the stage as if flying. The *machina* could also lower actors from the roof of the skene to the orchestra. The *machina* was heavy enough to carry a chariot and horses or several persons. Most frequently the character lowered represented a god from Mount Olympus who came to Earth to settle the affairs of human beings—and the problems of a playwright who could not resolve the conflict satisfactorily. From the use of this contrivance came the term *deus ex machina* (god from the machine), which is still used today to indicate some device an author introduces late in a play to resolve plot difficulties. Examples are the unknown relative who leaves a legacy, a long-lost letter, or the discovery of a relative given up for dead. Usually such a plot resolution weakens the play and works out acceptably only in farce, melodrama, or fantasy.

The Greek tragic actors wore masks with a built-in megaphone, padded costumes, and boots with thick soles called *cothurni,* or in Latin, *buskins.* The mask was enlarged and heightened by a crown, or *onkus.* The comic actors wore rather grotesque masks, usually padded in a humorously deformed way, and they wore a type of sandal called a sock. You are probably familiar with the "masks of comedy and tragedy," and some of you may even belong to a drama club named "Sock and Buskin" after the shoes of comedy and tragedy.

The actors and members of the chorus moved in stylized dances before huge audiences (it is believed that some theaters could seat over 17,000 patrons). There were fifty dancers in the early chorus, but that number was eventually decreased to twelve or fifteen. Gradually the responsibilities of the chorus diminished as actors took over the key roles.

The chorus, however, was an integral part of the early Greek theater. It served to explain the situation, to bring the audience up to date, to make a commentary on the action from the point of view of established ideas or the group it represented, and to engage in dialogue with the actors. Vestiges of the Greek chorus are found in theater even today: the chorus in Anouilh's *Antigone,* the Stage Manager in *Our Town,* and El Gallo in *The Fantasticks* are three well-known examples of a modern chorus embodied in one character.

Greek Tragedy

The main conflicts of the Greek tragedies evolved from the clash between the will of the gods and the ambitions and desires of humanity. The plays showed how useless were the efforts of human beings to change fate. The greatest writers of Greek tragedy were Aeschylus (525–456 B.C.), Sophocles (497–405 B.C.), and Euripides (485–406 B.C.).

Aeschylus was a warrior-playwright who held firmly to the Greek religion of his day. He added the second actor and reduced the chorus to twelve. He is noted for the elevation and majesty of his language, which has never been surpassed. Many critics refer to him as the "father of tragedy." Of his seventy to ninety plays, only seven remain. *Prometheus Bound* is the tragedy of the mythological "Firebearer" who felt compassion for his creation, human beings. Zeus, infuriated by Prometheus's defiance, had him chained to a rock at the edge of the world. Aeschylus also left us the only existing trilogy, the *Oresteia*. The first play, *Agamemnon,* is the story of the return of Agamemnon from Troy and his murder at the hands of his wife, Clytemnestra, and her lover, Aegisthus. The second play, *The Libation Bearers (Choephori),* tells of the revenge Orestes and Electra take upon Aegisthus and their mother, Clytemnestra. The third play, *The Furies (The Eumenides),* tells of Orestes' torment by the Furies, his trial, and his acquittal.

The greatest of the Greek tragedians, ranked with Shakespeare as one of the greatest playwrights of all time, was Sophocles. This writer of perfectly crafted plays added the third actor and introduced dramatic action leading to a definite plot structure of unity and beauty. He achieved an amazing balance between the power of the gods and the importance of humanity, believing that human beings have a little of the divinity in them that elevates their struggles against fate. Questioning, yet reverent, Sophocles allowed his characters to ask "Why?" within the framework of their acceptance of the will of the gods and fate. As a result, his characters are among the strongest ever to walk upon the stage. He wrote at least 110 plays, of which only 7 have survived. However, we do know that Sophocles won the first prize eighteen times.

Sophocles's *Oedipus Rex* stands as one of the world's most powerful plays of dramatic irony. Aristotle described it as the most ideal tragedy he had ever seen. It is the tragic story of a man in search of Truth. His fate, to unwittingly kill his own father and marry his mother, has been preordained by the gods. It is not until he gouges out his own eyes that Oedipus perceives the Truth his human eyesight was blind to.

Sophocles's *Antigone* is also ranked among the great tragedies. Antigone is Oedipus's daughter. Her two brothers, Eteocles and Polynices, are left to rule jointly. However, civil war breaks out when Eteocles refuses to step down when his term on the throne comes to an end. The two brothers meet on the battlefield and slay each other. Their uncle, Creon, takes over the throne and decrees that Polynices' body must remain unburied. The Greeks believed that desecration of the dead was offensive to the gods and that the soul of a body not given proper burial was doomed to wander eternally. Antigone defies Creon's decree in order to fulfill her higher loyalties to family and gods. She attempts to bury Polynices, is caught, and is placed in a cave to die. It is not until his own world crumbles about him that Creon realizes that the laws of humanity cannot supplant the laws of the gods. A widely produced modern version of *Antigone* by Jean Anouilh is extremely popular now, especially in colleges and high schools.

Euripides was a playwright who seriously questioned life. He became more concerned with the human-interest element than with the religious views of his day. He emphasized human relationships and became a master of pathos. He wrote over ninety plays, but only four won first place. One of his plays, *The*

Masks similar to those used in ancient Greek drama were worn in the production of Oedipus Rex *at the Stratford, Ontario, Festival Theatre in Canada.*

Trojan Women, is one of literature's strongest indictments against war. As the atrocities of murder, pillage, and slavery unfold outside the walls of burning Troy, the audience is deeply moved by the pathos of women and war. Euripides's *Medea* is the tragedy of a woman who seeks revenge on her husband, Jason. In her desire to make Jason pay the highest price for his infidelity, Medea sacrifices that which is dearest to her also—their two sons. These two plays still rank among the most poignant portrayals of women in dramatic literature.

The elevation of humankind as noble beings, the elevation of language, and the elevation of human conflicts lifted Greek tragedy to heights attained since only by Shakespeare.

Greek Comedy

The outstanding author of Greek comedy was Aristophanes (450–380 B.C.), who contributed forty plays, eleven of which still remain. Aristophanes was a skilled satirist and a keen observer of humanity. He considered nothing sacred. His barbed wit mocked the leaders of Athens and the gods themselves in a rollicking, bawdy fashion. Three of his best known plays are *The Frogs,* a writer's contest between Aeschylus and Euripides in Hades judged by Dionysus himself; *The Clouds,* a travesty on Socrates and Greek education; and *Lysistrata,* a scathing attack on war.

Aristophanes was the chief writer of "Old Comedy." Many of the Roman and Renaissance writers were influenced by the "New Comedy," whose best-known author was Menander (342–291 B.C.). Only one complete script, *The Curmudgeon,* is known, and only three fragments remain of his other plays. Menander's comedies seem gentle compared to those of Aristophanes. The satire of Aristophanes gave way to sentimental comedy based on a love story. By this time, the chorus had disappeared and stock characters had made their appearance upon the stage.

Roman Theater

Roman drama was a decadent imitation of Greek drama. It deteriorated at last into sensual interpretive dances called pantomimes, vulgar farces called mimes, and colossal gladiatorial contests in which the slaughter of human beings and beasts became the emotional delight of the audience. The Roman theater at first resembled the Greek, with a heightened skene elaborately decorated with arches and statues of varying sizes. Gradually the theater was extended into a circular arena surrounded by towering tiers of seats. Strangely enough, when Rome had no theaters, two writers of comedy stood out—Plautus and Terence. Two hundred years later, when Rome had constructed huge amphitheaters, only Seneca, a writer of bombastic tragedies, attempted anything like a play. Seneca's plays are usually referred to as "closet" dramas—plays meant to be read rather than acted. Although these three playwrights offered little compared to their Greek predecessors, their plays did influence later writers, including Shakespeare.

It is easy to see that a playwright could not compete with the real conflicts of life and death in the arena, the thrills of the chariot races in the Circus Maximus, or real naval battles on the open seas. The only kind of performance the Roman audience wished to see was that which was filled with vulgarity. The worship of Dionysus had deteriorated into Bacchanalian orgies. The cruelty of the great spectacles and the coarseness of the dramatic entertainment were representative of the moral decay of Rome, which brought about the hostility of the rising Christian church. During the Dark Ages following the decline of Rome, only wandering players called *histriones* and minstrels called *jongleurs* kept the drama alive with their dancing, singing, juggling, acrobatics, and marionette shows. Sad as it seems, from 400 B.C. to the Elizabethan Age of England nearly 2,000 years later, not a single great play was written.

Medieval Drama

The drama owed its revival, like its origin, to religion. During the period extending roughly from the fifth to the fifteeenth centuries, drama developed along slightly different lines in the various European nations. In each case, however, its rebirth came about through the Christian church, a strange coincidence considering that the church associated the worship rites of Dionysus and Bacchus with those of Baal. Nevertheless, the priests gradually introduced *tropes,* liturgical chants added to the mass, in order that the many people who could neither read nor write might learn of the great events in Biblical history.

From mere tableaux at the altar and the stations of the cross, these church plays evolved into elaborate productions that drew increasingly larger crowds and necessitated out-of-doors presentations. Latin was used, as in the masses, and the performers were nuns, priests, and choirboys.

Gradually church drama expanded to present more and more Bible stories. Plays were translated from the Latin, and little by little, lay members of the parishes took part in the performances. The Miracle and Mystery plays were based on the lives of the saints and on stories in the Bible. The *Passion Play,* which is concerned with the last week in the life of Christ, is an example of these medieval church dramas. It still is given in Europe at Oberammergau, Germany, by the citizens of the Bavarian village where it was first performed in 1634. It has been produced every ten years since 1760, on the opening of each decade. The 1980 performance drew approximately six hundred thousand spectators. In the United States, the Black Hills Passion Play group at Spearfish, South Dakota, performs all summer and in Florida during the winter.

A scene from the Passion Play, given every ten years at Oberammergau, Germany. The last production of the Passion Play was in 1980.

The early Miracle and Mystery plays were performed with mansions, a series of acting stations placed in a line. The mansions, or houses, were Biblical localities such as Heaven, Limbo, Pilate's House, Jerusalem, The Temple, and Hell's Mouth. The plays often portrayed the many temptations and challenges facing humans between Heaven and Hell. Hell's Mouth seemed to be of keen interest to the medieval audiences. It breathed fire and smoke, its jaws opened and closed, and as the wicked were pushed in by the Devil's tribe, the pitiful cries of the eternally damned would be heard. Lee Simonson's *The Stage Is Set* gives a delightful account of the elaborate effects and quaint stage directions for Hell's Mouth.

By the twelfth century, the medieval trade unions, or *guilds,* had taken over the presentation of most of the plays during the festival of Corpus Christi. Each guild, according to the craft of its members, presented one part in the story. The bakers presented *The Last Supper;* the goldsmiths, *The Three Wise Men;* the shipwrights, *The Construction of the Ark;* and the cooks, *The Harrowing of Hell.*

Each guild had its own *pageant wagon,* or stage on wheels. The pageant wagon was divided into two levels. The upper level was a platform stage, and the lower level, curtained off, served as a dressing room. The wagons would travel from town to town in a procession. The audience could remain in one spot while the pageant wagons moved through town one by one. The entire sequence of plays was called a cycle. The guilds vied with one another to see which could stage the most elaborate production.

The cycles were highly developed in England, and manuscripts are still preserved from Chester, York, Coventry, and Wakefield. However, the release of control by the church allowed an increasing amount of secular material, especially humorous incidents, to creep into performances. For example, in the Chester *Noah's Flood,* the water is rising rapidly but Noah's wife refuses to get on the ark without her gossipy friends. *The Second Shepherd's Play* is 90 percent secular burlesque focused upon a clever rogue named Mak, who steals a sheep, hides it in a crib, and passes it off as his son. His deception is discovered, and just before a brief nativity tableau, Mak is punished for his theft with a blanket-tossing.

Gradually groups of strolling players began presenting the Miracle and Mystery plays. They drew criticism from the church fathers, and the number of performances declined. These wandering troupes, without sanction of either the church or state, were, however, the originators of the first acting companies, which later were taken under the patronage of the nobility.

The Morality play followed the themes of the Miracle and Mystery plays. But the Morality play was primarily ethical in purpose, dealing with the principles of right and wrong. The plays usually took the form of allegories dramatized by symbolic characters who represented abstract qualities. The most important survival of the Morality plays is *Everyman,* described in Chapter 6.

Other dramatic forms developed in the fifteenth century. They included interludes, short humorous sketches performed between serious plays; chronicle plays, based on historical events; and masques, highly artistic spectacles written and performed for the glorification of the nobility. The backgrounds for the masques were designed by renowned artists like Leonardo da Vinci.

THE RENAISSANCE AND DRAMA

The historical period known as the Renaissance (meaning ''rebirth'') began in Italy in the early fourteenth century. Painting, sculpture, and architecture flourished, but dramatic literature did not.

The Renaissance in Italy

Italy did develop theater architecture and stage equipment, introducing sets with perspective and colored light. Among Italy's architectural contributions to theater were the Teatre Farnese at Parma and the famous Teatro Olimpico, still preserved at Vicenza.

The early offerings of Italian playwrights, however, were only weak imitations of classical plays, paltry obscenities, or poorly constructed scripts.

The *commedia dell' arte* provided much of the new interest in the theater. The commedia was professional improvised comedy. The term *comedy of art* meant just that—these troupes had mastered the art of playing out their comic *scenarios,* plot outlines posted backstage before each performance. There were no fully composed play scripts as we know them. Instead, the scenarios were quite detailed plot outlines that included *lazzi* and certain memorized lines. The *lazzi* were special humorous bits of stage business, usually set apart from the main action. A well-known *lazzi* was one in which the stage action continued while a comic actor laboriously caught a fly. Set speeches, such as the expressions of love, jealousy, hate, and madness, were memorized and used for designated scenes. Also committed to memory were comments on extraneous matters that could be inserted wherever convenient and stock jokes, proverbs, songs, and exit speeches.

Each troupe was led by a manager who usually was the author in the company. The plots were almost always comic intrigue involving fathers putting obstacles in the way of their offsprings' romances. Servants were very important figures in the plot, often proving instrumental in successfully completing the matchmaking. All

In the Teatro Olimpico, perspective paintings of streets placed behind the entrances at the back of the stage give the illusion of depth.

the characters of the commedia were stock types identified by their costumes and masks. There were usually two young male lovers, called *innamorati,* and their female counterparts, the *innamorate*. All four were beautifully dressed and spoke in refined language; their parts did not require masks. The love matches were hampered by the fathers, and the young man often found himself competing against his own father as a suitor.

The only other character to perform unmasked was the *fontesca,* a serving maid. She appears in many plays as Columbina, a clever and high-spirited flirt. The *fontesca* was the forerunner of the witty soubrette of musical comedy, such as Ado Annie in *Oklahoma!*

The *zanni* were the male servants, excellent at ad-libbing and acrobatics. Most *zanni* belong to the same character-type as Mak—the rogue or clever rascal. It is difficult to categorize them by name, but there were basically two kinds of *zanni;* the clever prankster, agile in mind and body; and the dullard, blundering in thought and action. Of the first type, Arlecchino was probably the most popular. He is more commonly known to us by his French name, Harlequin. Little panto-mimes and playlets based on the style of the commedia are often called Harle-quinades. However, the diamond-patterned costume we associate with Harlequin came late in the history of the commedia.

Opposite Arlecchino was Brighella—slow, dishonest, cruel, and vulgar. Another name used for a servant was Pulchinello. This malicious character with his hooked nose and high-peaked hat was the ancestor of Punch of the Punch and Judy shows. Still another of the male servants was Pedrolino, who later became known as Pierrot, the moonstruck eternal lover—melancholy and gentle, but always too romantic and too sad. Later, a sincerely devoted sweetheart, Pierrette, was paired with him. One other variation of the *zanni* must be mentioned—Pagliacci, the man who must make others laugh while his own heart breaks.

Pantalone was an old man—the father competing romantically against his own son, the husband deceived by a young wife, or an overly protective father zeal-ously guarding his young daughter from suitors. His costume consisted of a black coat with flowing sleeves, a red vest, and the breeches from which we have taken the words *pantaloon* and *pants*. His mask was brown, with a large hooked nose and long gray beard. The Pantalone is a common character in later drama. We see him as Polonius in *Hamlet* and as Aragon in *The Miser*. Another old man, Dottore, was the man of law or science impressed with his own knowledge. Garbed in his doctor's hat and robe, the Dottore inserted many Latin phrases into his pretentious boasting. Professor Willard in *Our Town* is a modern example of Dottore.

The last two characters of importance were Capitano, a boastful coward who quaked at his own shadow, and Scaramouche, a mustached scoundrel who became the ancestor of the villain of the Victorian melodramas. The great ''save-your-own-skin'' death speech of Falstaff is typical of the ''brave'' Capitano.

The Renaissance Elsewhere on the Continent

Written drama evolved in Spain, where Cervantes (1547–1616), Lope de Vega (1562–1635), and Calderón (1600–1681) contributed to the mounting interest in theater. *The Man of La Mancha,* the modern musical adaptation by Dale Wasserman of Cervantes' famed *Don Quixote* promises to survive as a classic in its own right.

France developed the professional theater under the patronage of the state with such great plays as *The Cid* by Corneille (1606–1684), *The Miser, The Misanthrope,* and *The Imaginary Invalid* by Molière (1622–1673), and *Phaedra* by Racine (1639–1699).

So many of Molière's sparkling comedy-dramas are being presented today in the regional theaters across the country that they are becoming more familiar to American audiences than many contemporary plays.

Strolling players kept the drama alive during this period, appearing before the public in village squares and before the nobility in their castles. They created melodramatic history plays, rowdy comedies, and romantic love stories that were the origins of the great dramas of later generations.

The Renaissance in England

The climax of the dramatic renaissance came during the Elizabethan age in England. This was a period in which the drama was the expression of the soul of a nation, and the theater became a vital force in the lives of the people.

The first English comedy was *Ralph Roister Doister* produced in 1553, which the author, Nicholas Udall, modeled on Plautus's plays. It was followed by *Gammer Gurton's Needle,* authorship uncertain, which became famous after its first production at Cambridge. The first true English tragedy was *Gorboduc,* which was performed in 1561. Among the many writers in this period were John Lyly *(Endymion),* George Peele *(The Old Wives' Tale* and *King Edward the First),* Robert Greene *(Friar Bacon and Friar Bungay),* John Webster *(The Duchess of Malfi),* Thomas Dekker *(A Shoemaker's Holiday),* Thomas Heywood *(A Woman Killed with Kindness),* Philip Massinger *(A New Way to Pay Old Debts),* Thomas Kyd *(The Spanish Tragedy),* and Francis Beaumont and John Fletcher *(The Knight of the Burning Pestle* and *The Maid's Tragedy).*

Three Monumental Elizabethan Dramatists

Towering above all the other brilliant actor-playwrights responsible for the glory of the period, three men—Marlowe, Jonson, and Shakespeare—produced plays that have never lost their appeal.

Christopher Marlowe (1564–1593) introduced the first important use of blank verse, the "mighty line" of English poetic drama. Combining extraordinary use of language and the excitement of melodramatic plots, he wrote *Tamburlaine the*

Great, The Jew of Malta, and *Edward II*. These plays present the glory and the horror of the age. They suited the physical and theatrical power of the actor Edward Alleyn, for whom they were written. However, it is *Doctor Faustus,* the story of a man who sells his soul for 24 hours of damning knowledge, that brilliantly bridges the gap between the medieval age and the Renaissance.

Ben Jonson (1573–1637) was the first master of English comedy. He wrote *Volpone, The Alchemist,* and *Every Man in His Humour.*

To the Elizabethan, the word *humour,* as used in the phrase "He's in a good humour," did not refer to an attitude of amusement. The Renaissance was a period in which anatomical study, as well as the arts, developed. Physicians were amazed by the amount of fluids (humours) found in the human body. Scholars believed that all matter was made up of four elements—air, earth, fire, and water. It was also assumed that the human body was composed of these same four elements, each having its own effect on the personality. Air was identified with blood and caused the *sanguine* humour—light-hearted, airy, happy-go-lucky. Fire was associated with bile and brought about the *choleric* humour—angry, hot-tempered, impetuous. Water was identified with phlegm and caused the *phlegmatic* humour—dull, listless, lethargic.

The humour of most interest in Elizabethan plays is that of black bile, identified with earth, which resulted in the *melancholy* humour. The melancholy character fell into three main types: the lover, the malcontent, and the intellectual. Hamlet is an excellent example of the intellectual melancholy humour. Although most stage figures have a predominating humour, a balanced personality was the most desirable. This is evidenced by Antony's tribute to Brutus in *Julius Caesar:* ". . . the elements [were] so mixed in him that Nature might stand up and say to all the world, this was a man."

Jonson widened the scope of the humours to include any strong personality trait, especially a weakness, foible, or folly that could make a character a cause of laughter.

William Shakespeare (1564–1616) was the greatest Elizabethan dramatist as well as the greatest dramatist of all time. He followed his dramatic career as playwright, actor, and manager for only 20 years. In that time, he wrote thirty-six plays. Not only is Shakespeare the towering literary figure of all the ages, but his characterizations, beautiful poetry, and never-to-be-forgotten lines echo a majesty best expressed by the "Bard's" friendly rival, Ben Jonson, who said that Shakespeare "was not of an age but for all time."

The Shakespearean Playhouse

The first English public playhouse, the Theatre, was built across the Thames River from London in 1576 by James Burbage. He was the manager of the company later housed in the famous Globe Theatre, with which Shakespeare was

In Shakespeare's play Henry IV (Part One), *Hotspur, played by Laurence Olivier, jests tenderly with his wife (Margaret Leighton) before the battle in which he is killed.*

associated as actor-playwright. The theaters were modeled after the medieval inn yards where the wandering acting companies had played for years. The inns had open courtyards where the audience could stand around a platform stage or sit in the galleries surrounding the courtyard.

The playhouses were round or octagonal in shape and had three tiers of galleries. The stage has been called an "unlocalized platform stage" because this 5- to 6-foot high acting area used little scenery to indicate locale. A sign or an actor's line was usually enough to inform the audience of geographical locations. The area surrounding the stage was called the pit, and the motley playgoers who paid a modest fee to stand there were called groundlings. The groundlings were, for the most part, tradesmen, apprentices, soldiers, sailors, and country folk who had come to the great city of London. In some of his plays, Shakespeare commented sharply on the lack of discernment in this fickle mob that reeked of garlic and body odor, ate and drank during the performances, and reacted loudly to what they liked or disliked. Wandering through this crowd were the "cut-purses," or what we might call Elizabethan pickpockets. The more refined audience occupied the gallery seats, for which an additional fee was charged. The most expensive seats were on the stage itself.

Over the stage was the Heavens, a roof supported by two ornate columns. The underneath side of the Heavens was painted blue, with a golden sun in the center surrounded by stars and the signs of the zodiac. An actor who spoke of the heavens and the earth, had only to point to the roof overhead and the stage floor beneath to create the illusion of a microcosmic universe. The "back wall" of the stage looked like the outside of a multistoried building.

The area backstage was called the tiring house. In the center rear was a curtained recess called the inner below, or study. This area could be used for "reveal" scenes, such as a bedroom or the tent of Antony. There were second-floor acting areas also: a central area consisting of the shallow balcony; the tarras, separated by a curtain called the arras from a recess called the chamber. On either side of the chamber were the window boxes, probably used for such settings as the balcony scene of *Romeo and Juliet*. A third level, when present, could be used for acting when necessary, but seems to have served primarily as the musician's gallery. In all these acting levels, there were trapdoors, some mechanically operated. They were used in scenes like that of the grave diggers in *Hamlet*.

Over the third level was what appeared to be a small house, which was appropriately called the scenery hut. This structure housed stage machinery and a cannon. From the peak of the roof a flag was flown to inform the residents of London when a play was to be given. Since there was no artificial lighting, plays were presented in the afternoon, which accounts for the description of the Globe as a "wooden O"—a circular building open to the sky.

All female roles were played by specially trained boys. Costumes were often very beautiful, since they were provided by the wealthy patrons who sponsored the acting companies and who competed with one another for the success of their troupes. Of course this meant that little attempt was made to costume the actors with historical accuracy. Roman citizens in *Julius Caesar* appeared in the gorgeous satins, velvets, and plumes of the sixteenth century. The audiences loved color, sound, and pageantry. A march of armies garbed in the royal colors, the ringing of the alarum bell, and the firing of the cannon heightened the action on the stage.

SHAKESPEARE, THE PLAYWRIGHT

As you begin your study of Shakespeare, there are a few things you should remember. The ideal way to become acquainted with Shakespeare is to see his plays, not merely to read them or read about them. The plays were written by a practical man of the theater who wrote them to be seen—not read—by a loud, boisterous audience accustomed to shouting its approval or hissing its displeasure. A play had to be exciting, moving, and violent, filled with fury, humor, and truth, in order to keep such an audience interested. The characters Shakespeare wrote of were moved by emotions—love, jealousy, ambition, joy, and grief—that are as universal today as they were 400 years ago.

Play Structure

Shakespeare did not divide his plays into acts and scenes. His characters came and went, explaining in their conversation where they were as well as who they were. In the Elizabethan theater, there was no curtain to be drawn, so there were no dramatic curtain lines; each scene blended into the next. However, Shakespeare often used a rhymed couplet to show when a scene was over, and this is one clue that producers and editors have used in dividing the plays into acts and scenes.

His plays are famous for their openings, in which the master dramatist did so much to set the characters, the preliminary situation, and the mood of the play as a whole. The exposition usually takes several scenes because the action is invariably complicated.

The rising action begins in the first act and reveals the main problem of the play, the opposing forces, and the conflict, which may be between two characters or groups of people or within the soul of the leading character. The climax usually comes in the third act, when the eventual outcome of the play is definitely fore-shadowed and the main groups of characters are brought together in a single dramatic situation.

The action is built, often by the use of minor plots, to maintain interest through the fourth and fifth acts. The play concludes with the resolution, and the ending is usually as effective as the beginning. Note how the closing scene helps make a complete unit of the play.

Characters

It is, of course, in his unsurpassed power of characterization that Shakespeare's genius most brilliantly expresses itself. His stories were seldom original, but when the magic of his hand touched plots and characters, they were transformed into masterpieces that eclipsed the sources from which they sprang. In turn, his masterpieces inspired works of art by the world's greatest composers, painters, and poets.

The characters form the center of the interest of Shakespeare's plays. Note exactly how each is introduced and how well defined the personality becomes immediately. Shakespeare used the soliloquy and accurate descriptions by other actors to delineate his characters, for there were no programs to make any printed explanations. Notice how clear-cut the minor characters are, defining themselves in their few lines as vividly as do the main characters in their thousands of lines.

Theme

The theme, or underlying idea of the play, may be found by analyzing the leading characters, their motivations and goals, and the manner in which they solve, or fail to solve, their main problem. Usually the theme is expressed in one important line, but often it is repeated in varied forms for emphasis. Frequently it is condensed in the title of the drama.

In every play, there are scores of brilliantly worded ideas about which whole dramas could be built, but there is always one dominant thought about which the

Burgher women and a country woman as they might have appeared in Shakespeare's Merry Wives of Windsor

action centers. In fact, the fascination of working out these key ideas of the great dramas has caused whole volumes to be published by famous critics and actors.

Language

When you read a Shakespearean play, you will be struck by the power and the beauty of the language if you do not worry too much about its form. Most school editions of the plays have excellent notes that will help you over the difficulties of Elizabethan speech. You will be amazed, however, to find how modern in spirit the language is. You will, of course, pick out the figurative language in a play and see how greatly it adds to the beauty and force of Shakespeare's ideas. You will also listen to the music of the language and note how the pronunciation and emphasis of words form a definite rhythm. See how the movement of the lines and the choice of words express the spirit of a scene and suggest the manner in which it must be played.

Chronology of the Plays

Since the exact dates for the composition of Shakespeare's plays are not known, an approximate chronology has been devised by scholars from available evidence. In the following list, the plays appear in the order generally agreed upon. (The starred titles are those most suitable for use in class reading.)

1590 *Love's Labour's Lost*	1599 *As You Like It**
1591 *The Comedy of Errors*	1600 *Twelfth Night**
Henry VI	1601 *Julius Caesar**
1592 *Two Gentlemen of Verona*	1602 *Hamlet**
Richard III	1603 *Troilus and Cressida*
Romeo and Juliet*	1604 *Measure for Measure*
1593 *King John*	*Othello*
Richard II	1605 *Macbeth**
Titus Andronicus	1606 *King Lear*
1594 *A Midsummer Night's Dream**	1607 *Timon of Athens*
1595 *All's Well That Ends Well*	1608 *Pericles*
The Taming of the Shrew*	*Antony and Cleopatra*
1596 *Henry IV*	1609 *Coriolanus*
1597 *The Merry Wives of Windsor*	1610 *Cymbeline*
The Merchant of Venice*	1611 *The Winter's Tale*
1598 *Much Ado about Nothing*	*The Tempest**
Henry V	1616 *Henry VIII*

The Continued Success of Shakespeare's Plays

The reason for the success of Shakespeare's plays is their adaptability to all types of production because of their universal appeal. That appeal is based on the fact that Shakespeare was an actor as well as a playwright, and he knew his theater as no other person ever has. His practical business sense and stability of character prevented his becoming involved in the reckless excesses of the other actor-dramatists of his time, who failed to reach their full potentialities. He wrote many passages about the stage and its relation to people, among them these:

> All the world's a stage
> And all the men and women merely players.

> I hold the world but as the world, Gratiano,
> A stage where every man must play a part.

> Life's but a walking shadow, a poor player
> That struts and frets his hour upon the stage
> And then is heard no more.

How greatly has the world profited by the fact that Shakespeare's genius lay in both acting and writing plays of infinite variety. Otherwise, he, too, might only have strutted and fretted his hour upon the stage and then been heard no more.

LATER DRAMA IN ENGLAND

Naturally the American stage has always reflected its British origins, but with the current interchange of actors, producers, and famous companies, we are gradually thinking of an English-speaking theater rather than of a British or an American one. Therefore, you should know a great deal about the history of drama in Great Britain to understand better the present and future trends in the United States.

Restoration Drama

Important innovations were made during the Restoration. Women were allowed to appear as players by the English Royal Patent of 1662, which said that ''all women's parts should be performed by women'' and provided that plays and acting might be esteemed ''not only harmless delights but useful and instructive representations of human life.'' Elaborate scenery and mechanical equipment, earlier introduced from Europe by Inigo Jones for court masques, came into general use. The licensing of theaters still continued, though only two playhouses were officially sanctioned, the famed Drury Lane Theater and the Covent Garden.

In the 1700s, professional stage plays were presented in London, England, at the Drury Lane Theater, one of the first ''legitimate'' theaters in the world.

From these patent theaters came the term *legitimate theater*, which we use now simply to refer to professional stage plays.

Among the Restoration dramatists are a few whose plays have survived until today. William Wycherley (1640–1716), in *The Country Wife*, started the fashionable trend in comedies. William Congreve (1670–1729) ranks as one of the great masters of comedy. The brilliant art and pace of his *Love for Love* and *The Way of the World* set a standard for later comedies of manners. George Farquhar (1678–1707), in his *The Beaux' Stratagem*, brought a refreshing breath of the country into the dissolute city life depicted on the stage. This play strongly influenced later playwrights. John Gay (1685–1732) was primarily a poet, but his biting satire, *The Beggar's Opera*, was revamped in 1928 by Bertolt Brecht as *The Threepenny Opera*, with the bewitching music of Kurt Weill. Both forms are frequently revived today.

Eighteenth- and Nineteenth-Century English Drama

The eighteenth century produced only two outstanding playwrights. Richard Brinsley Sheridan (1751–1816) wrote two scintillating social comedies: *The*

School for Scandal and *The Rivals,* which features the immortal Mrs. Malaprop, the world's greatest misuser of words.

Oliver Goldsmith (1728–1774) was a dramatist whose fame rests on one play, *She Stoops to Conquer.* Every character is a "rich" part, from Tony Lumpkin to Kate Hardcastle, who pretends to be a servant to win a bashful suitor.

The London stage of the nineteenth century established the trends that have given it the prestige it holds today. Gilbert and Sullivan created their clever comic operas, such as *The Mikado, H. M. S. Pinafore,* and *The Pirates of Penzance.* Oscar Wilde, with his genius for epigrams and brilliant dialogue, wrote *The Importance of Being Earnest.*

George Bernard Shaw (1856–1950) ranks as the greatest playwright of his long period of eminence and has been acclaimed next to Shakespeare among English dramatists. Although he is primarily a philosopher frankly declaiming his theories, his satiric humor and fascinating characters will keep alive such plays as *Saint Joan, Candida, Man and Superman, Caesar and Cleopatra, Pygmalion, Androcles and the Lion,* and *Arms and the Man.*

Drama in England Today

England is the center of theater lovers today. They are drawn to London by the assurance that they will find a large number of productions of all types to choose from, where versatile and superlative acting is assured at reasonable prices. The Arts Council of Great Britain established The National Theatre under the direction of Laurence Olivier, the first actor to be made a peer. The National Theatre is an elegant theater complex which replaced the famous Old Vic.

English summer theater festivals are flourishing. Of these the Royal Shakespeare Memorial Theatre at Stratford-on-Avon, the Edinburgh International Festival, and the Malvern Festival offer the most varied and exciting fare.

Drama students should be familiar with the plays of John Osborne, who introduced the "angry young men," and of J. B. Priestly, T. S. Eliot, Harold Pinter, Robert Bolt, Tom Stoppard, Anthony and Peter Shaffer, and Alan Acykbourne.

DRAMA IN IRELAND

Drama in southern Ireland has had a brief but brilliant history, starting with the plays of William Butler Yeats and Lady Gregory at the turn of the century. Yeats was dedicated to poetic drama retelling the ancient tales of Ireland. His *At the Hawk's Well* beautifully combined myth, dance, and poetry. Lady Gregory excelled in one-act plays based on peasant life in the villages, such as *The Rising of the Moon.* John Millington Synge is considered by many to be the finest of the Irish dramatists, but his compatriots objected to his portrayal of them in several plays. His *The Playboy of the Western World* and *Riders to the Sea* are frequently produced today. Sean O'Casey, with *Juno and the Paycock, Within the Gates,* and *The Plough and the Stars,* was the prominent midcentury voice of the Irish theater.

DRAMA ON THE CONTINENT

Drama has flourished throughout Europe for three centuries. The chief contributions of the European dramatists has been in initiating trends that have been followed in all countries. No longer can we divide any discussion into the drama of the various countries, because today they are interrelated.

Notable Dramatists

In France, Molière, Voltaire, Victor Hugo, and Alexandre Dumas broke away from classical traditions and produced exciting drama. Edmund Rostand created the immortal character Cyrano de Bergerac, the poet-warrior with the huge nose, whose romance has become world famous. Jean Giraudoux *(Tiger at the Gates, The Madwoman of Chaillot)* and Jean Anouilh *(The Lark, Antigone, A Time Remembered)* have also been popular in the United States. Their plays have been translated by such dramatists as Christopher Fry and Lillian Hellman. Jean-Paul Sartre's *No Exit* and *The Flies* reflect his existentialist viewpoint.

In Germany, the colossal figure of Goethe towers above all others with his *Faust.* His poetic drama, telling the tragedy of the man who sold himself to the Devil to get all worldy desires in a new-lived youth, was written in glorious verse and has inspired three grand operas as well as literary works in other languages.

Gerhart Hauptmann in the nineties began the new era of realism in the German theater. His work culminated in *The Weavers,* one of the great dramas setting forth a social issue built around a "group protagonist." Bertolt Brecht wrote for the epic theater. *Mother Courage, The Caucasian Chalk Circle,* and *The Good Woman of Setzuan* are among his plays most often produced in the United States.

In Czechoslovakia, the Capek brothers achieved fame working together and separately on expressionistic plays of social impact, such as *R.U.R.,* the theme of which is machines taking over humanity.

In Spain, after the great early period, José Echegaray was the only dramatist whose plays were acted abroad until Jacinto Benavente won the Nobel Prize for Literature for *The Passion Flower.* Symbolist playwright Federico García Lorca's *Blood Wedding* is frequently seen in university theaters.

From Italy, comes Luigi Pirandello, whose conviction that people are not what they appear to be is described in his "naked masks" theory. His plays are exceedingly complicated and difficult on the whole. However, *Six Characters in Search of an Author* and *Henry IV* are frequently produced.

Henrik Ibsen of Norway (1828–1906), sometimes called ''the father of modern drama,'' introduced realism in conversation and presentation. His chief theme— that the individual rights of each person must be protected and developed—had a special appeal for Americans. Ibsen wrote two magnificent poetic dramas, *Peer Gynt* and *Brand,* but it was his *A Doll's House, Ghosts, Hedda Gabler, An Enemy of the People,* and *The Master Builder* that account for his world influence.

Konstantin Stanislavski (1863–1938) of Russia was the other European whose influence in this country cannot be estimated. His ''Method'' has established the acting theory centered on the inner understanding of a role plus the perfecting of physical response when presenting the role to an audience. The Moscow Art Theatre, founded and directed by him, became the finest in the world from the viewpoint of ensemble acting and realistic production. To name only a few Russian dramatists, there are Gogol with *The Inspector General;* Turgenev, *A Month in the Country;* Tolstoy, *The Power of Darkness;* and Andreyev, *He Who Gets Slapped.* The greatest of all the Russian dramatists was the early realist Anton Chekhov (1860–1904), who wrote *The Sea Gull, The Three Sisters, Uncle Vanya,* and *The Cherry Orchard.*

The plays of Molière, Voltaire, Victor Hugo, and Alexandre Dumas would have played at the Variétés Amusantes (now called the Théâtre-Français), shown as it appeared in 1789.

To the Westerner, the appeal of the drama of the Far East lies largely in the gorgeous costumes, which are complemented by masks or elaborate makeup, and in the expressive pantomime. This scene is from the Chinese theater spectacle The Sun and Moon.

DRAMA IN ASIA

To the Westerner, the appeal of the drama in the Far East lies largely in the gorgeous costumes that are complemented by masks or elaborate makeup, in the brilliant color, and in the grotesque and expressive pantomime. Asian drama is presented in a highly traditional manner inherited from the distant past. The subject matter deals with historical and religious legends not easily understood by a foreigner. The length of the performances, the high-pitched voices, and the discordant music are often very wearing to Westerners, but there is an exotic charm in every program.

The Chinese theater, using the same symbolism and techniques as it has for centuries, can still be seen in Hong Kong and occasionally in Honolulu. Historical plays featuring the actions of generals, long journeys by characters, and many battle scenes predominate.

All forms of the drama of Japan have been brought to the United States in the last few years and shown on stage and television. There are three forms of drama distinctly Japanese: The Nō (Noh), the Bunraku or Doll Theater, and the Kabuki.

The Nō theater is the oldest form of drama to be preserved in its exact form, with words, dance, and music rhythmically coordinated as they were in productions 600 years ago. The traditional forms have been handed down by generations of actors strictly trained from childhood in what is practically isolation. The special theater is like a temple, with the 18-foot square stage extending into the audience and supported by four wooden pillars that form a part of the action. The characters—all of whom are played by men—include an old man, an old woman, a young man, a child, a monster, a formidable god, a gentle god, and an animal. The essence of Nō lies in creating beauty of motion and speech. The plots are short and very simple, and the language is intricate. The spectators follow the libretto closely.

The Bunraku features marionettes about 4 feet tall, carved in wood and gorgeously gowned. They are so realistic that they move their fingers, mouths, eyes, and eyebrows with lifelike expressiveness. Each doll is manipulated by three attendants who are dressed in black and wear gauze masks to symbolize their invisibility. Amazingly they soon seem to disappear. The dialogue is read in turn by five narrators in elaborate costumes. This form of theater was brought from Korea to Japan in the sixth century. The traditional movements and play forms of the Kabuki drama originated in the Doll Theater.

The Kabuki came into being in the sixteenth century and was originally an imitation of both the Doll Theater and the Nō drama. Women first produced and acted the plays, but today only men are the players. The actors spend their lives in the theater. They begin as children and continue to act in historical and domestic plays and dance-dramas until they are in their seventies. The infinitely detailed pantomime and the superlative acting, enhanced by elaborate costuming and makeup painted with brushes, are true theater.

DRAMA IN THE UNITED STATES

The theater in America, because of its British origin, has naturally been strongly influenced by the dramatists and actors of England from Colonial days to the present.

Early American Drama

The first theater in America was built in Williamsburg, Virginia, in 1716, but all traces of it had disappeared by the time the entire city was restored in the 1920s. The Dock Street Theater of Charleston, South Carolina, was erected in 1736. Although twice rebuilt, it is still in use. The Southwark was built in Philadelphia in 1766 and is acclaimed as the first permanent theater in the country. In New

York the first important theater was erected in 1767 on John Street by David Douglass, who had also built the Southwark in Philadelphia.

The first American dramas were produced by the American Company, managed by David Douglass. The first play was *The Prince of Parthia* by Thomas Godfrey, given on April 24, 1767, at the Southwark. It was strictly an imitation of British blank-verse tragedies and had only one performance. *The Contrast* by Royall Tyler opened at the John Street Theater on April 16, 1787, and was an instant success. It was a comedy and introduced Jonathan, the original typical Yankee—shrewd, wholesome, and humorous—who has appeared in many guises ever since. However, *Fashion* by Anna Cora Mowatt, produced in 1845, is considered our first native comedy on the same theme—poking fun at social pretenders—and it is frequently revived. *Uncle Tom's Cabin,* dramatized by George Aiken from Harriet Beecher Stowe's novel of 1852, holds the record as our most widely produced melodrama.

The first actors were English professional troupes who presented popular London plays. The legendary family that links the early American stage with the modern is the Barrymores. John Drew was an Irish actor who came to America in 1846; he married Louise Lane, our first distinguished actress-manager. She had three children: John Drew, Sidney, and Georgiana, who married Maurice Barrymore, a dashing Irish actor. The Barrymores were the parents of Lionel, Ethel, and John Barrymore, who were for years America's leading actors.

Edwin Booth (1833–1893) was the greatest romantic actor America has produced. His illustrious career nearly suffered an eclipse when he retired after his brother, John Wilkes Booth, also a well-known actor, assassinated Abraham Lincoln. Edwin Booth later returned to the stage but never appeared again in Washington.

Steele MacKaye (1842–1894) was one of the most fascinating characters in our theater. He was a playwright and an actor and was the first American to appear as Hamlet in London. His inventions, which foreshadowed the mechanics of the modern stage, included elevator stages, overhead lighting, and folding theater chairs. He also started America's first dramatic school, the American Academy of Dramatic Art.

The Commercial Theater

The term *commercial theater* denotes every form of dramatic entertainment designed primarily to make money. Professional playwrights, producers, and actors make and lose fortunes in a gamble with the public.

Vaudeville was for many years tremendously popular, and playing the Palace on Broadway was the supreme desire of every entertainer. Stock companies in almost all cities, with their weekly change of play, have been, and are still, the finest possible training ground for actors. Established companies, managed on a subscription basis, have played a vital and distinguished role in Broadway's history. The Theater Guild, founded in 1919, was destined to become the most illustrious producing company America has known. George Bernard Shaw owed his popularity in this country to its splendid presentations of his plays. Eugene O'Neill (1888–1953), acclaimed as one of America's leading dramatists, had many of his finest dramas first produced by the Theater Guild. *Strange Interlude, Mourning Becomes Electra, Dynamo, Ah, Wilderness!, The Iceman Cometh, Anna Christie, The Emperor Jones,* and *The Hairy Ape* are but a few of his great plays. O'Neill was awarded the Nobel Prize in literature and four Pulitzer prizes, the last one granted posthumously for *Long Day's Journey into Night.*

The Group Theater was founded in 1931 by Harold Clurman, Lee Strasberg, Cheryl Crawford, and a number of dedicated actors, directors, and scenic artists interested in applying the Stanislavski Method in American productions. A long succession of strong problem plays was presented, including those by Clifford Odets and William Saroyan, with creative sets by Mordecai Gorelik and direction by Elia Kazan. Odets's *Waiting for Lefty* and Saroyan's *The Time of Your Life* achieved lasting recognition. Economic pressures caused the group to disband in 1941. Six years later, Lee Strasberg and Cheryl Crawford established the Actors' Studio, which has exerted a strong influence on the American stage. Among the well-known actors and actresses to study there are Marlon Brando, Geraldine Page, Paul Newman, Joanne Woodward, Marilyn Monroe, Julie Harris, and Ben Gazzara.

Modern Theater

The twenties and thirties brought the United States into the mainstream of world drama. The theater flourished on Broadway because enthusiastic audiences were attracted by many fine plays of varied types, by the painstaking production of the directors and scenic artists staging them, and by a growing number of excellent actors and actresses interpreting them with skill and inspiration. Amateurs across the country established successful groups producing first-class plays artistically, and the educational theater came into being with students in universities and high schools, for the first time, studying plays from the standpoint of acting and producing, not just reading them as a form of literature.

Off-Broadway plays became in the fifties a new source of inspiration for the American theater, with creative producers, actors, and backstage artists bringing fresh talent to reviving our great plays and encouraging new ones to be written. Greenwich Village has been the center for progressive artists since the early twenties, so it was naturally the first area where less expensive, more original, and interesting presentations found a satisfactory environment. By the sixties, off-

Elizabeth Swados's Runaways *began at Joseph Papp's Public Theater in Greenwich Village in New York City. The production's popularity grew so rapidly that* Runaways *moved to Broadway for a successful run.*

Broadway theaters had opened all over New York in any available building—cafés, churches, lecture halls, lofts.

The Lincoln Center for the Performing Arts houses the Metropolitan Opera, the New York Philharmonic Orchestra, the New York City Opera, and the New York City Ballet. Its Vivian Beaumont Theater was planned as its official repertory theater, but difficulties have faced the opening seasons, causing changes in directors and policies.

Regional and Repertory Theaters

The hope of the American theater lies in the growth of the regional movement, which is rapidly bringing drama to all areas. In a sense, this movement is an outgrowth of the amateur movement, for it gives professionally inclined members of existing community groups an opening they have never had.

You are probably wondering about the two terms *regional* and *repertory*. To state the difference briefly, the regional theaters present any type of play for as long as they wish and can repeat a play when and if they think it wise. Repertory companies set up a definite number of productions, which they repeat at regular intervals or rotate as advertised at the beginning of each season. Both are known as resident theaters when guest stars are not used, and they specialize in ensemble acting. They both usually have subscription memberships. Individual admissions, at higher cost per performance than the memberships, may or may not be sold.

The first regional theater to be built was the dream of the Minnesota Theatre Company, which was organized to give Tyrone Guthrie an opportunity to start a theater in a typical American city far from Broadway. It was named the Tyrone Guthrie Theatre. In 1963, the first season presented an international group of fine plays from contrasting epochs—*Hamlet, The Miser, The Three Sisters,* and *Death of a Salesman.* The theater has maintained the high standard then established. The building resembles the one Guthrie had already designed for the Stratford Festival Theatre, now officially titled the Stratford National Theatre of Canada, at Stratford, Ontario. The thrust stage and other features have proved of durable value.

The standards of the Tyrone Guthrie Theatre are based on the classics because, as Guthrie said in his first program, "They are what the best minds in previous generations have united to admire. Only through the classics can intelligent standards of criticism be established."

The hope of American theater lies in the growth of such regional theaters as the Dallas Theater Center, where classics such as Anton Chekhov's Three Sisters *are periodically revived.*

The Negro Ensemble Company of New York has established itself as an excellent repertory theater and training group under the direction of Douglas Turner Ward. Home by Samm-Art Williams and such fine young actors as Charles Brown gained national recognition with Tony nominations during the 1980 New York theater season.

It is impossible to list all the theaters that show promise of surviving as permanent institutions, but you should know where you can see some excellent productions in outstanding theaters.

The Arena Stage in Washington, D.C., the Dallas Theater Center, the Alley Theater of Houston, and the Seattle Repertory Theater are among the earliest to achieve success and are all continuing to offer seasons of exciting plays. The Negro Ensemble Company of New York has established itself as a first-class repertory theater and training group under the direction of Douglas Turner Ward. It is presenting plays expressing the real lives and spirit of the black people of America while developing new playwrights and actors. The American Conservatory Theater under the stimulating direction of William Ball is presenting splendidly paced, articulate productions in two theaters in San Francisco and in tours across the country.

Performing arts centers are being established in many cities since the origin for the idea of building Lincoln Center away from Broadway developed into a reality. They all include a number of handsome buildings in a central location to house the phases of the arts which are of interest to the people of the community. Usually these are an opera house; a theater with two auditoriums—one large enough for repertory seasons, with storage and wardrobe room for many classical and period plays, and the other smaller, for experimental and contemporary drama; a concert hall; an art academy; and any additional schools, museums, and art galleries desired.

The Los Angeles Music Center was the second performing arts center to be completed and put to use. In it, the theater is the Mark Taper Forum, a perfectly equipped theater, with a large thrust stage. There is also a smaller theater where the New Theater for Now provides a laboratory for new forms and concepts.

The Inner City Cultural Center in Los Angeles is another that has a repertory theater, also on a smaller, more intimate scale, where plays of racial and international interest, as well as classical plays, can be featured.

The Denver Center for the Performing Arts is a recently developed cultural complex. It includes four theaters, a concert hall, and a cinema.

The Utah Festival of the Arts in American Fork, Utah, presented in the summer of 1980 a *tableau vivant,* which means a "living picture." Special lighting effects, costumes, and makeup were used to create the living pictures of great works of art and sculpture.

Another development in regional theater is the growth of dinner theater. Offering a package price for a meal and a professional play, dinner theaters have captured a suburban audience that might not have ventured into a city to see a play. In addition, the emergence of dinner theater has provided a new place for actors, designers, and technicians to work at their art.

You will undoubtedly hear fine music and see great plays and operas in these centers for the rest of your life. More and more centers are already in the planning stage and others are being built.

The Amateur Theater

Amateur means "one who loves." In America, the number of amateurs who give hours and hours of their leisure time to putting on plays is a national fact of importance. If you really want to enjoy acting in, directing, or staging plays, you will become involved in the amateur field.

The little theaters were a part of the life of almost every city and town in the twenties and thirties. They were usually formed by groups of congenial people who loved the theater and enjoyed bringing the best Broadway plays to their communities. The one-act play came into prominence in the twenties, largely because tournaments where only one-act plays could be entered were held in many states.

Community theaters gradually superseded the little theaters. They are more democratic, drawing players from all sections of cities and catering to larger and more varied audiences. In many places where no professional theaters are located, community theaters present current plays during their Broadway runs.

University Theater

Some of the finest theater buildings in the world have been constructed on the campuses of American universities, and university departments of drama are covering every field of theater. Thousands of teachers of dramatics are graduating every year to enter both the high school and elementary fields. Professional aspirants are getting practical experience in every type of play—period, classical, contemporary, and children's theater.

Guest stars have become resident instructors and actors under special arrangements made through the Extension Department of Equity. Thus dramatics majors get firsthand instruction and information from the guest stars.

Repertory theaters of fine quality have become a part of many of the adjoining communities with subscription audiences. The Repertory Theater of St. Louis has one of the latest of Guthrie's theaters. The University of Washington in Seattle has for years had three working theaters: The Penthouse, where Glen Hughes first introduced the Theater-in-the-Round; the Showboat; and the Playhouse. The Carnegie-Mellon University in Pittsburgh, Pennsylvania, continues the noteworthy dramatic training of the former Carnegie Institute of Technology. The University of Denver maintains its reputation of years with a series of fine plays each season and the introduction of a professionally oriented program.

The Juilliard School, after years of fame as one of the great schools of music, located in Lincoln Center, has recently opened a Drama Department under John Houseman.

The first American College Theater Festival was held in the spring of 1969, backed by the American National Theater and Academy (ANTA) and the American Educational Theater Association (AETA) and sponsored by the Smithsonian Institute, the Friends of the Kennedy Center, and American Airlines. There were ten plays selected for the Washington, D.C., Festival from about twenty campuses. It is a continuing impetus toward a high standard of production as well as fresh creativity.

Government Participation

The U.S. government and drama have not been closely associated until recently, but in 1965 an important change took place. The National Foundation on the Arts and Humanities was signed into law. Its purposes are to assist creative artists, to develop wider audiences, and to stimulate appreciation of artists and their work.

State foundations on culture and the arts, under which hundreds of city and community councils are now established, have been set up by governors across the country. Large grants have been made to regional theaters in the hope that the

Theater is alive and well and flourishing in American universities and colleges in every region of the country. Ring Around the Moon *by Jean Anouilh was one of several full-length productions presented at Catholic University in Washington, D.C.*

theaters will be a permanent means of bringing drama to every community. Whether a national theater will grow out of this movement remains to be seen. The theater around the world has been supported financially by patrons and governments since the early beginnings, and the United States is beginning to follow suit.

The American National Theater and Academy (ANTA) is the forerunner of the National Foundation. It receives no subsidy from the government and is supported by voluntary subscription, memberships, and donations. It is designed to serve all facets of the American theater and acts as coordinator, consultant, and guide through its National Theater Service.

The John F. Kennedy Center for the Performing Arts in Washington, D.C., was created as the National Cultural Center, and government land on the Potomac was granted as a site. It was formally opened in September 1971.

Ten units housed under one roof at Kennedy Center include the opera in the central hall, the Concert Hall, the Eisenhower Theater for drama and film production, and the Studio Playhouse on the roof above the theater. The Studio Playhouse will be used as an experimental, film, and children's theater and for poetry and drama reading.

Theater of the Future

Out of our current drama, certain trends will probably survive. The increasingly popular dance drama is developing a theater of its own. Electronic effects are giving emotional backgrounds to productions such as *Beatlemania, Evita,* and *Dracula.* Audiences are tiring of the shock values of the performances of the late sixties and early seventies and are showing a growing interest in revivals of the best plays and musicals of past decades.

The 1979–1980 theater season in New York City revived such musicals as *Camelot, Oklahoma!, Peter Pan,* and *West Side Story.* A comedy of the 1930s, *Morning's at Seven,* enjoyed a successful rebirth. And old-fashioned burlesque burst upon the Broadway scene in *Sugar Babies.*

What form the productions of the future will take will depend on the taste of the public. The commercial theater in many cities is losing some of its hold, and nonprofit theater of some sort is growing. With the increasing spread of regional

The theater of the future seems to be headed in two directions—revivals of past favorites and innovative productions whose casts come from minority groups. Morning's at Seven (left) by Paul Osborn was revived on Broadway in 1979. FOB (right), a play with an entirely Asian cast, was presented at New York's Public Theater by Joseph Papp.

theaters all over free Europe, England, and America and the interchange of plays in festivals and conferences growing more frequent every season, there is justifiable hope that drama of the world will hold the best of the past, will safely survive the changes of the present, and will create ever-expanding means of expressing the dreams of humanity.

It is impossible to determine the future. Never have young people had more need for a firm foundation of knowledge on which to base their judgment of what they choose to see in the theater. You are fortunate in being introduced to the world of the theater in a dramatics class where you can become familiar with great dramas and learn to distinguish between the best and the worst theatrical practices of today.

DISCUSSION

1. What are some of the most recent developments in American theater? What do you think some future ones will be?

2. Are there any modern American plays or movements that you think will strongly affect those of the future?

3. What kind of influence do you think the contemporary American stage exerts on today's daily life?

4. Why do you think Shakespeare's plays continue to be successful on stage, screen, and television? Which ones that you have seen have you enjoyed most? Why?

5. Compare productions seen by members of the class in conventional Elizabethan style and in modern styles. Have you seen any productions using electronic sight and sound effects? Have you seen any adaptations recently in musical comedy, opera, motion pictures, or on television?

6. Do you enjoy most the drama of the stage, the screen, or television? Why?

7. If you could choose any one period in the history of the theater in which to be an actor, which period would be your choice? Why?

BIBLIOGRAPHY

Cheney, Sheldon: *The Theatre: Three Thousand Years of Drama, Acting, and Stagecraft,* McKay, New York, 1959.

Gassner, John: *Masters of the Drama,* Dover, New York, 1953.

Gorelik, Mordecai: *New Theatres for Old,* Dutton, New York, 1962.

Hewitt, Barnard: *Theatre U.S.A., 1668 to 1957,* McGraw-Hill, New York, 1959.

Nicoll, Allardyce: *Development of the Theatre,* Harcourt, Brace, New York, 1958.

Quennell, Peter: *Shakespeare, a Biography,* World Publishing, Cleveland, 1963.

Rowse, A. L.: *William Shakespeare, a Biography,* Harper & Row, New York, 1963.

Shakespeare, William: *The Complete Works,* World Publishing, Cleveland, 1965.

Webster, Margaret: *Shakespeare without Tears,* Fawcett, New York, 1955.

————: *The Same Only Different,* Knopf, New York, 1969.

Overleaf: *Lead Wanda Ritchart arriving in New York City, from the hit musical* 42nd Street.

PART THREE

Producing the Drama

CHAPTER TEN

Fundamentals of Play Production

Play production offers many opportunities that you may well find more stimulating and exciting than acting. All the activities involved in the design and construction of sets and costumes, the handling of lighting equipment, and the managing of affairs backstage and in the front of the house are of absorbing interest when the preparation for a play once gets under way.

At present, your main interest probably centers around the plays given by your own school. School stages may range from simple ones in classrooms to theaters having a fully equipped switchboard, recording and sound equipment, fine dressing rooms, and ample work and storage space. If your school does not have all these facilities, do not be dismayed. A small stage, crowded backstage area, and the minimum of stage lights are limitations that may challenge your imagination and ingenuity. As a result, your productions may well be superior to those presented more easily with first-class physical equipment. Whatever the size and equipment of your theater, having a share in a big public production is a rewarding experience.

Putting on a public production of a long play means several weeks of intensive work by a large group of people. Before that period, much preliminary planning and preparation must be done. To get the most from the experience, follow all the activities from the beginning, carrying out your own special duties with enthusiasm and responsibility.

In school dramatics, the director usually plans the production in accordance with the schedule for school events and often works with a student executive committee in the selection of individual production staff members and their assistants. The director and this executive committee also set up special committees to assist in all, or some of, the following production procedures: play reading and selection, casting, costuming, properties, publicity, business management, and stage crew work. All the people chosen should be dependable and enthusiastic, since a great deal of the authority in production rests with them.

THE PRODUCTION STAFF

The number of people on the production staff will be determined by the size of the production, the availability of capable people, and the needs of the individual school or class. In the school theater, various departmental activities often center about public production. The dramatics class may furnish the cast and the direction. The art department may design and/or paint the set. The shops may make and handle the scenery and provide stage carpenters. The home economics classes may make the costumes or do alterations. The music department may provide the incidental music. In the case of an operetta or musical, the music department usually furnishes singers, instrumentalists, and musical direction.

The Denver Center Theater Company presents Molière's The Learned Ladies. *Note the effectiveness of costuming, scenery, and lighting.*

A brief discussion of the tasks of each position to be filled will give you an idea of the work involved in producing a play.

The Producer

The producer of a high school production is usually the director. In the professional theater, the producer agrees to back a show by finding financial investors called "angels." The producer also hires the director and the production staff, sets the budget, and pays the bills.

The Director

The director of your public productions in high school is usually your dramatics teacher. Many high schools today have a trained, and frequently professionally experienced, teacher-director.

In the professional theater, the director is usually credited with the play's success or failure. Actors also seek out fine directors under whom to work. Actors take minor parts frequently for the privilege of sharing the experience of creating the perfect performance of a play—the ideal of every dedicated person involved in theater.

The ideal director inspires actors with confidence in their abilities and intelligence in building their roles, molding all phases of production into a unified whole. Ardent, concentrated attention to every detail maintains enthusiasm and dedication on the part of every individual involved in each situation and eliminates distracting and nerve-racking crises. The director is responsible for onstage empathies and backstage morale. The director's objective at all times must be to produce the playwright's intentions as faithfully as possible by an intensive study of the script, including the author's style, the play's theme, and the characters' relationships. The director's word is law! Only the director has visualized the production as it should be in performance.

In high school productions, the students usually have a much larger input, and the director is a teacher-director. Therefore, putting on a play is far more a cooperative, delightful experience of a team working together in an exciting game. You are fortunate to be having the companionship and excitement of high school dramatics as your introduction to theater.

The Assistant Director

In the school theater, the position of assistant director (AD) is held by a capable student. This must be a person whom the director finds dependable and whom the students respect. The AD will serve as a liaison between the director, cast, and crew, taking charge of rehearsals in the absence of the director. This is a position you must aspire to if you are interested in all phases of the theater.

MASTER PRODUCTION SCHEDULE CHECKLIST

1. Production budget established
2. Play-reading committee selected
3. Committee reports
4. Final selection of play
5. Staff organized
6. Research
7. Production rights obtained
8. Scripts ordered
9. Meeting of director, technical director, and stage manager
10. Promptbook prepared
11. Floor plan designed
12. Basic design presented—scenery, lights, costumes
13. Tryouts
14. Cast selected
15. Stage and costume crews recruited
16. First publicity release
17. Costume measurements taken
18. Light plot prepared
19. Floor plan laid out on rehearsal floor
20. Blocking rehearsals begun
21. Tickets ordered
22. Publicity committee organized

23. Scenery begun
24. Program prepared for printing
25. Working rehearsals
26. First costume fittings
27. Arrangements made for publicity photos
28. Props secured
29. Second publicity release
30. Tickets placed on sale
31. Construction of scenery completed
32. Special effects (recordings and the like) secured
33. Lighting, cue sheets, and prop plots completed
34. Tickets distributed and/or racked
35. Rental or purchase of costumes and accessories arranged
36. Second costume fitting
37. First lighting check
38. Polish rehearsal and rehearsal timed
39. Rehearsal with props
40. Set completed
41. Major press releases
42. Technical rehearsals
43. Costume parade
44. Final set touches
45. Dress rehearsals

(continued)

MASTER PRODUCTION SCHEDULE CHECKLIST (continued)

46. Performances

47. Costume and prop check-in

48. Bills paid and tickets audited

49.
   a. Scenery struck and stored
   b. Props put away
   c. Borrowed items, such as furniture and the like, returned

   d. Rented costumes packed and returned
   e. Own costumes cleaned and stored
   f. Dressing rooms cleaned
   g. Thank-you letters sent

50. Final financial statement drawn

The Prompter

This position should also be held by a dependable student who will attend every rehearsal. During rehearsals, the prompter, or holder of the book, keeps the director's promptbook and makes penciled notes on interpretation, movement, and business, light and sound cues, and warning signals. This is done under the supervision of the director.

A numbering system is recommended for marking the blocking—the movements, positions, and crosses. In this system, each movement on each page is given a number of easy reference by actors and director. Sound and light cues and other special effects are numbered in different colors. By using floor-plan sketches in the promptbook, the prompter can clarify any questions concerning stage groupings, crosses, and changes.

The prompter must mark every pause so that an unnecessary prompt will not be given. During the performance the prompter can often save the show if emergencies arise by giving correct cues and lines. If the cast starts to skip passages, the prompter can feed the vital lines to keep the meaning clear for the audience. If the prompter fails at these crucial times, the entire production can be ruined. Audiences will often remember and laugh about one moment of confusion after they have forgotten all the fine points of a production.

Some directors do not use the prompter during the performance, preferring to have the actors know they are on their own. Others feel that a skilled prompter is essential. If your school does use a prompter, this is a position from which you may learn a great deal. It is a job that requires both reliability and intelligence.

The Scenic Artist and the Technical Director

The scenic artist, or the designer, usually designs the settings but in many cases may also design the costumes, the makeup, and the lighting. Though these designs may be simple or complex, they must always give the play visual dimensions in harmony with the aims of the director.

The work of the technical director (TD) is also vitally important. It is the TD who executes the designs of the scenic artist, with the assistance of a crew for building sets, painting drops, creating costumes, and hanging lights. In some cases, the scenic artist and the technical director are the same person. Though their functions are different, they both aim at serving the director's intentions as effectively, simply, and beautifully as possible to achieve a unified production.

The Stage Manager

Aided by the stage crew, the stage manager (SM) takes complete charge backstage during rehearsals and performances. In some cases, the SM and the crew act as both the stage carpenters who build the set and the grips who change the scenery. The stage manager also keeps a promptbook containing all cues and effects. The SM makes up cue sheets or charts containing the cues for lights, sound, and curtain. For the stage crew, the SM makes up a chart of set and prop changes to guide them through the play. During the performance, the stage manager usually sits at a prompt table in the stage right wing just upstage of the proscenium. From that vantage point, the SM gives all cues (lights, sound, curtain) to the technical crew. In addition, the stage manager must handle any and all emergencies that arise during the performance. A good stage manager is essential to a smooth production.

In the professional theater, the stage manager has to be versatile and experienced in all phases of theater production. The SM not only runs the show backstage but also acts as a director for brush-up rehearsals, breaking in new cast members, and keeping the production fresh and sharp.

The Backstage Assistants

The property person and property assistants get the furniture and props the designer has planned, store them backstage, arrange them, prepare a prop table, and give the hand props to the actors backstage just before entrances. These hand props should be kept on the side of the stage where the actors who use these props will make entrances. Props must be carefully replaced and never touched except when in use. The wardrobe person and makeup crew serve under the stage manager. The efficiency, ingenuity, and dependability of these backstage assistants during long hours of hard work are determining factors in a successful production. Without them, the play cannot go on.

The Business Manager

The business manager is responsible for the financial arrangements of the production. In accordance with school policy, the business manager may be in charge of all funds, pay all bills, and handle the printing and selling of tickets. The business manager and the director should gauge probable receipts and achieve a reasonable profit by watching production and publicity expenses. An income statement such as the one opposite will help in the financial record keeping of a production.

In the school theater, the business manager has the difficult task of issuing tickets to many salespersons and checking on sales. The business manager should give out all passes to the show with the permission of the director and should issue stage-door slips to those working backstage. It is most important that people who do not have specific duties in the dressing rooms or backstage area not be admitted during performances. (If stage-door slips are not used, a program listing members of the staff may be substituted. A responsible person may use it to check entrances and exits at the stage door.)

The business manager is also in charge of printing the programs, which should be designed in harmony with the production. The cast is usually listed in order of appearance. The business manager should be accurate in listing names of cast members, production staff, committee chairpersons, backstage crew, and acknowledgments for favors and assistance from businesses and individuals. Selling advertising to pay for the program is usually a matter determined by school authorities. If advertising is used, the business manager supervises it.

The Publicity Manager

The publicity manager must promote the show in the school and in the community. Good publicity is vital to the financial success of the play. If they are properly approached, the public press, newspapers published at other schools, local radio stations, and church publications will give space and time to notices about public school productions. In these days of broadcasting systems, tape recordings, and other devices in many high schools, there are almost limitless possibilities for promoting a play.

The publicity manager and assistants have a real opportunity to make original and artistic contributions to the success of a production. The advertising staff would do well to consult the art department of the school. With serious dramas, advertising in keeping with the spirit of the play may include well-designed individual notices sent to all drama enthusiasts in the community. For comedies,

Income Statement

John Adams High School Production
Brigadoon

December 31, 198___

Revenue:

Tickets sold_____ @ $_____ = $_____

Other income:

    Concessions $_____

    Program ads   _____

Total Income: $_____

Expenses:

    Royalty $_____

    Play books   _____

    Tickets   _____

    Programs   _____

    Advertising   _____

    Scenery   _____

    Properties   _____

    Costumes   _____

    Makeup   _____

Miscellaneous:

    Custodial fees $_____

    Police department   _____

    Fire department   _____

    Ushers   _____

    Box-office staff   _____

Total Production Costs $_____

Net Income (Total income less total $_____

production costs)

cartoons of the cast and humorous items about the funniest rehearsal situations can be featured, possibly with lively quotations from the play. The title of the play itself, the author, the skill or prominence of the performers, the past achievements of the director, and striking scenic effects can also furnish material for publicity.

If there is a good possibility of filling the house more than once, plans should be made for several consecutive performances before any advertising goes out. The repetition of a play several days or weeks after a single highly successful performance is seldom satisfactory because both cast and public lose interest rapidly. Also, the expense of renting costumes and furniture again takes what little money has been made. It is always better to have one packed house than several half-empty ones.

The House Manager

The house manager is responsible for the seating and comfort of the audience, the competence and training of the ushers, and the distribution of the programs. Ushers in uniform, evening dress, or appropriate costumes can add to the pleasure of the audience.

Other Personnel

School productions frequently involve still more people. Fire fighters and police officers are on hand if they are notified when a production is scheduled. Sometimes members of the faculty are required to be in attendance in the dressing rooms and backstage areas, and they often take or sell tickets out front.

The school orchestra or recordings may furnish music for the curtain raiser or intermissions. If so, the selections should be approved by the director far in advance, and they should be properly rehearsed. Music should also be in keeping with the production and subordinate to it, not added as a special feature. Announcements or stunts between acts should be avoided.

DISCUSSION

1. In your school, what are some of the special problems connected with putting on a play? Are they being solved? Is the entire student body interested in them? Are the people in the community interested?

2. Discuss the school plays you have attended or assisted with, and note the part the backstage people had in their success or failure.

3. For what purpose are the proceeds of your dramatic productions used? Are they used exclusively for improving the stage and its equipment, as a means of raising money for other school activities, or for charity? How do you think they ought to be used?

4. Discuss possible difficulties that might arise during a performance. Show how the prompter and/or the stage manager might avoid or overcome them.

PREREHEARSAL ACTIVITIES

After the director and the executive committee have set up the special committees and after individual production staff members have been selected, the next step is to choose a play. This is usually done by the reading committee and the director.

Choosing a Play

Choosing a play is a crucial problem. Before a choice can be made, many plays must be read. A poor choice can ruin the reputation of the producing group; a good one can establish it. The producing group must know the purpose of the proposed production. Is it primarily a school project, recognized as an important group activity? Or is it to raise funds for a specific purpose or organization? A play must be found that will fulfill its designated purpose, appeal to its particular audience, and be adaptable to the ability of the actors, the size and equipment of the stage, and the limits of the budget.

In their desire to reduce the royalty charge and to entertain the public, inexperienced groups sometimes choose silly farces that do not warrant an expenditure of time and energy. Rather than compromise on the quality of the script, it is better to present classics (most of which require no royalty) or cut production expenses sufficiently to pay the royalty on a contemporary play by a first-class writer. Remember that there are many classics that the other students and the parents will thoroughly enjoy. There are also many plays of the last century, now released from royalty charges, that your audience would enjoy. Try to avoid plays that a large portion of your audience may have seen recently, and try to provide variety in the annual programs of your school.

The size of the cast requires attention in the choice of a play. When the cast is large, more students receive the benefits of training and experience. However, large casts make for difficult rehearsals and staging. Ability to create the necessary stage settings and the possibility of adequate interpretation by available actors must be considered.

Securing Production Rights

Before a play is finally selected, the director or some authorized person should write to the author or publisher controlling the acting rights of the play. The director should state the time and number of performances planned and request authorization to present the play. There are many regulations restricting the presentation of plays by amateurs, especially in larger cities where stock and road companies appear. Therefore, full permission should be obtained for a public performance before preparations start.

Planning the Production

The director must first study the play from every angle to determine the style and atmosphere to be carried out in the sets and costumes. The director must understand the theme and decide how best to express it; decide how to emphasize the conflict, suspense, and climax of the plot; and analyze the characters and their relationships with one another. For a period play, the director must study the historical background, social conditions, and attitudes of the people represented, as well as the costumes, furnishings, and manner of speech and movement.

Early in the director's work on a play, a tentative budget must be planned. The director must estimate the probable size of the audience and take into account sets and props that may be obtained without expense. The director should set up a master production schedule such as the one on page 243. Careful scheduling is often the difference between a smoothly run production and a chaotic one.

After studying the play, the director makes a floor plan. This is an overhead view of the set and helps the director plan the action that will take place on the stage. During this early period, the director should have frequent conferences with the scenic artist and stage manager concerning many aspects of the production. Problems of handling the show backstage must be discussed.

The entrances and exits must be practical and logical. The location and size of the furniture should be planned to create helpful, meaningful units for definite bits of action and to form attractive and balanced stage pictures. The light sources must be considered and marked on the floor plan. Windows provide daytime light; lamps, fireplaces, and perhaps chandeliers give light at night. Sufficient backing for windows and doors must be considered in planning the action, and the director must make these needs clear to the scenic artist. The backstage storage areas for furniture, props, and sets must be diagrammed. After the director, the scenic artist, and the stage manager have made overall plans, the director will visualize important scenes carefully and plan for effective grouping. Unimportant characters can be momentarily emphasized by being placed upstage or apart from the others.

Making the Promptbook

The promptbook, started by the director during the planning period and containing the entire play script, is the backbone of a production. Into this book go the director's plans as well as the telephone numbers and addresses of all the people involved in the production. The easiest way to make a promptbook is to paste the pages of the play in a large loose-leaf notebook. This system requires two copies

*Stress 7 mirror lines and actions**

(*Enter* JACK.)

GWENDOLEN. (*Catching sight of him.*) Ernest! My own
Ernest!

x's her w/ open arms

JACK. Gwendolen! Darling! (*Offers to kiss her.*)*1
strikes melodramatic pose of indignation

warn:
Alg-ENT #4

GWENDOLEN. (*Drawing back.*) A moment! May I ask if
you are engaged to be married to this young lady? (*Points
to* CECILY.)*2

w/ fan

JACK. (*Laughing.*) To dear (little) Cecily! Of course not!
What could have put such an idea into your pretty (little)
head?

Play up little's

as if "Just as I thought" — Jack
kisses her (#5) and keeps arm around
waist

GWENDOLEN. (Thank you.) You may. (*Offers her
cheek.*)

CECILY. (*Very sweetly.*) I knew there must be some mis-
understanding, Miss Fairfax. The gentleman whose arm
is at present around your waist is my dear guardian, Mr.
John Worthing. (*x DL*)#6

GWENDOLEN. I beg your pardon?

Jack runs finger
nervously around
inside of collar

CECILY. This is Uncle Jack.

Melodramatic shock
pose - back of hand
to forehead -
flutters fan

GWENDOLEN. (*Receding.*) Jack! Oh! *7 x's DR
Turns back on J.

(*Enter* ALGERNON.)

CECILY. Here is Ernest. *G and J - "Jake"*

ALGERNON. (*Goes straight over to* CECILY *without noticing anyone else.*) My own love! (*Offers to kiss her.*)
*1 *x's to her w/open arms - mirror*
of Jack

CECILY. (*Drawing back.*) A moment, Ernest! May I ask *2
you—are you engaged to be married to this young
lady?

Points w/ fan

"Jake"

ALGERNON. (*Looking round.*) To what young lady? Good
heavens! Gwendolen!

Sample promptbook page

of the play. If there is only one copy available for this purpose, page-size windows can be cut in the sheets of the notebook and each page of the script can be fastened with cellophane tape or glue into these windows.

Large margins around the script are essential for the sketches, cues, and notes, first made by the director in the preliminary planning and then added to and changed during rehearsals. The marginal notes show script cuttings, stage directions, and markings of difficult passages for pauses, phrasing, and emphasis. The sketches or diagrams of floor plans and sets show positions of furniture and actors in every scene. Stage groupings of actors can be drawn with the initials of the characters' names marked in little circles. Most directors like to sketch important crosses and countercrosses in the promptbook and mark actors' movements with symbols. For example, "XR from C" means that the actor moves to the right from a position in stage center. "Enter UL, exit DR" means that the actor comes in from the farthest upstage entrance on the left and crosses the stage diagonally, going out nearest the audience on the right.

Cues marked in the margin include those for lights, curtains, and other effects both on and off the stage. As rehearsals progress, individual cue sheets are made from the book by the stage manager. These sheets are given to the electrician, the wardrobe people, the prop committee, the sound technician, and others whose tasks require written directions. When marking the promptbook, pencil rather than pen should be used so that changes may be made when necessary. It is advisable to use different colors for particular types of cues and warning signals, such as red for lights, blue for curtain, and green for entrances and exits. A sample promptbook page appears on page 251.

When a play is finished, the promptbook should be completed with a copy of the program and photographs of the production. Frequently a school play is repeated in 5 or 6 years without much duplication in the audience. Although every production has a new promptbook, the original can be most useful for reference purposes.

CASTING THE PLAY

Few phases of production are more important to the ultimate success or failure of a play than the choice of the cast. Casting demands tact, sincerity, fairness, and sound judgment. It is sometimes helpful to have a student casting committee assist the director in conducting tryouts by supervising the completion of tryout forms, such as the one found opposite. Final decisions on casting are made by the director, based on estimates of which candidates can best capture the spirit of the play. A successful production demands that actors be equipped physically, mentally, and temperamentally to give convincing interpretations of the roles assigned to

TRYOUT INFORMATION CARD

NAME (LAST NAME FIRST)		CLASS	AGE	PHONE
ADDRESS		SEX	HEIGHT	WEIGHT

PREVIOUS ACTING EXPERIENCE

WHAT VOCAL PART DO YOU SING? S A T B	WHAT MUSICAL INSTRUMENT DO YOU PLAY? EXPERIENCE:

WHAT DANCE TRAINING HAVE YOU HAD?

LIST YOUR CLASS SCHEDULE:

1	4	7
2	5	8
3	6	9

WILL YOU BE ABLE TO ATTEND ALL REHEARSALS?   YES_____   NO_____
IF NOT, WHAT CONFLICTS ARE THERE?

ARE YOU INTERESTED IN WORKING ON ANY OF THE FOLLOWING COMMITTEES?

MAKEUP	PROPERTIES	SCENERY CONST.
PUBLICITY	COSTUMES	STAGE CREW

ARE YOU INTERESTED IN BEING STUDENT DIRECTOR?

PROMPTER?   TECHNICAL DIRECTOR?   STAGE MANAGER?

DIRECTOR'S COMMENTS:
  VOICE: PHYSICAL APPEARANCE:
    QUALITY: IMAGINATION:
    PITCH: ANIMATION:
    VARIETY: STAGE PRESENCE:

PARTS CONSIDERED FOR:

them. Personality development belongs in classroom dramatic work, not in public productions.

Auditions

One of the most important experiences for an actor is the audition. Some of the most talented actors fail to get parts because they give poor auditions. Many stage hopefuls find themselves on the other side of the footlights because they choke at their audition.

Those of you wanting to pursue acting as a professional career should have a resumé, such as the one found on the next page, and a portfolio. Your resumé includes an 8 × 10 inch headshot photograph of you as you appear offstage, not as a character in costume. The resumé also includes all the important information a casting director wants to know: name, address, phone number, type of voice (if you sing), vital statistics, experience, education and professional training, and special skills. Since all actors are typed by class of performer, include at the top of the resumé your type classification. For example, if acting is your strongest skill, followed by dancing, followed by singing, your classification would be actor-dancer-singer. Similarly, there are dancer-singer-actors, singer-actor-dancers, actor-singer-dancers, and so on.

The portfolio you present at an audition should include other photographs of you as you appeared in specific roles. If possible, select roles that show you to have a range of abilities from drama to comedy to musical comedy. Include reviews of your performances and sample programs of the plays in which you appeared.

In some public schools, auditions are limited to drama or speech students. In others, they are open to all students. This is a matter to be decided by the director or by the individual school. Perhaps the director will want to use a point system of stage experience and service to help determine eligibility for an important role. In some schools, scholastic standing in other departments and good citizenship are considered before an applicant is allowed to try out. In any case, eligible applicants must be made to understand that casting is usually probationary until the director has been able to determine the actor's ability to take direction, willingness to work, and understanding of the task.

Every possible means of publicizing the roles to be filled should be used prior to the tryouts. Posters, articles in the school paper, and posted mimeographed descriptions of the characters are all good ways of circulating the information. If possible, the director will place a copy of the play on reserve in the school library for all applicants to read or will make the play available in some other way.

The tryout arrangements must be determined by the number of people who wish to read for the play, the length of time that can be devoted to casting, and the kind

```
JOYCE JACKSON              ACTRESS-SINGER-DANCER         HOME PHONE: (203) 658-7028
4950 Cove Road                                           SER. PHONE: (203) 799-9190
Stamford, CT 06904         Legit. Soprano: low G-high C

Age Range: 16-30    Height: 5'6"    Weight: 108    Hair: Blonde, long    Eyes: Blue    Dress: 7/8
```

EXPERIENCE

```
HANSEL AND GRETEL               Wicked Witch                Courtyard Playhouse, N.Y.C.
GUYS AND DOLLS                  Sarah Brown                 Rochester, Minn., Civic Theatre
110 IN THE SHADE                Lizzie                      Highland Summer Theatre, Minn.
THE FANTASTICKS                 Luisa                       Highland Summer Theatre
DARK AT THE TOP OF THE STAIRS   Flirt Conroy                Highland Summer Theatre
DIRTY WORK AT THE CROSSROADS    Nellie Lovelace             Ohio Valley Summer Theatre
NAUGHTY MARIETTA                Marietta                    Ohio Valley Summer Theatre
THE SOUND OF MUSIC              Maria                       Mosby Dinner Theatre, Virginia
OKLAHOMA!                       Understudy for Laurey and   Mosby Dinner Theatre
                                Dancing Laurey(played by
                                Kathleen Conry of Broadway's
                                NO, NO, NANETTE)

ANYTHING GOES                   Hope Harcourt               Club Bone Dinner Theatre, N.J.
LIL ABNER                       Daisy Mae                   Club Bone Dinner Theatre
MARY POPPINS                    Mary Poppins                Club Bone Dinner Theatre
LAUGHING GAS (original musical) Mrs. Krause                 Cavalier Productions, Virginia
RUMPELSTILTSKIN                 Maiden Queen/Mother         National Parks and Planning
                                                            Commission, Washington, D.C.
HAPPY BIRTHDAY, AMERICA!        Voice-overs                 Library Theatre, Washington, D.C.
AMAHL AND THE NIGHT VISITORS    Mother                      Kenyon, Minnesota
MAN OF LA MANCHA                Antonia & Housekeeper       Boulder, Colorado
```

NIGHTCLUB AND CABARET

```
HOLIDAY INN                     "Rooftop Revival" singing group show      Denver, Colorado
                                Featured singing duo, musical comedy,     Washington, D.C.
                                operetta and popular
INN OF TRENTON and              "Broadway Showstoppers" Revue
PRINCETON UNIVERSITY
```

EDUCATION AND TRAINING

```
DEGREE:    Bachelor of Music Ed. in Voice, University of Colorado
GRADUATE   Acting- Mankato State College, Minn., under Dr. C. Ron Olauson
STUDY:     Ohio University under Robert Winters
           Private study with Richard G. Holmes(Senator Dawes in Broadway's
           INDIANS), Washington, D.C.
DANCE:     Ballet- 8 years       Modern- 2 years        Tap- 1 year
SINGING:   8 years classical and musical comedy training, some belting
MODELING:  J.C. PENNEY CO., 3 years floor modeling and fashion shows - Denver, Colorado
           Print and promotional work in Colorado for Wells, Rich, Green Inc. of N.Y.C.
           First Runner-up, JANTZEN SMILE GIRL, Colorado Region
           Subject of prize-winning photos in Eastman-Kodak's National Photographic Contest
OTHER      Play piano; Teach piano and voice; Sing in Italian, German, Spanish, French
SKILLS:    Accents: Norwegian, Swedish, Cockney, Irish, Southern
           Excellent snow skier and swimmer
           Own and drive a car
           public elementary school teacher
```

Sample theatrical resumé

of play to be presented. It is always preferable to hold tryouts in the auditorium or theater in which the play is to be performed. Sometimes, however, this is not possible.

When the applicants have assembled, the director can explain all details of the tryouts, discuss the play briefly, and describe the characters. Applicants should be asked to fill out cards giving name, address, phone number, height, weight, past experience in school plays, and any previous commitments that might interfere with attendance at rehearsals. The casting committee can take charge of getting this information.

Careful organization is essential to keep the tryouts moving rapidly and effectively. Here again the casting committee can assist the director.

Methods of conducting auditions vary with directors. Auditions can be either open or closed. To a professional, an *open* audition is for nonunion actors; a *closed* audition is open only to union members. In the high school, an open audition means that anyone in the student body is eligible to try out. A closed audition means that only certain students may try out—members of the drama club or the senior class, for example. A second classification of auditions is prepared or cold. A *prepared* audition permits the actor to bring in material that has been thoroughly worked out, including memorization and action. A prepared tryout is sometimes called a textual tryout because the audition material comes from a manuscript or printed play. Textual tryouts may be either monologues or scenes. A *cold* audition is one in which the actor is given material never seen before. The actor is expected to read the unfamiliar material with imagination, feeling, and confidence. Unless the casting director summarizes the situation and the characters, the actor is usually not penalized for making errors in interpretation. If the cold tryout uses a scene, the actor has the disadvantage of playing with another actor whose acting skills are unknown. On the other hand, the actors have the advantage of having someone to play against. Sometimes a cold tryout is not textual, but improvisational. In an *improvisational* audition, the actor is assigned a character and given a brief description of a situation. Then the actor must improvise a scene around the assigned character and situation.

Some directors like to combine audition formats. This is especially true of tryouts for musicals. In musicals the actors very often have to be able to act, sing, and dance.

Callbacks

After the best possibilities for all roles have been selected, second or perhaps third callbacks should be held for final selection of the candidates who might work together in regard to physical appearance, voice, and personality. By this time, any problems concerning rehearsal attendance, dependability, responsiveness to suggestions, and general attitudes should be determined as far as possible.

Perhaps the most important aspect of auditions is that they be conducted in a friendly and relaxed atmosphere. Each student who tries out must know that she or he is being given a fair chance. Good auditions can set morale at a high level for the rest of the production.

You and Your Audition

In order to have the best audition possible, the first thing you must know well is yourself. You must be honest in your self-appraisal, neither conceited nor overly modest. Know what kind of actor you are and what kinds of roles you can play. You may aspire to play every great role ever written, but if you are truly objective, you know that you are best suited for certain roles. Bear in mind that auditioning is a selling job and you are the product that must be sold. This selling process begins when the director first sees you.

Dress appropriately for the audition. Correct dress shows you off to your best advantage. Line, color, and style are important. Avoid wearing offbeat clothes, jewelry, or shoes. They tend to be distracting, drawing attention away from you. If you know the play, you can help the director visualize you in a part if your auditioning clothes suggest the part you desire. However, be careful that you do not overdo the suggestion.

Observe the time limits that you are given. Contrary to inexperienced actors' beliefs, most directors know within the first 15 seconds whether or not an actor is right for a part. Length is not necessarily strength in an audition.

Know the production that you are auditioning for whenever possible. Know the character or characters you really believe you can play and want to play. If you bring a prepared audition, select a monologue or single-character scene that suits the play and character for which you are auditioning. A comic monologue is inappropriate for a drama. A contemporary drama monlogue is inappropriate for classical tragedy.

If you are asked to do both comedy and drama, do your strongest selection first. If you are permitted, prepare a series of short monologues rather than one long one. Work up at least ten to twelve auditioning pieces that last a few seconds to a minute each. Be certain there is enough to each to really show what you can do. In this way, you can show a director in 5 minutes your range of acting abilities. This is especially important in casting for a whole season or for a repertory group.

Finally, develop a good audition attitude. Look forward to auditioning. Shake off the nervousness. Show a little hunger for the part. Be ready, willing, and eager to take a part, whatever part is offered to you. But also learn to take rejection. For one reason or another, you may be turned down. If you have the talent and the desire, bounce back to audition again and again. If the message you are receiving is saying that you may not have what it takes, accept that reality.

REHEARSING

If you are wise, you will attend every rehearsal, whether you are due on stage or not, in order to become a part of the play as a whole, appreciate the director's motivation for movements and tempos, and sense the satisfactory empathies being sought, to which the audience will respond later. You can also profit by the director's suggestions to the other actors and thus avoid their mistakes and profit by their achievements. One of the advantages of a school production is that the director has often had many of the actors in dramatics class and knows what to expect of them in regard to stage techniques. Much time is saved in avoiding explanations of stage terms. As an onlooker, you can become conscious of the importance of developing a scene without needless interruptions by members of the cast who bring up personal problems of interpretation onstage. All discussion and arguments should be offstage during rehearsal breaks.

Reading Rehearsals

The first rehearsal is most important. At it the director should expect all members—cast, stage manager, and crew; all understudies; the technical director; and the chairpersons of committees involved in the backstage activities—to be present. The director should make it clear that the pleasure of play production lies in the efficient, happy, conscientious working together of everyone toward the objective of putting on the best production of that particular play with that particular group under the particular stage circumstances. The director should point out the factors that make a fine performance. These factors are perfect timing, excellent individual characterizations, and careful coordination of onstage and backstage activities. It is through this working together of cast and crew that the play's theme is brought out and the play's spirit is maintained.

At this first rehearsal, some directors prefer to read the play themselves, thus setting at once the interpretation of the entire play and of individual roles. Others prefer to give the cast the opportunity to suggest their own characterizations by reading the parts assigned, while the director merely points out important details of phrasing, timing, and inflections. Whatever the method, the rehearsal should build up a clear-cut conception of the play and of conduct during rehearsals. All present should take careful notes in pencil.

In the first hours of work on the play, the director can sense the actors' ability to understand lines and project personality. The director can also judge the actors' willingness to respond to direction and to what extent they pay attention. If there is ample time, a number of reading rehearsals can ''set'' the characters and the lines. More reading rehearsals are necessary when dialects or stage diction are required. In any case, a number of reading rehearsals makes actors feel more secure about interpretation when rehearsing on the stage.

Rehearsal Schedules

A time schedule for the entire rehearsal period should be worked out and copies made for participants to give their parents. This procedure helps parents understand how much time will be involved in the production. When making this rehearsal schedule, the director considers the time allotted for preparing the production, the length and difficulty of the play, and the availability of the cast. For instance, if the audition-rehearsal-performance period has been set at 7 weeks, after-school rehearsals should probably be planned for 3 hours a day, 5 days a week. The individual director can adjust the schedule to fit the particular situation.

In such a schedule, the first week should complete the tryouts and the reading rehearsals. The second week includes blocking and business rehearsals and a line check for the first and second acts. The third week should complete blocking and business rehearsals for the third act, full line check, and intitial run-throughs. The fourth and fifth weeks constitute working rehearsals of the entire play.

If the auditorium has not been available previously, a long Saturday rehearsal should be held at the end of the fourth week. At this time, whatever is technically difficult should be rehearsed. All available sounds, lights, props, scenery, furniture, and costumes should be used. The sixth week is for polishing rehearsals,

Lewis Merkin and Valerie Curtin in a reading rehearsal of Children of a Lesser God *by Mark Medoff presented at the Mark Taper Forum in Los Angeles. This award-winning play was praised not only as a fine piece of dramatic literature but also for the outstanding performances by the leading actors—Phyllis Frelich and Lewis Merkin—who are both deaf.*

including stagecrew rehearsals and run-throughs with props and at least some costumes.

The dress rehearsals with full stage crew and the performances take place in the seventh week. On Monday of this last week, the staff should hold its last rehearsal in which interruptions can be made, problems discussed, final costumes and props checked, and all details settled.

If there is only one dress rehearsal, it should come on the Wednesday night before the Friday night performance. Tuesday may be spent in getting everything in final shape. It is wise to invite a few people to a dress rehearsal to accustom the

---

Sample 7-Week Audition-Rehearsal Schedule

Week 1:	Auditions and first rehearsal (3 hours each)
Monday	Auditions
Tuesday	Auditions
Wednesday	Callbacks (if necessary)
Thursday	Cast posted
Friday	Reading rehearsal

Week 2:	Blocking and line-check rehearsals (2½–3 hours)
Monday	Blocking Act I
Tuesday	Rehearse Act I
Wednesday	Line-check Act I
Thursday	Blocking Act II
Friday	Rehearse Act II

Week 3:	Blocking and line-check rehearsals (2½–3 hours)
Monday	Line-check Act II
Tuesday	Run through Acts I and II
Wednesday	Block Act III
Thursday	Line-check Act III
Friday	First run-through

Week 4:	Working rehearsals (3 hours)
Monday ⎫ Tuesday ⎬	Special scenes—chase, fight, and so on—rehearsed privately
Wednesday	Act I concentrated

---

cast to playing before an audience. It is sometimes wise to leave the night before the performance free for final adjustments.

Students involved in a production should be urged not to be absent from school because of their participation in a play. Much discrediting of school dramatics results from unnecessary cutting of classes and upsetting of routine when a play is being produced. With wise management and administrative cooperation, a big production can be put on without complicating the daily schedule. The auditorium should be closed to all other activities during the last three weeks, and enough time must be given the technical director and crew to "hang the set."

Thursday	Act II concentrated
Friday	Act III concentrated
Week 5:	Working rehearsals (full stage crew present—3 hours)
Monday	Acts I, II, III in sequence
Tuesday	Acts II, III, I—in that order
Wednesday	Acts III, I, II—in that order
Thursday	Problem scenes only
Friday	Final working run-through
Week 6:	Polishing rehearsals (all crews present—3 hours)
Monday	Run-through and dress parade
Tuesday	Run-through with lights
Wednesday	Run-through with scenery
Thursday	Run-through with lights and scenery
Friday	First complete run-through
Week 7:	Polishing rehearsals and performances (4–5 hours)
Monday	Second complete run-through
Tuesday	Final run-through
Wednesday	First dress rehearsal
Thursday	Final dress rehearsal
Friday	Performance
Saturday	Performance

Blocking Rehearsals

Blocking the movement and planning stage business follow the reading rehearsals. The major blocking areas of the traditional and the arena stages are shown on pages 263 and 295. Work on the interpretation of lines should be delayed while attention is focused on movement and stage groupings. The director will have already worked out plans for using the stage area, emphasizing important groupings, and keeping effective stage pictures. However, in the early rehearsals most directors are willing to discuss possible changes and incorporate spontaneous reactions of the actors. When the fundamental blocking of the first act has been set, the blocking of the second act should follow. The two acts can then be put together at one rehearsal. Following this, the third act should be set, and the first and second reviewed. As soon as the business of the first act is clarified, the lines and blocking may be memorized.

When planning stage business, the director must be sure that all gestures and movements are meaningful. In order to avoid later delay, the director should try to eliminate tendencies of the actors to fidget, shift weight, and gesture ineffectively. If the actors have studied dramatics, they should understand that every gesture and cross must be motivated and definite and that the center of interest should be accentuated at all times. The director must adhere to fundamental directions when dealing with inexperienced people to avoid confusing them with too much detail.

If blocking rehearsals cannot be held in the auditorium, the assistant director should arrange a rehearsal area that has exactly the same dimensions as the stage. The assistant director should then indicate the entrances and exits with chalk or tape and obtain furniture that resembles the pieces that will eventually be used.

During this period, a feeling of comradeship should develop. Both the actors and crew members should feel free to approach the director with their problems and suggestions and receive considerate attention and advice. If the director remains poised and pleasant, many of the complications that attend school dramatics may be avoided. The director is largely responsible for establishing morale, because his or her methods will be copied unconsciously by the cast and the crew.

The artistic principles prompting the director's planning for unity, proportion, and balance in the grouping of characters and furniture against the intended setting should be made clear to the actors at this time. It is often difficult to have them make the necessary movements an intrinsic part of the dialogue. Many directors then ''give the actors the stage'' and let them read their lines and move about as they please, and frequently their instinctive reactions are the right ones. Other directors have the actors improvise the scene without the script in their hands, and their natural reactions are often both pleasing and effective and can be incorpo-

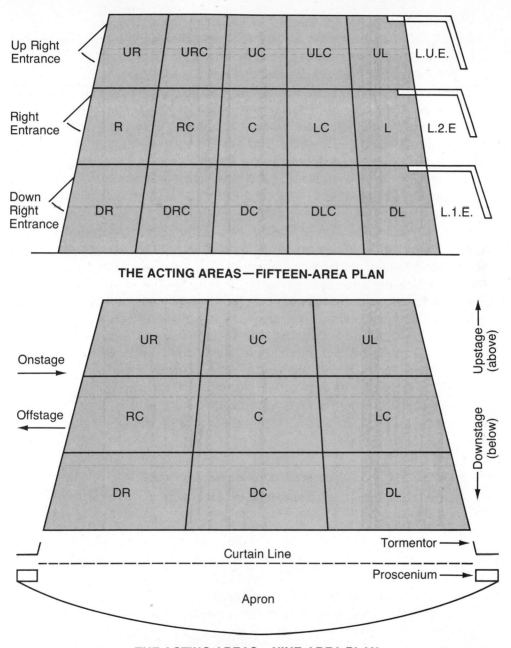

THE ACTING AREAS—FIFTEEN-AREA PLAN

THE ACTING AREAS—NINE-AREA PLAN

The upper diagram also indicates directions from the actor's point of view. The lower diagram shows entrance positions used with the old wing setting—L.1.E. (left first entrance), etc.—and early box sets—down right entrance, etc. These symbols are still used with many musical plays.

rated into the planning. Such methods avoid the puppetlike following of directions, not felt necessary by actors, which ruin the immediacy of a scene.

Working Rehearsals

After all the action has been blocked out, the most creative part of rehearsing begins. Interpretation is developed, and words and action are put together. All the acting techniques previously discussed are brought into play and are coordinated with the director's carefully thought-out plans. Some directors use the terms *essential* and *accessory* to describe action. The former is set by the director; the latter is worked out as a means of character delineation by the actor.

The interpretations of the roles are set during the working rehearsals. The influence of the Stanislavski Method has complicated this phase of early rehearsals, for some Method actors get too deeply involved in their own inner reactions. Always keep in mind that the director is in absolute control of the production, for the director alone has planned the stage settings, action, and tempo to create an artistic whole of which the actors are only one part. The director is also privileged to change his or her mind without question. However, individual and group discussions should be arranged, or encouraged informally offstage, where ideas can be

A theater class preparing for a play at the College of New Rochelle

exchanged and questions answered. Actors might find that writing character sketches of their roles before such discussions helps clarify their thinking.

After the stage business has been blocked for the whole play, memorization should be nearly completed. Usually a date is set after which no scripts can appear onstage. Only then can real characterization begin. At this point, actors should be left relatively free to move and speak, for spontaneous physical and vocal responses frequently improve a scene. In fact, actors should be left as free as possible in their interpretation of lines, but they must not be permitted to fix a false inflection or swallow important words and phrases. Having the actor rewrite a passage often will help that actor appreciate the exact meaning of the lines. It is sometimes helpful if the director stops the actor suddenly and says, "Wait a minute. Where are you going after this scene? What were you doing just before this entrance? What are you saying? What is happening to your character in this scene?" Only as a last resort should the director read the lines.

Speeding up or slowing down words and action to attain a certain mood or meaning is often difficult for amateurs. It is during the working rehearsals that the actors must develop tempo—learn to pick up cues rapidly, listen effectively, hold for a laugh or a pause, point lines, break up long speeches with action, and use appropriate body movement.

This phase of interpretation is especially critical. There is a tendency to return to first inclinations under the pressure of performance, so no false inflections or moves, especially gestures, must become set. With troublesome lines, sometimes bridging is helpful. *Bridging* is adding words before or after the difficult ones. Beginners must be helped to help each other by feeding cues properly, by listening effectively but not conspicuously, or by taking themselves out of a scene when necessary. Most amateurs have trouble giving sufficient time on pauses. Here it is frequently helpful to have them count, usually from one to three beats or even longer, for a desired effect. Restraining bodily movements in order to give a telling gesture or a glance a chance to register is very important.

The location of the director is crucial during working rehearsals. Most directors sit on the stage beside the prompter during early rehearsals and quietly interrupt to ask relevant questions and to give directions. Other directors place the prompter on one side of the stage and seat themselves about halfway back in the auditorium in order to check the entire stage area. Usually a combination of methods is preferable. If sitting too near the actors, the director does not get a good perspective of the stage pictures, the sense of unity of the action as a whole, and the clear and harmonious blending of the voices. On the other hand, if the director is near, the intimate question-and-answer procedure can be used to inspire the actor in trouble to think out a problem. A good procedure is to work intimately with a scene, bringing out details and correcting mistakes, and then retire to a distance and watch the entire action from different vantage points, while checking the clarity of key lines and words, the spacing of the actors, and the continuing effect of stage pictures. The director can then have the difficult bits of action repeated correctly until they are set.

Especially in period and stylized plays, mock costumes and props should be used as soon as possible. Usually the assistant director is responsible for obtaining long skirts, proper shoes, coats, swords, hats, cups and saucers, cigarette cases— whatever the play requires—and for storing them after rehearsals.

In addition to the general rehearsal schedule, a second, specialized schedule should be worked out for actors who are together in a number of scenes. These scenes or fragments of scenes can be rehearsed separately by the assistant director. This schedule of simultaneous rehearsals avoids long waits and the resulting boredom and restlessness. Important roles can often be rehearsed separately. Love scenes and other intensely emotional scenes should always be directed privately until the action is crystallized and the responses are natural and convincing.

Projection of lines is the means by which the play is heard and understood and is an absolute necessity, frequently disregarded by actors today. If you have taken seriously the exercises and text of Chapter 4 and have been practicing vocal exercises regularly, you should understand the fundamental principles. Your work now is to correlate the physical processes of correct breathing and articulation with the psychological consciousness of speaking to everyone in the audience. Remembering the last person at the farthest point in the auditorium, and at the same time considering everyone else as well, will enable you to project key words and sentences clearly. You should by this time be breathing correctly and relaxing your inner throat muscles from force of habit, while at the same time you are clarifying the important words with flexible lips and tongue.

Speaking intelligibly, not necessarily loudly, depends, of course, upon the exact meaning of what you are saying. From the first rehearsal, you should have begun marking the words and phrases that must be stressed and taking your breath in pauses to emphasize meanings. These pauses should also be marked while you are working out your characterization. The most common fault of amateurs is to drop the last words of every sentence instead of breathing between thought groups, for often the most vital words are at the end and must be heard.

Unless you are specifically told by the director to speak upstage, it is wise to speak front or diagonally front (three-quarter front), turning your head toward the person you are addressing on sentences of little consequence. Remember also that many small words, such as articles, prepositions, and minor adjectives and adverbs, can be "thrown away," just as are the unaccented vowel sounds in many words. Too precise pronunciation of all words is a fatal mistake and should be used only in caricature for a definite effect.

A scene from Carnegie-Mellon University's production of And Miss Reardon Drinks a Little *by Paul Zindel*

Polishing Rehearsals

It is in the polishing rehearsals that the real joys of directing and acting are experienced. These rehearsals must be characterized by complete concentration, sustained discipline, and joyous participation on the part of all persons concerned. With lines memorized and action set, all phases of the production can be brought together in an artistic whole.

From the standpoint of the actor, these rehearsals should bring the creative satisfaction of developing the subtle shades of vocal inflection and pantomime that make the character live for both the actor and the audience. Mannerisms of movement, distinctive physical attitudes, and subtle coloring of lines can develop through identification with the role only when the actor feels perfectly at ease in the environment of the setting.

Approximate costumes and accessories, such as wigs and body padding, should be worn at polishing rehearsals. The essential elements of the production should be in place. Exits and entrances, windows, staircases, fireplaces, and basic furniture should be onstage. Telephones and lamps should be in position, and sound effects necessary for cues should be set. Only then can the actors find themselves in the environment of the play and become a part of it. Once the mechanics of fitting themselves into the sets have been mastered, the actors can complete their search for identity with their roles in relation to the play as a whole.

It is in these final rehearsals that subtle touches of improvisation perfectly in accord with the entire production creep into both acting and directing to enhance its appeal. These must be absorbed and not lost by overrehearsing. Overrehearsing occasionally results in a whole company's going stale. The director must establish the tempo of the production as a whole, speeding up cues, eliminating irrelevant action, clarifying speech while assisting the cast to point their lines and hold their pauses. Voices, color, and lights must be blended harmoniously. Even the music between acts, if there is any, should be in accord with the type, mood, and period of the play.

If the play is dragging because of pauses between sentences, it is helpful to have a rapid-fire line rehearsal, with the actors conversationally running through the play without any action or dramatic effects. To pace the timing and to make sure of clarity, some directors listen to difficult scenes without watching them.

To a director, the most important element in play production is rhythm. The rhythm of a play is the overall blending of tempo, action, and dialogue. It is during the polishing rehearsals that the rhythm of the play is set and maintained. Sound and light cues must be carefully timed. Telephones, lamps, fireplaces, and sound effects should function smoothly. A single extraneous sound, a slight motion, an unmotivated gesture, or a poorly timed sound cue can destroy the effect of a scene. The director must scrutinize every stage picture from all parts of the auditorium.

About 10 days before the first performance, the complete play must be put together in rehearsal. When the actors make their proper entrances and exits, wear costumes, and use props, the director can see exactly what is still needed to make the play a success. From this time on, the rehearsals must be by acts, played through without interruption. Separate rehearsals for difficult scenes can be held as needed, however.

In the polishing process, some scenes are built up by having the lines top preceding ones, some are speeded up by rapid picking up of cues, and some are slowed down by effective pauses. It is possible to err in any of these directions. It is said that George M. Cohan's acting in his younger days was known for its overly brisk pace and rapid timing. However, once he discovered the effectiveness of the pause, he used it so often that it added 18 minutes of playing time to *Ah, Wilderness!*

Members of the prop committee should have all props ready, and the wardrobe committee should have all costumes and accessories finished and on hand during polishing rehearsals. Curtain calls must be rehearsed, intermission time checked, and time allowances made for changes of costume.

Technical Rehearsals

During the weeks of rehearsal, the scenic artist and stage manager have designed and constructed the sets and planned the lighting. Fundamental scenic units should be onstage as soon as possible in order for necessary adjustments to be made. Ideally the stage should be available for the 3 weeks before the performance, with entrances, exits, stairways, functional windows, doorways, doorbells, and practical sources of light all ready for use. As soon as possible, the cast and backstage crews should be working together so that costumes, makeup, scenery, properties, and furniture can be considered simultaneously from the standpoint of color, light, and form.

Stage plots must be made by the stage manager for each scene, showing exact positions and angles of flats and furniture. Each piece should be numbered and stagehands appointed to place and remove it and store it backstage properly.

Crew rehearsals must establish a sequence of action that must be carefully rehearsed so that changes can be made in seconds rather than minutes. The same members of the crew should always handle the curtain, lights, and props, because exact timing must be established for every scene. Mistakes are disastrous and can ruin a whole performance.

Special lighting rehearsals are imperative, for only experimentation can assure the most effective results. Stage lighting today is an art in itself. Light often replaces paint for rapidly changing effects. It takes hours of adjustment before shadows are removed, special areas are highlighted, artificial sources of lighting are made to appear natural, and exact moods are established. Light must not be allowed to leak through flats, reflect from mirrors onstage, or splash on the proscenium, apron, or orchestra pit.

Technical rehearsals are crucial to the success of any production, especially one in which special effects are important. In this opening scene from Peter Pan *by J. M. Barrie, the actors must learn to feel comfortable as they are whisked about the stage on overhead wires.*

Only a standby cast need be called to help in the experimentation. Usually the crew can act as stand-ins for lighting placement and adjustment. School lighting equipment is often inflexible, and the regulations concerning its use are quite stringent. If there is any question of overloading the circuits, it should be settled before a lighting rehearsal begins.

Dressing the stage is too often neglected in the later rehearsals when it should be done. It is often difficult to obtain the correct pictures, hangings, props, and household effects and to arrange them so that the stage looks ''lived in'' but not cluttered. It may take a week or more to locate just one article.

Securing curtains of the right color and texture is always a problem, but a good stage design demands that they be well chosen and properly draped. Backing for windows and doorways must be carefully planned. Often shrubbery, garden walls,

Evita, the award-winning rock opera appearing on Broadway, relies a great deal on special effects and dramatic lighting. Whenever screens and film clips are part of a live theater production, timing is essential. The screen must lower and the film must appear at precisely the right moment. It takes many hours of technical rehearsals to perfect the timing.

and skylines seen through the stage windows must be properly lighted to show the time of day and to create the mood. It also may be necessary to have backstage floodlights to kill any shadows that might precede the actors onstage. Ample space must be allowed for the cast to get on and off the stage in character. The cast must learn a safe means of using any stage stairways and balconies, even in the dark.

These matters must be settled before the dress rehearsals. However, the planning is worth the effort if it avoids hectic dress rehearsals and a slipshod performance. "Eventually, why not now?" is an excellent motto for everyone connected with a play to keep in mind, for it is easier to attend to the inevitable details beforehand than on the day of performance.

Technical rehearsals are the first rehearsals on the stage with complete stage equipment. They are not always possible to arrange, and the group sometimes has to go directly from the polishing to the dress rehearsals. Far too often the auditorium is not available until the final week before the first performance.

The first time the cast and technical crew work together with the set there is likely to be chaos. There will probably be confusion and delays in getting lamps to work, doors to open, curtains to come down exactly on time, and props to be in the right place at the right time. During these technical rehearsals, the grips, fly operators, wardrobe people, and property crew must get their performance duties clearly in mind and their materials organized. Actors should be trained to return props to the appointed tables backstage.

A long technical rehearsal on Saturday of the week before the performance is invaluable. All details of setting, costume, and makeup will not be ready, but the essentials should be. A run-through of the whole play with changing of costumes, coordination of all effects, and curtain calls should begin fairly early in the morning. The assistant director, stage manager, and prompter work together to keep things going smoothly onstage. The director should move through the auditorium checking sight lines, acoustics, and total effects and taking notes to share with the cast after the final curtain. Every person involved will write down the director's suggestions.

In the afternoon, weak scenes can be redone, important scenes restaged, and all loose ends and details settled. If possible, photographs should be taken for the press at this time, with the leads in costume and makeup.

Dress Rehearsals

If possible, three dress rehearsals should be held, the last with an invited audience so that the cast can learn to point lines and hold the action for laughter and applause. An audience at the last dress rehearsal provides an occasion, too, for the house manager and ushers to learn their duties and familiarize themselves with the seating arrangement.

Galileo *by Bertolt Brecht presented by Catholic University. Dress rehearsals are real performances. The actors may or may not present their dress rehearsals before an audience.*

Usually photographs of the cast in various scenes are taken at a dress rehearsal. The picture-taking should be done either before or after the rehearsal so that the timing of the production and the establishment of moods are not interrupted. Every person involved in the dress rehearsals should have an instruction sheet listing the time actors are due for makeup; responsibilities for props, costumes, and stage equipment; and backstage regulations about outsiders who may wish to call or deliver flowers.

The final dress rehearsal should begin on time and go straight to the end without interruption. The cast and crew should be instructed not to correct mistakes obviously, but to go right along adjusting whatever is seriously wrong as best they can while the action continues. The main consideration is to avoid awkward pauses and the repetition of lines or action.

Backstage organization must be efficient. There must be a chain of command from the director down so that everyone has specific responsibilities. The director is the final authority, checking the makeup, costumes, props, lights, and stage before going out front. Then the assistant director takes over backstage, receiving suggestions from, or sending questions to, the director concerning the lights, furniture, and other matters. Next in command is the stage manager, who has full responsibility for the backstage area. The SM checks the lights and stage before the curtain goes up, sees that the cast is ready, gets the crew members in their places, and gives the signals for lights, curtain, and sound effects. Once the show opens, the stage manager is the only backstage authority.

The prompter should not be interrupted once the curtain is up. All pauses and lines should be clearly marked in the promptbook so there will not be a temptation to prompt during a dramatic moment of silence. The prompter must be alert every instant that the play is in progress. Any prompting should be for the actors, not for the audience. The prompter should be not only inaudible but also invisible to the spectators.

When the final dress rehearsal is finished, the actors should leave the dressing rooms in perfect order, put away their makeup, and hang their costumes neatly. The wardrobe crew can then check to see if any pressing or mending is needed.

After the curtain calls have been rehearsed, the cast should wait for the director backstage. During final rehearsals, some directors sit at the back of the house and dictate notes, which are written on separate sheets of paper for each performer. As these are given out, the director explains the correction and may ask the actor to run through the line or business. Other directors prefer that the cast write down the comments and remember them. Both cast and crew should feel encouraged and confident after a dress rehearsal. If there is continued cooperation, a good dress rehearsal should ensure a satisfactory performance.

BIBLIOGRAPHY

Cartmell, Van H.: *Amateur Theatre: A Guide for Actor and Director,* Van Nostrand, Princeton, New Jersey, 1961.

Chilver, Peter: *Staging a School Play,* Harper & Row, New York, 1968.

Cole, Toby, and Helen Chinoy: *Directors on Directing,* Bobbs-Merrill, Indianapolis, 1963.

Dean, Alexander, and L. Carra: *Fundamentals of Play Directing,* 3rd Edition, Holt, New York, 1974.

Dietrich, John E.: *Play Direction,* Prentice-Hall, Englewood Cliffs, New Jersey, 1953.

Dolman, John, Jr.: *The Art of Play Production,* 3rd Edition, Harper, New York, 1973.

Gassner, John, and P. Barber: *Producing the Play,* Holt, New York, 1953.

Gielgud, John: *Stage Directions,* Putnam, New York, 1966.

Heffner, Hubert, Samuel Selden, and Hunton Sellman: *Modern Theater Practice: A Handbook of Play Production,* 5th Edition, Appleton-Century-Crofts, New York, 1973.

Nelms, Henning: *Play Production,* Barnes & Noble, New York, 1958.

Nuttall, Kenneth: *Play Production for Young People,* Plays, Boston, 1966.

CHAPTER ELEVEN

Stage Settings

An appreciation of the significance and beauty of stage settings should be one of the rewards of your study of the theater. The profusion of striking color and scenic effects in television productions and in motion pictures, as well as the spectacle of lavish musical plays, have increased the interest in scenic art on the part of performers and audiences alike. Scenery and lighting have become an integral part of contemporary play writing and production. No longer must the "set" be a platform with a nondescript background or a drop with a poorly painted perspective of a locale totally unrelated to the play.

All students of drama should have a basic knowledge of stagecraft and design for four reasons: (1) to develop an appreciation of the importance of scenery to fine productions; (2) to better understand the relationship of each element of production to total theater; (3) to introduce you to another realm of the dramatic arts in which you may participate; and (4) to provide knowledge that may enable you to share in further theater activities in college and community life. Wishing to act without knowing your theater environment is like wishing to sail with knowing the bow of a boat from the stern.

Even if you do not feel artistically inclined, you will find there are many things to be done backstage by those with a little knowledge, a lot of enthusiasm, and a willingness to learn. It takes many workers behind the scenes—stagehands, property people, carpenters, costume and set designers, tailors, painters, and lighting technicians, to name a few—to make possible the bows of a few performers at curtain call. Backstage theater experience may bring you the satisfaction and joy of knowing that you have played a part in making a successful show possible. Such experience may also help you discover talents and acquire skills that will be useful to you beyond your theater experience.

STAGE TERMINOLOGY

To understand the various phases of scenic design and the kinds of stage equipment that have been developed in the last 350 years, you should be familiar with the following terms.

act curtain: The curtain, hung just upstage of the proscenium, that opens or closes each act or scene.

acting area: The portion of the stage used by the actors during the play.

apron: The section of the stage in front of the curtain.

asbestos or *fire curtain:*   A fireproof curtain closing off the stage from the auditorium.

auditorium: Where the audience sits.

backdrop (drop):   A large piece of cloth upon which scenery is painted, fastened at top and bottom to battens, and hung at the back of the stage setting.

backing (masking):   Flats or drops behind scenery openings to mask the backstage area.

backstage: That part of the stage—left, right, and rear—that is not seen by the audience; also the dressing rooms, greenroom, prop room, shops, and storage areas.

batten: A long piece of wood or pipe from which scenery, lights, and curtains are suspended; also used at top and bottom of a drop.

book: To hinge two or three flats together so that they will stand free or fold up; also the script in a musical play.

border (teaser):   A short curtain hung across the stage above the acting area to mask the overhead lights from the audience; also refers to overhead strip lights.

box set: A two-wall or three-wall set composed of flats representing an interior of a room, often covered by a ceiling.

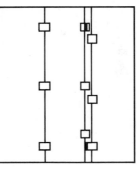

Book

brace: An adjustable, polelike support for flats.

clout nail: A special, soft, self-clinching nail used in flat construction.

convention: An accepted rule or tradition.

counterweight system: A system of lines and weights that gives mechanical advantage to the raising and lowering of scenery.

curtain: Playbook instruction to close the curtain.

curtain line: The imaginary floor line the curtain touches when closed.

cyclorama or *cyc:*   A background curtain hung around the three sides of the stage.

dutchman: A canvas strip 4 to 5 inches wide to cover the gap between flats.

elevation: An eye-level-view drawing showing the flats arranged in a continuous row to be used in a set.

false proscenium: A frame built inside the proscenium to reduce the size of the stage opening.

flat: A wooden frame covered with cloth used as the basic unit of structure of a box set.

flies or *loft:*   The area above the stage in which scenery is hung.

floor plan: A drawing of the overhead view of a set showing the exact location of all entrances, walls, and furniture.

fly: To raise or lower scenery.

gauze or *scrim:*   A drop, usually seamless, made of special fabric that seems almost opaque when lit from the front and semitransparent when lit from behind.

grand drape: A curtain at the top of the proscenium, usually made of the same material as the act curtain, used to lower the height of the stage.

greenroom: A backstage lounge used as a reception or waiting room for the actors.

gridiron or *grid:*   A series of heavy beams or metal framework just under the roof of the stage to which are attached the pulleys or blocks through which lines pass to raise or lower scenery.

grip: A stagehand who moves scenery.

ground cloth or *floor cloth:*   A canvas covering for the floor of the acting area.

ground row: A low profile of scenery that can stand by itself, used to mask the bottom of the cyc or backdrop.

jack: A triangular brace for supporting scenery.

jigger: A board used as a spacer in three-fold flats.

jog: A narrow flat, usually less than 2 feet in width, used to form such things as alcoves and bay windows.

lash line: Rope used for lashing flats together.

legs: Pieces of cloth, usually hung in pairs, stage left and stage right, to mask the backstage area.

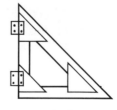

Jack

parallel: A specially constructed collapsible platform.

permanent setting: A setting that remains the same throughout a play, regardless of change of locale.

perspective: A head-on view of a set having the illusion of depth.

pit: The part of the auditorium where the orchestra may be located—often an area below floor level.

places: An order for actors and crew to get to their positions.

plastic: A three-dimensional article or structure.

portal: A drop that has its lower middle section removed so that the drop will mask only the top and sides of the stage.

practical-usable: A term applied to such parts of the set as doors and windows that must open and shut during the action, a rock that can bear a person's weight, and lamps that can be turned on.

profile (cut-out): A two-dimensional piece of scenery, such as a hedge or bush.

proscenium: The arch or frame enclosing the visible stage, the opening between the stage and the auditorium.

rake: To slant or set at an angle. A raked stage is inclined from the footlights to the rear of the stage.

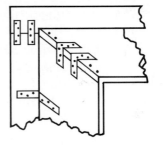

Profile

ramp: A sloping platform connecting the stage floor to a higher level.

returns: Flats placed at the downstage edges of the set extending into the wings right and left.

reveal: A thickness piece placed in door, window, and arch openings to give the illusion of the third dimension to walls.

set pieces: Individual pieces of scenery, such as trees, rocks, and walls, that stand by themselves.

sight line: A line for the side walls and elevation of the set established by taking a sighting from the front corners and upper balcony seats.

sky cyc: Smooth cloth hung at the back and sides of the stage and painted to give the illusion of the sky.

Reveal

stage: The space where the actors perform, usually a raised platform.

stagecraft: The art and craft of putting on a production.

strike: The stage manager's order to remove an object or objects from the stage or to take down the set.

tab: A narrow drop.

theater: A building used for the presentation of plays.

tormentors: Side pieces—flats or drapes—just back of the proscenium used to narrow the opening.

trap: A door or opening in the stage floor.

traveler: A stage curtain upstage of the act curtain that opens to the right and left rather than moving up and down.

trip: To double a drop for raising when there is insufficient fly space.

wagons: Low platforms on casters.

wing setting: A set made with pairs of wings on both sides of the stage, used with a matching backdrop.

wings: The offstage areas to the right and left of the set; also one or more flats, usually hinged at an angle but sometimes parallel to the footlights, used as entrances but which conceal backstage areas.

working drawing: A detailed drawing showing how a piece of scenery is to be constructed.

PURPOSES OF SCENERY

The first and most important function of scenery is to provide a place to act, a place designed to emphasize action and conflict. The setting should define the locale of the play in terms of time: the era or historical period, the time of day, the season of the year, and the changes in time that may occur during the play. The important environmental surroundings should be made clear: the climate and geographical conditions, the socioeconomic situation, the cultural background, or perhaps the political-governmental system of the area. The set should also indicate whether the setting is interior or exterior, rural or urban, real or imaginary.

A set should help inform the audience about the characters, particularly the effects of the environment upon them, and how, in turn, their personality traits affect the surroundings. We have all observed that the laziness, preciseness, carelessness, eccentricity, and so on, of a person is reflected in that person's home and its furnishings. In *You Can't Take It with You,* the strange conglomeration of mismatched objects found in the family living room clearly indicates the let-one-do-as-one-pleases attitude of the Sycamores.

A set often reveals the interrelationships between people, their rank, station, influence, or position in the family, office, royal court, or community. The audience can concentrate more easily on characters, symbolic elements, or a focal point of interest on the stage if the scenery is effectively designed. Scenery should provide a means for focusing audience attention on the actor. Elevating the actor on stairways and platforms provides a strong stage position. Furniture and actors may be arranged to facilitate triangular blocking with the key actor at the point of the triangle. And well-placed doorways and other openings can dramatically frame the actor.

In *Our Town,* Thornton Wilder brought about a strong concentration of the action and lines with a set design that has impressed most audiences as having "no design." *Our Town* has inaccurately been called "the play without scenery," but the experienced drama student will see that there *is* scenery—the scenery that

A scene from Death of a Salesman. *In designing this set, Jo Mielziner selected details that would create the atmosphere of the Loman home but that would not distract attention from the play itself.*

Wilder felt necessary for the universality he sought. In fact, he used the most effective designer playwrights have called upon for centuries: the imagination of the audience. *Our Town* has been a most popular play for high school productions, unfortunately not because of its beauty and greatness, which are often missed because of what appears to be an obvious ''simplicity,'' but because it doesn't take any scenery. Many directors and their casts have failed to recognize that the concentration on the actors brought about by such a stage design demands an even stronger interpretation of the roles than in plays with conventional scenery.

Scenery should indicate the style of the production. A play is usually *presentation* or *representational*. Presentational style ''recognizes'' the audience as an audience and the play as a play; therefore, the actor may speak directly to the audience. Shakespeare's plays are presentational; as are many modern plays. Representational staging assumes the fourth wall, and the actor is careful not to cross the curtain line. The actor ''plays'' as if the audience does not exist and as if their laughter and applause do not exist. Of course, stage settings are not totally realistic, especially when presented on a proscenium stage. Theater conventions, those rules and traditions that apply to staging, determine general positions for set pieces and entrance areas. For example, all, or nearly all, furniture faces the audience. Exterior doors are usually off stage right; most interior doors are stage left or upstage. Fireplaces tend to be placed on stage right walls. French doors are usually stage left. Living room and dining room furniture often appear in the same area. When this occurs, a sofa may be down right while the dining table may be down left. These are only a few of the staging conventions used in the theater.

A set may also reflect the style of a historical period. A number of theaters have been built with thrust stages, thus enabling the actor to apply the acting conventions of any era without seeming out of place.

One of the most important functions of scenery is to create mood and atmosphere. The tone of an entire production may be established by well-designed scenery. The reaction of the audience to the actors and the script may be determined to a great extent by the "mental framework" a set may create. For example, if the set is painted in bright yellows, oranges, and pinks, the audience will expect the play to be correspondingly light and cheery. On the other hand, if a set is painted in violets, dark blues and greens, grays and black, the audience will expect the play to be heavy and serious. The emotional impact of a scene can be effectively heightened when the background is in keeping with the feeling of the action. The scenic designer utilizes the known psychological effects of artistic principles to arouse a subconscious emotional reaction from the audience. All sets should be aesthetically satisfying, even when an atmosphere of fear, chaos, or mystery is to be created.

SCENIC DESIGN

Scenery must be in keeping with the author's intent and the director's interpretation. It must always serve the actor, never dominate. Scenery must not clash with costumes or become an obstacle course when blocking. Scenery should never be distracting, inconsistent, or "pretty for pretty's sake." In addition, a set must be functional. It must aid the action of the play, never hinder it. It must fit all the needs of the play, yet maintain an essential simplicity in design, construction, and shifting. Remember: A basic rule for all aspects of theater from acting to stagecraft is "use the least to say the most."

Proper design adds the color and life to a production that makes theater an exciting experience for the audience. Costumes will seem more appropriate and attractive against a fitting background. A careful selection of stage furnishings makes the set and its people seem complete and correct. However, the scenic artists must always bear in mind that a good design can only be as elaborate or difficult as the talent and experience of the crew can handle well.

SCENIC DESIGN AND THE STUDENT OF DRAMA

The basic high school drama course is concerned more with the principles of design and scenic construction than with the actual building of sets. However, knowledge of the development of scenic design and some principles of construction are valuable whether or not you plan to take a course in stagecraft. You may want to work on backstage crews or on such committees as construction, properties, costumes, or makeup. Every performer needs to know the role and function of the director, scenic designer or technical director, and the stage manager and the stage crew in order to appreciate the contribution each makes and to achieve the spirit of cooperation essential to successful productions.

In bringing a play to life, the scenic designer is next to the director in importance. The aim of both is to create a world of illusion that theatergoers will accept and enjoy. The director works primarily with the bodies and voices of the actors; a designer works with mass, color, and line. Together they create the proper atmosphere to express the meaning of the play. The scenic designer does not build real rooms, houses, or mountain tops but uses painted canvas, creative lighting, and special effects to stir the imagination of the audience so that it is transported to the realm where the playwright's dream seems a reality. The scenic designer works with the four areas of scenery, lighting, makeup, and costumes to create satisfying empathetic illusions. The more satisfying the empathies that are established, the better the production.

THE DEVELOPMENT OF SCENIC DESIGN

From primitive campfires to the modern theater house, devoted theater technicians have improved scenery and light design in the desire to convey meanings through visual sensations. The first important step was the "skene" building, which the Romans subsequently enlarged. Later came the "stations" of the miracle plays, with the special mechanical effect of Hell's Mouth.

Renaissance Designs

Stage design as we know it came into being in Italy in 1508 at the royal court of the Duke of Ferrara. The stage there was modeled after the ancient Roman theaters, solidly built and heavily decorated with elaborate niches, columns, and statues. One such Renaissance stage, the Teatro Olimpico, is perfectly preserved in Vicenza. Behind the entrances appeared streets in perspective from stucco and paintings. Buildings covered with statues of diminishing size lined the streets. The amazing effect is that of a city stretching into the distance because the streets branch off at angles.

From the large central entrance of the Teatro Olimpico the proscenium arch developed. The first real proscenium was in the Farnese Theater of Parma, where an elaborate architectural structure surrounded a frame with a curtain. Behind this frame, the actors performed against painted scenes. To facilitate scenery changes, *periaktoi* like the revolving prisms of the Greek theater were sometimes used.

Another Renaissance invention, which spread to England and was still used in London early in this century, was the raked stage. In a further attempt to make false perspective complete, the stage floor was slanted upwards toward the back of the stage. From this the terms *upstage* and *downstage* came into being; the actor was actually walking up or down the stage.

The tiring house facade of the Elizabethan playhouse emphasized simplicity and used a minimum of scenic effects, but the Renaissance masques were famous for their beautiful scenery. Some of the most extravagant masques were designed by Inigo Jones, an English architect, who introduced the proscenium to England. These elaborate productions, which extended into the seventeenth century, demanded detailed scenery quite different from the permanent setting of the Elizabethan theater house.

Backdrops became very popular, and large theaters were built to accommodate the extensive rigging needed to raise and lower the scenery. Wing settings were a continuation of the attempt to achieve perspective. However, the desire for perspective sets led to the fanning out of the auditorium and resulted in poor sight lines. The demand for many scenic backgrounds brought the introduction of shutters—flats that moved back and forth on tracks or grooves—and nested wings—several wings placed one behind the other to allow quick scene changes. Even revolving stages were tried during the Renaissance stage experimentations.

Restoration Stages

The Restoration period in England found most of the acting taking place on raked aprons, with little action behind the proscenium "in" the scenery. The proscenium at this time was a very thick wall compared to our picture frame stages—so thick that one or two doors were placed in each side wall of the proscenium to enable the actors to enter on the apron rather than in back of the frame.

The Nineteenth Century

In the nineteenth century, an effort was made to suit the scenery to the play. However, typical interior sets were still made of canvas drops and wings painted to represent walls, windows, curtains, furniture, potted palms, mirrors, and all the other details of a conservatory or a parlor. Exterior scenes were also painted. For example, the conventional garden and forests consisted of painted trees, shrubs, fountains, gates, and pathways. Street scenes had painted buildings, store windows, signs, and street lamps. Entrances were made through wings parallel to the back wall. These were often painted like the backdrop, with furniture and draperies for interiors and cut-out greenery for exteriors. Some of these sets are still used in isolated "opery" houses, and imitations are made for revivals of the old-fashioned melodramas.

One of the notable changes in the mid nineteenth-century theaters was the gradual shrinking of the apron and the subsequent addition of orchestra seats in the space formerly occupied by the stage. The flapping canvas wings and backdrops with their painted doors and windows and illogical shadows were no longer satisfying to the designers, who were seeking greater accuracy in historical and realistic representation. The wings gradually "closed," forming "real" left and right walls on the stage. Thus, the box set came into existence and the beginnings of realism had taken root.

The Twentieth Century

The cry for realism was answered in France by André Antoine and in the United States by David Belasco. Their stage sets were so photographically accurate that their style of design was called naturalism. However, Belasco was so concerned with exact detail that his scenery distracted the audiences from the action of the play. Many stories have been told of Belasco's stress on accuracy, including individual selection of books and what-nots for shelves and the dismantling and reconstructing of real rooms. The important contribution of the naturalists was that their ultrarealistic sets worked toward making the realistic drama ring true.

Most realistic stage sets today are designed with selective realism. This modified form of realism developed because the many details of naturalism confused the audience. An impression of actuality is better theatrically and artistically. The designer selects scenic elements that convey the idea of the locale. The designer does not attempt to create an exact replica.

Eli Wallach and Zero Mostel in a scene from Rhinoceros. *Realistic details are used in furnishing the set.*

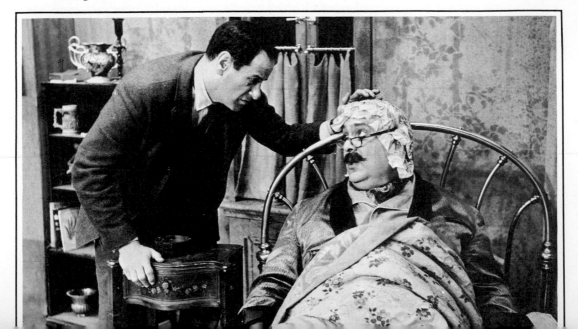

The modern realistic interior set in a proscenium theater has all essential entrances, doorways, windows, and so on, placed in a two-sided or three-sided room. The room is usually placed off-center and at an angle instead of squarely on the stage in the old-fashioned manner. The fourth wall is imaginary, of course, and its presence is only a suggestion. Furniture usually faces that fourth invisible wall, through which the audience observes the action. There have been attempts, almost every one unsuccessful, to treat the fourth wall as a wall by placing a sofa with its back to the audience or by having an actor look out an imaginary window. The selective realists for the most part have agreed that "a set is a set," and the audience must accept it as a room. Natural sources of light—windows, lamps, skylights—have helped establish the illusion of reality.

The properly designed stage set can become an ideal background for the author's theme, as well as a pleasing picture for the audience to enjoy. At the same time, it represents the actual living quarters of people and discloses their tastes, financial status, cultural level, and habits of living.

Exterior sets are at best only suggestive. Plastics (three-dimensional structures) and cut-outs (two-dimensional profiles) are placed against a drop or sky cyc. A ground row is used to break the line between the floor and the drop and to give the illusion of distance. As much as possible, the use of wings is avoided and some other means of masking the sides of the stage is incorporated into the set.

The twentieth century has seen many experiments in scenic design. Two European designers of symbolic sets rebelled against ultrarealism. Adolphe Appia concentrated on three-dimensional forms, which he contended were essential for the performance of the three-dimensional actor. Appia emphasized the importance of the actor and used dramatic lighting innovations to focus attention on the performer. The other designer, Gordon Craig, believed the essential message of a play could be conveyed most effectively by the scenic designer. He even suggested eliminating the actors and replacing them with super-marionettes. If Craig's ideas had been implemented, the director-scenic artist would have become the god of all things theatrical.

The revolutionary ideas of Appia and Craig were carried out in this country in a modified form, especially in productions of the plays of the great American dramatist Eugene O'Neill. Flexible sets were made of screens, platforms, columns, and stairs. Psychologically, meaningful lighting and color schemes expressed the spirit and mood of the plays. The staging was in direct contrast to the lifelike physical detail of the realistic style.

MAJOR TWENTIETH-CENTURY STYLES

In twentieth-century Europe and America, the new ideas developed gradually into several major styles. You will want to know something about the distinctive qualities of these.

In Jo Mielziner's set for Winterset, *the height of the buildings and the hugeness of the bridge support have a symbolic relationship to the overpowering and tragic situation the central character faces.*

Symbolism

In scenic design, symbolism is the visualization of a play's idea or atmosphere through a visible sign of an idea or object. A symbol is a token of meaning; that is, it is one thing that stands for something else. For instance, a lone, twisted tree might represent a wasteland and also suggest barrenness in the hearts of central characters. Effective lighting can also be used in symbolism. For example, a lowering shadow can represent an approaching disaster—emotional or real. A shaft of light through a colored window can indicate a great cathedral. In *Riders to the Sea,* the white boards may seem like bleached bones, a fishing net may suggest the entrapments of life, and the dying fire may parallel the death of the last son.

Expressionism

Expressionism is exaggerated symbolism that strives to intensify the emotional impact of a play by distorting a major scenic element. For instance, in *The Adding Machine,* one of the scenic pieces is a gigantic adding machine. Its size emphasizes the fact that it dominates the lives of the central characters.

Impressionism

The impressionistic style seeks to make the audience react and see as a character does when stirred by intense feelings such as anger, horror, and fear. Unusual

Mordecai Gorelik designed this expressionistic setting for Robert Ardrey's play Thunder Rock. *The action takes place in a lighthouse. Note the way the tower is framed and the effective use of a soaring stairway.*

rhythms, exaggeration of minor details, and violent contrasts of light and design are used, enabling the theatergoer to see through the character's eyes and actually realize the impressions that character is receiving. For example, in Eugene O'Neill's *The Emperor Jones,* the jungle seems to creep up and surround Jones as he tries to escape the island's voodoo power.

Constructivism

Constructivism is a technique that uses an architectural or mechanical skeleton as a background. The set often consists of a number of platforms and open frameworks connected by stairs, ladders, ramps, and arches, allowing the action to take place on different levels. Although originally used as a background for plays that dealt with economic and social problems, constructivism has also been effectively used with other types of plays. It has frequently been used in conjunction with other scenic styles. For example, Jo Mielziner's design for *Death of a Salesman* (page 279) used a modified constructivism in the roof line of the Loman house.

Theatricalism

Theatricalism is a style of scenic design that makes no attempt to be realistic, but simply says ''This is a stage set.'' Theatricalism may incorporate elements or techniques from other styles of scenic design, but it stresses the illusory nature of the theater and the functional value of scenery. Any combination of props or scenic elements may be used if they serve the purpose. *Our Town* used ladders for rooms and a board placed across two chairs as the soda fountain in a drugstore.

Stylization

Stylization is a nonrealistic approach to design that strives to set a mood or pattern for the play. The designer often reveals a personal artistic style through distorted shapes and colors or a motif repeated over and over again in the scenery, makeup, and costumes. Stylization has been successfully used in ballets, fantasies, dream sequences, and children's plays. The mood it creates is usually light, happy, quaint, or fanciful, such as is found in the ballet sequence from *Oklahoma!*

Formalism

Formalism is a style of design that has been with us for 2,500 years. It depends mainly upon a neutral background that can become whatever the players suggest it might be. Formalism uses ramps, platforms, columns, and staircases against an unchanging facade or cyclorama background. The set provides the actor with a dramatic place to perform but without elaborate scenery or distracting embellishments. The thrust stages, such as the Tyrone Guthrie Theatre in Minneapolis, lend themselves well to formal or theatrical design.

TYPES OF SETS

Box Sets

The box set has been the most common type of interior set since it replaced the old wings and drops of the nineteenth century, although it, too, has been replaced by other forms in recent years. The box set consists of two or three walls built of flats and often covered by a ceiling.

Unit Sets

The unit set utilizes certain basic structural units to create several settings. Unit sets are quite practical for schools that wish to present multiset plays or a program of one-act plays, or to build units for a little theater that can be arranged to fit the needs of almost any play. There are several kinds of unit sets. One type uses door or window flat units, which may be completely rearranged for each scene change. There are usually two door flats, one or two window-bookcase flats, and sometimes, for variety, a wall with an arch-French door opening. These openings may

Box set (above) and unit set (below)

UNIT PLAN "A" WITH FRENCH DOOR

UNIT PLAN "B" WITH BOOKCASE & FIREPLACE

simply be interchanged or may be "booked" together to form four-unit or five-unit walls; this can facilitate easy shifting and a variety of possible combinations.

A second important type of unit set consists of many openings, some of which are quite large. Once the set is erected for a play, it is not struck, but doors, windows, arches, curtains, and backing units are placed within or behind the openings to simulate scene changes.

A third type of unit set uses scenic units mounted on movable platforms. These may be shifted from one area of the stage to another, turned to a different position, or modified with simple set decorations, such as railings, window boxes, or drapes.

The Permanent Set

Another type of staging is the use of the permanent set, one that never changes during the play except in some instances when a set piece, stairway, or flown unit may be brought in. The Elizabethan playhouse was essentially a permanent set. Formalism works well for a permanent set. A simple doorway may serve as an

Permanent set (Elizabethan)

interior or exterior entrance, a gate or a passageway; a platform may be used as a porch, a boudoir, a garden, or a sofa. Locale is determined more by controlled light than by scenic representation.

A modification of the permanent set is the multiple set, which has several distinct acting areas, each of which may represent one or several locations. See-through walls, semipartitions, railings, and platforms can serve as dividers between acting areas. These strong dividers provide the main distinction between the permanent set and the multiple set. Flexible, controlled lighting equipment is once again quite necessary.

Profile Sets

Screens and profile sets, sometimes called *cut-down* or *minimum* sets, provide further opportunities for scenic variations. Screens consist of two-fold and three-fold flats, which are used either to form walls against a drapery background or to cover openings or furnishings as a quick means of changing scenes. Screens may be almost any height and width, but a height of 8 to 10 feet is usually the most

Screen set

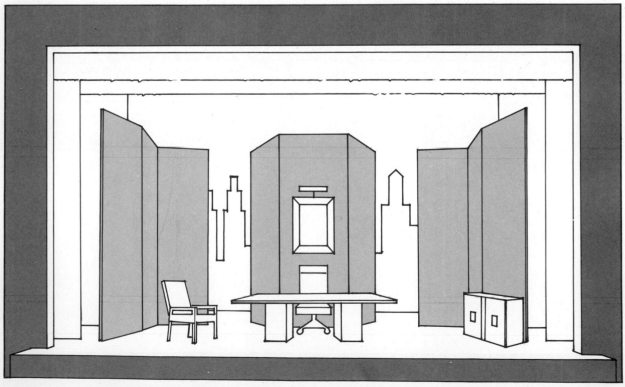

satisfactory. Although screens may be hinged or lashed together to form solid walls, that is seldom necessary, since two-fold and three-fold units are freestanding.

Cut-down scenery may be constructed of screens, but the chief difference between the two is that the cut-down set is more like the box set in that it forms the entire perimeter of the setting. Its height may vary from a mere 2 feet to 8 feet, depending upon the stage openings and furniture. Colors suggesting changing moods and emotions may be aimed against the background cyc to bring about a strong identification with the action.

Prism Sets

Prisms or *periaktoi* allow for fast changes with a minimum of equipment and space. The prisms are usually equilateral or isosceles triangles mounted to a wheeled carriage, which can be pivoted. Each *periaktos* is made up of three 6-foot flats or of two 4-foot flats and one 6-foot flat. At least four *periaktoi* are needed, but for more variety in combination and position and for more set possibilities, six or eight prisms may be used. Doorways may be created in several ways. The simplest method is to merely use a space between two prisms. Another method is to hook a normal door flat between two prisms. A third method uses inserts, sometimes called *plugs,* that may be hung between two *periaktoi*. The plugs may be shaped like ordinary doors or may be arched according to various architectural or stylistic designs. Window, bookcase, and fireplace flats may be used as one side of the *periaktos*. The prisms are especially valuable for schools that lack fly space, have trouble masking the sides of the stage, or need quick changes but have limited equipment.

Curtain (Drapery) Sets

In many forms, curtain sets have frequently been used as substitutes for constructed scenery. The typical school cyclorama rarely provides an adequate background for a play, but sometimes space, equipment, and budget force the director to use a modified curtain set. There are, however, many ways to use curtains. A formalistic set with ramps, platforms, columns, and so on, may be at its best against a curtain set. The placing of a few flats, such as doorways, windows, and fireplaces, between curtains can often turn a ''plain curtain set'' into an acceptable theatrical set. Nevertheless, curtains can never be transposed into convincing realistic sets. One of the disadvantages of a cyclorama is that the acting area is always the same size and shape. Therefore, many designers who have had to use curtain backgrounds have ignored the cyc and have used freestanding set pieces and furniture to ''shape'' their sets within the frame of the cyc.

An effective use of curtains may be employed by those fortunate enough to have a black cyclorama. Use of well-controlled lighting will make the actors and fur-

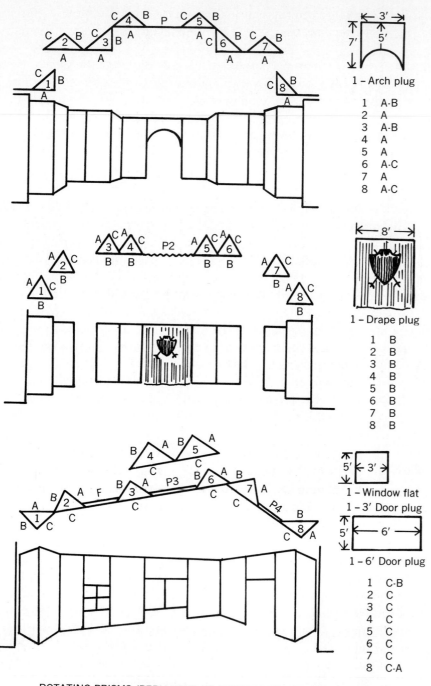

ROTATING PRISMS (PERIAKTOI) TO CREATE THREE DIFFERENT SETS

Drapery set

nishings stand out sharply against the void of the *space stage*. White furniture and clown white makeup can be particularly striking against such a background. A modification of the space stage, which can be used with any cyclorama, is the *skeleton* set, consisting simply of frames and openings, left empty or filled by draperies, backings, doors, and so on.

NEW TECHNIQUES OF STAGING

The *thrust stage* (horseshoe staging) has stirred the imaginations of scenic artists to develop new techniques of set design. Many of the nonproscenium theaters are modified picture-frame stages without the nonlocalized permanent acting backgrounds of true thrust stages; one example is the Tyrone Guthrie Theater. Since the audience surrounds the stage on three sides, conventional scenery cannot be used without blocking the audience's view, unless it is placed deep on the stage. Designers have used cut-down sets and screens quite successfully, but one of the most effective innovations is the floating screen or multiple plane set. This technique employs single flats or narrow drops 6 feet or less in width that are

The thrust stage has stirred the imaginations of scenic artists to develop new techniques of set design. The Dallas Theater Center is one example of the thrust stage.

placed at various depths parallel to the front of the stage. These floating screens provide concealed entrances for the actors and present a suggestive locale.

Arena staging (theater-in-the-round) uses a different approach. Since the audience completely surrounds the stage, no scenery can be erected, for it will block the view of the audience. Objects normally placed on walls, such as pictures and mirrors, are often casually laid on tables. A set of andirons and a grate may serve as a fireplace. Furniture may be placed in natural groupings but must allow the actors to move constantly in "S" and circular patterns.

PROCEDURES IN SCENIC DESIGN

The basic goal of scenic design is to enhance the production by creating a functional background for the action that does not intrude on that action. A set may have aesthetic appeal, establish tone and atmosphere, convey symbolism, and even aid in the expression of the theme. However, if the set does not provide the actors with a workable environment in which to move, it has failed in its primary function.

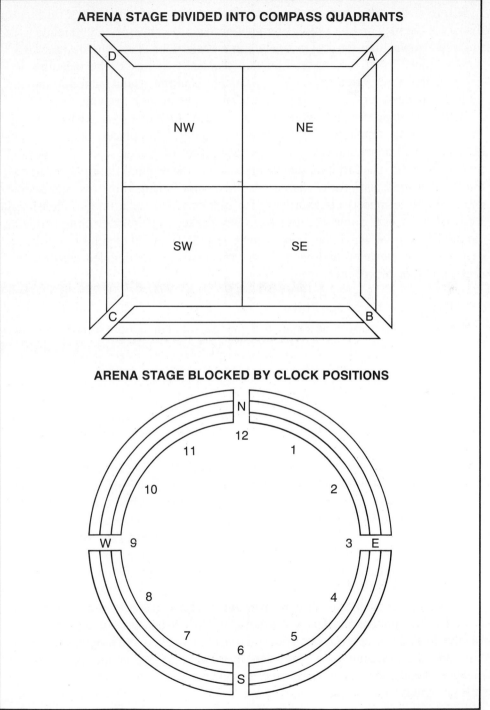

ARENA STAGE DIVIDED INTO COMPASS QUADRANTS

ARENA STAGE BLOCKED BY CLOCK POSITIONS

Before making any plan, the designer reads the play carefully several times and discusses the play and its style of production with the director. The director will provide a foundation for design, including a basic floor plan. The designer then makes a pencil sketch or watercolor that scenically expresses the meaning and spirit of the play. After considering available equipment and material and the budget, the designer enlarges this sketch into a perspective drawing.

Next the scenic designer works out a detailed floor plan—an exact diagram showing the position and size of entrances, windows, fireplaces, stairways, the backing for all doors and windows, and any pieces of plastic scenery or ground rows to be used. The furniture may be included in the original floor plan or in one made after rehearsals have started. At this point, many directors and scenic designers build model sets as a basis for blocking and for a three-dimensional study of the design. Some directors have a model set viewer, often complete with simple lighting, in which the model can be tested. The final step in design is the drafting of an elevation and working drawings, which are detailed construction illustrations or blueprints.

Predesign Considerations

Before designing a set, the scenic designer must obtain certain important information. First of all, the designer should know the size and shape of the auditorium, whether the floor is raked, and the type of seating arrangement. This is especially important in gymnasium-auditorium combinations and little theaters. Next, the designer must determine what space, including storage areas, will be available for the production; the dimensions of the apron and wings and the amount of fly space; and what equipment is available or can be obtained for use on this particular stage.

If there is fly space, the designer must know if the flies are high enough to handle a drop without tripping and whether the system is manual, sandbagged, or counterweighted. In most school situations, the designer should determine how many flats are available, their height and widths, and how many drops and scrims are ready for use. In addition, it is important to know how many special units, such as platforms, ramps, and staircases, are already constructed. And finally, the designer must consider lighting equipment and its flexibility before designing the set.

The budget for the production may greatly affect the elaborateness of the design as well as the number and kinds of sets to be used. When several sets are called for, the designer must always be concerned with the weight and mobility of scenic units and the availability of a traveler or apron space for acting during scene changes. Time and sound are two important factors to be considered whenever a shift in scenery takes place. An audience can become distracted during a long wait while scenery is shifted. Equally disconcerting is the amount of noise too often heard coming from the stage during a scenery change.

Basic Principles

The first consideration of scenic design is the play itself—its theme, type, and style. The designer must be aware of important scenes and special effects essential to that particular play, including lighting needs. The functional aspects of the set provide the information necessary for a preliminary design—location of doors, windows, fireplaces, elevated areas, essential props, and so on. Since a set is the background for actors, their experience, ages, sizes, costumes, and makeup must be considered.

Naturally, the designer must also consider the audience. Since they must see all important action, sight lines must be taken from the front corner seats and the highest balcony seats that may be sold. This means that the side walls must be raked (set at an angle) so that all entrances are visible to the entire audience. Likewise, elevated upstage platforms must be carefully positioned so that the upper balcony audience will not see ''headless'' actors.

The designer must not forget that lamps, columns, and other set pieces can hide the actor unintentionally. This might seem to be an obvious problem that could be eliminated in design or early rehearsals, but most acting groups borrow furniture or build set pieces that are not seen on the stage until a day or two before dress rehearsal; then it is rather late to change blocking or obtain another prop.

After evaluating these essentials, the designer can determine what kind of scenery would best suit the play and the director's purpose.

Artistic Considerations

Unity and emphasis are the two most important design principles to keep in mind when designing a set. *Unity* demands that all elements of the set form a perfect whole, centering around the main idea of the play. All furniture and properties must be in keeping with the background and, if possible, be a part of the stage design in period and composition. *Emphasis* focuses audience attention on some part of the stage (a hallway or a staircase), a piece of furniture (a piano or a desk), or an object on the set (a moose head or a rifle rack). A good set design emphasizes this center of interest by placing it in a prominent position, by painting it a color that makes it stand out from all else, by making it the focus of all lines of interest, or by playing light upon it. Everything else on the stage should be subordinated to the center of interest.

Proportion and balance are also important artistic principles to be observed. Proportion takes the human being as the unit of measurement. In realistic plays, all scenic elements are scaled to a person 6 feet tall. Nonrealistic sets may make people appear dwarfed or engulfed by rocks, huge columns, or towering buildings. Except in stylized settings, asymmetrical or informal balance is preferable to symmetrical.

In any case, the central axis must not be forgotten. The central axis is the focal point in the design, usually the deepest point just off-center. The "halves" of the stage on either side of this axis should be balanced but not exactly alike. The director and the scenic designer must work closely together because the position, number, and importance of people on stage form an intrinsic part of the scenic pattern.

For example, a strong character, who is to exemplify spiritual leadership and be the center of interest in a scene, can be placed on a height to one side against tall columns, a high arched doorway, or long drapes, with the other characters, perhaps a large crowd, below. The emphasis of the strong character's influence in the minds of the audience will offset the size of the crowd, and the stage picture will balance.

The next three artistic values are those of line, mass, and shape. The use of lines alters the sense of proportion and affects the observer psychologically. Long vertical lines in draperies, columns, or costumes suggest dignity, elevation, hope, or spirituality and may be used for temples and solemn places. Horizontal lines are emotional levelers, bringing about calm, evenness, and tranquility. Diagonal lines may suggest a driving force, strife, uncertainty, or concentration. Curved lines may give the impression of ease, wealth, and expanse. Curves and angles, usually combined with strongly contrasted colors, give a sense of intense excitement. Crooked or jagged lines suggest chaos, shattered dreams, injustice, or pain.

Mass takes into consideration the concepts of bulk and weight, both of which are difficult to determine without testing under the lights. Dark-colored objects usually appear heavier than light objects. Shape often influences both the concept of mass and the psychological reaction to objects on the stage. Remember that shape is outline, but mass is three-dimensional. Shapes may be geometric or free-form, natural or stylized, realistic or impressionistic. A circle may seem infinite, eternal, or feminine; a square or cube may appear staid or unimaginative; a triangle may seem uplifting or securely founded; a diamond may seem calming and restful.

The Use of Color

Color is one of the most important elements of staging, for the various colors and their combinations produce very different emotional effects. The relationship between characters or scenes and the colors used may be factors in a play's success. On the stage, color effects are achieved by playing colored lights on the pigments used in sets, costumes, and stage furnishings. Because colored light makes very definite and often surprising changes in the appearance of pigment, it is necessary to experiment with both to get the desired result. Though this may be a long and involved process, it is fascinating to see what happens to fabrics and painted surfaces under different lighting.

Color almost always arouses an emotional response, which can help establish the mood and atmosphere for each scene as well as for the whole play. Sets and costumes may be color-coded for both identification and emotional response. Color coding means that the emotional tone of a scene may be identified by its color dominance; for example, a ''pink scene'' may be that of romantic fantasy; a ''red scene'' may be one of anger and passion. Characters, too, may be color-coded in stylized productions. Costume colors may identify romantic pairings, members of the same family, an army, an ideological group, or simply the personality types of the characters.

In pigment, the primary colors are red, yellow, and blue. The secondary colors are orange, green, and violet. When dealing with light, the primary colors are red, green, and blue. And the secondary colors when dealing with light are yellow, blue-green, and magenta.

Colors differ from each other in hue, value, and intensity. *Hues* are the various colors seen in the spectrum of a beam of light that passes through a prism. Hue indicates the purity of color—the redness, blueness, and so on. Black is the absence of light and therefore is the absence of color. White is the fusion of all the spectral colors. As light falls on different surfaces, the colors are absorbed or reflected. A surface that absorbs all colors and reflects none is black. A surface that absorbs all the hues except green appears to be green because it reflects only that color.

The *value* of a color—its lightness or darkness—is determined by the amount of black or white mixed with it. Tints (light or pastel colors) contain a good deal of white. Shades (dark or deep colors) contain more black. The light colors generally suggest youth, gaiety, and informality. Dark colors suggest dignity, seriousness, and repose. Each color is said to have a value scale, running from white at one end to black at the other. If a costume or prop is to be emphasized, it should be placed against a background of different value or hue. If it is to be made inconspicuous, it should be shown against a background of its own value or hue so that, in effect, it disappears.

Intensity is the brightness or dullness of a color, often referred to as saturation. You can usually intensify a color by casting on it light of the same color. Intensity will be lessened if you add gray to the pigment or use a light of a complementary color. The complementary color for any one of the primary colors is achieved by mixing together the other two primaries. Thus, violet is the complement of yellow; orange, of blue; and green, of red.

A color wheel is an invaluable aid in designing, for it shows the relationships of the various hues. The colors next to each other on the wheel are *analogous*. For example, yellow, yellow-orange, and orange are analogous, since they all contain yellow. When analogous colors are used, a dash of complementary color will give a sense of balance.

Since neither pigments nor materials for coloring lights are likely to have pure color, endless experiments are required to get a desired effect. You can experiment with the effect of light on pigment on actual sets as they are built. Run through the color cycle of night to day—black, pale gray, light yellow, light red, deep red, orange, and full daylight. Then reverse this cycle and run from daylight to darkness through the sunset hues, ending with the green-blue conventionally used to simulate moonlight on the stage. A point to remember: Green-blue and blue-green are not the same color. The second named color is the dominant hue. Therefore, green-blue is blue with a tinge of green in it, and blue-green is green with a tinge of blue in it.

Colors are referred to as warm or cool. Red, orange, and yellow are warm colors. You see them in sunlight and fire. Blue, green, and violet are cool colors. You see them in deep pools and in shadows under leafy trees. Warm hues seem to advance, or move forward in space, because they attract attention quickly. Cool colors appear to recede, or move back in space, because they are less noticeable. However, a stage background or set piece painted in warm colors looks smaller because it seems nearer, while one painted in cool colors looks larger. A warm-colored costume or object generally catches the eye at once and looks important. Objects or persons dressed in cool colors are generally less noticeable to the audience. The warm colors are stimulating and exciting, appropriate for highly emotional scenes and for comedies. Cool colors give a sense of tranquility and are usually the predominant colors in serious comedies and in tragedies. One should bear in mind that too much stress on warm colors can be very irritating and too many cool colors are depressing. The photographs from the Broadway productions *Barnum* and *Talley's Folly* on pages 311 and 312 show the effects of warm and cool colors in scenic design.

The psychological effect of color has been made the subject of interesting experimentation. It is an accepted fact that different hues of various intensity exert a definite psychological influence and produce emotional responses. However, authorities do not agree on the exact nature of the effects on different people. On the stage, certain traditions are accepted based on known reactions to color. Their use is an important means of getting satisfactory empathetic responses in play production.

The following emotional values have been given to colors. These color meanings are useful in stage design.

blue—calm, cold, formal, spiritual, pure, truthful, depressing

orange—exhilarating, cheerful, lively

red—aggressive, passionate, bloody, angry

yellow—cheerful, happy, youthful, cowardly

pink—fanciful, romantic

green—youthful, eternal, reborn, jealous

soft green—restful, soothing

purple—mournful, mystic, regal

gray—neutral, depressing, negative, somber

brown—earthy, common, poverty-stricken

black—melancholic, tragic, gloomy, deathlike

white—truthful, pure, chaste, innocent, peaceful

In any stage set, there should be a controlling color scheme that carries out the predominant mood and atmosphere of the production. The most effective color schemes are those that give a single impression, although other colors are often used for contrast.

Other Aspects of Design

Variety through contrast and subordination is necessary if a design is to be interesting. Too often high school stage settings seem to have every scenic element emphasized in equal strength and dominance. This is not to say that a single motif carried through an entire scene of a production will not effectively underscore the unity and harmony of design. The key word in good design is simplicity. Cluttered sets, "busy" walls, or too many colors are not found in artistic stage sets.

CONSTRUCTING THE SET

The most common sets involve draperies, flats, or drops. The flat is the basic unit of construction for box sets, screens, prisms, and cut-down scenery. Since the majority of plays require an interior set, you should learn the procedures in flat building, assembling, and painting.

The most satisfactory height for flats to be used on the high school stage is 12 feet, although 10-, 14-, and 16-foot flats are not uncommon. Large stages with high prosceniums may accommodate flats up to 24 feet high. There are two different approaches, each having definite advantages and disadvantages, in determining the width of flats. One system includes the following as a basic number of flats:

PLAIN FLATS		SPECIAL FLATS	
Width	Number Needed	Type	Number Needed
1 ft	2–4	Door flats, 5–6 ft	2–3
1½ ft	2	Window-bookcase	
2 ft	2–4	flats, 5–6 ft	2
3 ft	6–8	Fireplace flat (optional), 5–6 ft	1
4 ft	6–8	Arch flat (booked), 8 ft	1
5 or 6 ft	6–8		
	24–34	French door– sliding door (booked), 8 ft	1
			7–8

This system requires a total of thirty to forty flats, depending upon the size of the stage. One of the advantages of this system is that you would have matching flats for alcoves, bay windows, periaktoi, and columns. Another advantage is that it is easier to plan wall dimensions and designate flats accordingly. However, care must be taken that the set does not turn out nearly symmetrical.

The 5'9" width is an arbitrary traditional figure, which does not normally concern high school groups. Years ago, professional scenery did not exceed 5'9" because that was the maximum width that could go through the doors of the old railway baggage cars. Also, it was the maximum width a flat could be made from a standard 72-inch width of muslin.

The second system consists of twenty plain flats starting with a 12-inch flat. Each successive flat increases the width by 3 inches: 12, 15, 18, and so on, up to 72 inches. Since there are no two flats exactly the same width, variety in the shape of the set is reasonably assured. Proponents of this system claim that the audience will not notice a 3-inch difference when flats are used for an alcove or a bay window. There are many times, however, when flats are to be matched. Therefore, if this system is followed, it is wise to pair some flats. The special flats for this system are the same as those in the first system described.

Construction of a Flat

The materials needed to build a flat consist of lumber, fabric, hardware, rope, and glue. The best kind of wood for stiles (the frame of the flat) is 1" × 3" white pine because of its workability and light weight. The grade of the lumber should

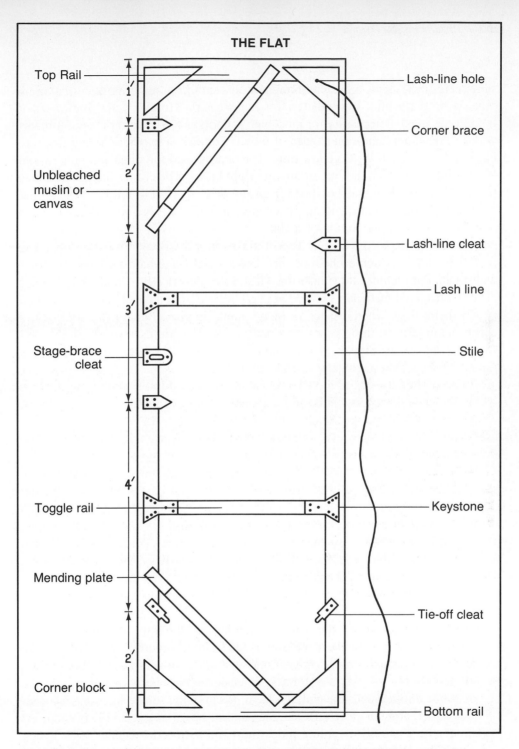

THE FLAT

Top Rail

Lash-line hole

Corner brace

1′

Unbleached muslin or canvas

2′

Lash-line cleat

Lash line

3′

Stage-brace cleat

Stile

4′

Toggle rail

Keystone

Mending plate

2′

Tie-off cleat

Corner block

Bottom rail

This diagram shows a flat 12 feet high and 4 feet wide with all hardware and plywood set in ³/₄ inch from all edges.

be screen stock, clear, or #1. Although the cost of this grade of lumber may seem high, a properly built flat will last for many years. However, the high cost of lumber has made it necessary for most high schools to use lower grades of lumber, wider dimensions, and other types of wood. For example, today many flats are built of #2 grade, 1″ × 4″ yellow pine. The boards used for stiles and rails should be absolutely straight and free of any but tight knots. The corner braces are made from 1″ × 2″ stock or may be ripped from any piece of 1″ × 4″ lumber. The corner blocks, keystones, and mending plates are cut from ¼″ plywood. Refer to page 303 for a detailed illustration of a flat.

The best fabric is canvas, but its cost makes it prohibitive to most groups. The next best choice is unbleached muslin. The special stage hardware needed for a well-made flat includes three lash-line cleats, two tie-off cleats, and a stage-brace cleat. Corrugated fasteners are used at every joint. Clout nails (1¼″ soft nails that clinch themselves when a piece of heavy metal is placed under the stile or rail before hammering), three-penny box nails, or screws are used to attach the plywood to the frame. Staples or tacks and glue are used to fasten the cloth to the finished frame. Although gelatine flake glue, which must be cooked in a glue pot or double boiler, has been the traditional stage glue, diluted vinyl glue adheres nearly as well, is easier to use, and does not set up as rapidly.

The first step in the construction of a flat is framing. The most common joint used is the butt joint. However, mitre joints are better, since they are stronger and do not chip or split as easily. When using butt joints, the top and bottom rails are cut the exact width the finished flat is to be. This allows the flat to slide without splitting the stiles. This also means that the boards used for the stiles must be cut the desired height of the flat less the width of two rails. Bear in mind that common names for lumber sizes do not reflect actual width and thickness. For example, 1″ × 3″ lumber is always less than 1 inch by 3 inches. It is ¾ inch by 2⅝ inches or less. Check exact lumber sizes with the lumber yard. Always measure carefully. Then check your measurements again before and after cutting. An old rule of thumb is "measure twice; cut once." A board sawed too short can never be used.

After the top and bottom rails and two stiles are cut, the frame is assembled. The most important tool for scenery building is the framing square. Unless you have a template, an adjustable framework serving as a mold, or can nail two boards at a 90° angle to serve as a square, framing is easier when one person can hold the square while another does the nailing. Then, keeping the square in place, a corner block is nailed on with eleven nails in the pattern shown on page 313. If you use a butt joint, the grain of the corner block must run across the joint.

Remember: Whenever you attach anything to the back of a flat, it must be set back ¾ inch from the edge. A scrap piece of 1″ × 3″ wood will serve as a guide.

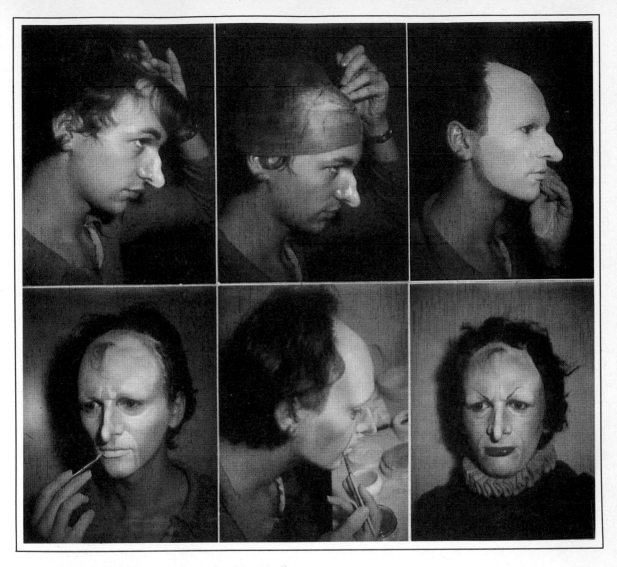

Nonrealistic makeup. An example of theatricalism.

Top left: Soaping out the front hair. Nose built up with nose putty.

Top center: Making outline of bald area on nylon stocking, which will cover soaped-out hair.

Top right: Applying the foundation with a sponge. Eyebrows have been blocked out.

Bottom left: Modeling the face with highlights.

Bottom center: Applying shadows.

Bottom right: Completed makeup, with painted eyebrows, rouge, and full lower lip. Makeup by student Lee Austin.

Makeup on pages 305 and 306 from Richard Corson's Stage Makeup, *sixth edition, published by Prentice-Hall, Inc., 1981. Reprinted by permission of the author.*

Realistic and nonrealistic makeup.

Top left: Medieval lady. Inspired by a fifteenth-century painting. Eyebrows and front hair soaped out. Makeup by student Dianne Hillstrom.

Top center: Leopard makeup for children's play. Entire makeup applied with cake makeup, using sponge and brushes. Makeup by student Dianne Harris.

Top right: Woman of Samoa. Shape of the face changed by highlighting cheekbones and shadowing jawbone and chin. Makeup by student Dianne Harris.

Bottom left: Portrait of a sixteenth-century lady. Inspired by a painting by Leonardo da Vinci. Creme makeup used for foundation, highlights, shadows, and rouge. Makeup by student Gaye Bowan.

Bottom center: Stylized makeup based on an Asian mask. Makeup by student Lee Austin.

Bottom right: Portrait of a lady. Inspired by a painting by Chardin. Creme makeup used for foundation, highlights, shadows, and rouge. Makeup by student Ruth Salisbury.

The Kabuki drama of Japan came into being in the sixteenth century and remains popular in Japan today. Only men perform in Kabuki drama. The actors begin acting in Kabuki drama as children and continue to act in historical and domestic plays and dance dramas until they are in their seventies.

The Crucifer of Blood *(a Sherlock Holmes mystery) by Paul Giovanni used striking special lighting effects to pull the audience into the supernatural atmosphere of the play. Top left: The scene is Pondicherry Lodge late at night. Light streaming through the latticed window creates an eerie mood. Top right: The scene is the River Thames. A smoke machine and overhead lighting create the dense fog expected on the Thames late at night. Bottom: Light radiating upward casts a golden glow, making the actors stand out in the darkness.*

Disegno di Zama. Moglie del gran Mogol Pᵃ Donna non eseguito N. 53.

Above: Costume for Zama, wife of the Grand Mogul, for Tamas-Kouli-Kan, 1772, at the Royal Theater, Turin, Italy. At right: Costume for Prince of Turin for Theodolinda, *1789, at the Royal Theater, Turin, Italy. The dominant colors in both costumes are red, orange, and yellow. Such warm colors usually arouse cheerful, passionate, and lively feelings in audiences.*

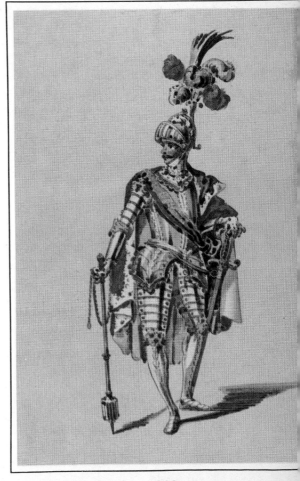

These are three different stages of a costume designer's creative process. Top left: A rough sketch showing important details of the costume. Top right: A finished sketch that also shows important costume features—the bodice and hem design. Bottom: A finished watercolor showing the complete costume as well as the type of character intended to wear the costume.

Color is one of the most important elements of staging, for various colors and their combinations produce very different emotions. The color schemes of the Barnum and Talley's Folly sets found on this page and on the next page show the contrasting moods created by different color combinations. Above: Barnum set as it appears in the scale model. The pastel colors suggest youth, gaiety, and informality, all of which are appropriate to a play built around a circus atmosphere. Below: The finished Barnum set. The vivid reds, oranges, and yellows of the costumes blend perfectly with the softness of the set's color scheme.

Above: The Talley's Folly *set—early evening. The dominant blue and soft greens convey a calm and spiritual atmosphere, while the browns project an earthy quality. At the start of the play, Matt is trying to woo Sally Talley, who remains aloof to him. Below: As Matt begins to win Sally over, the atmosphere of the play changes to romantic fancy, and the lighting changes from cool blue to warm pink.*

This setting-back allows two flats to be joined at a right angle without a crack appearing between the flats. Place a corner block at each corner in the same manner.

Next put in one or two toggle rails (bars). Toggle rails should be set at the same height so that keeper hooks may hold a stiffener board when the set is erected. Usually one toggle is sufficient for 8 × 10 foot flats, but for flats 12 feet and taller, use two toggles. The toggles should be cut the width of the flat less the width of the two stiles. Do not measure the toggle by the space between the stiles. If you have to, force the stiles in or out as necessary so that the total width is exactly the same as the top and bottom rails. Nail in the corrugators, and cover the joint with the keystones.

You can now install the corner braces. Notice that both are on the left side of the flat. If they were on opposite corners, the flat would torque (twist) diagonally. Corner braces need not be exact but are approximately the length of a rail and should extend from slightly past the midpoint of the rail to a point on the stile. A 40–60° angle is created if the corner braces are placed properly. Use corrugators and mending plates to secure the joint, and your flat is fully framed. Mending plates are 2 × 5 inch pieces of ¼″ plywood cut lengthwise with the grain.

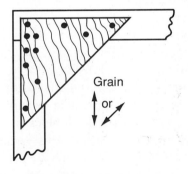

Corner block

The hardware is screwed on as indicated in the drawing of the flat on page 303. All measurements for the hardware can be approximated except for the tie-off cleats, which must be exactly 2 feet from the floor to facilitate lashing.

Flameproof the frame by washing the frame in a solution of 2 pounds of borax, 2 pounds of sal ammoniac, and 2 gallons of water. The flat may then be turned face side up and covered with muslin. The muslin should overlap all sides unless there is a finished edge, which may be placed ¼ inch in from the outer edge of one stile. Staples or tacks are spaced every 4 inches, ¼ inch from the inner edge of the stile. Fold the muslin back over the staples, and spread glue on the stile. As soon as the glue is applied, fold the cloth back down on the glue and smooth the cloth down with a wood block. Carefully stretch the muslin across the frame, allowing it to "belly" to the floor in the center. Be especially careful at the corners. There will be extra material because of the bellying of the cloth. Be sure the fabric does not pull or wrinkle. Repeat the stapling-gluing process until both stiles and the top and bottom rails are glued. Do not place any glue on the toggles or corner braces. Now staple ½ inch in from the outer edge of the frame around all four sides. The cloth can be flameproofed with the same formula that was used on the frame.

You are now ready to *size*—to paint on a glue-water mixture that seals the pores, provides a good painting surface, and stretches the muslin like an artist's canvas. The easiest sizing to use is made from a commercial cold-water size to which a little whiting has been added. Some brands of sizing need a little more water than the directions on the box call for. Your fingers should just tend to stick together when the sizing is properly thinned. After the sized muslin dries, use a razor knife to trim the selvage (waste) off ¼ inch from the outer edge of the stiles and rails. Do not trim the cloth flush with the outside edge of the flat or the cloth will be pulled loose by the handling of the flat.

All that remains to be done is to put a length of ¼-inch rope through the hole drilled in the upper right corner block, knot the end, and pull back tightly. Cut the rope 6 inches longer than the flat.

ERECTING THE SET

Flats may either be lashed or hinged together. If you plan to hinge all future scenery, every hinge should be matched, using loose pin hinges. Tight pin hinges are good only if the hinges are to be removed after the production. If only one set is required for the play and if it is permissable to nail into the stage floor, it is usually advisable to *floor block*—tack a small block of wood to the floor on both sides or each union where two flats meet. This keeps the walls straight and strengthens them. Stop cleats or stop blocks may be placed on the back of flats to prevent one flat from being pushed back of the other at sharp angle junctions. Walls that shake and rattle when a door is slammed have been identified with amateur theater far too often. Proper bracing will eliminate nearly all such distractions.

Adjustable stage braces provide support for the individual flat. One brace is used for each flat except door flats and occasionally window flats, which need two braces. The hook of the brace is inserted upside down and turned over firmly against the stile as shown on page 315. It is very important that the brace be correctly installed. If it is not, a hole in the muslin and a wobbly flat will be the price paid by a careless grip. The brace may be anchored to the floor by stage screws or a floor plate. If stage screws can be used, drill a hole before inserting the screw. If the wood is reasonably close-grained, the same hole may be used over

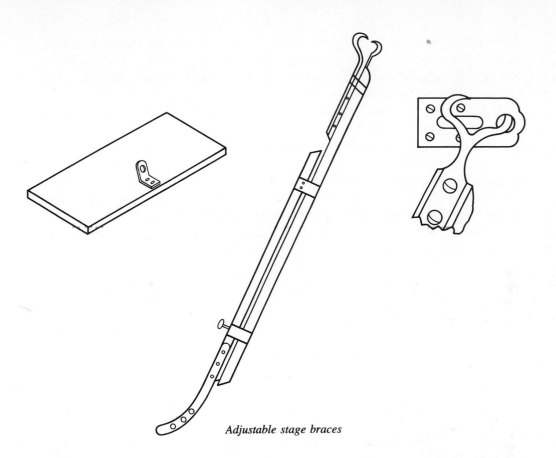

Adjustable stage braces

and over again for many years. (The dust from the stage will "fill" the hole sufficiently to secure the brace time after time.) If holes cannot be drilled in the floor, a wood block may be lightly tacked to the floor and the stage screw anchored into the block. Stage braces can be nailed directly to the floor. However, this is seldom satisfactory, since it does far more damage than either of the other methods described.

When there are restrictions against the use of any nails or screws in the floor or when the wood is too soft to hold a stage screw, there is an easy solution, which may be the best answer in almost all situations—the floor plate as shown above. A floor plate is simply a piece of plywood having a nonslip rubber pad on its under side and a special hardware adapter, which any school shop can make, bolted to the brace. Stage weights or concrete blocks are placed on top of the floor plate to hold it in place. However, a piece of 2″ lumber will work satisfactorily if there is not enough time to make floor plates.

Another type of bracing is the jack such as the one shown on page 276. A jack is a triangular wooden brace hinged to fold out of the way or even placed on wheels to allow large units to be moved more easily. Jacks are often used with set pieces and ground rows. Similar in function to the jack is the foot iron. The foot iron is an L-shaped piece of strap iron attached to the back of the flat and anchored to the floor with a stage screw. Foot irons are used mostly when there is insufficient space for jacks or braces.

Another means of strengthening walls is to use S or keeper hooks. Wherever there are two or more flats in a straight line, these handy pieces of hardware can be hooked over the top and toggle rails of each flat and a stiffener board dropped into the notch, making that entire wall section one "solid" unit. Some technicians prefer hinged stiffeners, but keeper hooks are convenient, quick, and effective.

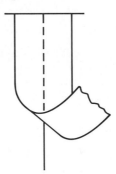

Dutchman

Once the set is assembled, apply the dutchman. A dutchman is a 4 to 5 inch strip of muslin used to cover the cracks between flats. A dutchman is never used on a set that is to be shifted except on booked flats or screens. Depending on whether the flats were painted before setup or are to be painted after being erected, the dutchman may be dipped in either scenic paint or sizing, placed over the crack, and brushed down smoothly. If flats are perfectly matched, a strip of masking tape can sometimes be substituted for the dutchman.

PAINTING SCENERY

Painting the set is certainly one of the important steps in the completion of a set, but it should not be the chore it often seems to be. One of the problems faced by amateur theater is the handling of scenic paints and glue. It takes only one sour batch of scenery paint to strain the relationships between the drama department and the rest of the school.

There are four approaches that may be taken. The first is to mix dry scenic paint according to the old procedures: mix the dry pigments thoroughly, add water (always add water to pigments), and stir. Add the binder, melted glue sizing, to this mixture until it feels slick when rubbed between the fingers. Test the color and consistency, remembering that scenic paint will dry lighter than it appears while wet. One of the problems associated with scenic paint is the preparation of the heated glue. Another is that scenic paint tends to bleed through new paint, and it is often necessary to wash old flats before applying a new coat of paint.

A second method uses one of the polyvinyl glues now on the market. There are polyvinyl liquid glues that require no cooking, and there are polyvinyl alcohol resins that must be cooked, but once prepared, can be stored indefinitely without decomposing. Check with paint manufacturers for new developments in this area.

A third choice is the use of casein or acrylic paints. These paints are made ready to use simply by adding water, but their cost is several times that of dry color and fewer colors are available. Casein is more water-repellent than dry color and can be used for scenery placed out-of-doors or in damp locations.

Latex paint can also be used. Its advantages and disadvantages are nearly equal. Latex paint is the most convenient when shop space is limited or only a small amount of scenery is to be painted. By shopping around, it is possible to buy fairly economical latex paint, which can be diluted considerably for stage use.

The advantages of latex, though few, are practical for many schools: it is readily available almost anywhere; it covers well and will not bleed through; it can be bought in basic tints, and with universal tinting colors, the spectral range is possible; and you can have latex paints mixed to order at any good paint or hardware store. On the other hand, it is expensive to paint with latex. If the paint is applied too heavily, the muslin eventually "holds" so much that the fabric-life is shortened. Universal tinting colors are very expensive in the deep tones. And when tinting colors are used at nearly full strength for special touches and accents, a dryer must be used or color rub-off is a problem.

Paint should be applied in random strokes or in figure eights. The base coat is usually better if uneven rather than a smooth, worked-out finish, which is "flat" and emphasizes all the flaws in the set. After the base coat has been applied, the set should be highlighted and shadowed and then textured. The texturing process is the most important in securing a good paint job. The texture coat covers flaws, dutchman, patches, and so on, so that the audience is not even aware such flaws exist.

Spattering, as shown on page 318, is the most common method of texturing. Use at least two colors, one a shade darker and the other a tint lighter than the base color. The complementary color may also be used to blend and harmonize the colors in the set. Dip a 4-inch brush into the paint and wipe it "dry" on the side of the pail. Stand about 6 feet from the set and strike the handle of the brush against the palm of the other hand, causing drops of paint to spatter the flats. This is a

Spattering   *Scumbling*

difficult technique to master, so practice on an old flat first. The dark spattering coat should normally be heavier at the top of the walls to make them appear shadowed.

Scumbling, as shown above, is a second method of texturing. A rag or a rolled-up piece of frayed burlap dipped in paint is rolled over the walls to make them look like rough plaster. Some scenic painters use this same term to describe a texturing technique using two brushes, each dipped in a different color; the painter brushes first with one color and then cross-strokes with the other.

Stippling uses a sponge, a crumpled rag, or the tips of a dry brush to gently touch the flat, leaving clusters of paint drops. The painting tool is constantly turned to avoid establishing a set pattern.

Featherdusting, as shown on the next page, is another popular and quick texturing technique. A featherduster is dipped into the paint, shaken off, and gently pressed against the surface that is to be textured. By turning the handle slightly, a different pattern appears each time the duster is applied. Featherdusting is especially good for foliage effects.

Dry brushing, as shown on the next page, may be used for wall texturing or for simulating wood grain. For walls, use a dry brush, stroke in one direction with a light color, and repeat with a dark color. For a woodgrain effect, use long, straight strokes with a dark color and then repeat the process with a lighter color.

Highlights and shadows, shown on the next page, are essential if the scenery is to be convincing and alive. Before painting these realistic dimensional touches, the painter must consider the primary light source, that is, the direction and cause of the predominant light. Moldings, paneling, wainscoting, shingles, siding, bricks, and rocks must be carefully painted, even when they are built in three dimensions. Stage lights often wash out natural shadows, making everything appear flat.

Profile scenery and drops, shown on page 277, are real challenges to stage painters because such scenery almost always represents some three-dimensional object or a perspective scene. Gridding is the process used to make the enlarging

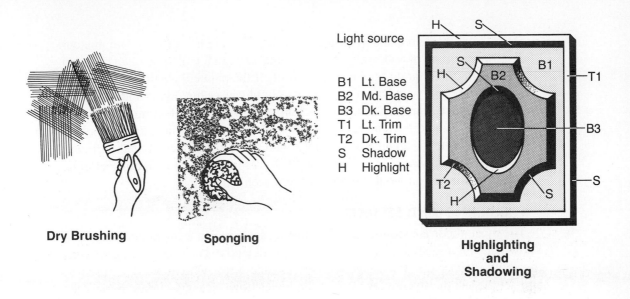

Dry Brushing   **Sponging**

Light source

B1 Lt. Base
B2 Md. Base
B3 Dk. Base
T1 Lt. Trim
T2 Dk. Trim
S Shadow
H Highlight

**Highlighting
and
Shadowing**

from a sketch to a drop. The drop is marked off into 1- or 2-foot squares and the sketch scaled proportionately as shown below. Then the drawing is transferred to the drop section by section.

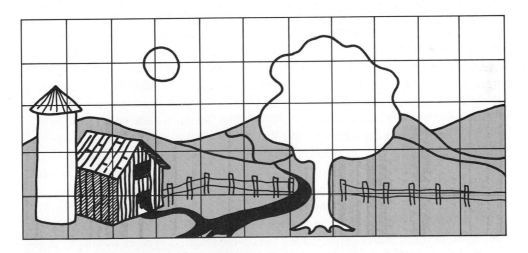

Transferring a backdrop design from the sketch to the drop through the use of a scaled grid

One of the most frequent examples of careless painting seen on the amateur stage is the painting of rock walls. Strange "masses" randomly placed in an equal amount of gray mortar do not look like a wall. If the painters would look at a real wall—how the rocks are laid in mortar, how light causes highlights and shadows, and how the texture and color of the rock give the viewer the feeling of bulk and weight—they would have a practical lesson in mass, line, color, and shape.

Scenery painting is an art that develops with time, experience, and experimentation. Watch what happens to colors and textures under various lighting effects, and consider how you would represent them scenically.

SHIFTING AND SETTING

The most important requirement for shifting scenery is a well-trained crew who know what their job is and how to get it done efficiently. The stage manager "runs the show" backstage. Backstage workers include grips, who move flats, prisms, and set pieces; the flycrew, who raise the lower flown scenery and draperies; the prop crew, who check properties in and out as they are set or struck; and the set dressers, who are responsible for setting and striking the finishing touches on a set, such as pictures, scarves, flowers, and so on.

Changing Scenery

There are many ways to change scenery, including those discussed earlier: unit, permanent, prism, and screen sets. A "booked" set may be dropped inside an existing set. Screens can also be used for a set within a set. Drops are the most frequently used type of flown scenery. Ground rows are usually brought in to mask the junction where drop meets floor, and wings or false prosceniums are used to mask the sides of the stage. Since most designers use wings sparingly, the masking of the wing areas is a real problem to the designer—the solution to which is often an even greater challenge to the crew. Masking the wings is a special problem associated with all exterior sets and now quite regularly with the musical play. Once again, a black cyclorama can help simplify the problems. Even a full sky cyc will close off the audience's view of the backstage areas. But a sky cyc may, in turn, make entrances and exits difficult.

Wagon sets are another means of executing scene changes. A set is placed on a wheeled platform, which can be rolled out on the stage. A type of wagon arrangement that often works quite well is the jackknife. The jackknife wagon, shown on page 321, is stored perpendicular to the curtain line on the side of the stage, usually behind the tormentor or false proscenium, and is pivoted out when needed. A second wall may be attached back-to-back to the wagon, making two sets possible for each wagon. Wagons require storage space in the wings, which may be lacking, but they are often the best solution when fly space is not available.

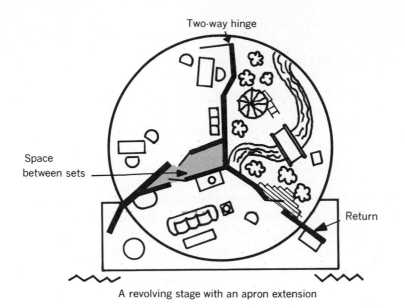

A revolving stage with an apron extension

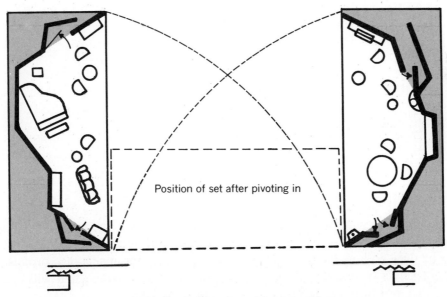

Jackknife staging using a false proscenium

Two ways of changing complete sets

Some directors have complained that the elevation of the wagon destroys the illusion they desire and eliminates the use of the apron unless the actor steps down from the wagon. This problem may be corrected in one of two ways. First, you may treat the wagon as a natural elevation, like a hallway above a sunken living room, or as a porch, with the apron as the lawn. The second method takes more work, but the results are worth it. The apron floor is built up with platforms that are flush with the front edge of the wagon. The apron is treated as an extension of the wagon set. Hinged returns may be added to the side walls of the set to frame the apron acting area.

A revolving stage may be used if you have the budget, equipment, time, and skill. As many as three sets may be placed on a revolving platform. However, revolving stages are expensive to build and take special mechanical equipment to rotate smoothly. It is possible to build stages that can be moved manually. If this is to be done, however, it would probably be simpler and certainly more economical

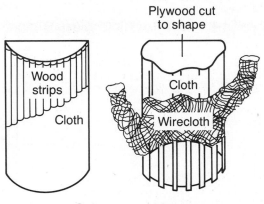

Columns-set pieces

to bolt wagons together to make a "revolving square." Such an arrangement would allow four scenes to be placed on the platform. Of course, once a set is out of view of the audience, it may be redressed for a new setting.

Special Set Pieces

Set pieces are scenery units that may be carried or rolled on the stage, such as benches, lamp posts, rocks, and trees. Before designing and building set pieces, it must be decided how the unit will be used—is it only for appearance or must it support weight or operate? Those that operate, such as windows that will open, lamps that will turn on, or a tree that will allow an actor to sit on a branch, are called practical or practical-usable. Because theater is illusion and time and expenses are always to be considered, few set pieces are built to be practical unless

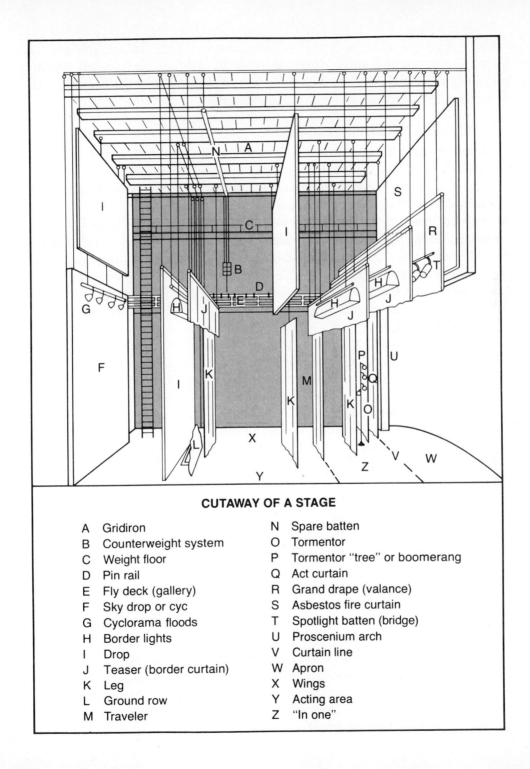

CUTAWAY OF A STAGE

A	Gridiron	N	Spare batten
B	Counterweight system	O	Tormentor
C	Weight floor	P	Tormentor "tree" or boomerang
D	Pin rail	Q	Act curtain
E	Fly deck (gallery)	R	Grand drape (valance)
F	Sky drop or cyc	S	Asbestos fire curtain
G	Cyclorama floods	T	Spotlight batten (bridge)
H	Border lights	U	Proscenium arch
I	Drop	V	Curtain line
J	Teaser (border curtain)	W	Apron
K	Leg	X	Wings
L	Ground row	Y	Acting area
M	Traveler	Z	"In one"

required to be so by the play. Columns (shown on page 322), rocks, and trees may be plastic, that is, three-dimensional, or simply two-dimensional cut-outs. Three-dimensional pieces allow for more light and shadow effects, but cut-outs may better convey stylization and the feeling of illusion.

COMMON SCENERY PROBLEMS

One of the problems encountered on most stages is that of insufficient space, particularly if the stage is shallow or lacks wing space. Many plays and most musical plays call for several sets and many changes. Sometimes the stage may be extended out into the pit area or built out over the front center seats. A runway may be built out from the center or may enclose the pit and, at the same time, the orchestra. Acting areas can often be added to the sides of the apron with platforms. Inadequate fly space may force the use of *trip* drops—doubled up for storage—or the use of short drops that can be raised as high as possible and concealed with low-hung teasers. It may even be necessary, as in arena staging, to make changes in full view of the audience. In some instances, the "invisible" stage hand may be your only recourse.

Your stage opening may be too large to make a standard set look its best. Many auditoriums have prosceniums as wide as 40 feet, yet most sets average 28 to 32 feet in width. The grand drape can often be lowered to change the height of the opening. A false beam or ceiling can replace the first teaser. A false proscenium can decrease both height and width, as can teasers and tormentors.

Masking the side areas can be a serious problem in musical plays and exterior sets. A false proscenium or drops with tabs similar to a false proscenium work reasonably well. Screens, wings, hanging banners, and backs of double-walled wagons may also work. Of course, a sky cyc can mask the wings quite well.

The acting surface in high school auditoriums often presents difficulties, for stage and platform floors may be rough, slick, or noisy. A canvas floor cloth, especially one that is reversible—brown on one side and green on the other—covers the stage floor and replaces carpeting or "grass." Carpets are fine if they lie flat or can be tacked down. Carpets deaden sound and provide a realistic appearance to a room that otherwise may seem unnatural to the audience, who can see the stage floor. Even wagons and parallels should be padded to lessen noise.

THINGS TO REMEMBER

There are certain bits of information that come in handy to stage designers and crews. Among these are the common lumber measurements and nail sizes. These should be posted in the shop. Since muslin draws up when sized, the ends of drops should be tapered by cutting the fabric on a 1-foot diagonal from top to bottom on each end. Another method requires using stretchers. These are boards installed vertically before sizing. The ends of the drops are stapled to the stretchers until all painting is completed. This will keep the drops from pulling and wrinkling.

It is not necessary to accept a set that shakes every time a door closes. Determine what bracing is needed and use it. Remember that standard dimensions apply to most common scenic props: chair seats are 16 inches from the floor; table and desk tops are 30 inches from the floor; chests are usually about 16 inches deep; stair treads are 10 to 12 inches deep and the risers are 6 to 7 inches high; finished door openings are 6 feet 8 inches high. Plywood comes in sheets 4′ × 8′ and may be ³⁄₁₆, ¼, ³⁄₈, ½, ⅝, or ¾ inch thick. Doorknobs and light switches also have standardized heights.

Use different levels, ramps, and stairs as much as possible for interest and variety. Stage doors normally open offstage-upstage except in mysteries when it is important that a character be concealed. Fireplaces are more usable on side walls than rear walls. Watch the location of mirrors so that they do not reflect lights or backstage areas into the audience's eyes.

Although most playbooks have a floor plan illustrated in the back, it is often foolish for schools to copy such a set. Most high schools do not have the time, budget, equipment, or space to build a Broadway set. The essential entrances, furniture, and props must be provided, but the creation of a scenic design should not be stifled by another designer's concept. If the audience spends much time

Robert Bolt's A Man for All Seasons *was planned for a one-set staging. Panel changes and carry-on props "shift" the scenes. The actors are Lester Rawlins, Olga Bellin, Paul Scofield, Sarah Burton, Albert Dekker, and George Rose (above).*

looking at the set and not at the actors, it is a poor design no matter how elaborate or attractive it may seem. Researching for a play is part of the fun and part of the learning; the library is usually the designer's best friend.

A SUMMARY STATEMENT

The student of drama should recognize that scenery is an integral part of modern play production but that scenic design has developed as a complement to the play and may lose its impact if looked upon as an end in itself. If scenery swallows up the performer, the costume, the makeup, or the acting; if the scenery is in poor taste or not aesthetically satisfying; if the mood of the play is lost by inappropriate surroundings; or if the set becomes a showpiece for a talented designer or exuberant art students, the purposes and intents of the playwright and director become distorted and meaningless.

Good scenery should add to and never detract from the overall merit of a production. Much of the scenery found in high school productions is inexcusably poor and ineffective. A little imagination, some inexpensive materials and equipment, and the enthusiasm and talents of high school students can easily bring to the audience a setting that enhances the total production by making it an "everything-seemed-to-go-together" performance.

In order to accomplish this goal, high school directors, designers, and production committees should work together to carefully select scenic elements, emphasizing those they wish to convey to the audience and minimizing or eliminating those that would not make a positive contribution to the play. It is often the frequently overlooked little things that may make a realistic set look complete—the right number and kind of pictures on the wall; the knick-knacks on the shelf; the flowers in the vases about the room; the choice of carpets, drapes, lamps, and furnishings; a flickering fire in the hearth; the shadow lines and texturing on the walls.

Conversely, it is usually the smallest number of elements with the greatest impact of identification and meaning that make a nonrealistic set the most satisfying—a lonely, twisted cedar makes one think of barren wastes; three lofty, graceful poplars may suggest an Italian formal garden; six towering pines may take the audience into the heart of the Black Forest; the knothole eyes and mouths of frightening Tree-Monsters may make us want to run from the magical forest of Oz.

Selectivity, simplicity, and consistency are the guide words of the stage designer. In addition, sets should be planned so that they may be set up and struck rapidly, carried easily, and packed away efficiently. Naturally they should be built firmly enough to stand steadily. They also should allow the actors to move easily and safely and to be seen effectively.

STAGE-SETTING PROJECTS

1. Select a play, study it carefully, decide upon style and type of scenery, and draw (a) a floor plan, (b) a simple perspective, and (c) an elevation.

2. Using your design, build a model set to scale.

3. Design a set for a fantasy, using a single motif or a one-color or two-color emphasis.

4. Design a set using ramps, platforms, staircases, and only a few simple set pieces.

5. Design a set for an arena production.

6. Design a thrust stage and facade for your own school stage for a Shakespearean play.

7. Work out a scene-shifting schedule, including crew needs, for a multiscene production.

8. Working in teams of two to four, build and paint a "practice" flat.

BIBLIOGRAPHY

Adix, Vern: *Theater Scenecraft,* Children's Theatre Press, Anchorage, Kentucky, 1956.

Buerki, Frederick A.: *Stagecraft for Nonprofessionals,* University of Wisconsin Press, Madison, 1955.

Cornberg, Sol, and Emanuel Gebauer: *A Stage Crew Handbook,* Harper & Row, New York, 1957.

Friederich, Williard, and John Fraser: *Scenery Design for the Amateur Stage,* Macmillan, New York, 1950.

Gillette, Arnold: *Stage Scenery: Its Construction and Rigging,* Harper & Row, New York, 1960.

Hake, Herbert: *Here's How: A Guide to Economy in Stagecraft,* French, New York, 1958.

Simonson, Lee: *The Stage Is Set,* Theatre Arts, New York, 1962.

CHAPTER TWELVE

Stage Lighting

Stage lighting is the most rapidly expanding phase of scenic art. It is taking the place of paint in many productions because white backgrounds can be instantly transformed by lighting in response to changes in mood, action, and location. In "total" theater, projections and motion-picture films are integral parts of the action. And in musical plays especially, dream sequences, dances, and tableaux are set apart by imaginatively designed lighting. Also, psychedelic effects combined with sound are affecting modern productions in varying ways.

There is no more intriguing phase of play production than working out truly effective lighting for different scenes, whether you have simple equipment or equipment that is the last word in flexibility and efficiency.

STAGE LIGHTING EFFECTS

Suppose, as the curtain opens, we look in on an antiquated English manor house. The room is dark except for a flickering glow from the fireplace. A dim figure appears in the archway, silhouetted against the diffused light of the entrance hall. The room instantly comes to life as the young woman presses the wall switch and the chandelier and the two sconces over the fireplace illuminate the right half of the stage. She presses another switch, and the lamp by the chair at stage left brightens the rest of the room. The actress swiftly crosses upstage to the high window and pulls the drapery cord. Immediately, the stage is flooded by bright sunlight reflected off the snow-covered terrain outside. She crosses down right to the fireplace and places two more logs on the dying fire. As she stirs up the coals, a reddish glow warms her young face. She turns, takes two steps toward the table, center, looks at her watch, and utters the first line of the play: "I *do* wish Martin would hurry. It's been nearly three hours since he called."

In a set such as this, lighting is used to highlight the area of action. Compare this setting for Death of a Salesman *with the one shown on page 279.*

The audience probably did not notice the room continue to brighten after the initial flash broke the darkness. It is unlikely, too, that they noticed the "sunlight" dimming slightly after the first rays had struck our heroine's face, nor would we expect them to question whether the fire continued to glow as brightly after she turned from the mantel toward the middle of the room into an area of strong light to say that first line. And, most assuredly, the audience never asked: "I wonder what lighting equipment was used for that effect?" All this an audience accepts as the effective illusion of modern stage lighting.

In the days of tribal ritual and primitive dance, the only lighting available was the natural light of the sun or moon and the artificial light provided by the campfire and torch. For hundreds of years, plays were performed almost exclusively in the daytime out-of-doors or in buildings open to the sky. The use of many candles and torches eventually made it possible to present plays in a completely enclosed structure. But it was not until gaslight replaced candles in 1803 that artificial light aroused much interest. By the 1820s Thomas Drummond, an Englishman, had developed one of the earliest spotlights, an oxyhydrogen flame directed against a piece of lime. Actors soon learned how to play in the "limelight."

However, with the greater use of artificial lighting came the increased danger of fire. The history of theater has been blackened by the ashen shells of once active playhouses. By the end of the nineteenth century electricity had revolutionized the lighting of the home and the stage. Today, we present well-lighted plays that may, with the proper equipment, be preset and computerized.

All students of drama—actors, directors, and crew—should understand the basic principles of light, its peculiarities, qualities, and effects on actor, audience, costumes, makeup, and pigments.

LIGHTING TERMINOLOGY

amperage: The strength of an electric current flowing through a wire.

arc or *carbon arc spotlight:* A very powerful spotlight with carbon rods as electrical conductors, used primarily as a long-distance follow spot.

boomerang (tree, tormentor tree): A polelike stand having horizontal arms (pipes) for hanging lighting instruments. A boomerang is usually located just upstage of the proscenium or tormentor.

border light or *borders:* A type of striplight hung from pipe battens above the stage.

breaker: An electrical device that cuts off the electric current when a circuit is overloaded. It may be reset once the problem is corrected.

bridge (x-ray): The first electrical pipe just upstage of the proscenium from which spotlights may be hung.

cable: Heavily insulated wire for joining instruments to electrical outlets or to a switchboard.

circuit: The complete path of an electrical current.

color frames: Metal holders that fit into a lighting instrument to keep a color filter in place.

connectors: Devices for joining cables to each other or for joining cables to instruments.

dimmer: An electrical device that controls the amount of current flowing into a lighting instrument, thus increasing or decreasing the intensity of the light.

ellipsoidal reflector spotlight: A highly efficient lighting instrument with a reflector shaped like an ellipsoid.

floodlight or *flood:* A high wattage (500 to 1,500 watts) lighting instrument with a metal shell open at one end, the inner surface of which is painted white, is polished metal, or has a mirror to reflect the nonfocused light.

floor pocket: A receptacle for stage plugs mounted in the floor.

follow spot: A long-range high-wattage (1,000 to 2,600 watts) lighting instrument capable of picking up or following a person moving on the stage, with a beam strong enough to stand out against normal stage lighting. These instruments may be either the carbon arc, quartz, or incandescent types.

footlights or *foots:* Striplights along the front of the apron that throw light up and back toward the acting area.

fresnel spot: A spotlight featuring a fresnel or stepped lens, which projects a clear, strong light with a soft edge.

fuse: A protective device set in an electric current and destroyed by the passage of excessive current.

gelatin and *glass roundels:* Transparent color media placed on lighting instruments to produce different colors.

kill: Command to turn a light off.

light cue sheet: The lighting technician's guide for all dimmer readings and settings at act or scene openings and all lighting changes.

light plot: Diagram showing the placing of the instruments and plugging system and where the beams from all the instruments fall. See page 332.

linnebach projector: A lantern for projecting images from a slide onto a backdrop from the rear of the backdrop.

load: The wattage of lights and electrical pieces of equipment supplied by one circuit; an overload will burn out a fuse or trip a breaker.

pin connector or slip pin connector: A special stage connector used for joining cables or instruments.

preset dimmer: A type of dimmer board that allows two or more lighting patterns to be set in advance.

quartz lamps: A new light bulb that has a quartz filament. It has a longer life and gives a much greater amount of illumination for the same wattage lamp than does an incandescent lamp.

splash (spill):   Light that strikes outside the intended area—as on the grand drape, proscenium, or upper walls.

spotlight or *spot:*   A metal-encased lighting instrument that can be focused, having a lens and a mirror that gives out a concentrated light and can be directed specifically. It is used to light acting areas. In wattage, it varies from 250 to 1,500.

stage plug: A special male connector consisting of a wood or fiber body and broad copper contact. Its use is declining.

striplights or *strips:*   Lamps arranged in metal troughs, usually with three or four circuits.

switchboard: The panel that holds the dimmers, switches, and fuses. Ideally, all stage circuits are united in this one board so that they may be controlled at one location. A board may have any number of circuits and/or dimmers. A portable switchboard is often the most satisfactory type for a school theater.

throw: The distance from a lighting instrument to the area to be lit.

tower: A platform on which lights may be hung.

twist lock connector: A type of stage connector that will not pull apart when inserted and twisted.

wash: To bathe walls in light.

wash out: The drain (absorption) of color by light, leaving the actor, costume, or scenery lifeless.

wattage: The measurement of electric power. All lighting instruments, lamps, dimmers, and fuses are given wattage ratings to denote their electrical capacities.

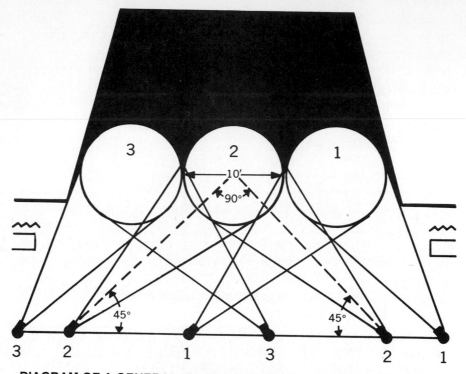

DIAGRAM OF A GENERAL LIGHTING PLAN FOR DOWNSTAGE AREAS

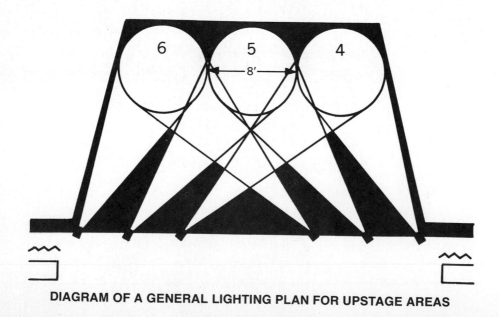

DIAGRAM OF A GENERAL LIGHTING PLAN FOR UPSTAGE AREAS

NECESSARY EQUIPMENT

The ideal lighting equipment for the school stage is that which is flexible, efficient, and economical. Of these, flexibility is the most important consideration in the selection of equipment and the primary factor to be considered when facing budgetary limitations. Flexibility is determined by (1) mobility—how easily the instrument may be moved about the auditorium according to the needs of various productions; (2) control—how easily the amount of light can be controlled, usually by a dimmer panel; and (3) multiple service—the capability of a lighting instrument to be used for area lights, border lights, cyclorama lights, and so on. The type of instrument that meets these three requisites most effectively is the versatile spotlight, which provides the best control of light distribution.

When determining the lighting equipment needed, you must consider the availability and number of dimmers, the size of the stage (especially the depth of the acting area as well as of the apron), the height of the theater ceiling or the distance to the balcony rail, the availability of mounting locations, and, of course, the budget. However, every high school should try to have the following minimum equipment.

A dramatic use of backlighting helps create a mysterious atmosphere in the Agatha Christie melodrama The Unexpected Guest, *presented by the Hartman Theater Company of Stamford, Connecticut.*

The light panel is the first equipment of importance. Its dimmer board allows the operator to choose which dimmer will control the brightness of the light of any given instrument. One of the best types suitable for the high school stage has plugs, connected to each outlet or instrument in the auditorium, that may be inserted into a "patchboard," much like a telephone switchboard.

The stage cable and connectors are most important to the safe conduction of electricity. The danger of overloads, shorts, and fires is very great on the stage, and proper means of completing an electrical circuit are often overlooked.

Common lighting instruments are as follows:

1. Ellipsoidal reflector spotlight of 500 to 1,000 watts, which provides the most important lighting. (These spotlights are mounted in the ceiling or on balcony rails.) Since these instruments normally operate in pairs, each pair lighting an area approximately 8 to 10 feet in diameter, six are needed for the normal set opening of 28 to 32 feet. But stages having 40-foot prosceniums should have eight ellipsoidals if the entire width is to be illuminated.

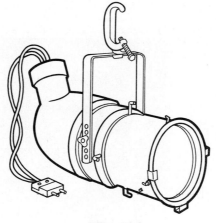

Ellipsoidal

2. Fresnels—On a pipe just behind the grand drape a minimum of eight to fourteen 500-watt fresnels should be located (250- to 400-watt baby spots may be substituted, although they are not as desirable).

3. Floodlights—Every stage needs at least two floodlights for special effects, such as sunlight and moonlight. If a cyclorama is to be lighted, more floods may be necessary. Some stage aprons are efficiently lighted by a special flood called the beam light. Three to four beam lights would be sufficient to cover the apron.

4. Border lights—Three to four 3-circuit border lights are necessary for general stage use and for scenic color blending.

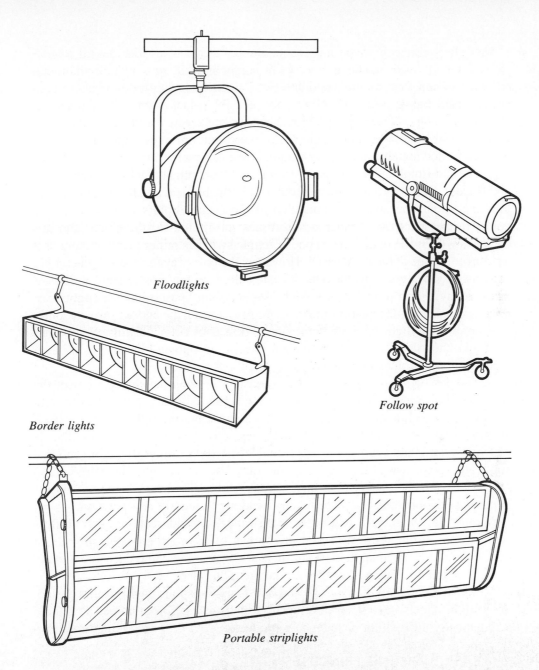

Floodlights

Follow spot

Border lights

Portable striplights

5. Follow spot—At least one follow spot is essential for every stage, although its use is rather limited in play production.

6. Portable striplights—These are preferable to permanently mounted footlights. These may be used as footlights, backing or entrance lighting, or cyclorama lighting. Again, three circuits are necessary.

Other desirable equipment includes additional ellipsoidal reflectors for mounting on the side walls of the auditorium or just behind the proscenium; additional fresnels for the first batten, including two 3-inch fresnels; the previously mentioned beam lights; a second follow spot; possibly black light units and special effects projectors. (These special effects instruments create the illusions of clouds, rain, flames, buildings, and scenic backgrounds but are quite expensive.)

Also needed are pipe clamps for hanging the instruments, color frames for each spotlight and flood, and color media (roundels for striplights; gelatin for the spots and floods). The best colors for the roundels in the borders and footlights are red, blue, and green because a combination of these three colors will make all the colors in the spectrum. Amber is sometimes substituted for the green, and this choice is wise if the light panel is one of toggle switches rather than dimmers or if a stronger overhead light is desired. However, the only way to produce green light is by using green color media. The delicate colors are the most preferred gelatins in use today. Flesh pinks, straws, ambers—especially bastard amber (light scarlet)—are some of the warm colors used. And special lavender, surprise pink, medium and daylight blue are some of the best cool color gelatins. Sometimes frost and chocolate are used for special effects, and green-blue makes a better night scene than blues or violets.

New types of lighting equipment are constantly being developed to meet the needs of the modern stage. One of the most revolutionary is the quartz-light equipment, which is initially expensive to purchase but more than pays for itself by providing a more efficient light at far less cost than incandescent bulbs. A 400-watt quartz light will more than double the light output of a conventional 500-watt fresnel, with four times the bulb life. The quartz light runs very hot, so new types of gels, which fade and warp less, have been developed. Another important advantage is that quartz lamps may be burned in any position.

Another development is that of the high-wattage incandescent or quartz follow spot, which, at one-third the initial investment of a carbon arc spot, provides a brilliant light nearly equal to most arc spots at ranges up to 150 feet, without many of the problems often associated with the arc equipment.

Although financially not feasible for most high schools, highly refined electronic light panels have been developed, which may be programmed to handle automatically all lighting changes in a production or series of productions.

BASIC LIGHTING PRINCIPLES

The most effective lighting takes into consideration the natural light sources on the set—the sun or moon, a window, a streetlight, lamps, chandeliers, fireplaces, televisions or radios, candles, lanterns. In order to avoid a pasteboard-figure effect, spotlights are usually operated in pairs, with warm colors coming from one

The most effective lighting takes into consideration the natural light sources on the set. In the musical review Ain't Misbehavin', *the lights frame the onstage band and add a lively background to a show with no scenery.*

side of the stage (the direction of the natural light) and cool colors from the opposite side (the direction of diffused or reflected light). Each spotlight is aimed in and down at a 45° angle toward the area to be lighted (see drawing on page 332). This results in the most dramatic effect of highlight and shadow. Always to be avoided is straight-on lighting from centrally located instruments, because it wipes out all form and depth. Observe people around you under varying light conditions to note the natural highlighting and shadowing that bring interest, variety, and dimension to the human face. It is these qualities that the lighting designer attempts to recreate.

The most important acting areas need to have stronger concentrations of light. Bringing a greater distribution (quantity) of light into a given acting area makes the actor playing in that area stand out in contrast to the other actors and the set. The technical director and the stage electricians may help shift the focus of attention back and forth by the smooth flow of light from one actor or area to another throughout the play.

Without doubt, lighting is the most important element in scenic design, for it affects the creation of mood and atmosphere. The exuberant nature of a musical play is heightened by the gaiety of a brightly illuminated stage. A mystery takes on a spine-tingling quality when the high walls and deep recesses of a deserted mansion are lost in the depths of shadow where undiscovered dangers may be lurking. An eerie fog, an iridescent liquid in a witch's cauldron, the ghostly whiteness of a full moon, the aura of intrigue and death in the shadowy alleys of the world of

Lighting affects the creation of mood and atmosphere. The exuberant nature of a bouncy musical, such as the Broadway production 42nd Street, *is emphasized by a brightly illuminated stage.*

counterespionage, or the light-hearted frivolity of the Mardi Gras—all of these may be created by the right distribution and brightness of light from carefully selected instruments. That is effective stage lighting.

As a general rule, tragedies and serious dramas emphasize cool colors, and comedies stress warm colors. However, the lighting designer should never allow actors to be lost in unintentional pockets of dark shadows. Nor should the lighting designer try to eliminate all shadows by generalized bright light. The result of this is one huge flat glow of light, which is the most common lighting error of the high school stage. This problem stems from the incorrect notion that lighting a set means turning all border and footlights on full. This garish amber-white light makes actors "dead" on the stage or makes them "disappear" into the set. Many of the most successful designers today use only spotlights and floods. Others add borders and foots for blending only. In any case, strong lights should be kept off the walls of a set. Most designers suggest keeping the upper walls in shadow.

Most lighting changes should be a gradual blending done by what is called a "cross-fade." This means simply that some lights are gradually "coming up" at the same time others are dimming down. The audience should not be consciously aware that a change is taking place. This means light changes should begin far enough in advance that the technician can accomplish the desired effects smoothly.

There are some general considerations to remember when working with stage lights. Brightly lighted scenes, especially of the type frequently found in musical plays, can cause changes in makeup and costumes. Strong amber can turn colorful fabrics into a drab brown; a strong red may wash the rouge out of the faces.

Night scenes are always difficult to light without having costumes and makeup turn black under a bluish light. When lighting scenes to be played in the "dark," it is always best to have some light even if no attempt is made to represent natural light sources. An unlighted stage is dead. Figures outlined against a moonlit window, a shaft of light through a window or skylight, a crack of light from under a door, or the glow of an old-fashioned street light may provide a realistic source for the stage light. However, if no other choice is left, a beam or two of colored light that is there solely for the reason that the actors must be seen may meet the requirements for light. The audience should never be left completely in the dark for more than a few seconds.

The effect of light on color is difficult to predict accurately because of the relationship between light and pigments and dyes, but there are some generalizations that may be made:

red light on red	=	red
red light on blue	=	violet
red light on green	=	gray

red light on yellow	=	orange
red light on purple	=	red
blue light on red	=	violet-black
blue light on blue	=	blue
blue light on green	=	green
blue light on yellow	=	green
blue light on orange	=	brown
amber light on red	=	brown
amber light on blue	=	greenish-orange
amber light on green	=	greenish-orange
amber light on violet	=	red
green light on red	=	black
green light on green	=	green
yellow light on blue	=	blue-green
yellow light on green	=	green
yellow light on violet	=	brown

Curtains, costumes, and furnishings are affected by light. The smooth, shiny fabrics reveal light and shadows. The heavy, coarse materials, no matter how inexpensive, absorb much light and often appear quite expensive to the audience; outing flannel may look like expensive velour. The important consideration is the brilliance of the color of the material and the color of the stage lighting for the scene in which the material is to be used. Patterns and prints cause many problems, as do several colors in the same costume. Lighting of period plays is always difficult, for the mixture of lace, silk, velvet, wigs, and makeup is a technician's nightmare.

SPECIAL LIGHTING EFFECTS

Lighting is probably the designer's most versatile source of special effects, accomplishing such feats as pinpointing a face in a crowd, changing the stage into a blazing inferno, "suspending animation" (as in the Soho Square scene of *My Fair Lady),* or creating the illusion of a silent movie by the use of a flicker wheel or strobe.

One of the most striking scenic-lighting combinations is that of using a scrim, or gauze drop. Lighting a scrim from the front makes it nearly opaque, and lighting it from behind makes it semitransparent. Scrims, properly lighted, may help create fog, mist, and dream scenes. Actors and cut-out scenery may be silhouetted against the scrim by back lighting. In the Broadway presentation of *The Sound of Music,* the designer elected to represent the Austrian Alps by an outline silhouette of mountains and trees. Maria was nearly imperceptible as she reclined on a

In the Yale Repertory production of August Strindberg's The Ghost Sonata, *the combined use of scrims and lighting create a ghostly, dreamlike scene.*

cut-out limb. Then both she and the lighting came to life with the song "The Sound of Music."

Painting or dyeing a scrim makes an impressive traverse curtain, which provides a fine background for short scenes, especially in musical plays. Such a painted scrim can also create the illusion of "passing through." In *The Music Man,* for example, a scrim might be painted to represent the outside of the Madison Public Library. With front lighting, the scrim looks like any ordinary drop, but when the lights come up in the library (behind the scrim), the audience members feel as if they have passed directly through the library's walls.

Another impressive use of a scrim and lighting has been used in the famous ballet scene of *Oklahoma!* Not only did proper lighting bring about the dreamlike quality of the dance, but the aiming of a spotlight down the fabric from directly above created a beautifully haloed "chapel of light" for the "wedding" sequence.

The Curious Savage has one of the most moving final scenes of plays frequently presented on the high school stage. By aiming a strong light from above and to the side, the "guests" of The Cloisters appear as figurines in the wished-for world of their inner dreams, where fantasy becomes reality and reality becomes unreal. It is only through lighting techniques that such illusions can be established.

One of the more unusual effects possible with light uses what is normally considered a negative effect of light. A standard makeup is applied, over which makeup using colors washed out under the normal stage light is placed. Makeup the same color as the lights has a tendency to disappear. By changing the dominant

Douglas Campbell and Frederic March are shown here in Gideon, *a play by Paddy Chayefsky. Lighting is used effectively to reveal their faces.*

lighting colors or by having the character move into the beam of a special spot, the actor may suddenly assume the mask of Death, the features of Satan, or the ugliness of a Mr. Hyde as the "invisible" makeup is seen.

When considering unique special effects, few techniques match the possibilities for the unusual that can be attained by the use of black light. Many new colors of luminous paint, paper, and fabrics have been developed, which have increased the flexibility and variety of blacklight (invisible ultraviolet or infrared lighting) uses.

PLANNING THE LIGHTING

The lighting for every production should be worked out carefully just as soon as the needs for costumes, makeup, scenery, and furnishings have been determined. Taking into consideration the information provided by the director and the scenic designer, the lighting technician works out the light plot and the lighting cue sheet (see illustrations on pages 343 and 344). The light plot shows the location of each lighting instrument and the area or object each illuminates. Almost all important acting areas need paired spotlights. However, some locations, such as doorways and windows, may be adequately lighted by one spot.

Once the light plot is prepared, the lighting technician can work out the cue sheet. The light plot indicates how the light board is to be set up for each scene. The cue sheet shows what changes are to take place; which controls, which instruments, what setting to use; and the length of time each change is to take. These are listed chronologically as they appear in the play, including warning cues, execution cues, and timing cues, that is, how to count the time during a change. The matter of timing is of great importance. One of the disadvantages of some electronic systems is that they are on timed settings, and if the production gets off schedule, the lighting cues do not synchronize and the lighting technician must override the system.

Lighting may be preplanned, but since the effects of light on any particular surface or color are unpredictable, the only way to properly light a production is to try out things under the lights. A play can easily have its impact destroyed by poor lighting.

All lighting cues need to be worked out in rehearsals, although it saves the time and the patience of the director and cast if most preliminary run-throughs and experimentations can be done in technical rehearsals held apart from the cast rehearsals.

LIGHTING CUE SHEET FOR:

CUE NO.	PAGE	CONTROL NO.	AREA	START CUE	START RDG.	COMPLETE CUE	COMPLETE RDG.
1	3	$M_1 M_2 M_3$	1,2,3	FOGHORN	0	BOATSWAIN'S WHISTLE	8
2	3	12,14	6,8	FRANK: "DO YOU THINK..."	0	PHIL: "I DON'T BELIEVE IT"	10
3	5	$M_1 M_2 M_3$ 12,14	1,2,3 6,8,	SCREAM (KILL)	8 10	(IMMEDIATE BLACKOUT)	0
4	8	$M_1 M_2 M_3$ $M_4 M_5$	1,2,3 4,5	CAR COMING UP DRIVE	0	CAR STOP	10

LIGHTING PLAN FOR:

DIMMER	AREA	INSTRUMENT NUMBER	INSTRUMENT TYPE	STAGE MAIN OR STAGE MASTER	INDEPENDENT OR PROPORTIONAL	GEL	SETTING
M1	#1 Michael's Room	—	—	—	—	—	10
11	"	9,12 / 15,17	500 W Fresnel / 500 W Fresnel	M	P	D. Pink / Sp. Lav.	6/6
21	"	10,13 / 16,18	500 W Fresnel / 500 W Fresnel	M	P	B. Amb. / St. Blue	10/10
31	Skylight Special	11 / 19	500 W Ellip / 500 W Ellip	M	I	Flesh / St. Blue	5/5
M2	#2 Hotel Lobby	2,3 / 7,8	750 W Ellip / 750 W Ellip	M	I	B. Amb. / D. Blue	8/8
12	"	14,19 / 23,25	500 W Fresnel / 500 W Fresnel	MS	I	D. Pink / Sp. Lav.	7/7
12	"	2,1 / 28	500 W Fresnel / 500 W Fresnel	MS	I	D. Pink / Sp. Lav.	8/8

The lighting technicians need to see that all equipment is in working order, that cables are not laid where they may be tripped over, and that exposed cables are taped down. Square knots or twist lock connectors should secure each connection, faded gels must be replaced, and any instruments that might have been accidentally moved by actors or crew during scene shifts have to be realigned. The lighting crew needs to be alert to the dangers of reflective surfaces—mirrors, highly polished furniture, glass-fronted cabinets, sequins, jewels, or anything else that might throw a blinding light into the eyes of the audience or reveal backstage areas.

There are three problems common to schools and little theater groups that should be discussed. The first concerns the matter of cues. The ideal location for the light panel is in a booth at the rear of the auditorium where the technician may watch the action on the stage and see the lighting effects as the audience sees them. However, most stages have the light panel at floor level or on an elevated platform stage right. Frequently the technician cannot see the actors and must depend on verbal cues, signals from other crew members in the wings or booth, or count cues.

There are two ways to avoid the embarrassment of an actor standing with a hand on a light switch for 5 seconds waiting for the lights to change. One solution, of course, is to wire the onstage lights directly to the power source so that they really work, as in a home. A second solution is to wire an onstage switch to a pilot or cue light located on the wall directly behind the switch or, better still, by the light panel itself. When a switch is thrown, the pilot operates just as the onstage lights do. The fraction of a second delay for the crew's reaction is imperceptible to the audience.

The second problem is more difficult to solve—that of the school having no dimmers or having the available dimmer linked directly to border or footlights only. An imaginative designer can devise various tricks to get the necessary lights on by flipping toggle switches, but, after a short time, the uniqueness of these tricks will wear off and the designer must return to "lights on, lights off." Homemade dimmers can be used, but a couple of small auto transformers would probably be the best low-cost investment. Several lights can be wired in a bypass system that uses the same dimmer. Unfortunately, good lighting effects demand a flexible dimmer panel, and makeshift substitutes are only substitutes.

The third common problem faced by many schools and community theater groups is the limitations of a low budget. However, small spotlights and floods are not too expensive, even for small schools, and their purchase makes fine money-raising projects for drama clubs, parents' groups, or class gifts. Still, some fine effects can be achieved by imaginative use of 150-watt PARs or reflector floods, which call for a very nominal cash outlay. It has been so widely acknowledged that good lighting is essential to modern theater that a series of good productions

may soon pay for a large portion of the cost of new equipment merely as a result of increased ticket sales.

Summary

1. Effective lighting demands control over the distribution, brightness, movement, and color of light on the stage.

2. Highlights and shadows are essential for depth, interest, and variety.

3. Light has strange effects on dyes, pigments, textures, and materials. This fact necessitates testing under production lighting.

4. Lighting is the designer's number one source of special effects.

5. Lighting, more than anything else on the stage, indicates mood, atmosphere, and time most effectively.

LIGHTING PROJECTS

1. Design the lighting plot for a play having an interior set, keeping in mind natural light sources (sunlight, lamps, fireplaces, and so on).

2. Design the lighting for an arena production to be presented in a lunchroom, gym, and so on.

3. Prepare lighting cue sheets based on the lighting design you have prepared.

4. Demonstrate the effects of different-colored lights on fabrics of different colors and textures.

5. Set up a demonstration to illustrate the lighting color wheel by projecting overlapped patterns of red, blue, and green filters onto a large sheet of white paper.

6. Use lighting as the basis for a set design to suggest depth, time changes, or acting planes.

BIBLIOGRAPHY

Fuchs, Theodore: *Stage Lighting,* Little, Brown, Boston, 1929.

McCandless, Stanley: *A Method of Lighting the Stage,* Theatre Arts, New York, 1954.

Parker, Oren W., and Harvey K. Smith: *Scene Design and Stage Lighting,* Holt, Rinehart, and Winston, New York, 1979.

Selden, Samuel, and Hunton Sellman: *Stage Scenery and Lighting,* Appleton-Century-Crofts, New York, 1959.

CHAPTER THIRTEEN

Costuming

One of the integral parts of play production that suffers most on the high school stage is costuming. The actor must realize that the costume is not merely a means of characterizing a role as attractively as possible, but that in its color and silhouette it is a vital part of the total stage design. One costume inharmonious in color or historical period, no matter how beautiful it may be in itself or how becoming to the actor, can ruin an atmospheric effect. The wise director will work out the costuming for an entire play well in advance of the dress rehearsal in order to avoid the necessity of last-minute changes. Because proper costuming is difficult and expensive, it is usually the first aspect of production to go under budget limitations.

EFFECTIVE COSTUMING

A stage costume should express the personality of the character, revealing social status, tastes, and idiosyncrasies. It should aid the audience's understanding of the actor's relationship to the other characters and to the play itself. The costume may be in harmony with others on the stage or in strong contrast to them. Color coding—matching characters by color or pattern—can provide a subtle means of identifying members of the same family or group, a pair of lovers, or masters and servants.

Since costuming is a part of the total design, you will probably have little to do with the design of your costume. Too often however in high schools, costumes are designed or rented only for period or stylized plays. When it comes to contemporary plays, the actors are frequently asked what they have in their own wardrobes. This is acceptable only if the student is portraying someone of the same age, personality type, social position, and so on, and this is rarely the case. For most plays the actor's personal wardrobe will never provide a suitable costume

Ancient Greek dress

without some modifications. Therefore, costumes should be designed for all actors in all plays. In any production, the effect of a costume on both the actor and audience is what counts on the stage. The taste of the artist, not the actor, must govern the choice of material and color, and the meaning of the play must dominate all decisions. Valuable heirlooms, lavish designs, and expensive fabrics are of no value unless they are appropriate in color, period, and design.

Amateurs are usually reluctant to appear anything but attractive on the stage, forgetting that the audience should react to the play, not to the individuals. No director will ever deliberately insist upon unbecoming or ludicrous lines or colors unless they are necessary to the corrrect interpretation of the play. However, the psychological reaction of being comfortably, becomingly, and suitably clothed greatly assists an actor's work. It is for this reason that you should understand the theories of costuming in order to cooperate intelligently in wearing whatever is designed for you in your role.

COSTUME DESIGN

The first step in costume design, as in all phases of theater production, is to study the play carefully. The costume designer should then meet with the director and technical director to discuss costumes in relation to the theme, style, period, colors, scenery, lighting, and budget. Together they can decide on types of materials for costumes that will suit the play in question in texture, finish, weight, fullness, and stiffness. Then measurements of the cast are taken and preliminary sketches are made.

Fabric samples should be tried under the lighting planned for the show. But remember that the lighting may be changed, and it is almost always the costumer who must make adjustments, seldom the painters or electricians. Once the fabrics are selected, the costumes may be sewn and fitted. It is wise to place the costumes under the lights again before making the final fitting and adding the trim. Once each costume is completed, it should be checked one last time under the lights before dress rehearsal.

Medieval dress (fifteenth century, Burgundy)

DOUBLET

RUFFS

FARTHINGALE

PUMPKIN
HOSE

CANIONS

Renaissance dress (sixteenth century)

Actors have a bad habit of not reporting lost buttons, tears, and other accidents to costumes. They should be reminded that such problems should be reported immediately so that the necessary repairs may be made before performance time.

An important point to bear in mind is that a historically accurate costume is not essential and might even have a negative effect on the production. Authentic costumes, especially those that expose parts of the body, such as Egyptian, Greek, or Roman costumes, may not look right on a particular actor. It is better to adapt the costume to the size, bone structure, and shape of the actor than to insist on historical correctness. Every historical or national costume has two or three indentifying characteristics that are sufficient to give the impression of that era or geographical region. A collar, cape, belt, or hat may be all the audience needs to accept the costume as being of a given time and place. The addition of a few little touches, such as jewelry, handkerchiefs, or gloves, will make the costume seem complete.

A complete costume is essential. All accessories should be part of a properly designed costume and should be obtained early enough for use in some rehearsals. Neglect of such details as shoes, hats, purses, fans, and parasols can ruin the harmony of the design and mood. Masks, wigs, and hairpieces are part of both costume and makeup, creating the complete costume.

It is equally important for the actor to have some substitutes to rehearse with if the real accessories are not available for use. An actor needs to get the ''feel'' of a costume. For a hoopskirt, a hoop alone may be used for rehearsing and will remind the actress that she will not be able to see her feet, that she may have difficulty maneuvering a 120-inch hoop skirt through narrow passages, and that she may have trouble getting close to a person or an object without the back of the hoop tipping up embarrassingly. When accessories are added at the last minute, many beginning actors find they must change some of their stage business and

Restoration dress (1660)

POWDERED WIG

TRICORN

JABOT

STOMACHER

PANIERS

CLOCKING

Eighteenth-century dress (1775)

even modify some of their blocking. It is a mistake to think that the addition of essential accessories on the day of dress rehearsal is good because it may give the performers a lift. Several weeks of rehearsal are necessary to develop the ease and naturalness essential to the use of a lorgnette, monocle, long cigarette holder, sword, or swagger stick.

The costume designer recognizes that clothing styles progress in definite patterns. This fact may be applied to the characters in a play. In any era, someone sets the fashion—perhaps a clothing designer, perhaps a person of renown, perhaps the star of a movie. This fashionable apparel is often first worn by professional models, then by the socially elite. Once a style is accepted in elite circles, fashionable people everywhere follow the new style, until finally the general population follows the trend. Then there are the people who are always outdated. They discard the previous style too late and consequently pick up the new style as it is waning. There are those who wear styles of a time 10 to 50 years prior to the play;

these are usually old-fashioned, eccentric, and economically or socially deprived people. Finally, there are those people who wear offbeat, unusual, or bizarre clothing. These are the people who may be classified as eccentrics and nonconformists. Remember also that styles are often revived and that conservative and flamboyant styles occur in cycles according to the philosophical tone of the times.

It is usually safer to costume plays of the last two or three decades in present-day attire unless some aspect of the play hinges on authentic costuming. For example, the middies of the girls in *Cheaper by the Dozen* add to the humor of the play, but a long, straight-line dress of the twenties for Mrs. Gilbreth might seem ridiculously out of place.

STOVEPIPE

CRINOLINE

FROCK COAT

Mid nineteenth-century dress

CRAVAT

CORSET

BUSTLE

Late nineteenth-century dress

Always consider the kind of action that will take place in the scene in which the costume will be used. A costume must be comfortable, easy to put on and take off, and strong enough to stand heavy strain. A skintight uniform may appear dashing, but may handcuff the actor completely in a fight scene. Costumes for dance sequences must be designed with the choreography in mind. If more than one costume is to be worn, each costume must be designed in such a way that the actor can change costumes in the time allowed. It must be admitted that playwrights do not always consider carefully the time needed for costume changes.

The total design of the play determines whether the costumes may be stylized. Some period plays adapt well to modern dress, the wearing of contemporary clothing instead of authentic period costumes. Formal attire (tuxedos and evening gowns) can be worn for many plays, particularly classical tragedies. Flowing robes, mosaic patterns, and variations in black and white fabrics may be used for certain stylized plays.

APPROPRIATENESS

Each historic period has its own distinctive line and form in dress. This is the *costume silhouette*. Look carefully at the silhouettes in this chapter, and notice how each period has its own characteristics. If a costume does not recreate the basic silhouette of the period, it is not effective, no matter how beautiful or elaborate it may be. This is a very important principle.

In style, material, and cut, a costume must be appropriate to the social background and period of the play. On the stage certain problems of dress are intensified. Actors and actresses should study their full-length reflections at a distance to get the proper perspective of themselves in costume. The director should observe every costume from various parts of the auditorium.

Small details become important onstage. For example, long skirts are more graceful than short ones, especially when the actress is seated. Draped scarves and stoles are very effective if they are skillfully handled. Trimming, to be noticed, must be somewhat conspicuous, but if it is overly so, it should be discarded.

Dress in the 1920s

Dress in the 1930s

Most people want to look their best when appearing in public, so costumes should fit well and bring out the best physical characteristics of the actor—unless a particular role dictates otherwise. It takes time in rehearsal to make a different style of clothing feel natural. The actor must lose self-consciousness in the costume if it is to look right. Sometimes a high school performer ''pulls back'' in the role because the costume feels uncomfortable—a girl may be embarrassed by a gown that is too ''revealing''; a boy may feel ill at ease in a Roman tunic. Often the student actors do not complain because they believe such a costume is what the director expects them to wear. But if the feelings of discomfort cannot be overcome by a better understanding of the role and the relationship of the costume to it, the director should consider modifying the costume slightly rather than send a tense, ill-at-ease actor onto the stage. In real life, clothes may not make the person, but on the stage they do. Fortunate indeed is the actor who has the knack of wearing clothes well and making them a part of the role.

Color and Material

Costumes for comedies, farces, children's plays, and fantasies are normally made of light material, are bright or pastel in color, and are frothy in design. Restoration comedy calls for satins, laces, and brocades, which are usually as overconscious of style as the characters themselves. High comedy deals with persons of taste and social grace; costumes for fashionable characters require careful selection of color and material and also special attention to line. In realistic plays, almost any material that will create garments suitable for the character and for the stage picture can be used. Symbolic and allegorical plays require even more thought concerning fabric, texture, and pattern, because the audiences will assume that the costumes used in such plays will help them interpret the inner meanings. Tragedies use grayed colors or dark tones in heavily weighted materials.

The personality of the character and the style of the play will determine whether a tailored cut or a touch of lace is needed. Even in plays in which we think the

Dress in the 1940s

LEG O' MUTTON
SLEEVES

SACK
SUIT

PARASOL

Dress from 1900 to 1910

styles of costumes are much alike, there must be variety in color, cut, line, material, and trim. The characters in every play must be treated as individuals to be identified in their stations of life, idiosyncrasies, or philosophies by some aspect in their costume design. At the same time, all costumes for the same play must go with each other in basic design.

Lines in garments should harmonize with those of the human body without constriction or exaggeration. A heavy-set person should wear costumes, hair styles, and hats accenting long, vertical lines. Tall, thin people should wear costumes, hair styles, and hats accenting horizontal lines, especially at the shoulder, and avoid long, clinging skirts, high hats, and V-necks. Black and dark colors are slenderizing, while white and light colors are broadening. Glaring colors, striking patterns, and lustrous materials attract attention and should be avoided by large persons unless they are especially appropriate to the characterization. Satin is a glossy material that in light colors makes a person appear larger, whereas velvet absorbs light, and dark velvet takes off pounds.

Prints must be carefully tested, for the stage lights turn small or light patterns into an undefined mass of color, which may create a grotesque effect. In general, blondes should wear cool colors, with touches of warm color contrast, and delicate designs and materials. Brunettes should wear warm colors, and they can risk brilliant fabrics and stronger color contrasts. Ordinarily redheads should emphasize their coloring by wearing yellow, orange, green, and golden brown.

Texture not only determines the outline of the costume but also has much to do with the effects of a material under the lights. Heavy or soft materials, such as velvet, burlap, cheesecloth, and flannel, react well under stage lighting, and the more inexpensive materials often appear richer than many costly fabrics. Drapery material and even carpeting have been used for costumes for this very reason. Knitted materials drape beautifully and cling to the figure, emphasizing lines.

Oilcloth, cardboard, plastics, rubber sheeting, felt, and other similar materials, including the special plastic molding materials now available, can be used for

Dress from 1910 to 1920

STOCK

CHEMISE

JOCKEY
BOOTS

Empire dress (1815)

trim, accent features, and appliqués. All sorts of familiar materials can be utilized in creating bizarre or unusual outfits.

OBTAINING THE COSTUMES

Work sheets and costume charts should be made for every costume in the production. The work sheets should describe the colors, fabrics, and accessories for each design. Ruled columns placed next to the items in the costume description are of great value. As each listed task is completed, the item can be checked off. Such charts can facilitate matters so that the costumes are ready before dress rehearsals.

One of the first problems to be settled is whether the costumes are to be rented, borrowed, or made. This decision must be made in time for the costumes to be collected with a minimum of effort and expense.

COSTUME PLOT FOR:							
CHARACTER	SCENE	COSTUME DESCRIPTION	MEAS. CARD	1ST FITTING	COMPLETE	OUT	IN
JULIE (CINDY PHELPS)	I, i	BLUE CHECKED GINGHAM PINAFORE w/ WHITE BLOUSE AND WHITE APRON. WIDE BRIMMED STRAW HAT. PARASOL	✓	✓	✓	✓	
"	I, ii	LT. GREEN BLOUSE WITH PUFFED SLEEVES. PINK SKIRT w/ BUSTLE. PURSE		✓	✓	✓	

Renting Costumes

If you decide to rent costumes, be careful. Rented costumes are expensive. Many times the costume company will not have what you want or all that you need when you need it. Be particularly cautious when costumers say they do not have quite what you request but will fix you up with something else.

If you send out of town for costumes, they may not fit properly. This is usually due to inaccurate measurements. The costume supervisor needs to know what measurements to take and how to take them. Refer to page 363 for instructions on how to measure for proper costume fit. Some costume houses will send costumes that are in poor condition. Substitutions are common, accessories are seldom what you expect, and the use of interchangeables—such as using the same hat for several purposes simply by changing the identifying trim—can result in a sameness you did not anticipate. Many costume houses send boot covers to be worn over regular shoes. Boot covers make poor substitutes for boots because they do not look natural when an actor walks. Also, boot covers are impossible to dance in. Only when you deal with very large firms can you hope to get the color or pattern you desire. Otherwise, you take what they have.

One of the chief drawbacks of rented costumes is that they may be available for only one dress rehearsal or at most for only 48 hours prior to the first performance without additional charge. Most costume houses'charge an additional fee for each performance day after the opening night. Some, however, will quote a flat rate per week including dress rehearsals and performances. Rental costumes are never available for publicity photos unless you rent them for that purpose. This can be done only if you are dealing with a local concern. In general, all costume orders

Taking Measurements

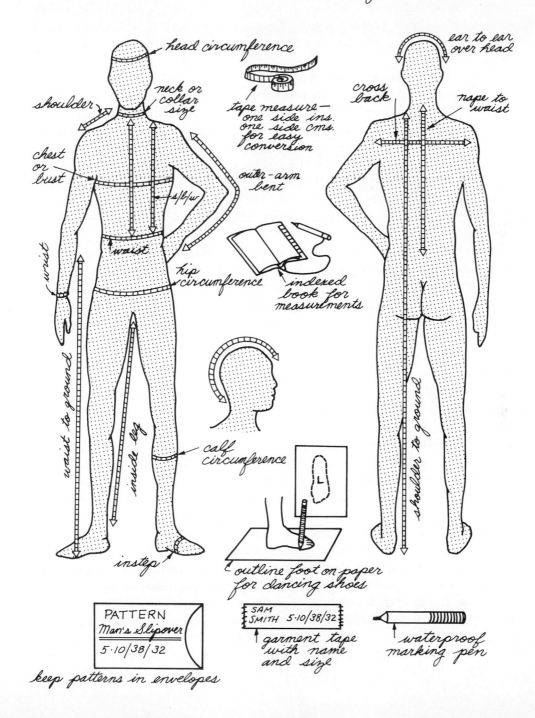

head circumference

ear to ear
over head

shoulder

neck or
collar
size

tape measure—
one side ins.
one side cms.
for easy
conversion

cross
back

nape to
waist

chest
or
bust

s/l/w

outer-arm
bent

wrist

waist

indexed
book for
measurements

hip
circumference

waist to ground

inside leg

calf
circumference

shoulder to ground

instep

outline foot on paper
for dancing shoes

L

PATTERN
Man's Slipover
5·10/38/32

keep patterns in envelopes

SAM
SMITH 5·10/38/32

garment tape
with name
and size

waterproof
marking pen

should be placed well in advance of dress rehearsal and performance dates. This means that measurements must be taken shortly after casting. Before committing yourself to a specific costume house, check to find out how far in advance orders must be placed. Your schedule may not allow for ordering from costumers too far away.

With so many reasons against renting why consider renting? Because fine costumes enhance the overall quality of a production. Formal evening dress, especially in period styles; uniforms and unusual national costumes; armor; and certain special properties are often unobtainable from any other source. If the budget is adequate, some of the leading costume houses can provide you with the costumes actually used in the Broadway or other well-costumed production; such productions may have had a high enough budget to order the kind of costumes prepared that no high school could afford to make. The trim for such elaborate costumes is quite expensive, and only large costumers can afford to trim the costumes properly.

When schools do not rent, there is always the temptation to take the easiest, cheapest route, which means you may make even more substitutions than the costumer or use some kind of apparel completely unsuitable for the play. Musical plays have sometimes lacked the sparkle and color so essential to their success simply because the costumes were simple substitutions. If you do rent, often it is best to deal with a large firm or, better still, two reliable companies. The choice of costumes of each company for certain historical periods is usually limited, and you do not want your audiences to tire of seeing the same costume over and over again. If at all possible, the director, designer, and costume manager should go to the costume company personally to select the costumes to be used.

Borrowing Costumes

Having the members of the cast and committee buy or borrow their own costumes may seem to be the simplest method of costuming a production, but it seldom is. It is very difficult to obtain garments that will achieve the planned and desired effect, even those that at first seem easy to get. In period plays, suitable costumes lent by generous friends are apt to be valuable and fragile, and no assurance can be offered that they will not be soiled or torn. Makeup stains that will not come out, delicate lace that is snagged, and materials that disintegrate under the strain of a performance are hard to explain to the owner of such treasured heirlooms. If you borrow costumes, treat them carefully.

Of course, when students borrow or buy their own costumes, it is obvious there is little or no budgeting cost other than the cleaning of the borrowed costumes. As previously mentioned, it is not easy for students to look older in their own clothes, and seldom would the wardrobes of character and actor match. Also, the actor may be more careful with a costume if it has been paid for or belongs to a friend or relative. Since cost is always a major factor, most modern costumes are borrowed.

Making Your Own Costumes

Making your own costumes almost always outweighs renting and borrowing if you insist on good design, materials, workmanship, and a definite time schedule. The cost of making costumes is about the same as, and often far less than, the rental fee, but the major difference rests in the end result—an addition to the costume wardrobe, or a high bill with nothing to show for it.

Making the costumes serves several purposes. Those students who design and make them gain valuable experience and have the pride and satisfaction of seeing the part a good costume plays in creating an effective stage picture. A more uniform pattern for the play in both color and line is possible, and the costume is made to fit the individual actor. Both the costumer and the actor take a personal interest in this facet of production, bringing about a mutual respect for each other's contribution to the play. It is exciting for the designer, as well as a relief to the publicity director, to have the actual costumes available for publicity photos. This is especially true if the publicity director plans to set up a poster featuring "real" scenes from the play.

If the costumes are to be made, a well-stocked wardrobe room is essential. If your school does not already have a costume room where costumes, accessories, materials, and supplies can be stored and cared for, you and your classmates should set up one. You will find your supply will grow quickly when the need for costumes becomes known in the community.

When you are ready to make the costumes, individual sketches and costume charts and sheets should include notes on the kind, amount, and cost of materials. Dyeing makes possible a more satisfactory and unified costume scheme. However, it requires skill in a complex activity, a place for the dyeing, and people willing to work until the job is completed. Before the dyeing is done, patterns should be cut to the exact measurements of the actors and be approved by the director, scenic designer, and actors. When all material has been dyed and checked under the stage lights, it may be cut from the patterns and sewed together.

The completed garments must be strong enough to stand the strain of rehearsals and performances, but they do not need to have elaborate, ornamental sewing. Pinking edges and basting rather than stitching are quite acceptable for much of costume making. Details, such as a row of buttons, are usually nonfunctional or "dummied" in order to save sewing time and facilitate quick changes. Costumes for dancers need extra material under the arms for greater freedom of movement. The main emphasis in costume planning should be on the total effect as seen from the auditorium. The perfection of a costume cannot be judged by the design alone. The costume must be observed in action on stage with the correct scenery and lighting. Costume design and construction are complex processes, but the effort is rewarded by the achievement of an original and artistic production.

Time is always the enemy in the production of a play, and this includes costuming. A schedule for measurement, fittings, and completion should be established and adhered to. Sufficient time must be allowed for checking material under lights, for alterations and corrections, and for the costume parade. One of the great advantages of making your own costumes is that if they are completed on schedule—at least a week before dress rehearsal—you can test them under the lights, make final adjustments, and add a touch of trim, accent, or jewelry as needed several days before rental costumes would be available.

In the long run, a combination of renting, borrowing, buying, and making your own costumes is probably the only satisfactory way to meet all the costume requirements for your dramatic program, particularly if you present musical plays.

Never overlook the possibilities of making over old clothes or revamping old costumes. It is a good practice to save fabric remnants for trim or accessories or perhaps to add to a costume of the same material at a later date. Men's old suits can be cut and remade into cutaways without a great amount of work. Even beautiful hats—always a costume problem—can be made from a few materials, a little imagination, 10 minutes in the library, and considerable patience.

Following Costume Patterns

The sample patterns on pages 367 to 370 have been drawn to a scale of ¼ inch to 2 inches; each square represents 2 inches. To reproduce these patterns, or create ones of your own, start with plain brown paper. Mark off the paper in 2-inch squares by measuring outward from the center front and the center back of the pattern, adjusting the pattern according to the size of the actor. Pin the pattern to your fabric, which has been placed on a large table. Cut around the pattern allowing extra fabric for ⅝-inch seams.

The most important measurements for women are the following: height, bust, waist, hips (approximately 7 inches below natural waistline), back of neck to waist, waist to shoe tops, across back from shoulder to shoulder, and arm length from top of shoulder to wrist. The most important measurements for men are the following: height, chest, waist, inseam, back of neck to waist, across back from shoulder to shoulder, collar size, and arm length from top of shoulder to wrist.

Greek

armhole   clasps   neck   clasps   armhole

man's length

seam   seam

Woman's robe
1 girdle

Man's tunic
girdle

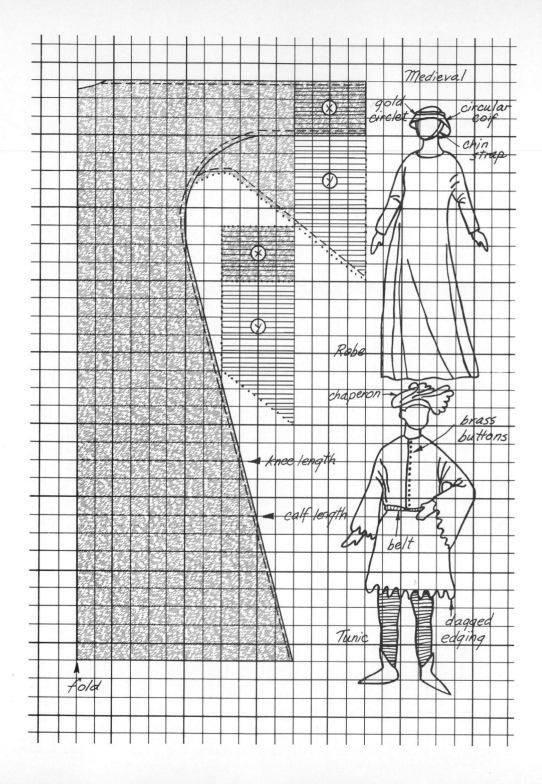

Medieval

gold circlet

circular coif

chin strap

Robe

knee length

calf length

chaperon

brass buttons

belt

Tunic

dagged edging

fold

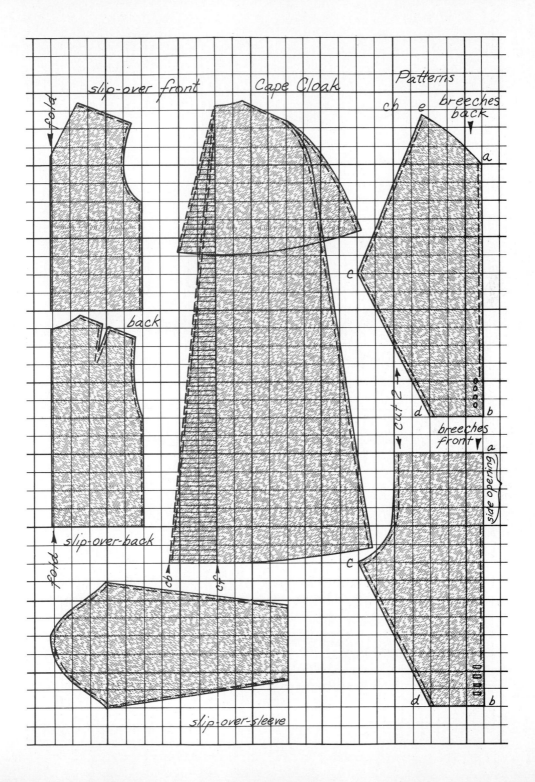

slip-over front   Cape Cloak   Patterns

fold

cb   e   breeches back

a

e

cut 2

side opening

d   b

breeches front   a

back

slip-over-back

fold

cb   cf

c

d   b

slip-over-sleeve

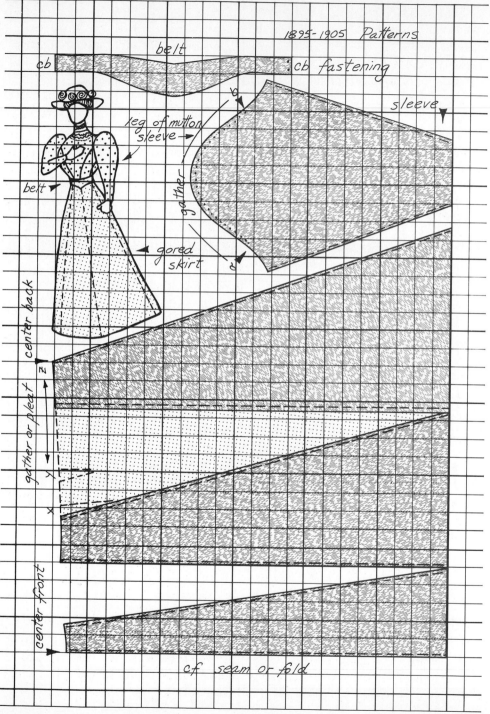

1895-1905 Patterns

belt

cb

cb fastening

sleeve

leg of mutton sleeve

belt

gather

gored skirt

center back

gather or pleat

center front

cf seam or fold

The pattern on page 367 for a woman's Greek robe or a man's Greek tunic can be altered for different effects. Increasing the width of the fabric will increase the sleeve length. By changing the length of the fabric, you can make the garment reach the knee, calf, or ankle. Sew this garment at the side seams, and gather it at the shoulders with clasps or fancy buttons to fashion the armholes.

The pattern on page 368 is a medieval robe with Magyar sleeves. This garment, with adjustments in overall length, sleeve design, and decorations, is suitable for both men and women. Pieces X and Y add length and fullness to the sleeves for either a woman's or a man's garment. The use of dagged edges, mock buttons, and a belt dress the garment for a man.

The pattern on page 369 shows a nineteenth-century man's full-length coat (with or without cape), a jacket, and a pair of breeches. For the jacket, make a simple slipover garment. By using braiding along the collar, front, bottom, and sleeve edges, you will get the visual effect of a jacket without the tailoring problems of making a real jacket. Mock buttons down the front will complete the jacket look.

To make Victorian breeches, sew the center back (e–c on the pattern) and center front seams (f–c on the pattern) first. Then sew the inside leg seams (c–d on the pattern). Finally, sew the leg side seams (a–b on the pattern), leaving open the button fastenings at the knee and the placket at one side. Use braiding to make a mock drop flap in the front.

The cloak can be made full length, knee length, or any other length desired. The horizontal markings on the pattern show an allowance for extra fullness recommended for an overcoat. The cloak section can be eliminated for a straight-line coat. For this garment, you will have to sew a back seam (cb, center back, on the pattern.) The center front of the coat is identified as cf on the pattern.

The pattern on page 370 is a gored skirt. You can fashion two types of skirts from this pattern: a six-gore skirt or a skirt with two darts at the hips. The darts are shown as X and Y on the pattern. The darted skirt requires gathering or pleating at the back, shown as Y–Z on the pattern. Also included are patterns for a belt or waistband and a leg-of-mutton sleeve.

For additional patterns and more detailed explanations, refer to Sheila Jackson's book *Costumes for the Stage*.

CARE OF COSTUMES

After the costumes have been obtained, they must be cared for during rehearsals and performances. A competent wardrobe manager should be chosen. The wardrobe manager will keep a costume plot as shown on page 362 and will choose responsible assistants in all the dressing rooms. The assistants help the actors with their changes, hang up clothes, keep all accessories close at hand, and see that everything is returned in good condition after the performance. The wardrobe manager sees that every costume is complete, in good repair, and identified by character and actor. Actors should have a designated place for their costumes, such as costume racks marked by tags or dividers. The wardrobe manager checks with the cast for problems that might have developed with zippers, tears, and the like, keeping needle and thread and a few handy supplies like hooks and eyes, buttons, or elastic on hand during all performances. All borrowed clothing should be dry-cleaned or washed before being returned to the owner. The wardrobe manager also sees that all school costumes are cleaned, repaired, and stored carefully for future use and that all rented costumes and accessories are returned promptly.

Dressing room floors should be covered with paper if long trains of fine materials are worn. The stage floor also should be kept clean; it should be vacuumed before dress rehearsals and performances. Protruding nails, unexpected steps, low ceilings, and other backstage hazards should be reduced to a minimum.

After almost every production, some costumes will need to be replaced or repaired. The decision as to whether or not such expenses are to come out of the proceeds should be made at the beginning of rehearsals.

THE ACTOR AND THE COSTUME

The actor must learn to wear a costume properly, bearing in mind the angle at which the audience will view the stage and performers as the actor turns, bends over, or crosses the legs. The actor must also think of the other performers—that they are not jabbed unintentionally with a sword; that buttons, medals, or jewelry do not snag or catch on another's costume; or that another performer's cape or train is not stepped on. The actor must seem natural and at ease in a costume, learning how to make a turn in a flowing or trailing costume. Girls must learn how to sit gracefully while wearing a hoop or several petticoats, and boys must learn how a "man of quality" sits without pinning the tails of his full evening dress under him. Snapping fans, removing scarves and gloves, handling capes and finger rings must be second nature to the actor if that actor is to appear convincing in a role.

In addition, the actor should feel responsible for personal costumes and properties, remembering that greasepaint, powder, spirit gum, and nail polish are almost impossible to remove and that torn fabrics can seldom be mended satisfactorily. Actors must personally see that every costume, accessory, and property is returned to the school, costumer, or friend exactly as it was received. But, above all, the actor should remember that the "total" actor is made up of a well-coordinated combination of voice, physique, makeup, and costume.

COSTUME PROJECTS

1. Design the costumes for the following types of plays: (1) contemporary, (2) period, (3) fantasy, (4) stylized.

2. Design costumes for a children's play, using unusual materials, such as boxes and paper sacks.

3. Color code the characters in a play by personality types or by relationships.

4. Demonstrate the simple altering of a modern garment to represent that of an earlier historical era.

5. Demonstrate the use of a fan, cane, parasol, sword, night stick, monocle, or lorgnette.

6. Demonstrate how movements are affected by hoops, trains, tails, or capes.

BIBLIOGRAPHY

Barton, Lucy: *Historic Costume for the Stage,* W. H. Baker, Boston, 1961.

Brooke, Iris: *English Costume in the Age of Elizabeth,* A. and C. Black, Ltd., London, England, distributed by Macmillan, 1956.

————: *English Costume of the Seventeenth Century,* A. and C. Black, Ltd., London, England, distributed by Macmillan, 1958.

————: *English Costume of the Eighteenth Century,* A. and C. Black, Ltd., London, England, distributed by Macmillan, 1958.

Hanse, Henry Harald: *Costumes and Styles,* Dutton, New York, 1956.

Jackson, Sheila: *Costumes for the Stage,* Dutton, New York, 1978.

Paterek, Josephine: *Costuming for the Theater,* Crown, New York, 1959.

Walkup, Fairfax: *Dressing the Part: A History of Costume for the Theater,* Appleton-Century-Crofts, New York, 1950.

Wilcox, R. Turner: *Five Centuries of American Costume,* Scribner, New York, 1963.

CHAPTER FOURTEEN

Makeup

Makeup should be one of the most rewarding phases of your dramatic experiences, because it opens up a field of study that conveys the excitement, fun, and challenge of theater illusion and communication. Unfortunately, many students of drama do not fully realize that most actors must design and apply their own makeup. Makeup techniques cannot be mastered merely by watching a demonstration or reading about them. To help yourself acquire this skill essential to every performer, you should study faces to see how they show the effects of age and emotion. Observe portraits, cartoons, magazines, and photographs.

Better still, observe real people. Take special notice of differences in skin color and texture; where wrinkles occur, bones are prominent, and flesh hangs in folds; and the direction and patterns of hair growth. You will discover that the changes that take place in facial expression are closely related to the changes in personality, stature, and voice that occur when an actor develops an effective characterization.

Bone structure is the key to facial makeup. Every student needs to know the bone-muscle relationship and how it alters with age and differs with nationality. It is essential that you study your own bone structure carefully before designing makeup for a role.

GENERAL CONSIDERATIONS

On the school stage, makeup must be handled with special care. Youthful faces do not always adapt themselves readily to older roles, and heavy makeup inexpertly applied looks ''tacked on.'' Only a slight amount of foundation should be used. It is much better to use too little than to use too much. For classwork, a little makeup and an appropriate hair style can suggest age and nationality effectively. However, every student of the drama should study and practice elaborate as well as simple makeup.

When you are to design makeup for a large production, your makeup requirements change considerably. The larger the auditorium or the more lights to be used, the more makeup is needed. Stage lights can wash the color from an actors face until the face has a pasteboard effect. Too much light from above results in deep shadows under all the bony prominences. Bright footlights make the face appear flat and lifeless. Most stages today do not have footlights. Without them, there must be proper lighting from the sides. Otherwise serious shadows distort the actor's face, the eyes can appear lost in deep sockets, and the nose may take on strange shapes.

The techniques of makeup application are closely related to the portrait artist's approach: the face is made a blank mask and then the principles of *chiaroscuro*—the use of highlight and shadow—are applied to model the features into the desired effect. Makeup should be designed on a makeup work sheet similar to the one on page 376. You may want to create your own work sheet using a sketch of your own face as the design model. Remember: Makeup does not make a character, but it does help present the external appearance of the internally created role.

A student applying clown make-up

MAKEUP WORKSHEET

PLAY:_____

CHARACTER: _____

ACTOR: _____

Foundation:_____

Eye shadow:_____

Eye liner:_____

Moist Rouge:_____
Dry Rouge: _____

Shadow: _____

Powder:_____

Hair:_____

Beard/mustache:_____

Forehead: _____

Eyes: _____

Cheeks: _____

Nose: _____

Mouth: _____

Prosthetics: _____

Special treatment: _____

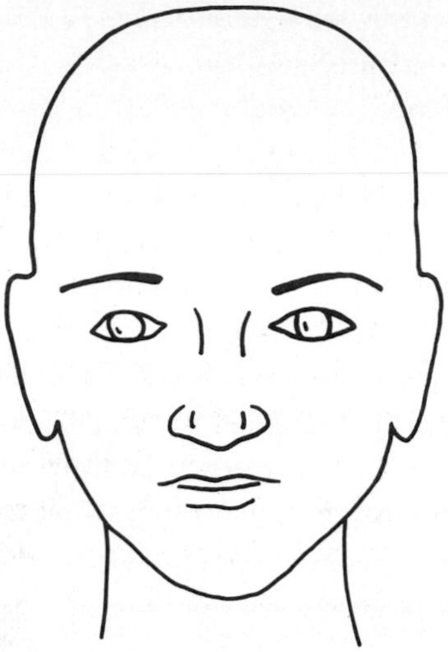

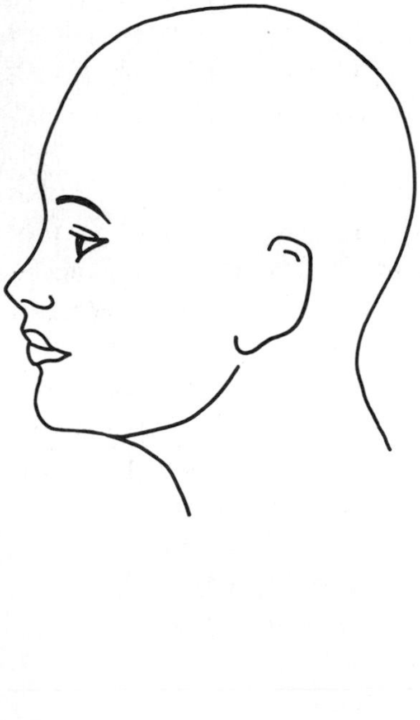

The Makeup Kit

Since most high schools use makeup crews to apply makeup for an entire cast, a well-stocked makeup kit is essential to every drama department. However, makeup is a very personal thing, and many amateurs and all stage professionals have their own personal kits.

Makeup is very expensive and very messy. Proper care of the makeup supplies, the kit, and the makeup room is most essential. Materials should be carefully laid out, all containers and tables should be cleaned up after use, lids and caps must be replaced on the right containers, and all supplies should be put back in the kit or storage cupboards.

Before a rehearsal or performance, the makeup crew should place the supplies neatly on a covered table. When makeup is being applied by a crew, materials must never be carried off by individuals. An ample supply of cold cream and cleansing tissue is always important. Though not on the table, the complete makeup supply must be readily available for emergencies. Only one or two experiences will teach the person in charge of makeup that if all the supplies are in sight, every one of them will be used, even if only slightly.

Makeup essentials are usually handled by a special committee, whose members are headed by someone experienced in makeup techniques who can design the makeup for the production. This committee should see that the makeup kit contains the following essentials:

foundation: Foundation, or base, makeup comes in creme, stick, or cake form. Shades ranging from light pink to dark sunburn to very dark brown are necessary for straight parts. For character parts, such as sallow or florid old age, there are various mixed tones. There are appropriate shades for different nationalities.

clown white: This is a special foundation color used for stylized makeup. It comes in greasepaint or pancake form.

face powders: They come in translucent or in shades to harmonize with the foundation.

moist rouge: Light, medium, and dark.

liners: These are greasepaints in such colors as blue, brown, green, violet, maroon, yellow, and white.

lipsticks: Women use moist rouge or stage lipstick; men use brownish rouge.

makeup pencils: Brown, maroon, red, and black eyebrow pencils are needed.

dry rouge: Light, medium, and dark.

mascara: Black, brown, and white.

cold cream, Albolene, baby oil, or *makeup remover:* Used for dissolving and removing makeup.

powder puffs: Large and small.

roll of absorbent cotton
powder brush: Used for removing excess powder.
hair whitener: White mascara; liquid white shoepolish, clown white, or wash-
   out hair colorants
hair colorants: Temporary hair color.
liquid body makeup: To match foundation.
eyeliner brushes or *round toothpicks, paper liners (stumps),* and *sable* or *camel's
   hair brushes:*   For making wrinkles, painting lips, lining eyes, and filling in
   eyebrows.
crepe hair: Gray, gray blends, light brown, medium brown, and black.
spirit gum and *alcohol* or *spirit gum remover*
liquid latex: For attaching beards and building up features.
nose putty, derma wax, black tooth enamel, white tooth enamel, and *artificial
   blood*
collodian: Flexible and nonflexible.
large mirrors
paper toweling: To protect the dressing tables.
cleansing tissues
*hand mirror, comb, brush, scissors, needles, black and white thread, straight
   pins, hairpins, bobby pins, safety pins,* and *soap*

STRAIGHT MAKEUP: PRINCIPLES AND PROCEDURES

Before beginning to make up, put on a smock, an apron, or a makeup cape.
Carefully bind back the hair or cover it with a cloth. Allow ample time for making
up—at least half an hour for a straight role and an hour for a character part. Men
should be clean-shaven but should never shave less than a half hour before applying makeup. Men should never get a full haircut less than 3 days before the
production because the back of the head and the temples may appear "skinned"
under the lights. Also, to protect the collars of white shirts and blouses, a piece of
adhesive tape may be placed over the fold of the collar.

Preparation for Makeup

Before applying makeup, cleanse the face thoroughly, removing all cosmetics.
Then moisten the fingertips with cold water and cool the surface of the face.
Persons with oily skins may need to use an astringent to assure a dry surface before
applying makeup.

Step One: The Foundation

The first step in the makeup process is the application of the correct foundation
(base) color. The foundation turns the face into a blank mask upon which facial

features are drawn with makeup. The foundation also provides pigment to replace that which is washed out by stage lights and gives a ''character color'' to help create a visual impression of a role.

There are three types of foundation popular in stage use today: cream makeup, soft greasepaint, and cake (pancake) makeup. *Creme* is the most preferred because of its ease of blending and use with soft liners. Creme comes in a plastic tube or jar and combines the advantages of soft greasepaint and cake. It is not overly greasy, but it does require powdering because it reacts to body heat and has a tendency to shine when moist. Consequently, some actors like to powder a creme foundation with translucent powder, pat the surface with a moist sponge, and then apply more makeup.

Creme base is usually applied directly with the fingers after a few spots have been dabbed on the face and neck. However, it may also be applied with a rubber or synthetic sponge. A thin coat should be spread over the face and all exposed parts of the head and neck areas, including the ears. The foundation should be worked gently into the hairline to avoid a halo effect around the face. Creme base should also be spread into the collar line, the back of the neck, and as far down the chest as is exposed or where body makeup will be applied. If the upper torso will be seen, stretch, gesture, or reach as you would in performance. This will help you determine how much of the chest and shoulders needs to be made up.

The foundation (base) color used should be selected according to the age, nationality, health, occupation, and experiences of the character. Generally speaking, men use darker foundations than women. Pinks are used for blondes and for children's roles. Sallows (yellowish tones) are used for characters who are ill, anemic, or shut in. Tans are used by those who are healthy, active, and outdoorsy. Ruddy (reddish) foundations are used for individuals who are blustery, alcoholic, robust, or weather-beaten.

Soft *greasepaint* is preferable for its economy as well as its ease in blending. Do not use any cold cream before applying soft greasepaint. Dab or streak small amounts on the forehead, cheeks, chin, and neck. Use greasepaint sparingly. A thin, even coat is desirable; a heavy mask is not. Heavy greasepaint causes considerable perspiration and running makeup. Also, lines will be difficult to draw, and the makeup will require constant retouching. Remove the makeup from your hands, moisten the fingertips with water, and begin spreading the greasepaint smoothly.

Cake (pancake) foundation was originally designed for motion picture makeup but has become quite popular with many actors, particularly school groups. Much of this popularity has been gained for the wrong reasons. Cake makeup goes on easily with a damp sponge or brush. A natural silk sponge works best for application. If cake highlights, shadows, and rouge are used, there is no need to powder. In fact, a light final coat of cake foundation sets and softens the total makeup effect. Since it is water-soluble, pancake makeup washes off without difficulty after the performance. However, in spite of ease of application and cleanup, the disadvantages of pancake makeup outweigh the advantages. Pancake melts under heat and runs under perspiration. In addition, pancake is very difficult to mix and does not blend with soft liners. Since most high school makeup kits have only grease liners, the *matte* (flat) finish of cake foundation makes an incompatible combination. Therefore, most makeup experts do not recommend pancake for young, inexperienced actors.

Step Two: Shadows and Highlights

The application of shadow and highlight is really the most important aspect of modeling the face. Highlighting and shadowing are used for three purposes: (1) to bring out the features in order that they may be seen; (2) to correct the features; and (3) to change the features to indicate age, character, or physical impairments. For shadowing, use a greasepaint at least three shades darker than the foundation color, or use brown, reddish-brown or maroon lining color. Never use gray except for extreme makeup, for it makes the face look skull-like or dirty.

Every shadow has its highlight. For highlighting, you may use a greasepaint at least three shades lighter than the foundation, or yellow or white liner. White is usually the easiest to use because it will pick up enough of the foundation color to blend effectively without appearing garish. If your chin, nose, or brows are too prominent, blend a shadow over that part of the face. If, on the other hand, some part of your face is not dominant enough, apply a highlight to that area. It is almost always necessary to shadow the sides of the nose in order for it to be seen under bright stage lights.

A sable or camel's hair brush is the most satisfactory tool for lining, but a round toothpick may work quite well if you are careful to make the lines thin and sharp before blending them out. Also, a makeup pencil may be used if the point is kept wedge-shaped and sharp.

Step Three: Rouge

Now apply moist rouge to cheeks and lips. For a feminine straight part, select a color that blends with the foundation color and costume. You should place the moist rouge where it will help shape your face to that of your character. If you have an oval face, apply the rouge in a crescent shape to the cheek bones and blend up and out. For a round face, blend the rouge along the cheek bone and then downward closer to the nose. For a long face, place the rouge high on the cheek bones and blend out toward the temples.

Blending is always important in makeup, but it is especially so in the application of moist rouge. You should never see where the rouge ends unless your character is a person obviously over-made up. Men and boys should use moist rouge sparingly—just enough for a healthy glow. Although rouge may be washed out under strong light, it often gives the same effect as shadowing. Use very little, if any, rouge for night scenes, since both blue and green lights will turn the red into a dark brown or black.

Step Four: Eyes and Eyebrows

The eyes and brows are made up next. The purpose of the eye shadow is to beautify the eyes, to make them seem larger, and to indicate character. Eye shadow is applied to the upper lids only, beginning with a heavy line next to the eye and fading out, blending the color over the eyelid. The choice of color is determined by the color of hair and costume, the personality of the character, and whether the eyes are supposed to look "made up." Blue, blue-green, blue-gray, violet, or brown may be used. Brown is the safest and most flattering color and should always be used for corrective male eye shadowing. Violet is used only when a weepy appearance is sought or the character is a fragile old lady whose foundation color is a delicate pink.

Be certain that the eye shadow does not kill any highlight below the eyebrow. The placement of the shadow can alter the appearance of the eyes to make them appear closer together or farther apart, or happy, sad, weary, suspicious, or squinty. In all cases the shadow should be blended so no definite line is seen.

The eyes are enlarged and accented by lining. Makeup experts disagree sharply regarding both the technique and placement of eye lining. Brown or black lining color may be used, but black is acceptable only for dark-complexioned actors, characters who would use heavy eye makeup, or for oriental eyes. If false lashes or heavy mascara will be applied later, the upper line is omitted by many actresses. Otherwise, you should use a sable brush or round toothpick to draw a line close to the lashes starting about two-thirds of the way in towards the nose and extending beyond the outer corner of the eye about ¼ inch. The lower line is drawn about one-third from the outer corner out to the upper line, fading out before it reaches the top line. Both lines should be softened by running the finger gently over them. If an eyebrow pencil is used, it must be sharp, or the lines will be too heavy.

To add sparkle to the eye, some makeup experts suggest a small red dot in the inner corner of the eye; others recommend a touch of rouge just below the outer corner or below the outer edge of the brow. The red dot, or *life spot* as it has been called, may help to serve another purpose: it can aid in determining how close or far apart the eyes seem to be. For Asian makeup, when latex lids or adhesive tape

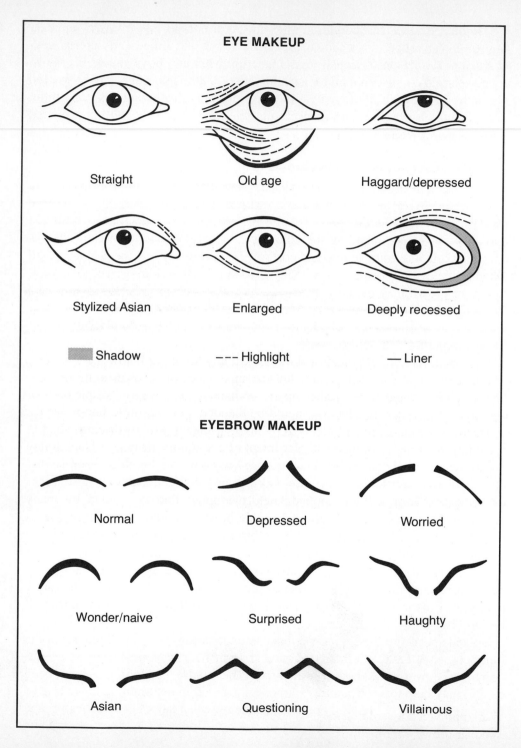

EYE MAKEUP

Straight

Old age

Haggard/depressed

Stylized Asian

Enlarged

Deeply recessed

▨ Shadow

––– Highlight

— Liner

EYEBROW MAKEUP

Normal

Depressed

Worried

Wonder/naive

Surprised

Haughty

Asian

Questioning

Villainous

are not to be used, a dot placed below the inner corner may contribute to the illusion of a slanted eye.

In straight parts, the eyebrows should frame the eyes rather than attract attention to themselves. Again, brown or black may be used in hairlike strokes following the shape of the eye. Most natural eyebrows do not have identical arches; therefore, by matching them, makeup can greatly improve their appearance. In character makeup, many different effects can be achieved by changing the eyebrows. Close, heavily drawn brows appear villainous. Lifting the brows into a round, thin arch gives an amazed or stupid expression. Twisted brows or brows dropped at contrasting angles make a face seem plaintive, menacing, or leering.

Step Five: Powdering

The most important step in the application of creme makeup or soft greasepaint is that of putting on the powder. Use translucent powder or a shade one tone lighter than the foundation. The powder, when properly applied, sets the makeup, softens the lines and colors, and gives a matte finish, which removes the shine of the makeup under the lights. Powder must be squeezed into the puff and the excess shaken off. Then the powder should be pressed or rolled into the makeup thoroughly but gently. Be very careful not to rub or smear the makeup.

The pressing in of the powder holds the makeup in place and prevents its running under the lights. Some makeup authorities suggest patting the powder on, but beginners often find they get spots of heavy powder that are difficult to remove. Be certain you have powdered all exposed skin areas you have made up, including the eyelids, ears, neck, and lips. Brush off the extra powder very lightly with the powder brush, but do not disturb the lines or leave streaks and powder spots.

Step Six: Lipstick and Finishing Touches

After the powder, you may apply the finishing touches. If the powder dulled the cheeks, dry rouge may be used to restore the color, but be sure no lines or spots of rouge are visible.

Girls should now apply mascara or false eyelashes. Use brown mascara instead of black unless you are a real brunette. False eyelashes, put on with liquid adhesive and carefully trimmed to suit the character and lighting, are often very effective and in many ways preferred over mascara.

Girls should use moist rouge or stage lipstick for the lips, for with the many pigments found in commercial lipsticks today, it is impossible to predict how they will react under modern lighting effects. Therefore, it is dangerous to use your "street" lipstick unless you have tested it under the stage lights and the director has approved the color. Boys, if they use lip makeup, should use brown or reddish-brown lining color.

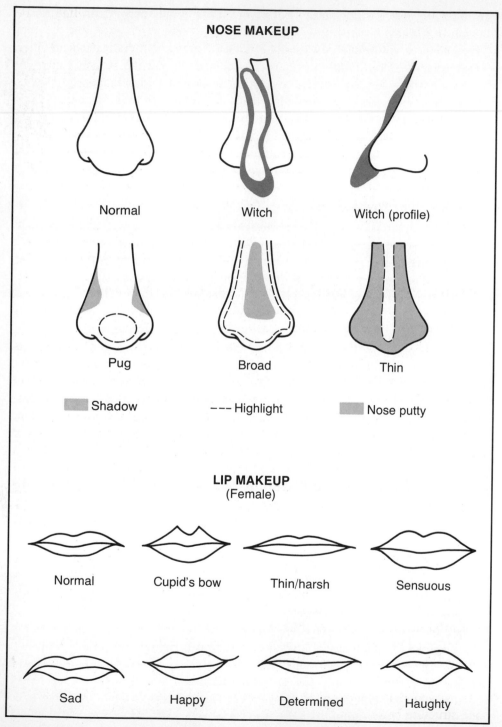

NOSE MAKEUP

Normal   Witch   Witch (profile)

Pug   Broad   Thin

Shadow   --- Highlight   Nose putty

LIP MAKEUP
(Female)

Normal   Cupid's bow   Thin/harsh   Sensuous

Sad   Happy   Determined   Haughty

For sanitary reasons, it is best for the actor to apply lipstick with the little finger or a lipstick brush. Lipstick brushes may be used for group makeup provided they are wiped clean and sterilized after each use. Girls should remember that the shape of the lips is determined by the role and not by their ordinary street makeup. The lipstick should be blended on the inside so that a definite line is not visible when the mouth is open. It is also important that the corners of the mouth receive just enough rouge to define the mouth against the foundation. The lower lip should be lighter in color than the upper lip. If the lips are too full, the foundation may be extended over them and ''new'' lips created. If the lips are thin, the rouge may be extended beyond the natural lip line to any shape desired, but not widened beyond the natural corners of the mouth. For character emphasis, the lips, particularly new lips, can be outlined with dark red or brown.

The line of the mouth can create many subtle expressions to heighten your characterization. For example, a full, sensuous mouth can be made puritanical by blocking out the curves and using light, straight lines in their place. By turning the corners of the mouth up slightly, an actor may be made to seem happy or pleasant even when not smiling. By turning the corners down, the actor may be made to seem always bitter or depressed. Avoid making your mouth the center of interest in your face, however, unless the part you are playing demands it.

Removing Makeup

After the performance is over, remove the makeup completely. Wearing makeup outside the theater marks you as an amateur and an exhibitionist. Use cold cream, Albolene, or makeup remover to soften the makeup and cleanse the skin. Use only the amount of makeup remover necessary to soften makeup. Too much makeup remover will dissolve the makeup so much that it will run and create a great smeared mess. Wipe off the liquified makeup with cleansing tissue or towels. Long strokes and a circular motion will prevent rubbing the makeup into the skin. Wash the face with soap and warm water and then rinse with cool water to close the pores.

SPECIAL MAKEUP PROBLEMS

Aging

Of all the makeup problems commonly encountered by the high school actor, the most difficult to handle effectively is the aging process. Young faces do not lend themselves well to the illusion of age. The methods suggested by some makeup authorities work well with older actors but do not result in a convincing appearance of middle or old age with most high school students.

The key to all makeup is bone structure. The actor needs to know her or his own bone structure before designing makeup for a role. Most serious acting students have facial masks made of their faces. A *facial mask* is a plaster casting taken of the face. The basic bone structure that the mask preserves does not alter much with time although the face may change considerably in appearance as years go by. These changes are due primarily to a pulling away of the muscles of the face, resulting in the sagging effect seen in old age.

Aging with makeup begins with the choice of foundation color. With age, the skin color tends to pale and deaden. Therefore, use light foundation colors, such as yellow, tan, or pale pink. However, it is through the modeling of the face that the real effects of aging are portrayed. This modeling involves the following three basic principles: lines, highlights, and shadows. *Lines* create wrinkles; *highlights* and *shadows* create folds of the skin, which deepen the wrinkles.

There are two basic methods for applying wrinkles. The first assumes you have already applied the highlights and shadows. If you have natural wrinkles, you can usually "mark" them in the foundation by raising the brows, squinting the eyes, smiling, and pulling the chin in. Then, while the lines are still visible in the greasepaint, draw the wrinkles on with brown liner. If you do not have natural wrinkles yet, you will have to follow the same procedure, but draw the lines while the muscles are still contracted.

The second method requires you to draw the wrinkles before applying the foundation. To use this method, spread brown liner over the areas where you plan to draw wrinkles. Form the wrinkles carefully, and wipe off the visible liner

Hal Holbrook prepares for his one-man show, Mark Twain Tonight. *Makeup transforms Holbrook into a seventy-year-old Mark Twain.*

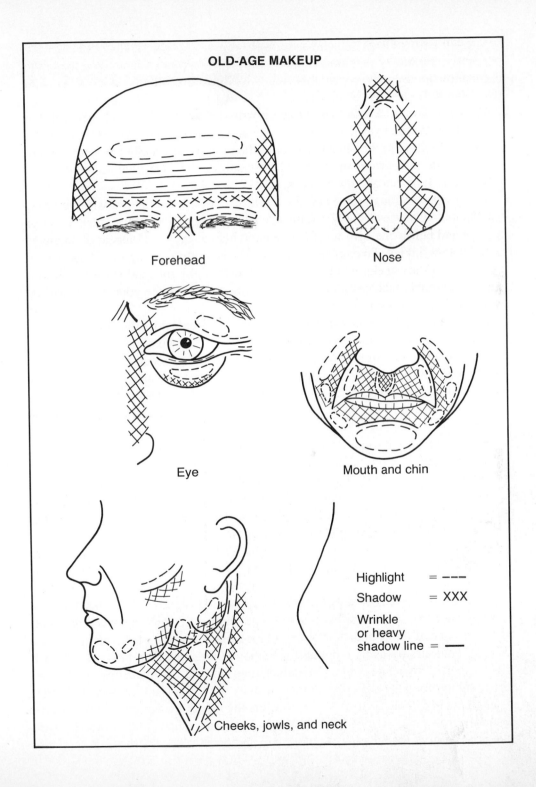

OLD-AGE MAKEUP

Forehead

Nose

Eye

Mouth and chin

Cheeks, jowls, and neck

Highlight = ---
Shadow = XXX
Wrinkle
or heavy
shadow line = ▬

before relaxing the face. When you relax the muscles, the natural wrinkles should be clearly marked by the remaining liner. Form the wrinkles again, and apply the foundation greasepaint. After this step, highlight the folds of skin, relax, and blend the wrinkles into shadows.

The most common locations for aging wrinkles are the forehead, between the brows, beneath the eyes (bags), the nasolabial folds (the smile wrinkle—from the nostrils extending to the outside corner of the mouth), vertically on the upper and lower lips, at the corners of the mouth, beneath the lower lip, under the jaw (the jowls), and horizontally on the neck.

Never draw too many lines on the forehead. Follow the natural wrinkle lines. You should also be especially careful when drawing age lines at the outer corner of the eye and below the eye, for if they are too heavy, they will appear as smudges rather than wrinkles. To emphasize sagging jowls, cotton, sponges, or tissues may be placed in the cheeks in addition to the use of highlights and shadows. If you elect this option, take extra care with your articulation since your mouth will be partially filled with cotton, sponges, or tissue.

It is the contrast in highlights and shadows that creates the illusion of old age. The older the character, the greater is this contrast. The bony prominences of the face receive the highlights, while the facial depressions receive the shadows.

The areas of the face to highlight are the frontal crest (the area above and below the eyebrows), the outer half of the eyelid, the outer curve of the eye pouches (bags), the bridge of the nose, the cheekbones, the nasolabial folds, the chin, the jowls, the Adam's apple (men only), and the wrinkles of the forehead and the eyes. When highlighting a wrinkle to make the wrinkle deep and sharply defined, a thin line of highlighter is drawn above the wrinkle line and blended outward until the highlight gradually fades into the foundation color.

The areas of the face to shadow are the depression in the forehead, the temples, the inner half of the eyelid next to the nose, the depression between the brows, the pouch (the soft area) beneath the eyes, the sides of the nose, the inside edge of the nasolabial folds, the cupid's bow of the upper lip, the depression beneath the lower lip, the hollows of the cheeks, the lower edges of the jowls, and the depressions of the neck.

There are additional factors to consider when creating an old-age makeup. As people age, their lips tend to become paler and thinner. To produce this effect with makeup, spread the foundation color to block out the edges of the mouth. Draw new lip contours by using a lighter foundation color, a reddish brown liner, or a light covering of white liner. Use darker rouge in old-age makeups. Apply the rouge lightly for a natural effect or more heavily if a "made-up" look is desirable. Hair changes with age. Gray, silver, or white the hair at the temples, in streaks, or overall. Brows may also be grayed or whitened and brushed gently inward toward the nose to give that shaggy appearance common in older people.

Skin tone changes with age. Stippling with a plastic sponge helps age the skin and is particularly effective for aging the smooth skin of youth. To stipple the skin, use two or three colors. Place a dab of each color in the palm of the hand. Take the sponge and dip it into each color. Then lightly touch the sponge to the face so that the little holes in the sponge leave tiny dots on the face.

A new technique that has grown popular in the theater today is using liquid latex to roughen skin texture. Liquid latex comes in tan, flesh, and white. Stipple the latex over a stretched section of skin and allow it to dry. When the skin relaxes, a wrinkled-textured face is the result, ready to be covered with greasepaint. However, this rough surface is more difficult to cover smoothly. A word of warning in using liquid latex. It must not get into the hair, even the "down" of a young face, because when the latex is removed the hair will be pulled.

Still another way to roughen the skin to show old age is to press cornmeal into a

The television production of Laurence Hausman's play Victoria Regina *won Julie Harris an Emmy Award. Here she is as the young queen and as the aging widow sixty years later. Helen Hayes played Victoria on Broadway.*

liquid latex base before it dries. For extreme old age, toilet tissue or cleansing tissue can be wrinkled and pressed into the latex. The cornmeal or tissue, whichever is used, is then covered with another coat of latex before applying the foundation color.

An often forgotten clue to age is the hands. They clearly reveal age and should always be made up for the portrayal of an older person. The tendons, knuckles, and other bones need to be highlighted. The sides, depressions, and wrinkles of the fingers need to be shadowed. To portray extreme old age, strongly pronounced blood vessels should appear on the backs of the hands.

One last word about old-age makeup. Like the hands, the legs are dead giveaways of age. A 16-year-old girl playing a 70-year-old woman must remember to change the appearance of her legs. One simple remedy is to wear cotton hose. A more dramatic solution may be required if the character will appear wearing sheer hose. In this situation, the legs must be aged by stippling and creating varicose veins.

Wigs and Beards

Hair is an integral part of both makeup and costume. Well-planned and carefully dressed coiffures can help transform high school girls into sophisticated middle-aged women, prim matrons, or exotic adventuresses. The use of easily removed hair tints can change a girl's stage personality. Hair whitener, white mascara, liquid white shoe polish, clown white, or wash-out colorants are used to gray or whiten the hair. The use of ordinary cornstarch or white powder is not recommended. Cornstarch has a tendency to deaden the highlights of the hair, and a cloud of white powder arises if anyone touches it. Costume changes over whitened hair are not difficult, particularly if the hair is covered with a protective scarf.

Wigs, hairpieces, and falls are quite helpful in changing hair styles to fit character types and historical periods. However, only expensive wigs appear natural and effective. They should be individually fitted, if the budget permits, and they should be adjusted and handled with great care. Wigs are put on from the front and fitted back over the head. The real hair, if it shows, must be tinted to match the wig. A bald wig must fit perfectly, and the places where it meets the forehead and neck must be cleverly concealed by makeup. One way to do this is to place a piece of adhesive tape over the edge of the *blender* and work the foundation greasepaint up over the tape onto the cloth. If inexpensive cloth wigs are to be used, the forehead edge of the blender can be cut unevenly and then glued down with spirit gum.

For men, eccentric haircuts and hairdos are often more realistic than wigs. Boys' hair problems are important, for a perfect makeup and an impeccable adult

With the help of makeup and costuming, Christopher Plummer (top, without make-up) becomes Sir Andrew Aguecheek in Twelfth Night *(left) and Philip the Bastard in* King John *(above).*

costume can be ruined by a boyish contemporary hairstyle. A good barber may cut the hair to suit the characterization. Boys can easily change the color of their hair with mascara or wash-out colorants. The hair should be freshly washed so that there is no natural oil on it. The mascara may then be applied with a wet toothbrush, brushing it back from the forehead.

Beards, mustaches, and sideburns require time and practice to apply realistically. Too many beards seem tacked to the point of the chin—probably because they were. Although professionally prepared beards and hairpieces are available, most are too expensive for school use. Wool crepe hair is used to create beards for the stage. Crepe hair comes in many colors, including grays, salt-and-pepper blends, blondes, light and dark browns, and black.

Crepe hair comes braided and is sold by the yard. It is curly when unbraided and must be straightened for most use. Either dampen the crepe hair and tie it across the arms or back of a chair to dry overnight, or iron the damp hair dry. Then the hair may be cut into lengths somewhat longer than the trimmed beard or mustache is to be. Several colors may be blended together for a more realistic appearance. Fan the hair between the fingers and thumb, and apply to the adhesive-coated area.

Spirit gum is still a popular adhesive, although liquid latex is being used by many actors. One disadvantage of latex is that it must never get into the actor's natural hair or brows. But it does have a strong advantage for those who must wear beards and sideburns for several performances. A piece of nylon stocking cut approximately the shape of the beard can be glued to the face with latex; the hair is then applied to the nylon. The beard and nylon are trimmed to shape, but instead of discarding the beard at the end of the performance, the nylon-backed hairpiece may be carefully peeled off to be used for the succeeding performances.

When making a beard, always consider the patterns and directions of natural hair growth. Before applying the hair, be certain that the face is clean-shaven and that all skin areas to which hair is to be attached are free from makeup if spirit gum is to be used. Apply only a small amount of hair at a time, starting at the point of the chin and shingling upwards. In a similar fashion, apply the hair beneath the chin. However, the shingling is from the point of the chin downwards. When all the hair is in place, press it to the face with a towel. It can then be combed and trimmed to shape.

An unshaven effect can be created by stippling gray-blue or brown lining color on the foundation with a rubber sponge just before powdering. An even more realistic effect can be achieved by cutting crepe hair into tiny bits, spreading the shredded hair over the surface of a smooth towel, and transferring the hair to the face, which has been sparingly coated with spirit gum or latex. For a heavy stubble, use pulverized tobacco.

Facial Features

Liquid latex can be used for molding eyelids, cheeks, noses, and other built-up features attached to the skin with additional latex. These molded pieces are called prosthetics.

Prosthetics are best made on a facial mask made by taking a plaster casting of the entire face, including the closed eyes. After the plaster has set you have an exact replica of the face. Shape the desired prosthetic piece in clay on the facial mask. Make a plaster casting of this clay model to provide a mold for the liquid latex. Pour the latex into the mold and allow it to set. When the hardened latex is removed, you have a prosthetic piece ready to be attached to the face.

When you use *nose putty* to change facial features, bear in mind that the putty must be kneaded into a pliable mass in the hands before it is placed on the face. Adding a little greasepaint or cold cream will make it more workable, and a little spirit gum will add to its adhesiveness. Nose putty may be used for building up noses, chins, cheekbones, and ears; for creating warts, scars, and other blemishes. Use alcohol or acetone to dissolve the spirit gum used to attach nose putty.

There are two types of collodion that are useful to the makeup artist—flexible and nonflexible. *Flexible collodion* is used for building up the flesh or texturing the skin. For example, a double chin may be built up with layers of cotton that have been coated with spirit gum. When the "chin" is as large as desired, the cotton is coated with diluted collodion (thinned with an equal amount of acetone), brushing outwards and extending the collodion about ½ inch beyond the cotton. *Nonflexible collodion* is used for making indentations and scars and for drawing up the flesh. To form a skin depression, apply the nonflexible collodion with a brush and allow each layer to dry until the indentation is deep enough. To draw up the flesh, stretch the skin in the area to be painted and allow the collodion to dry. Then relax the skin. Collodion may be peeled off or removed with acetone.

Adhesive tape can be a very effective aid to character makeup. Asian eyelids can be created by placing tape over the lids; the lift of Asian eyebrows may be achieved by a piece of tape that pulls the outer brow toward the temple. Tape may also "pull" parts of the face to suggest the effects of scars or paralysis.

Tooth enamel comes in black, white, ivory, or cream. The black enamel is used to block out teeth, to make teeth appear pointed or chipped, and to make large teeth seem smaller. The "white" enamels are used to cover discolored, filled, or capped teeth and braces. The teeth must be dry before the enamel is applied.

Some other techniques, which take time and practice to master, can be used. It is sometimes necessary to block out part or all of the eyebrows. Foundation greasepaint is satisfactory if the brows are not too dark or heavy; otherwise nose putty may be required. Then draw new brows with an eyebrow pencil. The photographs on page 305 show the steps taken to apply a character makeup.

Bizarre Makeup

Bizarre makeup may be tried if it is in keeping with the type of play and style of production. Stylized makeup, including "white masks," clownlike faces, and mosaics, can be quite effective on the stage. Special makeup has been developed for use with ultraviolet light. Changeable makeup really involves two makeup designs, one visible under ordinary light and the other visible under special lighting. For example, place a character wearing a special red greasepaint under red light, and that character will appear to be white or in straight makeup. Change to blue or green light and the red will appear to be black. Ultraviolet makeup can also be used for changeable illusions.

Animal makeup is fun and challenging. Most *animal makeup* can be suggestive rather than realistic. This allows the makeup designer to be creative in selecting makeup materials. For example, the designer can work with crepe hair, feathers, construction paper, foam rubber, Styrofoam, pipe cleaners, drinking straws, patches of cloth, and so on. Plastic bottles can be shaped into teeth. Liquid latex, nose putty, and derma wax can build up facial features or be molded into beaks, snouts, and horns.

Nonhuman illusions can be created with hoods and half masks. Upper head pieces constructed of foam rubber, Styrofoam, or paper can be worn like a hat or can be attached to a cap that will fit snugly on the actor's head.

The first step in creating an animal makeup is to develop a workable design that considers the identifying features of the animal and the actor. The makeup designer should begin with a photograph or sketch of the actor. Then a makeup worksheet similar to that shown on page 376 should be made. Next the designer should make a drawing of the animal's face that is the same size as the drawing of the actor's face. The prominent features of the animal should be outlined as a cartoon so that only those characteristics that readily identify the animal are exaggerated. This outline drawing should be transferred to a clear plastic sheet and superimposed over the actor's picture. This enables the makeup designer to see exactly where the animal features will appear on the actor's face. See page 306 for photographs of some bizarre makeups.

The Dark-Skinned Actor

The same basic makeup principles apply to dark-skinned actors as to the Caucasian actor. However, light-skinned actors almost always need a base, while the dark-skinned actor's own skin color may sometimes serve as the makeup foundation. Dark skin tones are not simply "brown" or "black." There is as much variation in dark skin as there is in light, and the underlying red, yellow, and "copper" pigments are important to proper makeup. Very dark skin has a tendency to "bleed" through a lighter foundation. Consequently, it may be necessary to apply a makeup sealer before applying the base. White, "flesh," yellow, rose, or a lighter foundation color may be used for highlighting. Maroon or maroon mixed with brown or black works well as a shadow color. Dark brown, maroon, or violet are good eye shadows. Black or dark brown should be used for eyeliner. At proscenium distance, the facial features of a dark-skinned actor can be lost to the audience. Therefore, a highlighting of the nostrils and the jawline may be required. The rouge should match the foundation color, but dark-skinned actors can also use rouges with orange as well as red pigment. Since dark-skinned people often have oily skins, careful drying or use of an astringent is recommended.

MAKEUP AND LIGHTING

One must always be aware of the effects of light on makeup. Amber light, which is frequently used on the stage, causes the complexion to yellow, the rouge to fade, and blue eye shadow to gray. Under blue lights, as in night scenes, blue is absorbed and red turns black. Be certain you know the lighting that will be used while you are onstage so that pigments can be selected or mixed in order that the light will reflect the proper colors. Finally, it is usually wise to plan a costume-makeup rehearsal to check the effects of light and costume on makeup.

Remember that in both class and school plays it is the actor, not the makeup and costume, who creates the real illusion. However, the care spent on a first-class ensemble of correct costume, makeup, hairdress, and accessories will give you an assurance that will help you create a convincing characterization. Makeup is an integral part of the actor's whole appearance. It is to be used and enjoyed as another tool in the actor's craft.

MAKEUP PROJECTS

1. Draw a facial "mask" of your own face, carefully indicating bone structure and features.
2. On the facial mask indicate the types and colors of makeup you would use if you were to make yourself up for a specific part in a play. Carefully show where it should be applied.
3. Design the makeup for a young woman in a night scene.
4. Design the makeup for all the characters in a stylized production.
5. Present a demonstration of some unusual makeup technique, such as the use of latex, nose putty, or collodion.
6. Prepare a full beard and mustache on a nylon backing for yourself or a classmate.

BIBLIOGRAPHY

Baird, John: *Make-up,* French, New York, 1941.
Buchman, Herman: *Stage Makeup,* Watson-Guptill, New York, 1971.
Corson, Richard: *Stage Makeup,* Prentice-Hall, Englewood Cliffs, New Jersey, 1975.
Strenkovsky, Serge: *The Art of Make-up,* Dutton, New York, 1937.

CHAPTER FIFTEEN

The Musical Play

Musical theater includes several forms. The oldest form is the *opera*. Since the voice and the orchestra are the only media of performance, opera is "total music." Even conversations are sung, not spoken as in other forms of musical theater. The *operetta* is another type of musical. Operetta music is lighter than operatic music and the singer/actor speaks lines rather than sings them. Operettas are usually built on flimsy plots that serve only to connect one song with another. Plot, character, and acting are incidental to the music, which is the most important element. The music must be well-written, and the performers must be accomplished singers. Some popular operettas are *The Desert Song, The Chocolate Soldier, The Student Prince, Babes in Toyland,* and *The Merry Widow.* An off-shoot of the straight operetta is *comic opera,* humorous or satirical operettas. For many years the comic operas of Gilbert and Sullivan have been very popular as high school shows. Among the favorites are *The Mikado, H. M. S. Pinafore,* and *The Pirates of Penzance.* Gilbert and Sullivan were the first successful musical theater writing team. A seldom-used form of musical theater is the *musical revue,* a loosely connected series of production numbers. The Ziegfield Follies was the most famous of these lavish extravaganzas.

The *musical comedy* is a combination of some elements from the musical revue and the operetta. Musical comedy plots still tend to be weak, while the music continues to be the main element. However, the creation of more believable characters speaking clever lines adds dimension to the musical comedy. The person most responsible for this change was Cole Porter. Singers need to be able to act as well as sing, but the primary demand is for talented song-and-dance performers. Some of the musical comedies presented by high schools are *Anything Goes, No,*

No, Nanette, Annie Get Your Gun, The Pajama Game, Damn Yankees, Guys and Dolls, and *L'il Abner.*

Show Boat is the musical that bridged the gap between the operetta, musical comedy, and today's musical play. The score of *Show Boat* is much like that of an operetta and the staging is like that of a musical comedy, but the story line and character development are very like that of the musical play.

Oklahoma! created the *musical play,* a form of musical theater characterized by an increased emphasis on real people in real situations. In the musical play, acting and choreography are an integral part of the production. Because a well-written musical play contains a good story, clever dialogue, interesting characters, well-designed choreography, bouncy tunes, and meaningful ballads woven into a sparkling package of color and spectacle that provides excellent opportunities for showmanship and talent, it has replaced many operettas and variety shows in the high school theater repertoire.

The musical play has become a major part of high school theater for other reasons. The sophistication of contemporary audiences demands more than a stage full of people in a simple review of pretty songs loosely tied together. In addition to greater audience appeal, a musical play involves many students on the stage, in the orchestra pit, and behind the scenes. It is a form of live theater that can pull people away from their television sets. Because the musical play is a total theater experience involving young people in all the facets of play production—singing, dancing, acting, stagecraft, and costuming—students are highly motivated to participate in such a play.

MUSICAL PLAY TERMINOLOGY

book: The script of a musical.

choreographer: A person who designs dance for the stage.

choreography: The dances designed for a production.

chorus: The singers other than the principals.

composer: A person who writes music.

conductor: A person who directs the orchestra.

crossover: A short scene played on a shallow stage while scenery is being changed behind a curtain.

librettist: A person who writes the book (script).

libretto: The book, including lines and lyrics.

lyricist: A person who writes words to music.

lyrics: The words to a song.

principals: The named characters in a musical play.

production number: A large-scale musical number involving a large group of performers in lavish costumes. Frequently a production number is a dance number.

score: The music as composed.

sides: Booklets containing half sheets of paper on which are written the cues and lines for one character.

soubrette: A secondary female lead, usually a comic role.

underscore: Music played to accompany dialogue.

vamp: Measures of music repeated until a singer or scene is ready to begin.

PRODUCING A MUSICAL PLAY

Staffing a musical play is considerably more difficult than staffing a straight play. A musical play usually calls for a play director, a vocal director, an instrumental director, a technical director, and a choreographer. In addition, there is a need for a costumer, a business manager, and a publicity director. However, only one person must be the *director,* and all the participants, no matter under which staff member they work most of the time, must recognize the director as being in charge of the entire production. Sooner or later, decisions will have to be made that only one person in authority can make. Everyone, students as well as staff, must accept the director's decision.

To direct a musical play, an individual must know all aspects of musical theater: acting, singing, dancing, orchestrating, and set designing. This does not mean that the director needs to be an expert in all these areas. However, she or he must be aware of all the components of the musical play. Sometimes the instrumental director or the vocal director may qualify to direct a musical play. Usually the only persons who truly qualify are the drama director and the choreographer, since they usually know more about all facets of musical theater.

Choreography has become such an essential part of the modern musical play that some of the most successful directors on Broadway started out as choreographers, Jerome Robbins, Gower Champion, and Bob Fosse, for example. With the emergence of such directors, musical plays have been created around dance and choreographic movement. *West Side Story* is an outstanding example. However, the choreography for a Broadway musical is designed for experienced professionals, not for high school performers with limited dance skills. Nevertheless, excellent and exciting dance numbers can be presented if the dances are suited to the abilities of the performers.

After the staff has been chosen, a *budget* must be prepared. The total expenses are considerably more for a musical than for a straight play (two to ten times as much). These expenses include costs not associated with the production elements

Choreography has become an essential part of the modern musical. The Wiz *was a long-running Broadway musical hit filled with lively and inventive dance numbers.*

of the play. For instance, royalty and script costs are significantly more complicated. The companies holding the rights to the majority of musical plays are Tams-Witmark, Rodgers and Hammerstein Repertory, Music Theater International, and Samuel French. Before producing a musical play, the publisher of the work must be contacted to grant permission to hold public performances of that play. Every publisher has a different formula for calculating royalty costs, which may include or exclude certain rehearsal material in the fee quoted.

A royalty fee is normally based on the number of seats sold and the ticket prices charged. The number of seats reported should represent what you determine your "house" to be. Otherwise, you will be charged for all your empty seats. For example, if you have an auditorium seating 1,500 but you plan to use only the front section seating 500, report your capacity as 500. Have tickets printed for 500 seats only. Do not sell more than those 500 seats unless you contact the publisher of the play and make the necessary royalty adjustments for the additional seats you intend to sell. Some royalty fees include music rental for one month; some charge the music rental separately. An additional fee is charged for a longer rehearsal time. Most schools need the music for at least 2 months.

Be sure you understand the script policies of each firm. Tams-Witmark provides vocal scores with the librettos with the fee. Rodgers and Hammerstein Repertory provide only vocal scores; librettos must be purchased separately. Music Theater International and Samuel French provide both vocal scores and librettos. Most companies will also send two piano scores. These will serve two rehearsal accompanists, but you will need to purchase additional piano scores separately through a music store for those members of the staff who want them.

Once the show has been selected and the rights to produce it obtained, the play must be *cast*. Under the best of circumstances, a musical play is much more difficult to cast than a straight play. Not only must acting ability be judged, but singing and dancing abilities must also be considered. Some shows require that the leads be skilled in all three of these areas; other shows require skills in only one or two of these areas. Too often a musical play is chosen that is too complex for a particular school to do well. It may require more strong characters than can be cast. The vocal requirements may be too demanding for high school voices. There may not be sufficient time to train students in the special skills the show requires, such as tap dancing. All too often and too late it is discovered that the best actor has "two left feet" or the individual with the finest voice is not an actor. Another often-forgotten factor in putting on a musical is the effect interpersonal relationships can have on a production. Since there are usually more cast members in a musical than in a straight play, there are more interpersonal relationships to consider when casting. Be aware of the personality mixture. Many potentially fine shows have been marred by squabbling among tempermental cast members.

In summary, when selecting a musical play for production, consider these questions:

Are the production costs within our budget limits?
Do we have the staff to direct this show?
Do we have the acting and musical abilities this show requires?
Do we have the time required to prepare this show?
Is this a musical play that will please both performers and audience?

Once the casting is completed, a *rehearsal schedule* must be planned. Obviously the size and scope of a musical play is greater than that of a straight play. Therefore, more rehearsal time will be needed. Most directors want a minimum of 8 weeks of rehearsal. For the first few weeks, it is more efficient to rehearse several groups simultaneously. The orchestra can rehearse by itself. The dancers can rehearse with the choreographer to piano accompaniment or a rehearsal tape of the orchestra. The chorus can rehearse with the vocal director. If possible, it is best to stagger rehearsal schedules so that the chorus members do not have to sit through an entire rehearsal just to sing one or two songs. The principals can rehearse with the play's director. Step by step, the separate elements are combined. Rehearsals of the vocal and dance numbers begin with the orchestra, the vocal numbers are rehearsed in the context of entire scenes, and finally, all the groups come together to rehearse the whole show.

The rehearsals involving everyone should take place for at least 2 weeks. Schedule a minimum of 4 days of dress rehearsal: 1 day for each of the two acts and two complete dress rehearsals. This may seem like too many dress rehearsals, but a musical play has so many elements to coordinate that anything short of three times through in costume with complete technical support will probably result in the opening night being the final dress rehearsal.

DIRECTING A MUSICAL PLAY

Directing a musical play is a very complex task. First, the director must consider the construction of this type of play. Most are written in two acts. A few shorter shows are written as one continuous act. Action, theme, and character in musical plays and some musical comedies are revealed through song lyrics. The songs in operettas, on the other hand, are entities in themselves. The plot, such as it is, continues "around" the song. Not so in musical plays. If members of the audience miss some of the lyrics, there will be gaps in their understanding and appreciation of the entire show. The themes of many musical plays are expressed through the lyrics of a key song. Rodgers and Hammerstein were noted for their

Directing a musical play is a very complex task because casts are large and because there may be as many as ten to thirty scene changes. Lionel Bart's Oliver *is an example. Here Fagin is explaining the fine art of the pickpocket to young Oliver.*

"theme" songs: "Climb Every Mountain," "You'll Never Walk Alone," "Some Enchanted Evening," and "Something Wonderful."

Musical plays usually have many scenes (ten to thirty or more). This means that some scenes must be played in front of a curtain or a drop on a shallow segment of the stage while scenery is being changed behind the curtain. This is called playing a scene "in one." A scene played "in one" takes place on that portion of the stage which is 8 to 10 feet deep and upstage of the curtain line. Musical theater stages are usually divided into three depths, each 8 to 10 feet deep. Performers may enter *one, two,* or *three* right or left. The terms go back to the days of the wing stage, when the wing spaces were called first, second, and third wings. Some "in one" scenes consist of characters walking across the stage together or entering from opposite sides and meeting on stage. Such scenes are called *crossovers*. Crossovers may also be played on the apron of the stage in front of the act curtain. Some librettists consider the length of scenery changes and write crossover scenes. Others make no allowances for scenery changes, assuming that a scene can be changed within the 7 seconds that is the usual time limit for scene shifts. Since few high school stages are equipped like those on Broadway, scenery changes often take longer. A director must work with the technical director to determine the exact scenery shift time so that the smoothness and rhythm of the production is not lost. The conductor may be asked to vamp the *change music* (the music played to cover the sound of scenery changes) if it becomes apparent that a shift cannot be completed quickly.

Stage positions are extremely important in directing a musical play. Center, down center, and down right are the locations for most solos. Down right is a very strong solo position. Since we are a left-to-right-oriented society, an audience always turns back to its left when there is a large open stage, as there usually is in musical plays. The chorus must be blocked in groups to avoid solid lines that look like a school chorus on stage. Groups should consist of one, two, three, four, five, or seven people. However, odd-number groupings are preferable. The asymmetrical look of odd-number groups provides a dynamic sight line, while the symmetrical look of even-number groups provides a static sight line. Getting these groups of chorus members on and off the stage presents a real traffic problem for the director. She or he must rehearse extensively on chorus entrances and exits so that these comings and goings are smooth and inconspicuous.

The chorus must learn to "turn scenes in" to the soloists. The chorus accomplishes this in various ways: by turning the shoulder closest to the soloist upstage, by dropping the downstage shoulder slightly, by getting into a bent-knee or semi-crouch position, by kneeling on the downstage knee, and even by reclining on the floor with the head toward the soloist. There is a tendency for the downstage end of a large chorus to "creep" too far downstage, shutting off the audience's view of the soloist. Choruses must be warned against this and be told to maintain their groupings and positions. Otherwise, they will drift together into one large mass.

Another difficulty in directing a musical play is teaching the performers to match their lines and actions to the underscore. Actors sometimes feel ''shut off'' by the orchestra, and the director needs to encourage them to project over the orchestra pit. If they still cannot be heard, the orchestra may have to be asked to play more softly. As a last resort, cut out the underscore entirely.

There are five simple techniques that the director should point out over and over again to the cast of a musical play: (1) attack the first beat of each measure; (2) sing ''through the eyes''; (3) play out to the audience; (4) be ''alive in character''; (5) look as if you are enjoying yourself.

One of the secrets of putting life into a musical play is placing a strong vocal attack on the first beat of each measure. Most show tunes are lively, bouncy, driving numbers, and the stress words come on the first beat. When there is a rest on the first beat, the mood of the song is usually gentle, unsure, questioning.

A second technique to use, which adds sparkle to a musical number, is singing ''through the eyes.'' This is a phrase that refers to the focus of the voice being in the ''mask of the face.'' Humming creates a buzzing sensation in the mask of the face. A well-trained singer strives to focus the voice properly so that it is projected clearly and forcefully, but without straining, over the orchestra pit.

A third technique for all members of the cast to remember is to play out to the audience. This is especially true when performing in a musical play where more theatrical conventions are common. The sense of intimacy of the straight play is not so much a part of a musical play, since most songs and dances are staged to be played directly to the audience rather than to other members of the cast.

A fourth technique directors try to instill in cast members is to be ''alive in character.'' This is especially difficult for chorus members, who often do not realize their importance to the total production. They may take an ''I'm just a member of the chorus'' attitude, which can kill a show. The director must stress the need for each chorus member to develop a well-defined character. ''Just a chorus member'' must become ''Sam Tilsbury, owner of the corner drug store in River City, whose wife, Martha Mae, just bought their son, Freddie, a double-belled euphonium from that fast talking two-bit swindler, Harold Hill.'' When there are twenty to sixty people onstage, it is easy for a few individuals to lose their concentration. The chorus needs to be reminded that an audience sweeps its eyes over the entire cast looking for someone really ''alive'' or really ''dead.'' Alive is better. One dead chorus member can spoil an entire scene.

The final technique that the director should teach to the chorus as well as to the principals is to enjoy, enjoy, enjoy. Excitement, enjoyment, and energy are con-

42nd Street was director-choreographer Gower Champion's last show. Here you can see a well-disciplined chorus "alive in character," playing out to the audience.

tagious. An audience is eager to be drawn into the spirit of a play. When a cast looks as if it is enjoying the performance, the audience, and each other, the audience, too, shares in this enthusiasm.

Some types of musical plays are particularly difficult to direct. A spoof is such a play. *Spoofs* are farcical and poke fun at certain subjects or time eras. For example, *Little Mary Sunshine* pokes fun at a style of musical film; *Once Upon a Mattress* laughs at fairy tales; *The Boy Friend* ridicules the 1920s practices of love and romance. If spoofs are overacted, they are absurd. If they are played straight, they are tediously outdated. *Satires* are also difficult. To direct a satire effectively, the director must make sure that the audience clearly understands what aspects of human behavior or human society are being held up to criticism. The director must pace a musical satire expertly so that the comic moments and the serious moments stand out at the appropriate times. *How to Succeed in Business without Really Trying* satirizes the shenanigans of getting ahead in the business world. *Pippin,* on the other hand, is a heavier musical satire. It comments on humankind's inhumanity, resulting from too little love and too much war. Some plays, even for musical plays, are controversial, and unless the director interprets such a work carefully, an audience may not be prepared for some of the disturbing elements portrayed through character, plot, song, and dance. *Cabaret* is such a play. Because it is rather moralistic for a musical, there is a temptation to stress the surface aspects of the play depicted quite vividly in the cabaret scenes. By emphasizing the frivolous, titillating, and bawdy side of *Cabaret,* the director will turn the audience away from the play's serious commentary on the destruction of human lives and values during that time just prior to the rise of Nazi Germany. The subtle humor of *1776* and the rowdy burlesque of *The Man of La Mancha* are sometimes lost when directors allow the cast to play them straight. Some musicals are "pace" shows. *George M* is such a play, requiring a brisk tempo. Other musicals are "heart" shows. *A Little Night Music* is such a play, requiring a special sensitivity to human emotions without becoming overly sentimental. Some musicals are "splash" shows. *Hello, Dolly!* is such a play, calling for large production numbers. Few directors can handle all the various types of musicals just described with equal skill. Therefore, choose carefully. Suit the musical to the director and the director to the musical, to paraphrase Hamlet.

Cab Calloway and Pearl Bailey in Hello, Dolly!, *the long-running musical hit*

STAGING A MUSICAL PLAY

There are many staging decisions associated with musical plays. The director's first decision will be to determine the number of *sets* needed for the production. Few high schools can build as many sets as the script calls for, and it may be necessary to combine, eliminate, or reuse some scenery. Often the only choice is to play a scene in front of a traveler or the act curtain. However, if too many scenes are played in front of curtains, the show looks dull. Before finalizing the number of sets required, the director, the set designer, and the technical director must decide how much time it will take to change from one scene to another. If the shift time is too long, the scenery should be modified. After determining the number of scenes and set changes required, the director must decide which scenes will use drops, which scenes will use wagons, which scenes will use set pieces, and which scenes will be played in front of a curtain.

Professional theaters often have sixty or more counterweight lines on which to hang scenery. Few high schools have more than one third that number, and many schools have no fly system at all for hanging drops. Of those schools that have some kind of system for hanging drops, some do not have counterweighted or sand-bagged systems and the only way to raise and lower scenery is manually.

Broadway shows often use a combination of portals and backdrops. *Portals* are drops looking much like tunnel portals with a teaserlike piece of cloth across the top and leglike extensions that come to the floor at each end. The portals solve the need to mask the wings, always a problem in musicals, by making a solid set that can be changed in seconds.

Another way to handle scenery is by using revolving and jackknife wagon stages. These stages are especially effective when a scene calls for a lot of furniture or set pieces and, with scenery mounted on them, they allow for quick scene changes. Wagons can also be mounted with walls that are hinged so that the flats can be flipped over, revealing the other side. Unfortunately, wagons take up considerable wing space, and many schools have limited side stage areas.

These fly space and wing area limitations force many schools to use other means of set changing. Prism sets *(periaktoi)* are alternatives for schools with no fly space and limited wing areas. Scenery can be painted on all three sides of the prisms and used in different combinations, as seen on page 292. Wagons with double-covered flats (flats with muslin on both sides) can be turned around to show a different scene on the reverse side. The plywood on the reverse side causes slight bulges, but they are not too noticeable, and the saving of construction and the weight of a double wall of flats is well worth the aesthetic sacrifice. Double-covering is a good way to use the muslin from old drops.

There are often special scenic demands that are difficult to handle on any stage; for example, fog or mist, flying apparatus, carousels, Wells Fargo wagons, auto-

HANGING PLOT FOR ___WILD SONG___

LINE NO.		USE	DISTANCE FROM CURTAIN LINE
16	〰	Cyc _ _ _ _ _ _ _ _ _ _ _ _ _ _ _ _ _	24'
15	—	Countryside drop _ _ _ _ _ _ _ _ _ _ _	26'6"
14	—	Gymnasium interior _ _ _ _ _ _ _ _ _ _	21'8"
13	—	Ballet drop _ _ _ _ _ _ _ _ _ _ _ _	20'
12	E	4ᵀᴴ electric (3ʳᵈ border) _ _ _ _ _ _ _ _	18'6"
11	⤙—	Leg #2 (strike) garden drop _ _ _ _ _ _	17'
10	〰	Teaser #3 _ _ _ _ _ _ _ _ _ _ _ _ _	16'
9	～	Scrim _ _ _ _ _ _ _ _ _ _ _ _ _ _ _	14'6"
8	〰	Traveler _ _ _ _ _ _ _ _ _ _ _ _ _	13'
7	E	3ʳᵈ electric (2ⁿᵈ border) _ _ _ _ _ _ _	11'6"
6	〰	Teaser #2 _ _ _ _ _ _ _ _ _ _ _ _	10'
5	—	Garden portal _ _ _ _ _ _ _ _ _ _ _	9'3"
4	⤙—	Leg #1 (strike) town hall exterior _ _ _ _ _	8'
3	E	2ⁿᵈ electric (1ˢᵀ border)_ _ _ _ _ _ _ _	6'
2	⤙—	Teaser #1 (strike) show curtain_ _ _ _ _	4'6"
1	E	1ˢᵀ electric – X-ray–500 watt presnels _ _ _	1'6"
0	〰	Act curtain _ _ _ _ _ _ _ _ _ _ _ _ _	0

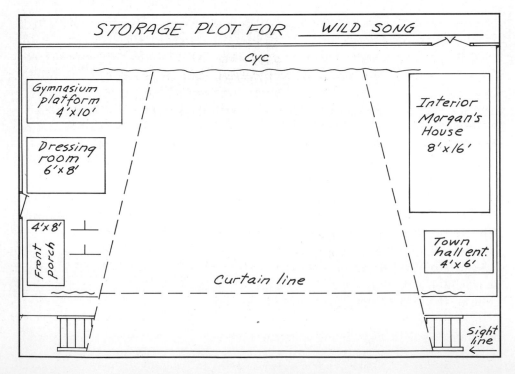

STORAGE PLOT FOR ___WILD SONG___

Cyc

Gymnasium platform 4'x10'

Dressing room 6'x8'

4'x8'
Front porch

Interior Morgan's House 8'x16'

Town hall ent. 4'x6'

Curtain line

Sight line

mobiles, and surreys. Sometimes it is better to work around such problems if you cannot treat them adequately on your stage. Rather than try too many poor substitutes, it may ultimately be better to try another show. Many of the answers to scenic problems depend upon the size and experience of the crew available to work the show.

Once all the scenery decisions are made, the technical director or the stage manager makes a *hanging plot* and a *storage plot* for the play. A hanging plot shows all the fly lines and what is on each. A storage plot shows the wing areas and how the scenic units are to be stored during the show. Refer to page 408 for an example of a hanging plot and a storage plot.

Lighting a musical play calls for more lighting equipment than needed for a straight play. There is usually a greater likelihood of shadows appearing on the stage in a musical because a limited number of instruments with a limited lighting range may have to be used to cover more stage areas. If the instruments are available, backlighting soloists and one-character and two-character scenes is quite effective. Backlighting throws light on the performer from above and slightly upstage. This causes a glow, or halo effect, that makes the actor stand out from the background or chorus. Backlighting should be used only with actors who have a strong stage presence, because the radiant glow can easily swallow up performers who have a weak stage presence.

Another lighting effect can be created with a follow spot. There are mixed feelings among high school directors regarding the use of follow spots. These spots do make soloists stand out. However, they also are an obvious artificial light source that can do strange things to the drop behind the performer. Also, when there is a chorus behind the soloist, the spotlight may cut off heads or other body parts of the chorus members. This particular side effect of a follow spot can be quite distracting. If a follow spot is used, most directors have the stage lights dimmed during a solo. This can be a slight dimming or as much as a three-quarter dimming. The lights are brought back up at the end of the solo after the applause. Of course, this dimming is recognized as a stage convention that is an acceptable lighting technique for musical plays.

Makeup and *costumes* for musical plays should be stronger and more exaggerated than those used in straight plays, since the many lights used in a musical play can deaden an actor's appearance. Costumes are more colorful and more highly stylized. Most musicals are bright, lively productions, and costume colors that would appear gawdy and unbelievable in a straight play seem totally acceptable in a musical play. Costumes for a musical may be quite elaborate, so it might be wise to consider renting them.

Dance costumes, especially for shows with several large production numbers, should be reversibles and coordinates. *Reversibles* are such clothing as vests, scarves, belts, and skirts that are made double-faced so that by reversing one or more of these articles of clothing, the illusion of a different costume is created. *Coordinates,* which can also be reversible, are separates or interchangeables. Costume coordinates such as hats, scarves, ties, vests, jackets, blouses, shirts, skirts, gloves, belts, spats, and shoes can be used in varied combinations.

All the costumes, whether rented or made, should be selected and approved by the director and the costumer. This will prevent costume imbalance. The principals' costumes should stand out from the chorus's costumes. However, it has been known to happen that a member or two of the chorus may stand out from the rest of the people on stage. This tends to occur when chorus members make their own costumes. As attractive as these homemade costumes might be, they must go. They upstage the principals by drawing audience attention to a chorus member and away from the principals.

One last note about costumes: do not try to costume everyone in every scene as done on Broadway. In a Broadway show, nearly every time a character comes onstage, he or she wears a new outfit. This is too costly, in time and money, for a high school production. One well-made, well-designed costume is far better than several mediocre ones.

THE ORCHESTRA

Although musical plays can be presented with piano accompaniment alone, an orchestra can greatly enhance the quality and impact of a production. Most musical plays open with an overture that features a medley of the show's total score. A similar, but briefer, orchestral piece, the *entr'acte,* precedes the second-act curtain. Unfortunately, orchestras often play too loudly, drowning out lines and lyrics, since few high school voices are strong enough to be heard over a "full pit." Good rapport must exist between the conductor and the director so that the priorities of the production can be met without creating animosity. If the orchestra is too loud, the director has the right to expect cooperation when the conductor is asked to lower the orchestra's volume.

One of the most critical problems facing a high school musical production is the limited vocal range of young voices. Rewriting the music or transposing it is normally a last resort. There is so much involved in rewriting the music for an entire orchestra that the time taken for this task is not well spent. Also, using just a piano for a particular number rewritten in a transposed key weakens that number when the rest of the show is fully orchestrated. The best way to handle the vocal restraints of high school singers is to choose a musical with a limited vocal range.

Acoustical problems are common to high school musical productions. Many schools do not have a recessed orchestra pit, so sound tends to attack the audience.

Other schools have tile, brick, or masonry on the auditorium floor and the apron of the stage. Such hard surfaces act as reflectors, and sound cannonades into the audience with deafening loudness. It sometimes helps balance sound if carpeting is placed on the floor of the orchestra pit, if there is one, and sheets of acoustical material or old stage curtains are draped over the front rows of seats. Some high schools solve their sound problems by building a shell around the orchestra so that the sound is slightly contained.

Communication between the pit and the stage is important. The conductor of the show, usually the instrumental director, must give clear signals to the performers on the stage. These signals must not be confused with those meant for the orchestra. Most conductors lead the orchestra with the right hand and cue the stage with the left. Whatever cuing system the conductor wishes to use, it should be made clear to the cast in early rehearsals. Giving the pitch to the stage performers is also quite vital in pit-to-stage communication. Often the score does not have a note for a soloist; he or she must "hear a note in the head" from another note played by the orchestra. Many high school performers do not have the musical experience necessary to pick up the pitch of a song in this way. Therefore, the conductor may have one of the instruments give the beginning note to the singer.

A musical revue is a good choice for a low-cost, small-cast high school production. Ain't Misbehavin', *the 1978 Tony Award-winning musical, revived the music of Fats Waller with a cast of five and a small onstage combo.*

WHAT CAN YOU DO?

The experience of presenting a musical play can be very rewarding. It is unfortunate that many schools feel they are too small or cannot afford the production costs. There are several shows that have small casts, require simple scenery and costumes, and can be done with minimum accompaniment. Among these shows are *The Fantasticks, You're a Good Man, Charlie Brown,* and *Dames at Sea.* There are also some musical plays with large casts that can be staged more economically than others. These include *Carnival, Once Upon a Mattress, The Pajama Game, Damn Yankees,* and *How to Succeed in Business without Really Trying.*

One of the real problems facing all high schools today is the fact that very few shows that have come off Broadway in recent years are suitable for high school production. School administrators, boards of education, teachers, and students must look very carefully at the available musical plays and decide which shows are fitting in subject matter and community taste and values.

MUSICAL PLAYS FOR HIGH SCHOOL PRODUCTION

Annotations: A = acting demanding; B = book difficult; C = choreography needed; CH = children needed; COS = costumes complex or numerous; D = dialect; LA = limited appeal; M = music difficult; NM = predominantly male cast; PC = production costs high; S = scenery complex; SC = small cast; SM = mature subject matter; SP = spoof or satire; ST = staging complex; V = vocal demands difficult.

Annie (CH,SC)
Annie Get Your Gun (COS,D,SC)
Anything Goes (C,SC)
The Boy Friend (C,SP)
Brigadoon (C,D,M,ST,V)
Cabaret (A,B,COS,LA,SM)
Camelot (A,B,COS,M,PC,SC,V)
Carnival (SC,V)
Dames at Sea (SC,SP)
The Fantasticks (NM,SC)
Fiddler on the Roof (A,D,ST)
Flower Drum Song (COS,D)
Funny Girl (A,D,SC,V)
George M (C,SC)
Godspell (SC,SM,ST,V)

Guys and Dolls (D,NM,SC)
Gypsy (A,SM)
Hello, Dolly! (A,C,ST,V)
How to Succeed in Business
  without Really Trying (M,SP)
The King and I (COS,D,M,PC,SC,V)
Kiss Me Kate (COS,V)
L'il Abner (D)
Little Mary Sunshine (COS,LA,SP)
Mame (A,COS,PC,SC)
The Man of La Mancha (A,ST,V)
The Music Man (A,C,SC,ST)
My Fair Lady (A,B,D,PC,SC,ST)
No, No, Nanette (C,COS,ST)
Oklahoma! (B,V)

Oliver (A,D,SC,V)
Once Upon a Mattress (COS,SP)
Paint Your Wagon (SM,ST)
The Pajama Game (B,SC,ST)
Pippin (COS,SM,SP)
*The Roar of the Greasepaint,
    the Smell of the Crowd* (LA,NM,SC)
1776 (A,COS,D,NM,V)

The Sound of Music (CH,D,SC,V)
South Pacific (D,NM,V)
Stop the World, I Want to Get Off (LA,SC)
The Unsinkable Molly Brown (A,B,SC,ST)
West Side Story (C,M,ST)
The Wiz (COS,PC,ST)
You're a Good Man, Charlie Brown (SC)

Overleaf: *"Voices" from the past in a scene from* Spoon River Anthology.

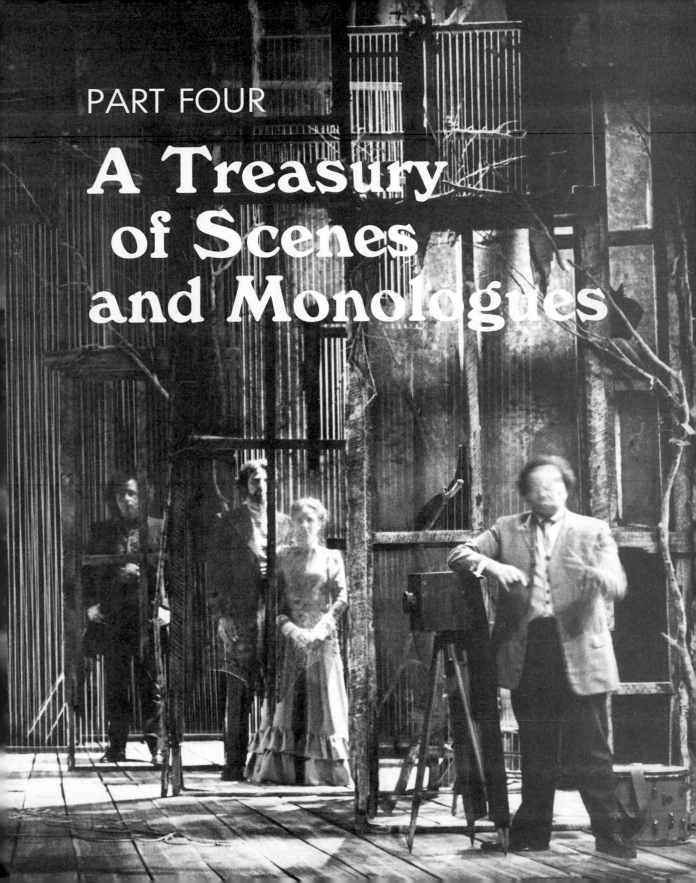

PART FOUR

A Treasury of Scenes and Monologues

Scenes for One Man and One Woman

Scenes for Two Women

Scenes for Two Men

Scenes for Mixed Groups

Monologues for Women

Monologues for Men

Long Plays for Production and Study

Scenes for One Man and One Woman

Romeo and Juliet

by William Shakespeare

    Romeo has met Juliet at a masked ball at her father's house and has fallen in love at first sight. After the ball, he goes to the Capulet garden. Juliet, standing on her balcony, confesses to the stars that she loves Romeo. Romeo overhears this private confession. The following scene is the balcony scene, the world's most famous love scene.

    (Capulet's orchard. ROMEO *advances from the wall.)*

ROMEO   He jests at scars that never felt a wound.

    (Juliet appears above at her window.)

But soft! What light through yonder window breaks?

It is the east, and Juliet is the sun!

Arise, fair sun, and kill the envious moon,

Who is already sick and pale with grief

That thou, her maid, art far more fair than she.

Be not her maid, since she is envious;

Her vestal livery is but sick and green,

And none but fools do wear it; cast it off.

It is my lady, O, it is my love!

Oh, that she knew she were!

She speaks, yet she says nothing; what of that?

Her eye discourses. I will answer it.—

I am too bold, 'tis not to me she speaks.

Two of the fairest stars in all the heaven,

Having some business, do entreat her eyes

To twinkle in their spheres till they return.

What if her eyes were there, they in her head?

The brightness of her cheek would shame those stars,

As daylight doth a lamp; her eyes in heaven

Would through the airy region stream so bright

That birds would sing and think it were not night.

See, how she leans her cheek upon her hand!

O, that I were a glove upon that hand,

That I might touch that cheek!

JULIET   Ay me!

ROMEO   She speaks!

O, speak again, bright angel! For thou art

As glorious to this night, being o'er my head,

As is a winged messenger of heaven

Unto the white-upturned wond'ring eyes

Of mortals that fall back to gaze on him

When he bestrides the lazy-pacing clouds

And sails upon the bosom of the air.

JULIET   O Romeo, Romeo, wherefore art thou Romeo?

Deny thy father and refuse thy name,

Or, if thou wilt not, be but sworn my love
And I'll no longer be a Capulet.

ROMEO *(Aside)* Shall I hear more, or shall I speak at this?

JULIET 'Tis but thy name that is my enemy.
Thou art thyself, though not a Montague.
What's a Montague? It is nor hand, nor foot,
Nor arm, nor face, nor any other part
Belonging to a man. Oh, be some other name!
What's in a name? That which we call a rose
By any other name would smell as sweet;
So Romeo would, were he not Romeo call'd,
Retain that dear perfection which he owes
Without that title. Romeo, doff thy name,
And for thy name, which is no part of thee,
Take all myself.

ROMEO   I take thee at thy word.
Call me but love, and I'll be new baptiz'd;
Henceforth I never will be Romeo.

JULIET What man art thou that, thus bescreen'd in night,
So stumblest on my counsel?

ROMEO   By a name
I know not how to tell thee who I am.

My name, dear saint, is hateful to myself,
Because it is an enemy to thee.
Had I it written, I would tear the word.

JULIET My ears have yet not drunk a hundred words
Of thy tongue's uttering, yet I know the sound.
Art thou not Romeo, and a Montague?

ROMEO Neither, fair saint, if either thee dislike.

JULIET How cam'st thou hither, tell me, and wherefore?
The orchard walls are high and hard to climb,
And the place death, considering who thou art,
If any of my kinsmen find thee here.

ROMEO With love's light wings did I o'erperch these walls;
For stony limits cannot hold love out.
And what love can do, that dares love attempt;
Therefore thy kinsmen are no stop to me.

JULIET If they do see thee, they will murder thee.

ROMEO Alack, there lies more peril in thine eye
Than twenty of their swords. Look thou but sweet,
And I am proof against their enmity.

JULIET I would not for the world they saw thee here.

ROMEO   I have night's cloak to hide me from their eyes,
    And but thou love me, let them find me here.
    My life were better ended by their hate,
    Than death prorogued, wanting of thy love.

JULIET   By whose direction found'st thou out this place?

ROMEO   By Love, that first did prompt me to inquire.
    He lent me counsel, and I lent him eyes.
    I am no pilot; yet wert thou as far
    As that vast shore washed with the farthest sea,
    I would adventure for such merchandise.

JULIET   Thou know'st the mask of night is on my face,
    Else would a maiden blush bepaint my cheek
    For that which thou hast heard me speak tonight.
    Fain would I dwell on form, fain, fain deny
    What I have spoke; but farewell compliment!
    Dost thou love me? I know thou wilt say "Ay,"
    And I will take thy word. Yet if thou swear'st,
    Thou mayst prove false. At lovers' perjuries,
    They say, Jove laughs. O gentle Romeo,
    If thou dost love, pronounce it faithfully,
    Or if thou think'st I am too quickly won,
    I'll frown and be perverse and say thee nay,—
    So wilt thou woo: but else, not for the world.
    In truth, fair Montague, I am too fond,
    And therefore thou mayst think my 'haviour light;
    But trust me, gentleman, I'll prove more true
    Than those that have more cunning to be strange.
    I should have been more strange, I must confess,
    But that thou overheard'st ere I was ware,
    My true love's passion; therefore pardon me,
    And not impute this yielding to light love,
    Which the dark night hath so discover'd.

ROMEO   Lady, by yonder blessed moon I vow,
    That tips with silver all these fruit-tree tops—

JULIET   O, swear not by the moon, th' inconstant moon,
    That monthly changes in her circled orb,
    Lest that thy love prove likewise variable.

ROMEO   What shall I swear by?

JULIET   Do not swear at all.
    Or, if thou wilt, swear by thy gracious self,
    Which is the god of my idolatry,
    And I'll believe thee.

ROMEO   If my heart's dear love—

JULIET   Well, do not swear. Although I joy in thee,

I have no joy of this contract tonight;

It is too rash, too unadvis'd, too sudden,

Too like the lightning, which doth cease to be

Ere one can say "It lightens." Sweet, good night!

This bud of love, by summer's ripening breath,

May prove a beauteous flower when next we meet.

Good night, good night! As sweet repose and rest

Come to thy heart as that within my breast!

ROMEO   O, wilt thou leave me so unsatisfied?

JULIET   What satisfaction canst thou have tonight?

ROMEO   Th' exchange of thy love's faithful vow for mine.

JULIET   I gave thee mine before thou didst request it;

And yet I would it were to give again.

ROMEO   Wouldst thou withdraw it? For what purpose, love?

JULIET   But to be frank, and give it thee again.

And yet I wish but for the thing I have.

My bounty is as boundless as the sea,

My love as deep; the more I give to thee,

The more I have, for both are infinite.

━━━━━━━━━━━━━━━━━━━━

Saint Joan

by Bernard Shaw

In this scene, Joan inspires the Dauphin, Charles VII, with the courage to fight Henry VI and his invading English armies at Orleans and to be crowned the true King of France at Rheims Cathedral.

JOAN *(to the Dauphin)*   Who be old Gruff-and-Grum?

CHARLES   He is the Duke de la Trémouille.

JOAN   What be his job?

CHARLES   He pretends to command the army. And whenever I find a friend I can care for, he kills him.

JOAN   Why dost let him?

CHARLES   *(petulantly moving to the throne side of the room to escape from her magnetic field)*   How can I prevent him? He bullies me. They all bully me.

JOAN   Art afraid?

CHARLES   Yes: I am afraid. It's no use preaching to me about it. It's all very well for these big men with their armor that is too heavy for me, and their swords that I can hardly lift, and their muscle and their shouting and their bad tempers. They like fighting: most of them are making fools of themselves all the time they are not fighting; but I am quiet and sensible; and I don't want to kill people: I only want to be left alone to enjoy myself in my own way. I never asked to be a king: it was pushed on me. So if you are going to say "Son of St. Louis: gird on the sword of your ancestors, and lead us to victory" you may spare your breath to cool your porridge; for I cannot do it. I am not built that way; and there is an end of it.

JOAN *(trenchant and masterful)* Blethers! We are all like that to begin with. I shall put courage into thee.

CHARLES But I don't want to have courage put into me. I want to sleep in a comfortable bed, and not live in continual terror of being killed or wounded. Put courage into the others, and let them have their bellyful of fighting; but let me alone.

JOAN It's no use, Charlie: thou must face what God puts on thee. If thou fail to make thyself king, thoult be a beggar: what else art fit for? Come! Let me see thee sitting on the throne. I have looked forward to that.

CHARLES What is the good of sitting on the throne when the other fellows give all the orders? However! *(he sits enthroned, a piteous figure)* here is the king for you! Look your fill at the poor devil.

JOAN Thourt not king yet, lad: thourt but Dauphin. Be not led away by them around thee. Dressing up dont fill empty noddle. I know the people: the real people that make thy bread for thee; and I tell thee they count no man king of France until the holy oil has been poured on his hair, and himself consecrated and crowned in Rheims Cathedral. And thou needs new clothes, Charlie. Why does not Queen look after thee properly?

CHARLES We're too poor. She wants all the money we can spare to put on her own back. Besides, I like to see her beautifully dressed; and I don't care what I wear myself: I should look ugly anyhow.

JOAN There is some good in thee, Charlie; but it is not yet a king's good.

CHARLES We shall see. I am not such a fool as I look. I have my eyes open; and I can tell you that one good treaty is worth ten good fights. These fighting fellows lose all on the treaties that they gain on the fights. If we can only have a treaty, the English are sure to have the worst of it, because they are better at fighting than at thinking.

JOAN If the English win, it is they that will make the treaty; and then God help poor France! Thou must fight, Charlie, whether thou will or no. I will go first to hearten thee. We must take our courage in both hands: aye, and pray for it with both hands too.

CHARLES *(descending from his throne and again crossing the room to escape from her dominating urgency)* Oh do stop talking about God and praying. I can't bear people who are always praying. Isn't it bad enough to have to do it at the proper times?

JOAN *(pitying him)* Thou poor child, thou hast never prayed in thy life. I must teach thee from the beginning.

CHARLES I am not a child: I am a grown man and a father; and I will not be taught any more.

JOAN Aye, you have a little son. He that will be Louis the Eleventh when you die. Would you not fight for him?

CHARLES No: a horrid boy. He hates me. He hates everybody, selfish little beast! I don't want to be bothered with children. I don't want to be a father; and I don't want to be a son: especially a son of St. Louis. I don't want to be any of these fine things you all have your heads full of: I want to be just what I am. Why can't you mind your own business, and let me mind mine?

JOAN *(again contemptuous)* Minding your own business is like minding your own body: it's the shortest way to make yourself sick. What is my business? Helping mother at home. What is thine? Petting lapdogs and sucking sugarsticks. I call that muck. I tell thee it is God's business we are here to do: not our own. I have a message to thee from God; and thou must listen to it, though thy heart break with the terror of it.

CHARLES I don't want a message; but can you tell me any secrets? Can you do any cures? Can you turn lead into gold, or anything of that sort?

JOAN I can turn thee into a king, in Rheims Cathedral; and that is a miracle that will take some doing, it seems.

CHARLES If we go to Rheims, and have a coronation, Anne will want new dresses. We can't afford them. I am all right as I am.

JOAN As you are! And what is that? Less than my father's poorest shepherd. Thourt not lawful owner of thy own land of France till thou be consecrated.

CHARLES But I shall not be lawful owner of my own land anyhow. Will the consecration pay off my mortgages? I have pledged my last acre to the Archbishop and that fat bully. I owe money even to Bluebeard.

JOAN *(earnestly)* Charlie: I come from the land, and have gotten my strength working on the land; and I tell thee that the land is thine to rule righteously and keep God's peace in, and not to pledge at the pawnshop as a drunken woman pledges her children's clothes. And I come from God to tell thee to kneel in the cathedral and solemnly give thy kingdom to Him for ever and ever, and become the greatest king in the world as His steward and His bailiff, His soldier and His servant. The very clay of France will become holy: her soldiers will be the soldiers of God: the rebel dukes will be rebels against God: the English will fall on their knees and beg thee let them return to their lawful homes in peace. Wilt be a poor little Judas, and betray me and Him that sent me?

CHARLES *(tempted at last)* Oh, if I only dare!

JOAN I shall dare, dare, and dare again, in God's name! Art for or against me?

CHARLES *(excited)* I'll risk it. I warn you I shant be able to keep it up; but I'll risk it. You shall see.

The Importance of Being Earnest

by Oscar Wilde

The Importance of Being Earnest *is a satirical farce. Oscar Wilde is using his play to ridicule the social manners of nineteenth-century England. His characters tend to be stereotypes representing the types of individuals he perceived as being absurd in society as he knew it. In the following scene, Lady Bracknell confronts Jack Worthing. She holds certain character traits and family backgrounds as being essential in young men if they are to be acceptable potential husbands for her daughter, Gwendolen. Lady Bracknell quite vigorously rejects Jack as an appropriate suitor for Gwendolen.*

LADY BRACKNELL *(sitting down)* You can take a seat, Mr. Worthing. *(looks in her pocket for a note-book and pencil)*

JACK Thank you, Lady Bracknell, I prefer standing.

LADY BRACKNELL *(pencil and note-book in hand)* I feel bound to tell you that you are not down on my list of eligible young men, although I have the same list as the dear Duchess of Bolton has. We work together, in fact. However, I am quite ready to enter your name, should your answers be what a really affectionate mother requires. Do you smoke?

JACK Well, yes, I must admit I smoke.

LADY BRACKNELL I am glad to hear it. A man should always have an occupation of some kind. There are far too many idle men in London as it is. How old are you?

JACK Twenty-nine.

LADY BRACKNELL A very good age to be married at. I have always been of opinion that a man who desires to get married should know either everything or nothing. Which do you know?

JACK *(after some hesitation)* I know nothing, Lady Bracknell.

LADY BRACKNELL I am pleased to hear it. I do not approve of anything that tampers with natural ignorance. Ignorance is like a delicate exotic fruit; touch it and the bloom is gone. The whole theory of modern education is radically unsound. Fortunately in England, at any rate, education produces no effect whatsoever. If it did, it would prove a serious danger to the upper classes, and probably lead to acts of violence in Grosvenor Square. What is your income?

JACK Between seven and eight thousand a year.

LADY BRACKNELL *(makes a note in her book)* In land, or in investments?

JACK   In investments, chiefly.

LADY BRACKNELL   That is satisfactory. What between the duties expected of one during one's lifetime, and the duties exacted from one after one's death, land has ceased to be either a profit or a pleasure. It gives one position, and prevents one from keeping it up. That's all that can be said about land.

JACK   I have a country house with some land, of course, attached to it, about fifteen hundred acres, I believe; but I don't depend on that for my real income. In fact, as far as I can make out, the poachers are the only people who make anything out of it.

LADY BRACKNELL   A country house! How many bedrooms? Well, that point can be cleared up afterwards. You have a town house, I hope? A girl with a simple, unspoiled nature, like Gwendolen, could hardly be expected to reside in the country.

JACK   Well, I own a house in Belgrave Square, but it is let by the year to Lady Bloxham. Of course, I can get it back whenever I like, at six month's notice.

LADY BRACKNELL   Lady Bloxham? I don't know her.

JACK   Oh, she goes about very little. She is a lady considerably advanced in years.

LADY BRACKNELL   Ah, now-a-days that is no guarantee of respectability of character. What number in Belgrave Square?

JACK   149.

LADY BRACKNELL   *(shaking her head)* The unfashionable side. I thought there was something. However, that could be easily altered.

JACK   Do you mean the fashion, or the side?

LADY BRACKNELL   *(sternly)* Both, if necessary, I presume. What are your politics?

JACK   Well, I am afraid I really have none. I am a Liberal Unionist.

LADY BRACKNELL   Oh, they count as Tories. They dine with us. Or come in the evening, at any rate. Now to minor matters. Are your parents living?

JACK   I have lost both my parents.

LADY BRACKNELL   To lose one parent, Mr. Worthing, may be regarded as a misfortune; to lose both looks like carelessness. Who was your father? He was evidently a man of some wealth. Was he born in what the Radical papers call the purple of commerce, or did he rise from the ranks of the aristocracy?

JACK   I am afraid I really don't know. The fact is, Lady Bracknell, I said I had lost my parents. It would be nearer the truth to say that my parents seem to have lost me . . . I don't actually know who I am by birth. I was . . . well, I was found.

LADY BRACKNELL   Found!

JACK   The late Mr. Thomas Cardew, an old gentleman of a very charitable and kindly disposition, found me, and gave me the name of Worthing, because he happened to have a first-class ticket for Worthing in his pocket at the time. Worthing is a place in Sussex. It is a seaside resort.

LADY BRACKNELL   Where did the charitable gentleman who had a first-class ticket for this seaside resort find you?

JACK   *(gravely)* In a hand-bag.

LADY BRACKNELL   A hand-bag?

JACK   *(very seriously)* Yes, Lady Bracknell. I was in a hand-bag—a somewhat large, black leather hand-bag, with handles to it—an ordinary hand-bag in fact.

LADY BRACKNELL   In what locality did this Mr. James, or Thomas, Cardew come across this ordinary hand-bag?

JACK   In the cloak-room at Victoria Station. It was given to him in mistake for his own.

LADY BRACKNELL   The cloak-room at Victoria Station?

JACK   Yes. The Brighton line.

LADY BRACKNELL   The line is immaterial. Mr. Worthing, I confess I feel somewhat bewildered by what you have just told me. To be born, or at any rate bred, in a hand-bag, whether it had handles or not, seems to me to display a contempt for the ordinary decencies of family life that remind one of the worst excesses of the French Revolution. And I presume you know what that unfortunate movement led to? As for the particular locality in which the hand-bag was found, a cloak-room at a railway station might serve to conceal a social indiscretion—has probably, indeed, been used for that purpose before now—but it could hardly be regarded as an assured basis for a recognized position in good society.

JACK   May I ask you then what you would advise me to do? I need hardly say I would do anything in the world to ensure Gwendolen's happiness.

LADY BRACKNELL   I would strongly advise you, Mr. Worthing, to try and acquire some relations as soon as possible, and to make a definite effort to produce at any rate one parent, of either sex, before the season is quite over.

JACK   Well, I don't see how I could possibly manage to do that. I can produce the hand-bag at any moment. It is in my dressing-room at home. I really think that should satisfy you, Lady Bracknell.

LADY BRACKNELL   Me, sir! What has it to do with me? You can hardly imagine that I and Lord Bracknell would dream of allowing our only daughter—a girl brought up with the utmost care—to marry into a cloakroom, and form an alliance with a parcel? Good morning, Mr. Worthing!

(LADY BRACKNELL *sweeps out in majestic indignation.*)

JACK   Good morning!

The Fantasticks

by Tom Jones and Harvey Schmidt

Matt and Luisa are a young couple in love. Their fathers have built a wall between their houses, supposedly to keep them apart.

LUISA   Matt!

MATT   Luisa!

LUISA   Shh. Be careful.
I thought I heard a sound.

MATT   But you're trembling!

LUISA   My father loves to spy.

MATT   I know; I know.
I had to climb out through a window.
My father locked my room.

LUISA   Oh . . . , be careful!
Suppose you were to fall?

MATT   It's on the ground floor.

LUISA   Oh.

MATT   Still, the window's very small.
I could get stuck.

LUISA   This is madness, isn't it?

MATT   Yes, it's absolutely mad!

LUISA   And also very wicked?

MATT   Yes.

LUISA   I'm glad.

MATT   My father would be furious if he knew.

LUISA   Listen, I have had a vision.

MATT   Of disaster?

LUISA   No. Of azaleas.
I dreamed I was picking azaleas.
When all at once, this Duke—
Oh, he was very old,
I'd say he was nearly forty.
But attractive.
And very evil.

MATT   I hate him!

LUISA   And he had a retinue of scoun-
drels,
And they were hiding behind the rho-
dodendrons,
And then, all at once,
As I picked an azalea—
He leapt out!

MATT   Golly, I hate him!

LUISA In my vision, how I struggled.
Like the Rape of the Sabine Women!
I cried "help."

MATT And I was nearby!

LUISA Yes. You came rushing to the rescue.
And, single-handed, you fight all his men,
And win—

MATT And then—

LUISA Celebration!

MATT Fireworks!

LUISA Fiesta!

MATT Laughter!

LUISA Our fathers give in!

MATT We live happily ever after!

LUISA There's no reason in the world why it can't happen exactly like that. *(Suddenly she stiffens.)* Someone's coming!

MATT It's my father.

LUISA Kiss me!

West Side Story

by Arthur Laurents and Leonard Bernstein

Tony and Maria met, danced, and fell in love at a dance. Like Romeo and Juliet,

Tony and Maria's love is ill-fated. The following scene is a contemporary balcony scene modeled after its classic counterpart.

11:00 P.M. A back alley. A suggestion of buildings: a fire escape climbing to the rear window of an unseen flat. As TONY *sings, he looks for where* MARIA *lives, wishing for her. And she does appear, at the window above him, which opens onto the fire escape. Music stays beneath most of the scene.*

(TONY *sings*) Maria, Maria. . . .

MARIA Ssh!

TONY Maria!

MARIA Quiet!

TONY Come down.

MARIA No.

TONY Maria. . . .

MARIA Please. If Bernardo—

TONY He's at the dance. Come down.

MARIA He will soon bring Anita home.

TONY Just for a minute.

MARIA *(Smiles)* A minute is not enough.

TONY *(Smiles)* For an hour, then.

MARIA I cannot.

TONY   Forever!

MARIA   *Ssh!*

TONY   Then I'm coming up.

WOMAN'S VOICE   *(From the offstage apartment)* Maria!

MARIA   *Momentito,* Mama. . . .

TONY   *(Climbing up)* Maria, Maria—

MARIA   *Cállate! (Reaching her hand out to stop him)* Ssh!

TONY   *(Grabbing her hand)* Ssh!

MARIA   It is dangerous.

TONY   I'm *not* "one of them."

MARIA   You are; but to me, you are not. Just as I am one of them— *(She gestures toward the apartment.)*

TONY   To me, you are all the— *(She covers his mouth with her hand.)*

MAN'S VOICE   *(From the unseen apartment)* Maruca!

MARIA   *Sí ya vengo,* Papa.

TONY   Maruca?

MARIA   His pet name for me.

TONY   I like him. He will like me.

MARIA   No. He is like Bernardo: afraid. *(Suddenly laughing)* Imagine being afraid of you!

TONY   You see?

MARIA   *(Touching his face)* I see you.

TONY   See only me.

MAN'S VOICE   *(Offstage)* Maruca!

MARIA   Wait for me! *(She goes inside as the buildings begin to come back into place.)*

MARIA   *(Returning)* I cannot stay. Go quickly!

TONY   I'm not afraid.

MARIA   They are strict with me. Please.

TONY   *(Kissing her)* Good night.

MARIA   *Buenas noches.*

TONY   I love you.

MARIA   Yes, yes. Hurry. *(He climbs down.)* Wait! When will I see you? *(He starts back up.)* No!

TONY   Tomorrow.

MARIA   I work at the bridal shop. Come there.

TONY   At sundown.

MARIA   Yes. Good night.

TONY   Good night. *(He starts off.)*

MARIA   Tony!

TONY   Ssh!

MARIA   Come to the back door.

TONY   *Sí. (Again, he starts out.)*

MARIA   Tony! *(He stops. A pause)* What does Tony stand for?

TONY   Anton.

MARIA   *Te adoro,* Anton.

TONY   *Te adoro,* Maria.
(She goes inside. He ducks out into the shadows. . . .)

Whose Life Is It Anyway?

by Brian Clark

Ken has been in an automobile accident that has left him completely paralyzed from the neck down. In the following scene, Ken shares his bitterness with Mrs. Boyle, a social worker trying to help him adjust to his severe handicap.

MRS. BOYLE   Why don't you want any more treatment?

KEN   I'd rather not go on living like this.

MRS. BOYLE   Why not?

KEN   Isn't it obvious?

MRS. BOYLE   Not to me. I've seen many patients like you.

KEN   And they all want to live?

MRS. BOYLE   Usually.

KEN   Why?

MRS. BOYLE   They find a new way of life.

KEN   How?

MRS. BOYLE   You'll be surprised how many things you will be able to do with training and a little patience.

KEN   Such as?

MRS. BOYLE   We can't be sure yet. But I should think that you will be able to operate reading machines and perhaps an adapted typewriter.

KEN   Reading and writing. What about arithmetic?

MRS. BOYLE   *(Smiling)* I dare say we could fit you up with a comptometer if you really wanted one.

KEN   Mrs. Boyle, even educationalists have realized that the three r's do not make a full life.

MRS. BOYLE   What did you do before the accident?

KEN   I taught in an art school. I was a sculptor.

MRS. BOYLE   I see.

KEN   Difficult, isn't it? How about an electrically operated hammer and chisel? No, well. Or a cybernetic lump of clay?

MRS. BOYLE   I wouldn't laugh if I were you. It's amazing what can be done. Our scientists are wonderful.

KEN   They are. But it's not good enough you see, Mrs. Boyle. I really have absolutely no desire at all to be the object of scientific virtuosity. I have thought things over very carefully. I do have plenty of time for thinking and I have decided that I do not want to go on living with so much effort for so little result.

MRS. BOYLE   Yes, well, we shall have to see about that.

KEN   What is there to see?

MRS. BOYLE   We can't just stop treatment, just like that.

KEN   Why not?

MRS. BOYLE   It's the job of the hospital to save life, not to lose it.

KEN   The hospital's done all it can, but it wasn't enough. It wasn't the hospital's fault; the original injury was too big.

MRS. BOYLE   We have to make the best of the situation.

KEN   No. "We" don't have to do anything. I have to do what is to be done and that is to cash in the chips.

MRS. BOYLE   It's not unusual, you know, for people injured as you have been, to suffer with this depression for a considerable time before they begin to see that a life is possible.

KEN   How long?

MRS. BOYLE   It varies.

KEN   Don't hedge.

MRS. BOYLE   It could be a year or so.

KEN   And it could last for the rest of my life.

MRS. BOYLE   That would be most unlikely.

KEN   I'm sorry, but I cannot settle for that.

MRS. BOYLE   Try not to dwell on it. I'll see what I can do to get you started on some occupational therapy. Perhaps we could make a start on the reading machines.

KEN   Do you have many books for those machines?

MRS. BOYLE   Quite a few.

KEN   Can I make a request for the first one?

MRS. BOYLE   If you like.

KEN   "How to be a sculptor with no hands."

MRS. BOYLE   I'll be back tomorrow with the machine.

KEN   It's marvelous, you know.

MRS. BOYLE   What is?

KEN   All you people have the same technique. When I say something really awkward you just pretend I haven't said anything at all. You're all the bloody same . . . Well there's another outburst. That should be your cue to comment on the light-shade or the color of the walls.

MRS. BOYLE   I'm sorry if I have upset you.

KEN   Of course you have upset me. You and the doctors with your appalling so-called professionalism, which is nothing more than a series of verbal tricks to prevent you relating to your patients as human beings.

MRS. BOYLE   You must understand; we have to remain relatively detached in order to help . . .

KEN   That's all right with me. Detach yourself. Tear yourself off on the dotted line that divides the woman from the social worker and post yourself off to another patient.

████████████████████████

The Rainmaker

by N. Richard Nash

It is a summer evening at the Curry ranch. An extreme drought has hit the plains states when Starbuck arrives claiming to be able to bring rain, for a fee. He is presently boarding with the Curry family. In the following scene, Lizzie Curry goes out to the bunkhouse with bed linens.

STARBUCK   Who's that? *(He rises tautly.)*

(LIZZIE *stands in the doorway, trying not to look into the room. She is carrying the bed linens. She knocks on the door frame.)*

LIZZIE   *(trying to sound calm)* It's me— Lizzie.

(STARBUCK *starts to put on his shirt. An awkward moment. Then* LIZZIE, *without entering the room, hands the bedding across the threshold.)*

LIZZIE   Here.

STARBUCK   What's that?

LIZZIE   Bed linens—take them.

STARBUCK   Is that what you came out for?

LIZZIE   *(after a painful moment)* No . . . I came out because . . . *(She finds it too difficult to continue.)*

STARBUCK   *(gently)* Go on, Lizzie.

LIZZIE   I came out to thank you for what you said to Noah.

STARBUCK   I meant every word of it.

LIZZIE   What you said about Jim—I'm sure you meant that.

STARBUCK   What I said about you.

LIZZIE   I don't believe you.

STARBUCK   Then what are you thankin' me for? What's the matter, Lizzie? You afraid that if you stop bein' sore at me you'll like me a little?

LIZZIE   No . . . *(and she starts to go.)*

STARBUCK   *(stopping her)* Then stay and talk to me! *(as she hesitates)* It's lonely out here and I don't think I'll sleep much—not in a strange place.

LIZZIE   Then I guess you never sleep. Running from one strange place to another.

STARBUCK   *(with a smile)* Not runnin'—travelin'.

LIZZIE   Well, if that's the kind of life you like . . .

STARBUCK   Oh, it's not what a man likes—it's what he's got to do. Now what would a fella in my business be doin' stayin' in the same place? Rain's nice—but it ain't nice all the time.

LIZZIE   *(relaxing a bit)* No, I guess not.

STARBUCK   People got no use for me— except maybe once in a lifetime. And when my work's done, they're glad to see me go.

LIZZIE   *(caught by the loneliness in his voice)* I never thought of it that way.

STARBUCK   Why would you? You never thought of me as a real rainmaker—not until just now.

LIZZIE   I still don't think it!

(Now she starts to go more determinedly than before. STARBUCK *stops her physically this time.)*

STARBUCK   Lizzie—wait! Why don't you let yourself think of me the way you want to?

LIZZIE   *(unnerved)* What do you mean?

STARBUCK   Think like Lizzie, not like Noah.

LIZZIE   I don't know what you're talking about.

STARBUCK   What are you scared of?

LIZZIE   You! I don't trust you!

STARBUCK   Why? What don't you trust about me?

LIZZIE   Everything! The way you talk, the way you brag—why, even your name.

STARBUCK   What's wrong with my name?

LIZZIE   It sounds fake! It sounds like you made it up!

STARBUCK   You're darn right! I did make it up.

LIZZIE   There! Of course!

STARBUCK   Why not? You know what name I was born with? Smith! Smith, for the love of Mike, *Smith!* Now what kind of handle is that for a fella like me? I needed a name that had the whole sky in it! And the power of a man! Star-buck! Now there's a name—and it's mine.

LIZZIE   No, it's not. You were born Smith—and that's your name.

STARBUCK   You're wrong, Lizzie. The name you choose for yourself is more your own than the name you were born with. And if I was you I'd choose another name than Lizzie.

LIZZIE   Thank you—I'm very pleased with it.

STARBUCK   Oh, no you ain't. You ain't pleased with anything about yourself. And I'm sure you ain't pleased with ''Lizzie.''

LIZZIE   I don't ask *you* to be pleased with it, Starbuck. I *am.*

STARBUCK   Lizzie? Why, it don't *stand* for anything.

LIZZIE   It stands for me! *Me!* I'm not the Queen of Sheba—I'm not Lady Godiva—I'm not Cinderella at the Ball.

STARBUCK   Would you like to be?

LIZZIE   Starbuck, you're ridiculous!

STARBUCK   What's ridiculous about it? Dream you're somebody—*be* somebody! But Lizzie? That's nobody! So many millions of wonderful women with wonderful names! *(in an orgy of delight)* Leonora, Desdemona, Carolina, Paulina! Annabella, Florinda, Natasha, Diane! *(then, with a pathetic little lift of his shoulders)* Lizzie.

LIZZIE   Good night, Starbuck!

STARBUCK   *(with a sudden inspiration)* Just a minute, Lizzie—just one little half of a minute. I got the greatest name for you—the greatest name— just listen. *(then, like a love lyric)* Melisande.

LIZZIE   *(flatly)* I don't like it.

STARBUCK   That's because you don't know anything about her. But when I tell you who she was—lady, when I tell you who she was!

LIZZIE   Who?

STARBUCK   *(improvising)* She was the most beautiful . . . ! She was the beautiful wife of King Hamlet! Ever hear of him?

LIZZIE   *(giving him the rope)* Go on! Go on!

STARBUCK   He was the fella who sailed across the ocean and brought back the Golden Fleece! And you know why he did that? Because Melisande begged him for it! I tell you, that Melisande— she was so beautiful and her hair was so long and curly—every time he looked at her he fell right down and died. And this King Hamlet, he'd do anything for her—anything she wanted. So when she said: "Hamlet, I got a terrible hankerin' for a soft Golden Fleece," he just naturally sailed right off to find it. And when he came back—all bleedin' and torn—he went and laid that Fleece of Gold right down at her pretty white feet. And she took that fur piece and wrapped it around her pink naked shoulders and she said: "I got the Golden Fleece—and I'll never be cold no more." . . . Melisande! What a woman! What a *name!*

LIZZIE *(quietly)* Starbuck, you silly jackass. You take a lot of stories—that I've read in a hundred different places—and you roll them up into one big fat ridiculous lie!

STARBUCK *(angry, hurt)* I wasn't lyin'—I was dreamin'!

LIZZIE It's the same thing!

STARBUCK *(with growing anger)* If you think it's the same thing then I take it back about your name! Lizzie—it's just right for you. I'll tell you another name that would suit you—Noah! Because you and your brother—you've got no dream.

LIZZIE *(with an outcry)* You think all dreams have to be your kind! Golden Fleece and thunder on the mountain! But there are other dreams, Starbuck! Little quiet ones that come to a woman when she's shining the silverware and putting moth flakes in the closet.

STARBUCK Like what?

LIZZIE *(crying)* Like a man's voice saying: "Lizzie, is my blue suit pressed?" And the same man saying; "Scratch between my shoulder blades." And kids laughing and teasing and setting up a racket. And how it feels to say the word "Husband!" . . . There are all kinds of dreams, Mr. Starbuck. Mine are small ones—like my name—Lizzie. But they're *real* like my name—real! So you can have yours—and I'll have mine!

(Unable to control her tears, she starts to run away. This time he grabs her fully, holding her close.)

STARBUCK Lizzie . . .

LIZZIE Please . . .

STARBUCK I'm sorry, Lizzie! I'm sorry!

LIZZIE It's all right—let me go!

STARBUCK I hope your dreams come true, Lizzie—I hope they do!

LIZZIE They won't—they never will!

STARBUCK Believe in yourself and they will!

LIZZIE I've got nothing to believe in.

STARBUCK You're a woman! Believe in that!

LIZZIE How can I when nobody else will?

STARBUCK *You* gotta believe it first!

(quickly) Let me ask you, Lizzie—are you pretty?

LIZZIE   *(with a wail)* No—I'm plain!

STARBUCK   There! You see? You don't know you're a woman!

LIZZIE   I am a woman! A plain one!

STARBUCK   There's no such thing as a plain woman! Every real woman is pretty! They're all pretty in a different way—but they're all pretty!

LIZZIE   Not me! When I look in the looking glass . . .

STARBUCK   Don't let Noah be your lookin' glass!

LIZZIE   He's not. My looking glass is right on the wall.

STARBUCK   It's in the wrong place. It's gotta be inside you.

LIZZIE   No . . .

STARBUCK   Don't be afraid—*look!* You'll see a pretty woman, Lizzie. Lizzie, you gotta be your own lookin' glass. And then one day the lookin' glass will be the man who loves you. It'll be his eyes, maybe. And you'll look in that mirror and you'll be more than pretty—you'll be beautiful!

LIZZIE   *(crying out)* It'll never happen!

STARBUCK   Make it happen! Lizzie, why don't you think "pretty" and take down your hair? *(He reaches for her hair.)*

LIZZIE   *(in panic)* No!

STARBUCK   Please, Lizzie! *(He is taking the pins out of her hair.)*

LIZZIE   No—no . . .

STARBUCK   Nobody sees you, Lizzie—nobody but me! *(taking her in his arms)* Now close your eyes, Lizzie—close them! *(as she obeys)* Now—say: "I'm pretty!"

LIZZIE   *(trying)* I'm—I'm—I can't!

STARBUCK   Say it! Say it, Lizzie!

LIZZIE   I'm . . . pretty.

STARBUCK   Say it again!

LIZZIE   *(with a little cry)* Pretty!

STARBUCK   Say it—mean it!

LIZZIE   *(exalted)* I'm pretty! I'm pretty! I'm pretty!

(He kisses her. A long kiss and she clings to him, passionately, the bonds of her spinsterhood breaking away. The kiss over, she collapses on the cot, sobbing.)

LIZZIE   *(through the sobs)* Why did you do that?

STARBUCK   *(going beside her on the cot)* Because when you said you were pretty, it was true!

(Her sobs are louder, more heart-rending because, for the first time, she is happy.)

STARBUCK   Lizzie—look at me!

LIZZIE   I can't!

STARBUCK   *(turning her to him)* Stop cryin' and look at me! Look at my eyes! What do you see?

LIZZIE   *(gazing through her tears)* I can't *believe* what I see!

STARBUCK   Tell me what you see!

LIZZIE   *(with a sob of happiness)* Oh, is it me? Is it really me? *(Now she goes to him with all her giving.)*

A Raisin in the Sun

by Lorraine Hansberry

Ruth and Walter live in a small apartment with their son, Travis, and Walter's mother and sister, Beneatha. In the following scene, Ruth and Walter try to understand what is happening to their marriage and their broken dreams.

WALTER   *(To* RUTH.*)* Who is Promeetheeius—? *(At sink with beer.)*

RUTH   I don't know, honey. Don't worry about it.

WALTER   *(Crosses above kitchen table. In a fury, pointing after* GEORGE.*)* See there—they get to a point where they can't insult you man to man—they got to talk about something ain't nobody never heard of! *(Crosses to sink.)*

RUTH   How you know it was an insult? *(To humor him.)* Maybe Promeetheeius is a nice fellow.

WALTER   *(Crosses below kitchen table.)* Promeetheeius!—I bet there ain't even no such thing! I bet that simpleminded clown—

RUTH   *(Rises, starts to* WALTER *L.)* Walter—

WALTER   *(Yelling.)* Don't start!

RUTH   Start what?

WALTER   Your nagging! Where was I? Who was I with—How much money did I spend?

RUTH   *(Plaintively.)* Walter Lee—why don't we just try to talk about it—

WALTER   *(Not listening.)* I been out talking with people who understand me. People who care about the things I got on my mind.

RUTH   *(Wearily.)* I guess that means people like Willy Harris. *(Crosses U.C., then above sofa.)*

WALTER   Yes, people like Willy Harris.

RUTH   *(Crosses R., back of sofa to laundry. With a sudden flash of impatience.)* Why don't y'all just hurry up and go into the banking business and stop talking about it!

WALTER   *(Crosses U.L. above table.)* Why?—You want to know why? 'Cause we all tied up in a race of people that don't know how to do nothing but moan, pray and have babies! (*The line is too bitter even for him and he looks at her and sits down.*)

RUTH   Oh, Walter— (*Softly.*) Honey, why can't you stop fighting me?

WALTER   (*Crosses D.L. to sink. Without thinking.*) Who's fighting you? Who even cares about you— (*This line begins the retardation of this mood.*)

RUTH   Well— (*She waits a long time and then with resignation starts to put away the laundry.*) I guess I might as well go on to bed— (*More or less to herself.*) I don't know where we lost it—but we have— (*Then to him as she crosses above sofa to C.*) I—I'm sorry about this new baby, Walter—I guess maybe I better go on and do what I started—I guess I just didn't realize how bad things was with us— (*Crosses R. front of sofa.*) I guess I just didn't realize— (*She picks up laundry basket and starts for R. bedroom, exits.*)

WALTER   (*He lifts his head and watches her going away from him in a new mood which began to emerge when he asked her "Who cares about you?" Crosses R. above table to C.*) Baby, it's been rough, ain't it? (*She hears and stops but does not turn around and he goes on to her back.*) I guess between two people there ain't never as much understanding as folks generally think there is. I mean like between me and you— (RUTH *enters. She turns to face him.*) How we gets to the place where we scared to talk softness to each other. (*He waits, thinking hard himself.*)

Why you think it got to be like that? (*He is thoughtful, almost as a child would be.*) Ruth, what is it gets into people ought to be close?

RUTH   (*Above sofa.*) I don't know, honey. I think about it a lot.

WALTER   On account of you and me, you mean. The way things are with us. The way something's come down between us.

RUTH   There ain't so much between us, Walter—Not when you come to me and try to talk to me. Try to be with me—a little, even.

WALTER   (*Standing front of chair L. of table. Total honesty.*) Sometimes— sometimes—I don't even know how to try.

RUTH   (*Crossing slowly L. toward* WALTER.) Walter—

WALTER   Yes—?

RUTH   (*Coming to him, gently and with misgiving, but coming to him.*) Honey—Life don't have to be like this. I mean sometimes people can do things so that things are better— (*She crosses to him slowly and they embrace. She gropes for what she wants to tell him.*) You remember how we used to talk when Travis was born—about the way we were going to live—the kind of house— (*She is stroking his head.*) Well, it's all starting to slip away from us.

The Philadelphia Story

by Philip Barry

Tracy Lord is a member of a very wealthy family. Mike Connor is a journalist. It is the eve of Tracy's wedding, and Mike has been assigned to cover the marriage ceremony for his magazine. The comings and goings of the very rich make for good magazine articles. In the following scene, Tracy and Mike begin to change their attitudes toward each other. Tracy is not what Mike expected, and Mike is not what Tracy expected.

TRACY   . . . Hello, you.

MIKE   . . . Hello.

TRACY   You look fine.

MIKE   I *feel* fine.

TRACY   Quite a fellah.

MIKE   They say.

(They drink.)

TRACY   Did you enjoy the party?

MIKE   Sure. The prettiest sight in this fine, pretty world is the Privileged Class enjoying its privileges.

TRACY   —Also somewhat of a snob.

MIKE   How do you mean?

TRACY   I'm wondering.

MIKE   Consider, Gentle Reader, they toil not, neither do they spin.

TRACY   Oh, yes they do! They spin in circles. *(She spins once and seats herself upon the steps at Left.* MIKE *goes to her.)*

MIKE   Nicely put. "Awash with champagne was Mrs. Willie Q. Tracy (born Geneva Biddle)'s stately pleasure dome on a hilltop in smart Radnor, P.A. on a Saturday night late in June; the eve of her great-niece's—" *(He sits beside her)* —Tracy, you can't marry that guy.

TRACY   George? —I'm going to. Why not?

MIKE   I don't know; I'd have thought I'd be for it, but somehow you just don't seem to match up.

TRACY   Then the fault's with me.

MIKE   Maybe so; all the same you can't do it.

*(*TRACY *rises and moves a little way along the path.)*

TRACY   No? Come around about noon tomorrow—I mean today. *(After a moment he rises and faces her.)*

MIKE   Tracy—

TRACY   Yes, Mr. Connor?

MIKE   How do you mean, I'm "a snob"?

TRACY   You're the worst kind there is: an intellectual snob. You've made up your mind awfully young, it seems to me.

MIKE *(goes to her)* Thirty's about time to make up your mind. —And I'm nothing of the sort, not Mr. Connor.

TRACY The time to make up your mind about people, is never. Yes, you are— and a complete one.

MIKE You're quite a girl.

TRACY You think?

MIKE I know.

TRACY Thank you, Professor. I don't think I'm exceptional.

MIKE You are, though.

TRACY I know any number like me. You ought to get around more.

MIKE In the Upper Clahss? No, thanks.

TRACY You're just a mass of prejudices, aren't you? You're so much thought and so little feeling, Professor. *(She moves Right, further away from him.)*

MIKE Oh, I am, am I?

TRACY *(wheels about on him)* Yes, you am, are you! Your damned intolerance furiates me. I mean *in*furiates me. I should think, of all people, a writer would need tolerance. The fact is, you'll never—you can't be a first-rate writer or a first-rate human being until

you learn to have some small regard for— *(Suddenly she stops. Her eyes widen, remembering. She turns from him.)* Aren't the geraniums pretty, Professor? Is it not a handsome day that begins?

(MIKE mounts the Porch, looks down upon her.)

MIKE Lay off that "Professor."

TRACY Yes, Professor. *(She mounts the Porch, faces him.)*

MIKE You've got all the arrogance of your class, all right, haven't you?

TRACY Holy suds, what have "classes" to do with it?

MIKE Quite a lot.

TRACY Why? What do they matter— except for the people in them? George comes from the so-called "lower" class, Dexter comes from the upper. Well?

MIKE Well?

TRACY —Though there's a great deal to be said for Dexter—and don't you forget it!

MIKE I'll try not to.

TRACY *(moves to the table)* Mac, the nightwatchman, is a prince among men and Joey, the stable-boy, is a rat. Uncle Hugh is a saint. Uncle Willie's a pincher. *(She fills her glass again.)*

MIKE So what?

TRACY There aren't any rules about human beings, that's all—You're teaching me things, Professor; this is new to me. Thanks, I am beholden to you. *(She raises her glass to him.)*

MIKE Not at all.

TRACY "Upper" and "lower," my eye! I'll take the lower, thanks. *(She brings the glass to her lips.)*

MIKE —If you can't get a drawing-room.

(She puts the glass down, untasted, and turns on him.)

TRACY What do you mean by that?

MIKE My mistake.

TRACY Decidedly.

MIKE Okay.

TRACY You're insulting.

MIKE I'm sorry.

TRACY Oh, don't apologize!

MIKE Who's apologizing?

TRACY I never knew such a man.

MIKE You wouldn't be likely to, dear—not from where *you* sit.

TRACY Talk about arrogance!

MIKE *(after a moment)* Tracy—

TRACY What do you want?

MIKE You're wonderful.

TRACY *(laughs)* Professor—may I go out?

MIKE Class is dismissed. *(She moves Left.)* Miss Lord will please wait.

(She stops, turns and meets his gaze steadily.)

TRACY Miss Lord is privileged.

MIKE *(speaks in a lower voice)* There's magnificence in you, Tracy. I'm telling you.

TRACY I'm—! *(A moment.)* Now I'm getting self-conscious again. I—it's funny— *(Another moment. Then she moves toward him, impulsively.)* Mike, let's— *(She stops herself.)*

MIKE What?

TRACY I—I don't know—go up, I guess. It's late.

MIKE —A magnificence that comes out of your eyes, that's in your voice, in the way you stand there, in the way you walk. You're lit from within, bright, bright, bright. There are fires banked down in you, hearth-fires and holocausts—

(She moves another step toward him, stands before him.)

TRACY You—I don't seem to you—made of bronze, then—

MIKE You're made of flesh and blood—that's the blank, unholy surprise of it. You're the golden girl, Tracy. full of love and warmth and delight— What's this? You've got tears in your eyes.

TRACY   Shut up, shut up!— Oh, Mike—keep talking—keep talking! *Talk,* will you?

MIKE   I've stopped.

(For a long moment they look at each other. Then TRACY *speaks, deliberately, harshly.)*

TRACY   Why? Has your mind taken hold again, dear Professor?

MIKE   You think so?

TRACY   *(moves Right, away from him)* Yes, Professor.

MIKE   A good thing, don't you agree?

(She leans against the column of the Porch, facing him.)

TRACY   No, Professor.

MIKE   Drop that Professor—you hear me?

TRACY   Yes, Professor.

(He moves to her slowly, stands almost against her.)

MIKE   That's really all I am to you, is it?

TRACY   Of course, Professor.

MIKE   Are you sure?

TRACY   *(looks up at him)* Why, why, yes—yes, of course, Profess— *(His kiss stops the word. The kiss is taken and returned. After it she exclaims softly.)* Golly. *(She gazes at him wonderingly, then raises her face to receive another. Then she stands in his arms, her cheek against his breast, amazement in her eyes.)* Golly Moses.

▬▬▬▬▬▬▬▬▬▬▬▬▬▬▬▬

The Diary of Anne Frank

by Frances Goodrich and Albert Hackett

The Frank and the Van Daan families are hiding from the Nazis in an attic over a place of business. In this scene, Anne Frank and Peter Van Daan realize what young love is in war-torn Europe.

ANNE   *(Looking up through skylight)* Look, Peter, the sky. What a lovely day. Aren't the clouds beautiful? You know what I do when it seems as if I couldn't stand being cooped up for one more minute? I *think* myself out. I think myself on a walk in the park where I used to go with Pim. Where the daffodils and the crocus and the violets grow down the slopes. You know the most wonderful thing about *thinking* youself out? You can have it any way you like. You can have roses and violets and chrysanthemums all blooming at the same time. . . . It's funny. . . . I used to take it all for granted . . . and now I've gone crazy about everything to do with nature. Haven't you?

PETER *(Barely lifting his face)* I've just gone crazy. I think if something doesn't happen soon . . . if we don't get out of here . . . I can't stand much more of it!

ANNE *(Softly)* I wish you had a religion, Peter.

PETER *(Bitterly)* No, thanks. Not me.

ANNE Oh, I don't mean you have to be Orthodox . . . or believe in heaven and hell and purgatory and things. . . . I just mean some religion . . . it doesn't matter what. Just to believe in something! When I think of all that's out there . . . the trees . . . and flowers . . . and seagulls . . . when I think of the dearness of you, Peter . . . and the goodness of the people we know . . . Mr. Kraler, Miep, Dirk, the vegetable man, all risking their lives for us every day. . . . When I think of these good things, I'm not afraid any more. . . . I find myself, and God, and I . . .

PETER *(Impatiently, as he gets to his feet)* That's fine! But when I begin to think, I get mad! Look at us, hiding out for two years. Not able to move! Caught here like . . . waiting for them to come and get us . . . and all for what?

ANNE We're not the only people that've had to suffer. There've always been people that've had to . . . sometimes one race . . . sometimes another . . . and yet . . .

PETER *(Sitting on upstage end of bed)* That doesn't make me feel any better!

ANNE I know it's terrible, trying to have any faith . . . when people are doing such horrible . . . *(Gently lifting his face)* but you know what I sometimes think? I think the world may be going through a phase, the way I was with Mother. It'll pass, maybe not for hundreds of years, but some day. . . . I still believe, in spite of everything, that people are really good at heart.

Scenes for Two Women

Antigone

by Jean Anouilh

Anouilh's Antigone *is based on the Sophocles tragedy of the same name. Antigone's two brothers, Eteocles and Polynices, were engaged in a power struggle after the death of their father, Oedipus, the King of Thebes. This struggle resulted in the brothers killing each other. The present King of Thebes, Creon, has ruled that only Eteocles shall be given a noble burial, while Polynices shall be left as carrion for the birds. In the following scene, Antigone plans, despite the pleadings of her sister, Ismene, to bury Polynices. Antigone knows that such an act will result in her death.*

ISMENE   Aren't you well?

ANTIGONE   Of course I am. Just a little tired. I got up too early. *(She relaxes, suddenly tired.)*

ISMENE   I couldn't sleep, either.

ANTIGONE   Ismene, you ought not to go without your beauty sleep.

ISMENE   Don't make fun of me.

ANTIGONE   I'm not, Ismene, truly. This particular morning, seeing how beautiful you are makes everything easier for me. Wasn't I a miserable little beast when we were small? I used to fling mud at you, and put worms down your neck. I remember tying you to a tree and cutting off your hair. Your beautiful hair! How easy it must be never to be unreasonable with all that smooth silken hair so beautifully set round your head.

ISMENE   *(Abruptly)* Why do you insist upon talking about other things?

ANTIGONE   *(Gently)* I'm not talking about other things.

ISMENE   Antigone, I've thought about it a lot.

ANTIGONE   Have you?

ISMENE   I thought about it all night long. Antigone, you're mad.

ANTIGONE   Am I?

ISMENE   We cannot do it.

ANTIGONE   Why not?

ISMENE   Creon will have us put to death.

ANTIGONE   Of course he will. That's what he's here for. He will do what he has to do, and we will do what we have to do. He is bound to put us to death. We are bound to go out and bury our brother. That's the way it is. What do you think we can do to change it?

ISMENE   *(Releases* ANTIGONE's *hand; draws back a step)* I don't want to die.

ANTIGONE   I'd prefer not to die, myself.

ISMENE Listen to me, Antigone. I thought about it all night. I'm older than you are. I always think things over and you don't. You are impulsive. You get a notion in your head and you jump up and do the thing straight off. And if it's silly, well, so much the worse for you. Whereas, I think things out.

ANTIGONE Sometimes it is better not to think too much.

ISMENE I don't agree with you! Oh, I know it's horrible. And I pity Polynices just as much as you do. But all the same, I sort of see what Uncle Creon means.

ANTIGONE I don't want to "sort of see" anything.

ISMENE Uncle Creon is the king. He has to set an example!

ANTIGONE But I am not the king; and I don't have to set people examples. Little Antigone gets a notion in her head—the nasty brat, the wilful, wicked girl; and they put her in a corner all day, or they lock her up in the cellar. And she deserves it. She shouldn't have disobeyed!

ISMENE There you go, frowning, glowering, wanting your own stubborn way in everything. Listen to me. I'm right oftener than you are.

ANTIGONE I don't want to be right!

ISMENE At least you can try to understand.

ANTIGONE Understand! The first word I ever heard out of any of you was that word "understand." Why didn't I "understand" that I must not play with water—cold, black, beautiful flowing water—because I'd spill it on the palace tiles. Or with earth, because earth dirties a little girl's frock. Why didn't I "understand" that nice children don't eat out of every dish at once; or give eveything in their pockets to beggars; or run in the wind so fast that they fall down; or ask for a drink when they're perspiring; or want to go swimming when it's either too early or too late, merely because they happen to feel like swimming. Understand! I don't want to understand. There'll be time enough to understand when I'm old. . . . If I ever *am* old. But not now.

ISMENE He is stronger than we are, Antigone. He is the king. And the whole city is with him. Thousands and thousands of them, swarming through all the streets of Thebes.

ANTIGONE I am not listening to you.

ISMENE His mob will come running, howling as it runs. A thousand arms will seize our arms. A thousand breaths will breathe into our faces. Like one single pair of eyes, a thousand eyes will stare at us. We'll be driven in a tumbrel through their hatred, through the smell of them and their cruel, roaring laughter. We'll be dragged to the scaffold for torture, surrounded by guards with their idiot faces all bloated, their animal hands clean-washed for the sacrifice, their beefy eyes squinting as they stare at us. And we'll know that no shrieking and no begging will make them understand that we want to live, for they are like slaves who do exactly as they've been told, without caring about right or wrong. And we shall suffer, we shall feel pain rising in us until it becomes so unbearable that we *know* it must stop. But it won't stop, it will go on rising and rising, like a screaming voice. Oh, I can't, I can't, Antigone! *(A pause)*

ANTIGONE   How well you have thought it all out.

ISMENE   I thought of it all night long. Didn't you?

ANTIGONE   Oh, yes.

ISMENE   I'm an awful coward, Antigone.

ANTIGONE   So am I. But what has that got to do with it?

ISMENE   But, Antigone! Don't you want to go on living?

ANTIGONE   Go on living! Who was it that was always the first out of bed because she loved the touch of the cold morning air on her bare skin? Who was always the last to bed because nothing less than infinite weariness could wean her from the lingering night? Who wept when she was little because there were too many grasses in the meadow, too many creatures in the field, for her to know and touch them all?

ISMENE   *(Clasps* ANTIGONE's *hands, in a sudden rush of tenderness)* Darling little sister!

ANTIGONE   *(Repulsing her)* No! For

heaven's sake! Don't paw me! And don't let us start sniveling! You say you've thought it all out. The howling mob—the torture—the fear of death . . . they've made up your mind for you. Is that it?

ISMENE   Yes.

ANTIGONE   All right. They're as good excuses as any.

ISMENE   Antigone, be sensible. It's all very well for men to believe in ideas and die for them. But you are a girl!

ANTIGONE   Don't I know I'm a girl? Haven't I spent my life cursing the fact that I was a girl?

ISMENE   *(With spirit)* Antigone! You have everything in the world to make you happy. All you have to do is reach out for it. You are going to be married; you are young; you are beautiful—

ANTIGONE   I am not beautiful.

ISMENE   Yes, you are! Not the way other girls are. But it's always you that the little boys turn to look back at when they pass us in the street. And when you go by, the little girls stop talking. They stare and stare at you, until we've turned a corner.

ANTIGONE   *(A faint smile)* "Little boys—little girls."

ISMENE   *(Challengingly)* And what about Haemon?

ANTIGONE   I shall see Haemon this

morning. I'll take care of Haemon. You always said I was mad; and it didn't matter how little I was or what I wanted to do. Go back to bed now, Ismene. The sun is coming up, and as you see, there is nothing I can do today. Our brother Polynices is as well guarded as if he had won the war and were sitting on his throne. Go along. You are pale with weariness.

ISMENE   What are you going to do?

ANTIGONE   I don't feel like going to bed. However, if you like, I'll promise not to leave the house till you wake up. Nurse is getting me breakfast. Go and get some sleep. The sun is just up. Look at you: You can't keep your eyes open. Go.

ISMENE   And you will listen to reason, won't you? You'll let me talk to you about this again? Promise?

ANTIGONE   I promise. I'll let you talk. I'll let all of you talk. Go to bed, now. (ISMENE *goes to arch and exits*.) Poor Ismene!

(ISMENE *enters again*.)

ISMENE   I can't sleep. I know. I'm terrified. I'm so afraid that even though it is daylight, you will still try to bury Polynices. Antigone, little sister, we all want to make you happy—Haemon, and Nurse, and I, and Puff whom you love. We love you, we are alive, we need you. And you remember what Polynices was like. He was our broth-

Several excellent scenes for women are in Anton Chekov's The Three Sisters.

er, of course. But he's dead; and he never loved you. He was a bad brother. He was like an enemy in the house. He never thought of you. Why should you think of him? What if his soul does have to wander through endless time without rest or peace? Don't try something that is beyond your strength. You are always defying the world, but you're only a girl, after all. Stay at home tonight. Don't try to do it, I beg you. It's Creon's doing, not ours.

ANTIGONE   You are too late, Ismene. When you first saw me this morning, I had just come in from burying him.

(ANTIGONE *exits through arch.*)

Twelfth Night

by William Shakespeare

Viola is masquerading as a young male servant in the household of Orsino, Duke of Illyria. Orsino is in love with Olivia, a rich countess. In the following scene, Viola comes with a message of love from Orsino. However, Olivia is not persuaded and begins to see Viola, as the young servant, as more desirable than the Duke.

(*Enter* VIOLA.)

VIOLA   The honourable lady of the house, which is she?

OLIVIA   Speak to me; I shall answer for her. Your will?

VIOLA   Most radiant, exquisite, and un-matchable beauty—I pray you tell me if this be the lady of the house, for I never saw her. I would be loath to cast away my speech; for, besides that it is excellently well penn'd, I have taken great pains to con it. Good beauties, let me sustain no scorn; I am very comptible, even to the least sinister usage.

OLIVIA   Whence came you, sir?

VIOLA   I can say little more than I have studied, and that question's out of my part. Good gentle one, give me modest assurance if you be the lady of the house, that I may proceed in my speech.

OLIVIA   Are you a comedian?

VIOLA   No, my profound heart; and yet, by the very fangs of malice I swear, I am not that I play. Are you the lady of the house?

OLIVIA   If I do not usurp myself, I am.

VIOLA   Most certain, if you are she, you do usurp yourself; for what is yours to bestow is not yours to reserve. But this is from my commission. I will on with my speech in your praise, and then show you the heart of my message.

OLIVIA   Come to what is important in't. I forgive you the praise.

VIOLA   Alas, I took great pains to study it, and 'tis poetical.

OLIVIA   It is the more like to be feigned; I pray you keep it in. I heard you were saucy at my gates, and allow'd your approach rather to wonder at you than to hear you. If you be not mad, be gone; if you have reason, be brief; 'tis not that time of moon with me to make one in so skipping a dialogue. . . . Tell me your mind.

VIOLA   I am a messenger.

OLIVIA   Sure, you have some hideous matter to deliver, when the courtesy of it is so fearful. Speak your office.

VIOLA   It alone concerns your ear. I bring no overture of war, no taxation of homage: I hold the olive in my hand; my words are as full of peace as matter.

OLIVIA   Yet you began rudely. What are you? What would you?

VIOLA   The rudeness that hath appear'd in me have I learn'd from my entertainment. What I am and what I would are as secret as maidenhead—to your ears, divinity; to any other's, profanation.

OLIVIA   Give us the place alone; we will hear this divinity. *(Exeunt Maria and Attendants)* Now, sir, what is your text?

VIOLA   Most sweet lady ———

OLIVIA   A comfortable doctrine, and much may be said of it. Where lies your text?

VIOLA   In Orsino's bosom.

OLIVIA   In his bosom! In what chapter of his bosom?

VIOLA   To answer by the method: in the first of his heart.

OLIVIA   O, I have read it; it is heresy. Have you no more to say?

VIOLA   Good madam, let me see your face.

OLIVIA   Have you any commission from your lord to negotiate with my face? You are now out of your text; but we will draw the curtain and show you the picture. *(Unveiling.)* Look you, sir, such a one I was this present. Is't not well done?

VIOLA   Excellently done, if God did all.

OLIVIA   'Tis in grain, sir; 'twil endure wind and weather.

VIOLA   'Tis beauty truly blent, whose red and white
Nature's own sweet and cunning hand laid on.
Lady, you are cruell'st she alive,
If you will lead these graces to the grave,
And leave the world no copy.

OLIVIA   O, sir, I will not be so hard-hearted; I will give out divers schedules of my beauty. It shall be inventoried, and every particle and utensil labell'd to my will: as—item, two lips indifferent red; item, two grey eyes with lids to them; item, one neck, one chin, and so forth. Were you sent hither to praise me?

VIOLA   I see you what you are: you are too proud;

But, if you were the devil, you are
fair.
My lord and master loves you—O,
such love
Could be but recompens'd though you
were crown'd
The nonpareil of beauty!

OLIVIA   How does he love me?

VIOLA   With adorations, fertile tears,
With groans that thunder love, with
sighs of fire.

OLIVIA   Your lord does know my mind;
I cannot love him.
Yet I suppose him virtuous, know him
noble,
Of great estate, of fresh and stainless
youth;
In voices well divulg'd, free, learn'd,
and valiant,
And in dimension and the shape of
nature
A gracious person; but yet I cannot
love him.
He might have took his answer long
ago.

VIOLA   If I did love you in my master's
flame,
With such a suff'ring, such a deadly
life,
In your denial I would find no sense;
I would not understand it.

OLIVIA   Why, what would you?

VIOLA   Make me a willow cabin at your
gate,
And call upon my soul within the
house;
Write local cantons of contemned
love

And sing them loud even in the dead of
night;
Halloo your name to the reverberate
hills,
And make the babbling gossip of the
air
Cry out 'Olivia!' O, you should not
rest
Between the elements of air and
earth
But you should pity me!

OLIVIA   You might do much.
What is your parentage?

VIOLA   Above my fortunes, yet my state
is well:
I am a gentleman.

OLIVIA   Get you to your lord.
I cannot love him; let him send no
more—
Unless perchance you come to me
again
To tell me how he takes it. Fare you
well.
I thank you for your pains; spend this
for me.

VIOLA   I am no fee'd post, lady; keep
your purse;
My master, not myself, lacks recom-
pense.
Love make his heart of flint that you
shall love;
And let your fervour, like my master's
be
Plac'd in contempt! Farewell, fair cruelty. *(Exit.)*

OLIVIA   'What is your parentage?'
'Above my fortunes, yet my state is
well:
I am a gentleman.' I'll be sworn thou
art;

Thy tongue, thy face, thy limbs, actions, and spirit,
Do give thee five-fold blazon. Not too fast! Soft, soft!
Unless the master were the man. How now!
Even so quickly may one catch the plague?
Methinks I feel this youth's perfections
With an invisible and subtle stealth
To creep in at mine eyes. Well, let it be.
What ho, Malvolio!

Romeo and Juliet

by William Shakespeare

Romeo and Juliet have been married secretly by Friar Lawrence. Nurse has been busy making arrangements for Romeo to be with his new bride. Juliet is eagerly awaiting Nurse's report of when Romeo will arrive. In the following scene, Nurse must reveal a painful truth to Juliet—Romeo has killed Tybalt and has been banished from Verona.

JULIET   O, here comes my nurse,
And she brings news; and every tongue that speaks
But Romeo's name speaks heavenly eloquence.
(NURSE *enters with cords.*)

JULIET   Now, nurse, what news? What hast thou there? the cords
That Romeo bid thee fetch?

NURSE (*Throwing them down*)   Ay, ay, the cords.

JULIET   Ay me! what news? why dost thou wring thy hands?

NURSE   Ay, well-a-day! he's dead, he's dead, he's dead.
We are undone, lady, we are undone!
Alack the day! he's gone, he's kill'd, he's dead!

JULIET   Can heaven be so envious?

NURSE   Romeo can,
Though heaven cannot: O Romeo, Romeo!
Who ever would have thought it? Romeo!

JULIET   What devil art thou, that dost torment me thus?
This torture should be roar'd in dismal hell.
Hath Romeo slain himself? say thou but 'I,'
And that bare vowel 'I' shall poison more
Than the death-darting eye of cockatrice:
I am not I, if there be such an I;
Or those eyes shut, that make thee answer 'I.'
If he be slain, say 'I'; or if not, no:
Brief sounds determine of my weal or woe.

NURSE   I saw the wound, I saw it with mine eyes,—
God save the mark!—here on his manly breast:
A piteous corse, a bloody piteous corse;
Pale, pale as ashes, all bedaub'd in blood,

All in gore-blood: I swounded at the sight.

JULIET   O, break, my heart! poor bank-rupt, break at once!
To prison, eyes, ne'er look on liber-ty!
Vile earth, to earth resign; end motion here;
And thou and Romeo press one heavy bier!

NURSE   O Tybalt! Tybalt, the best friend I had!
O courteous Tybalt! honest gentle-man!
That ever I should live to see thee dead!

JULIET   What storm is this that blows so contrary?
Is Romeo slaughter'd, and is Tybalt dead?
My dear-loved cousin, and my dearer lord?
Then, dreadful trumpet, sound the gen-eral doom!
For who is living, if those two are gone?

NURSE   Tybalt is gone, and Romeo ban-ished;
Romeo that kill'd him, he is ban-ished.

JULIET   O God! did Romeo's hand shed Tybalt's blood?

NURSE   It did, it did; alas the day, it did!

JULIET   O serpent heart, hid with a flowering face!
Did ever dragon keep so fair a cave?

Beautiful tyrant! fiend angelical!
Dove-feather'd raven! wolvish-ravening lamb!
Despised substance of divinest show!
Just opposite to what thou justly seem'st,
A damned saint, an honourable vil-lain!
O nature, what hadst thou to do in hell,
When thou didst bower the spirit of a fiend
In mortal paradise of such sweet flesh?
Was ever book containing such vile matter
So fairly bound? O, that deceit should dwell
In such a gorgeous palace!

NURSE   There's no trust,
No faith, no honesty in men; all per-jured,
All forsworn, all naught, all dissem-blers.
Ah, where's my man? give me some aqua vitae:
These griefs, these woes, these sor-rows make me old.
Shame come to Romeo!

JULIET   Blister'd be thy tongue
For such a wish! he was not born to shame:
Upon his brow shame is ashamed to sit;
For 'tis a throne where honour may be crown'd
Sole monarch of the universal earth.
O, what a beast was I to chide at him!

NURSE   Will you speak well of him that kill'd your cousin?

JULIET   Shall I speak ill of him that is my husband?

Ah, poor my lord, what tongue shall smooth thy name,

When I, thy three-hours wife, have mangled it?

But, wherefore, villain, didst thou kill my cousin?

That villain cousin would have kill'd my husband:

Back, foolish tears, back to your native spring;

Your tributary drops belong to woe,

Which you, mistaking, offer up to joy.

My husband lives, that Tybalt would have slain;

And Tybalt's dead, that would have slain my husband:

All this is comfort; wherefore weep I then?

Some word there was, worser than Tybalt's death,

That murder'd me: I would forget it fain;

But, O, it presses to my memory,

Like damned guilty deeds to sinners' minds:

'Tybalt is dead, and Romeo—banished;'

That 'banished,' that one word 'banished'

Hath slain ten thousand Tybalts. Tybalt's death

Was woe enough, if it had ended there:

Or, if sour woe delights in fellowship

And needly will be rank'd with other griefs,

Why follow'd not, when she said 'Tybalt's dead,'

Thy father, or thy mother, nay, or both,

Which modern lamentation might have moved?

But with a rearward following Tybalt's death,

'Romeo is banished,' to speak that word,

If father, mother, Tybalt, Romeo, Juliet,

All slain, all dead. 'Romeo is banished!'

There is no end, no limit, measure, bound,

In that word's death; no words can that woe sound.

Where is my father, and my mother, nurse?

NURSE   Weeping and wailing over Tybalt's corse:

Will you go to them? I will bring you thither.

JULIET   Wash they his wounds with tears: mine shall be spent

When theirs are dry, for Romeo's banishment.

Take up those cords: poor ropes, you are beguiled,

Both you and I; for Romeo is exiled:

He made you for a highway to my bed;

But I, a maid, die maiden-widowed.

Come, cords, come, nurse: I'll to my wedding-bed;

And death, not Romeo, take my maidenhead!

NURSE   Hie to your chamber: I'll find Romeo

To comfort you: I wot well where he is.

Hark ye, your Romeo will be here at night:

I'll to him; he is hid at Lawrence'
cell.

JULIET   O, find him! give this ring to
my true knight,
And bid him come to take his last farewell.

━━━━━━━━━━━━━━━━━━

Trifles

by Susan Glaspell

*The farmer's wife has been arrested
for murdering her husband. In the following scene, the sheriff and his deputies are
searching the farmhouse for evidence
while Mrs. Peters and Mrs. Hale neaten
up the kitchen.*

MRS. HALE   She liked the bird. She was
going to bury it in that pretty box.

MRS. PETERS   *(In a whisper)* When I
was a girl—my kitten—there was a
boy took a hatchet, and before my
eyes—and before I could get there—
(Covers her face an instant.) If they
hadn't held me back I would have—
*(Catches herself, looks upstairs, fal-
ters weakly.)*—hurt him.

MRS. HALE   *(With a slow look around
her)* I wonder how it would seem never
to have had any children around.
(Pause.) No, Wright wouldn't like the
bird—a thing that sang. She used to
sing. He killed that, too.

MRS. PETERS   *(Moving uneasily)* We
don't know who killed the bird.

MRS. HALE   I knew John Wright.

MRS. PETERS   It was an awful thing was
done in this house that night, Mrs.
Hale. Killing a man while he slept,
slipping a rope around his neck that
choked the life out of him.

MRS. HALE   His neck. Choked the life
out of him. *(Her hand goes out and
rests on the birdcage.)*

MRS. PETERS   *(With rising voice)* We
don't know who killed him. We don't
know.

MRS. HALE   *(Her own feeling not interrupted)* If there'd been years and years
of nothing, then a bird to sing to you, it
would be awful—still, after the bird
was still.

MRS. PETERS   *(Something within her
speaking)* I know what stillness is.
When we homesteaded in Dakota, and
my first baby died—after he was two
years old, and me with no other then—

MRS. HALE   *(Moving)* How soon do you
suppose they'll be through looking for
the evidence?

MRS. PETERS   I know what stillness is.
(Pulling herself back) The law has got
to punish crime, Mrs. Hale.

MRS. HALE   *(Not as if answering that)* I
wish you'd seen Minnie Foster when
she wore a white dress with blue rib-
bons and stood up there in the choir
and sang. *(A look around the room.)*
Oh, I *wish* I'd come over here once in a
while! That was a crime! That was a
crime! Who's going to punish that?

MRS PETERS (*Looking upstairs*) We mustn't—take on.

MRS. HALE I might have known she needed help! I know how things can be—for women. I tell you, it's queer, Mrs. Peters. We live close together and we live far apart. We all go through the same things—it's all just a different kind of the same thing. (*Brushes her eyes, noticing the bottle of fruit, reaches out for it.*) If I was you, I wouldn't tell her her fruit was gone. Tell her it *ain't*. Tell her it's all right. Take this in to prove it to her. She—she may never know whether it was broke or not.

MRS. PETERS (*Takes the bottle, looks about for something to wrap it in; takes petticoat from pile of clothes; very nervously begins winding this around the bottle. In a false voice*) My, it's a good thing the men couldn't hear us. Wouldn't they just laugh! Getting all stirred up over a little thing like a—dead canary. As if that could have anything to do with—with—wouldn't they *laugh!*

Pride and Prejudice

dramatized by Helen Jerome

The following scene is from Act III of Helen Jerome's dramatization of Jane Austin's novel Pride and Prejudice. *Lady Catherine has visited Elizabeth Bennet to demand that Elizabeth abandon any plans to marry Mr. Darcy, Lady Catherine's nephew. Elizabeth, however, is not persuaded, despite Lady Catherine's vehement objections.*

LADY CATHERINE (*Seats herself, quite unperturbed*) Sit over there, Miss Bennet, where I can see you plainly.

(ELIZABETH *does so, amusedly.* LADY CATHERINE *eyes her an instant, reproof in her orbs.*)

ELIZABETH I am feeling far from frivolous, I can assure you, ma'am.

LADY CATHERINE Then you know why I am here? (ELIZABETH *shakes her head, surprised.*) Has not your conscience told you?

ELIZABETH (*Astounded*) My conscience?

LADY CATHERINE (*Angrily*) Miss Bennet, I am not to be trifled with. I am celebrated for my frankness. (*Fixes* ELIZABETH *with a gorgon glance.* ELIZABETH *stares at her wide-eyed.*) Don't assume those innocent airs. . . . *I'm* not a man! They will have no effect whatever on *me.* (ELIZABETH *raises her brows and waits in silence.*) A report has reached me that you hope to be married to my nephew, Mr. Darcy. (*Looks narrowly at* ELIZABETH.) I would not insult him by asking about the truth of this . . . besides, he has left Rosings . . . and I believe joined the Bingleys at Netherfield. (*Looks suspiciously at* ELIZABETH, *who just gives an imperceptible start of surprise.*) I have come post haste from Rosings to let you know my exact sentiments.

ELIZABETH (*Wonderingly*) What a long

way to come for such a purpose, Lady Catherine. Would not a letter have been just as efficacious? *(Smiles.)* Especially as I know nothing of such a rumour.

LADY CATHERINE Will you swear there is no foundation for it?

ELIZABETH   Oh, no. I do not pretend to be as celebrated for frankness as your ladyship. So there are certain questions I may not choose to answer . . . that is one of them.

LADY CATHERINE How—how *dare* you? I insist on knowing: has my nephew made you an offer of marriage?

ELIZABETH But your ladyship has already declared that to be impossible.

LADY CATHERINE It certainly *should* be. But your arts may have entangled him into forgetting what he owes to his family.

ELIZABETH *(Rising, going to her favorite place near the mantel, leaning against it, nonchalantly)* Then surely I should be the last to admit it. *(Laughs.)*

LADY CATHERINE *(Furiously)* Miss Bennet, do you know *who* I am? I have not been accustomed . . . *(Pauses, almost in a fit)* I am the nearest relative he has and entitled to know his dearest concerns.

ELIZABETH *(Calmly)* Then question *him*. You certainly are not entitled to know *mine*.

LADY CATHERINE This marriage to which you have the effrontery to aspire . . . will *never* take place. *Never!* Mr. Darcy is engaged to *my daughter*. *(Rises, stands hands on hips, facing* ELIZABETH.*)* Now what have you to say?

ELIZABETH Only that if this is true, why are you worrying? How could he make an offer to me? . . . Or has he a case of bigamy in view? *(Smiles.)* It is still a crime in England, you know.

LADY CATHERINE *(Hesitatingly)* Well, they were intended for each other since infancy . . . my sister, the Lady Anne . . . hoped it with her last breath. *(Stands over* ELIZABETH *threateningly.)* Didn't you hear me say at Rosings, before the gentlemen came in after dinner, that I wish him to marry my daughter?

ELIZABETH *(Placidly)* Certainly. You gave expression to that wish several times. But if there were no *other* objections to my marriage with Mr. Darcy . . . your *wish* certainly would carry little weight.

LADY CATHERINE *(Threateningly)* Very well. If you persist. Don't expect to be received by his family . . . or his friends . . . *or* . . . *me!* Your name will never be mentioned by any of us! *(Nods several times to emphasize.)*

ELIZABETH I must confess to your ladyship that this will not give me a moment's concern.

LADY CATHERINE *(Facing her with*

rage) I am *ashamed* of you. Is *this* your gratitude for my hospitality?

ELIZABETH   Gratitude! But, Lady Catherine, I regard hospitality as a mutual grace, and by no means consider myself as an object for charity.

LADY CATHERINE   *(Puffing about like a war horse)* Understand, my girl, I came here determined . . . I am not used to submitting to any person's whims nor brooking disappointments.

ELIZABETH   *(Demurely)* That is unfortunate. It is rather late in life for your ladyship to be receiving your first taste of it. . . .

LADY CATHERINE   Be silent. *(Storms up and down, then turns on* ELIZABETH.*)* The idea of you wanting to marry out of your own sphere!

ELIZABETH   *(Smiling)* Oh, I should not consider it so. Mr. Darcy is a gentleman. I am the daughter of one.

LADY CATHERINE   *(Coming close; with incredible vulgarity)* And pray what was your mother? A lady? *(Laughs scornfully.)* The daughter of a shopkeeper, with a brother . . . an *attorney!* You see, I am not deceived by your airs and graces. (ELIZABETH *looks at her silently.)*

ELIZABETH   *(Thoughtfully)* And you, Lady Catherine, the daughter of a peer! It's strange how little birth seems to affect questions of taste . . . or gentleness of heart.

LADY CATHERINE   As if you could possibly know anything about such things. *(Brushing all that aside with a gesture)* Answer me once and for all, are you engaged to my nephew?

ELIZABETH   I must ask you to speak in a lower key . . . my sister is asleep out there *(indicates conservatory)*. No, I am not engaged to anyone.

LADY CATHERINE   *(Pleased, ready to be conciliatory)* And will you promise me you never will be?

ELIZABETH   *(Quietly)* I will not.

LADY CATHERINE   Miss Bennet, I am shocked! *(Pauses, outraged, is about to rise, plumps down again.)* Then I refuse to leave until you have given me that promise.

ELIZABETH   *(Rising, going to bell rope, pulls)* I hope your ladyship will have a pleasant journey back to Rosings. *(To the servant at the door)* Hill, her ladyship's coach, if you please.

The Chalk Garden

by Enid Bagnold

Miss Madrigal is Laurel's governess. Laurel is fascinated by crime. She believes there is something most mysterious about Miss Madrigal's past. In the following scene, Laurel tries to pry information from Miss Madrigal about who she is, what she has seen, and where she has come from.

LAUREL   So you've been to a trial?

MADRIGAL   I did not say I hadn't.

LAUREL   Why did you not say—when you know what store we both lay by it!

MADRIGAL   It may be I think you lay too much store by it.

LAUREL   *(Relaxing her tone and asking as though an ordinary light question)* How does one get in?

MADRIGAL   It's surprisingly easy.

LAUREL   Was it a trial for murder?

MADRIGAL   It would have to be to satisfy you.

LAUREL   *Was it a trial for murder? (Sits above her on sofa.)*

MADRIGAL   *(Without turning around to look)* Have you finished that flower?

LAUREL   *(Yawning)* As much as I can. I get tired of it. *(Wandering to the window)* In my house—at home—there were so many things to do.

MADRIGAL   What was it like?

LAUREL   My home?

MADRIGAL   Yes.

LAUREL   *(Doodling on a piece of paper and speaking as though caught unaware)* There was a stream. And a Chinese bridge. And yew trees cut like horses. And a bell on the weathervane, and a little wood called mine—

MADRIGAL   Who called it that?

LAUREL   *(Unwillingly moved)* She did—my mother. And when it was raining we made an army of her cream pots and battlefield of her dressing table— I used to thread her rings on safety pins—

MADRIGAL   Tomorrow I will light that candle in the green glass candlestick and you can try to paint that.

LAUREL   *(Looking up)* What—paint the flame!

MADRIGAL   Yes.

LAUREL   *(Doodling again)* I'm tired of fire, too, Boss.

MADRIGAL   *(As she notices* LAUREL *doodling)* Why do you sign your name a thousand times?

LAUREL   I am looking for which is me.

MADRIGAL   Shall we read?

LAUREL   Oh, I don't want to read.

MADRIGAL   Let's play a game.

LAUREL   All right. *(With meaning)* A *guessing* game.

MADRIGAL   Very well. Do you know one?

LAUREL   Maitland and I play one called "The Sky's the Limit."

MADRIGAL   How do you begin?

LAUREL *(Sitting down opposite her)* We ask three questions each but if you pass one, I get a fourth.

MADRIGAL   What do we guess about?

LAUREL   Let's guess about each other? We are both mysterious.

MADRIGAL   *(Sententious)* The human heart *is* mysterious.

LAUREL   We don't know the first thing about each other, so there are so many things to ask.

MADRIGAL   But we mustn't go too fast. Or there will be nothing left to discover. Has it got to be the truth?

LAUREL   One can lie. But I get better and better at spotting lies. It's so dull playing with Maitland. He's so innocent. *(MISS MADRIGAL folds her hands and waits.)* Now! First question— Are you a—*maiden* lady?

MADRIGAL   *(After a moment's reflection)* I can't answer that.

LAUREL   Why?

MADRIGAL   Because you throw the emphasis so oddly.

LAUREL   Right. You don't answer. So now I get an extra queston. Are you living under an assumed name?

MADRIGAL   No.

LAUREL   Careful! I'm getting my lie-detector working. Do you take things here at their face value?

MADRIGAL   No.

LAUREL   Splendid! You're getting the idea!

MADRIGAL   *(Warningly)* This is to be your fourth question.

LAUREL   Yes. Yes. I must think—I must be careful. *(Shooting her question hard at* MISS MADRIGAL.*)* What is the full name of your married sister?

MADRIGAL   *(Staring a brief second at her)* Clarissa Dalrymple Westerham.

LAUREL   Is Dalrymple Westerham a double name?

MADRIGAL   *(With ironical satisfaction)* You've *had* your questions.

LAUREL   *(Gaily accepting defeat)* Yes, I have. Now yours. You've only three unless I pass one.

MADRIGAL   Was your famous affair in Hyde Park on the night of your mother's marriage?

LAUREL   *(Wary)* About that time.

MADRIGAL   What was the charge by the police?

LAUREL   *(Wary)* The police didn't come into it.

MADRIGAL   Did someone follow you? And try to kiss you?

LAUREL   *(Off her guard)* Kiss me! It was a case of Criminal Assault!

MADRIGAL *(Following that up)* How do you know—if there wasn't a charge by the police?

LAUREL *(Pausing a second. Triumphant)* That's one too many questions! *Now* for the deduction!

MADRIGAL You didn't tell me there was to be a deduction.

LAUREL I forgot. It's the whole point. Mine's ready.

MADRIGAL And what do you deduce?

LAUREL *(Taking breath—then fast as though she might be stopped)* That you've changed so much you must have been something quite different. When you first came here you were like a rusty hinge that wanted oiling. You spoke to yourself out loud without knowing it. You had been *alone.* You may have been a missionary in Central Africa. You may have escaped from a private asylum. But as a maiden lady you are an imposter. *(Changing her tone slightly—slower and more penetrating)* About your assumed name I am not so sure— *But you have no married sister.*

MADRIGAL *(Lightly)* You take my breath away.

LAUREL *(As lightly)* Good at it, aren't I?

MADRIGAL Yes, for a mind under a cloud.

LAUREL Now for your deduction!

MADRIGAL Mine must keep.

LAUREL But it's the game! Where are you going? *(Rises, steps down stage)*

MADRIGAL *(Pleasantly)* To my room. To make sure I have left no clues unlocked.

LAUREL To your past life?

MADRIGAL Yes, you have given me so much warning. *(Exits.)*

The Glass Menagerie

by Tennessee Williams

Amanda Wingfield raised her children, Tom and Laura, alone. Laura has grown up to be a very shy young woman largely as a result of her embarrassment over a deformed foot that makes her limp. Laura's escape from her handicap is a glass menagerie, a collection of delicate glass animals, that she tends lovingly. Amanda, worried about Laura's future, has sent her to typing school. However, Laura hates the school and has dropped out without telling her mother. In the following scene, Amanda has discovered Laura's deceit.

LAURA Hello, Mother, I was—

(She makes a nervous gesture toward the chart on the wall. AMANDA leans

against the shut door and stares at LAURA *with martyred look.)*

AMANDA   Deception? Deception?

(She slowly removes her hat and gloves, continuing the sweet suffering stare. She lets the hat and gloves fall on the floor—a bit of acting.)

LAURA   *(shakily)* How was the D.A.R. meeting? (AMANDA *slowly opens her purse and removes a dainty white handkerchief which she shakes out delicately and delicately touches to her lips and nostrils.)* Didn't you go to the D.A.R. meeting, Mother?

AMANDA   *(faintly, almost inaudibly)*—No—No. *(then more forcibly)* I did not have the strength—to go to the D.A.R. In fact, I did not have the courage! I wanted to find a hole in the ground and hide myself in it forever!

(She crosses slowly to the wall and removes the diagram of the typewriter keyboard. She holds it in front of her for a second, staring at it sweetly and sorrowfully—then bites her lips and tears it in two pieces.)

LAURA   *(faintly)* Why did you do that, Mother? (AMANDA *repeats the same procedure with the chart of the Gregg Alphabet.)* Why are you—

AMANDA   Why? Why? How old are you, Laura?

LAURA   Mother, you know my age.

AMANDA   I thought that you were an adult; it seems that I was mistaken.

(She crosses slowly to the sofa and sinks down and stares at LAURA.*)*

LAURA   Please don't stare at me, Mother.

(AMANDA *closes her eyes and lowers her head. Count ten.)*

AMANDA   What are we going to do, what is going to become of us, what is the future?

(Count ten)

LAURA   Has something happened, Mother? (AMANDA *draws a long breath and takes out the handkerchief again. Dabbing process)* Mother, has—something happened?

AMANDA   I'll be all right in a minute, I'm just bewildered—*(Count five)*—by life. . . .

LAURA   Mother, I wish that you would tell me what's happened!

AMANDA   As you know, I was supposed to be inducted into my office at the D.A.R. this afternoon. But I stopped off at Rubicam's Business College to speak to your teachers about your having a cold and ask them what progress they thought you were making down there.

LAURA   Oh . . .

AMANDA   I went to the typing instructor and introduced myself as your mother. She didn't know who you were. Wingfield, she said. We don't have any such student enrolled at the school!

I assured her she did, that you have been going to classes since early in January.

"I wonder," she said, "if you could be talking about the terribly shy little girl who dropped out of school after only a few days' attendance?" "No," I said, "Laura, my daughter, has been going to school every day for the past six weeks!"

"Excuse me," she said. She took the attendance book out and there was your name, unmistakably printed, and all the dates you were absent until they decided that you had dropped out of school.

I still said, "No, there must have been some mistake! There must have been some mix-up in the records!

And she said, "No—I remember her perfectly now. Her hands shook so that she couldn't hit the right keys! The first time we gave a speedtest, she broke down completely—was sick at the stomach and almost had to be carried into the wash-room! After that morning she never showed up any more. We phoned the house but never got any answer"—while I was working at Famous and Barr, I suppose, demonstrating those—Oh!

I felt so weak I could barely keep on my feet!

I had to sit down while they got me a glass of water!

Fifty dollars' tuition, all of our plans—my hopes and ambitions for you—just gone up the spout, just gone up the spout like that. (LAURA *draws a long breath and gets awkwardly to her feet. She crosses to the victrola and winds it up.*) What are you doing?

LAURA   Oh! (*She releases the handle and returns to her seat.*)

AMANDA   Laura, where have you been going when you've gone out pretending that you were going to business college?

LAURA   I've just been going out walking.

AMANDA   That's not true.

LAURA   It is. I just went walking.

AMANDA   Walking? Walking? In winter? Deliberately courting pneumonia in that light coat? Where did you walk to, Laura?

LAURA   All sorts of places—mostly in the park.

AMANDA   Even after you'd started catching that cold?

LAURA   It was the lesser of two evils, Mother. I couldn't go back up. I— threw up—on the floor!

AMANDA   From half past seven till after five every day you mean to tell me you walked around in the park, because you wanted to make me think that you were still going to Rubicam's Business College?

LAURA   It wasn't as bad as it sounds. I went inside places to get warmed up.

AMANDA   Inside where?

LAURA   I went in the art museum and the birdhouses at the Zoo. I visited the penguins every day! Sometimes I did without lunch and went to the movies. Lately I've been spending most of my afternoons in the Jewel-box, that big glass house where they raise the tropical flowers.

AMANDA   You did all this to deceive me, just for deception? (LAURA *looks down*.) Why?

LAURA   Mother, when you're disappointed, you get that awful suffering look on your face, like the picture of Jesus' mother in the museum!

AMANDA   Hush!

LAURA   I couldn't face it.

(Pause. A whisper of strings)

AMANDA   *(hopelessly fingering the huge pocketbook)* So what are we going to do the rest of our lives? Stay home and watch the parades go by? Amuse ourselves with the glass menagerie, darling? Eternally play those worn-out phonograph records your father left as a painful reminder of him.

We won't have a business career— we've given that up because it gave us nervous indigestion! *(laughs wearily)* What is there left but dependency all our lives? I know so well what becomes of unmarried women who aren't prepared to occupy a position. I've seen such pitiful cases in the South—barely tolerated spinsters living upon the grudging patronage of sister's husband or brother's wife!— stuck away in some little mouse-trap of a room—encouraged by one in-law to visit another—little birdlike women without any nest—eating the crust of humility all their life!

Is that the future that we've mapped out for ourselves?

! swear it's the only alternative I can think of!

It isn't a very pleasant alternative, is it?

Of course—some girls *do marry.* (LAURA *twists her hands nervously.*) Haven't you ever liked some boy?

LAURA   Yes. I liked one once. *(rises)* I came across his picture a while ago.

AMANDA   *(with some interest)* He gave you his picture?

LAURA   No, it's in the year-book.

AMANADA   *(disappointed)* Oh—a high-school boy.

LAURA.   Yes. His name was Jim. *(*LAURA *lifts the heavy annual from the claw-foot table.)* Here he is in *The Pirates of Penzance.*

AMANDA   *(absently)* The what?

LAURA   The operetta the senior class put on. He had a wonderful voice and we sat across the aisle from each other Mondays, Wednesdays and Fridays in the Aud. Here he is with the silver cup for debating! See his grin?

AMANDA   *(absently)* He must have had a jolly disposition.

LAURA   He used to call me—Blue Roses.

AMANDA   Why did he call you such a name as that?

LAURA   When I had that attack of pleurosis—he asked me what was the matter when I came back. I said pleurosis—he thought that I said Blue Roses! So that's what he always called me after that. Whenever he saw me, he'd holler, "Hello, Blue Roses!" I didn't care for the girl that he went out with. Emily Meisenbach. Emily was the best-dressed girl at Soldan. She never struck me, though, as being sincere. . . . It says in the Personal Section— they're engaged. That's—six years ago! They must be married by now.

AMANDA   Girls that aren't cut out for business careers usually wind up married to some nice man. *(gets up with a spark of revival)* Sister, that's what you'll do!

(LAURA utters a startled, doubtful laugh. She reaches quickly for a piece of glass.)

LAURA   But, Mother—

AMANDA   Yes? *(crossing to photograph)*

LAURA   *(in a tone of frightened apology)* I'm—crippled!

AMANDA   Nonsense! Laura, I've told you never, never to use that word. Why, you're not crippled, you just have a little defect—hardly noticeable, even! When people have some slight disadvantage like that, they cultivate other things to make up for it—devel-op charm—and vivacity—and—charm! That's all you have to do! *(She turns again to the photograph.)* One thing your father had *plenty of*—was charm!

The Importance of Being Earnest

by Oscar Wilde

The Importance of Being Earnest *is a satirical farce ridiculing the social manners of nineteenth-century England. In the following scene, Cecily and Gwendolen meet for the first time. Both believe they are engaged to be married to Ernest Worthing. However, Cecily's Ernest is really Algernon Moncrieff, Gwendolen's cousin and Jack Worthing's friend. Gwendolen's Ernest is really Jack Worthing, who has been leading a double life. He is Jack in the country, and he is Cecily's guardian and Ernest in the city, where he met and fell in love with Gwendolen. For this scene to be effective, both young women should be played with a tongue-in-cheek attitude. Oscar Wilde created them to be farcical characters, fussily feminine, emotionally flighty, and pettily competitive.*

(Enter GWENDOLEN. *Exit* MERRIMAN.*)*

CECILY   *(Advancing to meet her.)* Pray let me introduce myself to you. My name is Cecily Cardew.

GWENDOLEN   Cecily Cardew? *(Moving to her and shaking hands.)* What a very sweet name! Something tells me that we are going to be great friends. I like you already more than I can say. My first impressions of people are never wrong.

CECILY   How nice of you to like me so much after we have known each other such a comparatively short time. Pray sit down.

GWENDOLEN   *(Still standing up.)* I may call you Cecily, may I not?

CECILY   With pleasure!

GWENDOLEN   And you will always call me Gwendolen, won't you?

CECILY   If you wish.

GWENDOLEN   Then that is all quite settled, is it not?

CECILY   I hope so.

(A pause. They both sit down together.)

GWENDOLEN   Perhaps this might be a favorable opportunity for my mentioning who I am. My father is Lord Bracknell. You have never heard of papa, I suppose?

CECILY   I don't think so.

GWENDOLEN   Outside the family circle, papa, I am glad to say, is entirely unknown. I think that is quite as it should be. The home seems to me to be the proper sphere for the man. And certainly once a man begins to neglect his domestic duties he becomes painfully

effeminate, does he not? And I don't like that. It makes men so very attractive. Cecily, mamma, whose views on education are remarkably strict, has brought me up to be extremely shortsighted; it is part of her system; so do you mind my looking at you through my glasses?

CECILY   Oh, not at all, Gwendolen. I am very fond of being looked at.

GWENDOLEN   *(After examining* CEC-ILY *carefully through a lorgnette.)* You are here on a short visit, I suppose.

CECILY   Oh, no, I live here.

GWENDOLEN   *(Severely.)* Really? Your mother, no doubt, or some female relative of advanced years, resides here also?

CECILY   Oh, no. I have no mother, nor, in fact, any relations.

GWENDOLEN   Indeed?

CECILY   My dear guardian, with the assistance of Miss Prism, has the arduous task of looking after me.

GWENDOLEN   Your guardian?

CECILY   Yes, I am Mr. Worthing's ward.

GWENDOLEN   Oh! It is strange he never mentioned to me that he had a ward. How secretive of him! He grows more interesting hourly. I am not sure, however, that the news inspires me with feelings of unmixed delight. *(Rising and going to her.)* I am very fond of you Cecily; I have liked you ever since I met you. But I am bound to state that now that I know that you are Mr. Worthing's ward, I cannot help expressing a wish you were—well, just a little older than you seem to be—and not quite so very alluring in appearance. In fact, if I may speak candidly——

CECILY   Pray do! I think that whenever one has anything unpleasant to say, one should always be quite candid.

GWENDOLEN   Well, to speak with perfect candor, Cecily. I wish that you were fully forty-two, and more than usually plain for your age. Ernest has a strong upright nature. He is the very soul of truth and honor. Disloyalty would be as impossible to him as deception. But even men of the noblest possible moral character are extremely susceptible to the influence of the physical charms of others. Modern, no less than Ancient History, supplies us with many most painful examples of what I refer to. If it were not so, indeed, History would be quite unreadable.

CECILY   I beg your pardon, Gwendolen, did you say Ernest?

GWENDOLEN   Yes.

CECILY   Oh, but it is not Mr. Ernest Worthing who is my guardian. It is his brother—his elder brother.

GWENDOLEN   *(Sitting down again.)* Ernest never mentioned to me that he had a brother.

CECILY   I am sorry to say they have not been on good terms for a long time.

GWENDOLEN   Ah! that accounts for it. And now that I think of it, I have never heard any man mention his brother. The subject seems distasteful to most men. Cecily, you have lifted a load from my mind. I was growing almost anxious. It would have been terrible if any cloud had come across a friendship like ours, would it not? Of course you are quite, quite sure that it is not Mr. Ernest Worthing who is your guardian?

CECILY   Quite sure. *(A pause.)* In fact, I am going to be his.

GWENDOLEN   *(Inquiringly.)* I beg your pardon?

CECILY   *(Rather shy and confidingly.)* Dearest Gwendolen, there is no reason why I should make a secret of it to you. Our little county newspaper is sure to chronicle the fact next week. Mr. Ernest Worthing and I are engaged to be married.

GWENDOLEN   *(Quite politely, rising.)* My darling Cecily, I think there must be some slight error. Mr. Ernest Worthing is engaged to me. The announcement will appear in the *Morning Post* on Saturday at the latest.

CECILY   *(Very politely, rising.)* I am afraid you must be under some misconception. Ernest proposed to me exactly ten minutes ago. *(Shows diary.)*

GWENDOLEN   *(Examines diary through her lorgnette carefully.)* It is certainly very curious, for he asked me to be his wife yesterday afternoon at 5:30. If you would care to verify the incident, pray do so. *(Produces diary of her own.)* I never travel without my diary. One should always have something sensational to read on the train. I am so sorry, dear Cecily, if it is any disappointment to you, but I am afraid *I* have the prior claim.

CECILY   It would distress me more than I can tell you, dear Gwendolen, if it caused you any mental or physical anguish, but I feel bound to point out that since Ernest proposed to you he clearly has changed his mind.

GWENDOLEN   *(Meditatively.)* If the poor fellow has been entrapped into any foolish promise I shall consider it my duty to rescue him at once, and with a firm hand.

CECILY   *(Thoughtfully and sadly.)* Whatever unfortunate entanglement my dear boy may have got into, I will never reproach him with it after we are married.

GWENDOLEN   Do you allude to me, Miss Cardew, as an entanglement? You are presumptuous. On an occasion of this kind it becomes more than a moral duty to speak one's mind. It becomes a pleasure.

CECILY   Do you suggest, Miss Fairfax, that I entrapped Ernest into an engagement? How dare you? This is no time for wearing the shallow mask of manners. When I see a spade I call it a spade.

GWENDOLEN   *(Satirically.)* I am glad to say that I have never seen a spade. It is obvious that our social spheres have been widely different.

(Enter MERRIMAN, *followed by the footman. He carries a salver, table-cloth, and plate-stand.* CECILY *is about to retort. The presence of the servants exercises a restraining influence, under which both girls chafe.)*

*(*MERRIMAN *begins to clear and lay cloth. A long pause.* CECILY *and* GWENDOLEN *glare at each other.)*

GWENDOLEN   Are there many interesting walks in the vicinity, Miss Cardew?

CECILY   Oh, yes, a great many. From the top of the hills quite close one can see five counties.

GWENDOLEN   Five counties! I don't think I should like that. I hate crowds.

CECILY   *(Sweetly.)* I suppose that is why you live in town? (GWENDOLEN *bites her lip, and beats her foot nervously with her parasol.)*

GWENDOLEN   *(Looking around.)* Quite a well-kept garden this is, Miss Cardew.

CECILY   So glad you like it, Miss Fairfax.

GWENDOLEN   I had no idea there were any flowers in the country.

CECILY   Oh, flowers are as common

here, Miss Fairfax, as people are in London.

GWENDOLEN Personally I cannot understand how anybody manages to exist in the country, if anybody who is anybody does. The country always bores me to death.

CECILY Ah! This is what the newspapers call agricultural depression, is it not? I believe the aristocracy are suffering very much from it just at present. It is almost an epidemic amongst them, I have been told. May I offer you some tea, Miss Fairfax?

GWENDOLEN *(With elaborate politeness.)* Thank you. *(Aside.)* Detestable girl! But I require tea!

CECILY *(Sweetly.)* Sugar?

GWENDOLEN *(Superciliously)* No, thank you. Sugar is not fashionable any more.

(CECILY looks angrily at her, takes up the tongs and puts four lumps of sugar into the cup.)

CECILY *(Severely.)* Cake or bread and butter?

GWENDOLEN *(In a bored manner.)* Bread and butter, please. Cake is rarely seen at the best houses nowadays.

CECILY *(Cuts a very large slice of cake, and puts it on the tray.)* Hand that to Miss Fairfax.

(MERRIMAN does so, and goes out with footman. GWENDOLEN drinks the tea and makes a grimace. Puts down cup at once, reaches out her hand to the bread and butter, looks at it, and finds it is cake. Rises in indignation.)

GWENDOLEN You have filled my tea with lumps of sugar, and though I asked most distinctly for bread and butter, you have given me cake. I am known for the gentleness of my disposition, and the extraordinary sweetness of my nature, but I warn you, Miss Cardew, you may go too far.

CECILY *(Rising.)* To save my poor, innocent, trusting boy from the machinations of any other girl, there are no lengths to which I would not go.

GWENDOLEN From the moment I saw you I distrusted you. I felt that you were false and deceitful. I am never deceived in such matters. My first impressions of people are invariably right.

CECILY It seems to me, Miss Fairfax, that I am trespassing on your valuable time. No doubt you have many other calls of a similar character to make in the neighborhood.

Wine in the Wilderness

by Alice Childress

Tommy, a factory worker, meets Cynthia, a social worker, and Cynthia's husband, Sonny-Man, a writer. Cynthia and Sonny-Man know that a friend of theirs,

Bill Jameson, an artist, is looking for a black woman to model for him. Tommy is exactly the kind of woman he has been looking for. In the following scene, Cynthia is trying to protect Tommy from getting emotionally involved with Bill, since he really is primarily interested in her as a model, not as a woman.

CYNTHIA *(A bit uncomfortable)* Oh, Honey, . . . Tommy, you don't want a poor artist.

TOMMY Tommy's not lookin' for a meal ticket. I been doin' for myself all my life. It takes two to make it in this high-price world. A black man see a hard way to go. The both of you gotta pull together. That way you accomplish.

CYNTHIA I'm a social worker . . . and I see so many broken homes. Some of these men! Tommy, don't be in a rush about the marriage thing.

TOMMY Keep it to yourself, . . . but I was thirty my last birthday and haven't even been married. I coulda been. Oh, yes, indeed, coulda been. But I don't want any and everybody. What I want with a no-good piece-a nothin'? I'll never forget what the Reverend Martin Luther King said . . . ''I have a dream.'' I like him sayin' it 'cause truer words have never been spoke. *(Straightening the room)* I have a dream, too. Mine is to find a man who'll treat me just half-way decent . . . just to meet me half-way is all I ask, to smile, be kind to me. Somebody in my corner. Not to wake up by myself in the mornin' and face this world all alone.

CYNTHIA About Bill, it's best not to ever count on anything, anything at all, Tommy.

TOMMY *(This remark bothers her for a split second but she shakes it off)* Of course, Cynthia, that's one of the foremost rules of life. Don't count on *nothin'!*

CYNTHIA Right, don't be too quick to put your trust in these men.

TOMMY You put your trust in one and got yourself a husband.

CYNTHIA Well, yes, but what I mean is . . . Oh, you know. A man is a man and Bill is also an artist and his work comes before all else and there are other factors . . .

TOMMY *(Sits facing* CYNTHIA*)* What's wrong with me?

CYNTHIA I don't know what you mean.

TOMMY Yes you do. You tryin' to tell me I'm aimin' too high by lookin' at Bill.

CYNTHIA Oh, no my dear.

TOMMY Out there in the street, in the bar, you and your husband were so sure that he'd *like* me and want to paint my picture.

CYNTHIA But he does want to paint you, he's very eager to . . .

TOMMY But why? Somethin' don't fit right.

CYNTHIA *(Feeling sorry for Tommy)* If you don't want to do it, just leave and that'll be that.

TOMMY Walk out while he's buyin' me what I ask for, spendin' his money on me? That'd be too dirty. *(Looks at books. Takes one from shelf)* Books, books, books everywhere. "Afro-American History." I like that. What's wrong with me, Cynthia? Tell me, I won't get mad with you, I swear. If there's somethin' wrong that I can change, I'm ready to do it. Eighth grade, that's all I had of school. You a social worker, I know that mean college. I come from poor people. *(Examining the book in her hand)* Talkin' 'bout poverty this and poverty that and studyin' it. When you in it you don't be studyin' 'bout it. Cynthia, I remember my mother tyin' up her stockin's with strips-a rag 'cause she didn't have no garters. When I get home from school she'd say, . . . "Nothin' much here to eat." Nothin' much might be grits, or bread and coffee. I got sick-a all that, got me a job. Later for school.

CYNTHIA The Matriarchal Society.

TOMMY What's that?

CYNTHIA A Matriarchal Society is one in which the women rule . . . the women have the power . . . the women head the house.

TOMMY We didn't have nothin' to rule over, not a pot nor a window. And my papa picked hisself up and run off with some finger-poppin' woman and we never hear another word 'til ten, twelve years later when a undertaker call up and ask if Mama wanta come claim his body. And don'cha know, mama went on over and claim it. A woman need a man to claim, even if it's a dead one. What's wrong with me? Be honest.

CYNTHIA You're a fine person . . .

TOMMY Go on, I can take it.

CYNTHIA You're too brash. You're too used to looking out for yourself. It makes us lose our femininity . . . It makes us hard . . . it makes us seem very hard. We do for ourselves too much.

TOMMY If I don't, who's gonna do for me?

CYNTHIA You have to let the black man have his manhood again. You have to give it back, Tommy.

TOMMY I didn't take it from him, how I'm gonna give it back?

Butterflies Are Free

by Leonard Gershe

Mrs. Baker has overprotected her blind son, Don, for most of his life. Only recently has he been able to convince his mother that he should have the opportunity to have an apartment of his own and learn to care for himself completely. Jill is a neighbor in Don's apartment building. They met and discovered that they enjoyed each other's company. In the following scene, Mrs. Baker is once again trying to protect her son. She believes that Jill is the wrong woman for Don and will hurt him deeply. So Mrs. Baker is eager to convince Jill to get out of Don's life.

MRS. BAKER *(Mumbling to herself.)* Mrs. Benson!!!

JILL *(Opening her door.)* Yes?

MRS. BAKER *(Is startled for a moment, but recovers, quickly. In friendly tones:)* Could you come in for a moment, Mrs. Benson?

JILL *(Uneasily.)* Well, I have my audition. I should leave in about fifteen minutes. I don't know New York and I get lost all the time.

MRS. BAKER *(Ingratiatingly. Steps toward* JILL *a bit.)* Don't you worry. I'll see that you get off in time. *(*JILL *enters, reluctantly, stands behind table.)* I thought you and I might have a little talk. You know—just girls together. Please sit down. *(*JILL *remains standing, avoiding too close contact with* MRS. BAKER.*)* Would you like a cup of coffee? Tea?

JILL No, thank you . . . *(Crosses off platform to* L. *of sofa.)* but if that apple is still there.

MRS. BAKER *(Crosses to refrigerator, gets apple and lettuce on plate, crosses to sink.)* I'm sure it is.

JILL *(Crosses between sofa and coffee table to ladder, sits step.)* Where's Don?

MRS. BAKER Shopping. *(Washes apple and polishes it with dish towel.)* You must be so careful to wash fruits and vegetables, you know. They spray all those insecticides on everything now. I'm not at all sure the bugs aren't less harmful. *(Crosses to* JILL *with apple.)* I like apples to be nice and shiny. *(Holds the apple out to* JILL, *who looks at it and then at* MRS. BAKER *oddly.)*

JILL This reminds me of something. What is it?

MRS. BAKER I have no idea.

JILL You . . . handing me the apple . . . nice and shiny. . . . Oh, I know! Snow White. Remember when the witch brought her the poisoned apple? Oh, Mrs. Baker, I'm sorry. I didn't mean that the way it sounded. I know you're not a witch.

MRS. BAKER Of course not. And I know you're not Snow White.

JILL *(Takes the apple, rises, crosses below* MRS. BAKER, *through kitchen to* D. L. *post.)* I may have to wait hours before I read. I'll probably starve to death before their eyes.

MRS. BAKER *(Crosses to kitchen, takes lettuce, picks off a few pieces, washes them, puts them on plate.)* You're going to get that part, you know.

JILL What makes you so sure?

MRS. BAKER Well, you're a very pretty girl and that's what they want in the theatre, isn't it?

JILL *(Crosses below to* D. R. *post, away from* MRS. BAKER.) Today you have to have more than a pretty face. Anyway, I'm not really pretty. I think I'm interesting-looking and in certain lights I can look sort of . . . lovely . . . but I'm not pretty.

MRS. BAKER *(Crosses with lettuce, sits* C. *sofa.)* Nonsense! You're extremely pretty.

JILL *(Laugh)* No, I'm not.

MRS. BAKER Yes, you are.

JILL *(Turns, leans post.)* No, I'm not. I've got beady little eyes like a bird and a figure like a pogo stick. *(Waits for a reaction from* MRS. BAKER. *There isn't one.)* Well? Aren't you going to deny you said that?

MRS. BAKER *(Unperturbed.)* How can I, dear? Obviously, you heard it.

JILL *(Crosses above director's chair.)* There are plenty of true things you can put me down with. You don't have to put me down with lies.

MRS. BAKER You know what I like about you?

JILL Uh-huh. Nothing.

MRS. BAKER Oh yes. I like your honesty . . . your candor. You're really quite a worldly young woman, aren't you, Mrs. Benson?

JILL I suppose I am. *(Crosses above ''picnic,'' away from* MRS. BAKER.) I wish you wouldn't call me Mrs. Benson.

MRS. BAKER Isn't that your name . . . Mrs. Benson?

JILL But you don't say it as though you mean it.

MRS. BAKER I'm sorry. Why don't I call you Jill? That's more friendly . . . and I'll try to say it as though I mean it. Now, Jill. *(*JILL—R. *turn, back to audience.).* . .

MRS. BAKER I was interested in seeing what you and Donny might have in common. He likes you very much.

JILL *(Crosses* U. *end of coffee table.)* And I like him very much. He may very well be the most beautiful person I've ever met. Just imagine going through life never seeing anything . . . not a painting . . . or a flower . . . or even a Christmas card. I'd want to die, but Don wants to live. I mean really live . . . *(Crosses onto platform to above table.)* and he can even kid about it. He's fantastic.

MRS. BAKER Then you would want what's best for him, wouldn't you?

JILL *(Crosses* U. S. *end of coffee table.)* Now, we're getting to it, aren't we? Like maybe I should tell him to go home with you. Is that it?

MRS. BAKER Donny was happy at home until Linda Fletcher filled him with ideas about a place of his own.

JILL *(Crosses through kitchen to above*

table.) Maybe you just want to believe that he can only be happy with you, Mrs. Baker. Well, there are none so blind as those who will not see. *(Crosses* D. L. *post.)* There. I can quote Dylan Thomas AND Little Donny Dark.

MRS. BAKER *(Rises, takes lettuce to counter.)* You constantly astonish me.

JILL   Well . . . we women of the world do that.

MRS. BAKER *(Crosses to "picnic," picks up pillows and cloth, folds cloth.)* Funny how like Linda you are. Donny is certainly consistent with his girls.

JILL   Why do you call him Donny?

MRS. BAKER   It's his name. Don't I say it as though I mean it?

JILL   He hates being called Donny.

MRS. BAKER *(Crosses to sofa, pillows at each end, crosses to counter, puts cloth on it.)* He's never mentioned it.

JILL   Of course, he has. *(Crosses off platform to* D. *end of sofa.)* You just didn't listen. There are none so deaf as those who will not hear. You could make up a lot of those, couldn't you? There are none so lame as those who will not walk. None so thin as those who will not eat . . .

MRS. BAKER *(Crosses off platform to* U. C.*)* Do you think it's a good idea for Donny to live down here alone?

JILL   I think it's a good idea for *Don* to live wherever he wants to . . . and he's not alone. I'm here.

MRS. BAKER *(Crosses* U. *end of coffee table.)* For how long? Have you got a lease on that apartment?

JILL   No.

MRS. BAKER   So, you can leave tomorrow if you felt like it.

JILL   That's right.

MRS. BAKER   You couldn't sustain a marriage for more than six days, could you?

JILL *(Upset. Crosses* D. R.*)* My marriage doesn't concern you.

MRS. BAKER   It didn't concern you much, either, did it?

JILL   Yes, it did!

MRS. BAKER *(Crosses above director's chair.)* Have you though about what marriage to a blind boy might be like? . . .

MRS. BAKER   . . . You've seen Donny at his best—in this room, which he's memorized . . . and he's memorized how many steps to the drugstore and to the delicatessen . . . but take him out of this room or off this street and he's lost . . . he panics. Donny needs someone who will stay with him—and not just for six days.

JILL   You can stop worrying, Mrs. Baker. Nothing serious will develop between Don and me. I'm not built that way.

MRS. BAKER   But Donny *is* built that way.

JILL   Oh, please—we're just having kicks.

MRS. BAKER   Kicks! That's how it started with Linda—just kicks . . . but Donny fell in love with her . . . and he'll fall in love with you. Then what happens?

JILL   *(Crosses below to* D. *end of sofa.)* I don't know!!

MRS. BAKER   *(Crosses* U. *end of sofa.)* Then don't let it go that far. Stop now before you hurt him.

JILL   What about you? Aren't you hurting him?

MRS. BAKER   I can't. I can only irritate him. You can hurt him. The longer you stay the harder it will be for him when you leave. Let him come with me and you go have your kicks with someone who won't feel them after you've gone!!

JILL   I'm not so sure you can't hurt him. Maybe more than anybody. *(Crosses above table.)* I think you deserve all the credit you can get for turning out a pretty marvelous guy—but bringing up a son—even a blind one—isn't a lifetime occupation. *(MRS. BAKER turns* U., *away from* JILL.) Now the more you help him, the more you hurt him. It was Linda Fletcher—not you— *(MRS. BAKER turns and looks at* JILL *slowly.)* who gave him the thing he needed most—confidence in himself. *(Crossing away* L.) You're always dwelling on the negative— always what he needs, never what he wants . . . always what he can't do, never what he can. *(Crosses* D. *end of sofa.)* What about his music? Have you ever heard the song he wrote? I'll bet you didn't even know he could write songs! *(Crosses above table.)* You're probably dead right about me. I'm not the ideal girl for Don, but I know one thing—neither are you!! And if I'm going to tell anyone to go home, it'll be you, Mrs. Baker. YOU go home!! *(Turns and exits into her apartment, closing door behind her.* MRS. BAKER *watches her go.*

Scenes for Two Men

Othello

by William Shakespeare

    Othello has promoted Cassio to a position that Iago believed should have been his. He vows revenge against both Othello and Cassio. His plot is to convince Othello that his wife, Desdemona, has been unfaithful to him. And Iago names Cassio as the other man. In the following scene, Iago plants the seeds of doubt in Othello's mind.

IAGO   My noble lord———

OTHELLO   What dost thou say, Iago?

IAGO   Did Michael Cassio, when you wooed my lady,
Know of your love?

OTHELLO   He did, from first to last: why dost thou ask?

IAGO   But for a satisfaction of my thought;
No further harm.

OTHELLO   Why of thy thought, Iago?

IAGO   I did not *think* he had been acquainted with her.

OTHELLO   O yes; and went between us very oft.

IAGO   *Indeed!*

OTHELLO   Indeed, ay, indeed; discern'st thou aught In that? Is he not honest?

IAGO.   Honest, my lord?

OTHELLO   Honest! ay, honest.

IAGO   My lord, for aught I know.

OTHELLO   What dost thou think?

IAGO   Think, my lord!

OTHELLO   Think, my lord!
By heaven, he echoes me,
As if there were some monster in his thought
Too hideous to be shown. Thou dost mean something;
I heard thee say but now, thou likedst not that,
When Cassio left my wife; what didst not like?
And, when I told thee he was of my counsel
In my whole course of wooing, thou criedst "Indeed!"
And didst contract and purse thy brow together,
As if thou then hadst shut up in thy brain
Some horrible conceit. If thou dost love me,
Show me thy thought.

IAGO   My lord, you *know* I *love* you.

OTHELLO   I think thou dost;
And, for I know thou'rt full of love and honesty,
And weigh'st thy words before you giv'st them breath,

Richard Dreyfuss as Iago in Shakespeare's Othello, *presented by Joseph Papp for the New York Shakespeare Festival.*

Therefore these stops of thine fright me the more;
For such things in a false disloyal *knave*
Are tricks of *custom,* but in a man that's *just*
They are close delations, working from the heart
That passion cannot rule.

. . .

IAGO I do beseech you,
Though I perchance am vicious in my guess—
As I confess, it is my nature's plague
To spy into abuses, and oft my jealousy
Shapes faults that are not—that your wisdom yet,
From one that so imperfectly conjects,
Would take no notice, nor build yourself a trouble
Out of his scattering and unsure observance.
It were not for your quiet nor your good,

Nor for my manhood, honesty, or wisdom,
To let you know my thoughts.

OTHELLO   What dost thou mean?

IAGO   Good name in man and woman,
dear my lord,
Is the immediate jewel of their souls:
Who steals my purse steals trash; 'tis
something, nothing;
'Twas mine, 'tis his, and has been
slave to thousands;
But he that filches from me my good
name
Robs me of that which not enriches
him
And makes me poor indeed.

You Can't Take It with You

by Moss Hart and George S. Kaufman

*Mr. Henderson of the Internal Revenue
Service calls on Grandpa Vanderhof, who
has never filed an income tax return.*

HENDERSON   *(Pulling a sheaf of papers
from his pocket)* Now, Mr. Vanderhof,
(A quick look toward hall) we've written you several letters about this, but
have not had any reply.

GRANDPA   Oh, that's what those letters
were.

ESSIE   *(Sitting on couch R.)* I told you
they were from the Government.

HENDERSON   According to our records,

Mr. Vanderhof, you have never paid
an income tax.

GRANDPA   That's right.

HENDERSON   Why not?

GRANDPA   I don't believe in it.

HENDERSON   Well—you own property, don't you?

GRANDPA   Yes, sir.

HENDERSON   And you receive a yearly
income from it?

GRANDPA   I do.

HENDERSON   Of—*(He consults his
records.)*—between three and four
thousand dollars.

GRANDPA   About that.

HENDERSON   You've been receiving it
for years.

GRANDPA   I have. 1901, if you want the
exact date.

HENDERSON   Well, the Government is
only concerned from 1914 on. That's
when the income tax started. *(Pause)*

GRANDPA   Well?

HENDERSON   Well—it seems, Mr.
Vanderhof, that you owe the Government twenty-four years' back income
tax. Now, Mr. Vanderhof, you know
there's quite a penalty for not filing an
income tax return.

GRANDPA   Look, Mr. Henderson, let me ask you something.

HENDERSON   Well?

GRANDPA   Suppose I pay you this money—mind you, I don't say I'm going pay it—but just for the sake of argument—what's the Government going to do with it?

HENDERSON   How do you mean?

GRANDPA   Well, what do I get for my money? If I go to Macy's and buy something, there it *is*—I see it. What's the Government give me?

HENDERSON   Why, the Government gives you everything. It protects you.

GRANDPA   What from?

HENDERSON   Well—invasion.   Foreigners that might come over here and take everything you've got.

GRANDPA   Oh, I don't think they're going to do that.

HENDERSON   If you didn't pay an income tax, they would. How do you think the Government keeps up the Army and Navy? All those battleships . . .

GRANDPA   Last   time   we   used battleships was in the Spanish-American War, and what did we get out of it? Cuba—and we gave that back. I wouldn't mind paying if it were something sensible.

HENDERSON   Sensible?   Well,   what

about Congress, and the Supreme Court, and the President? We've got to pay *them,* don't we?

GRANDPA   Not with my money—no, sir.

HENDERSON   *(Furious. Rises, picks up papers.)* Now wait a minute! I'm not here to argue with you. *(Crossing* L.*)* All I know is that you haven't paid an income tax and you've got to pay it!

GRANDPA   They've got to show me.

HENDERSON   *(Yelling)* We *don't* have to show you! I just told you! All those buildings down in Washington, and Interstate Commerce, and the Constitution!

GRANDPA   The Constitution was paid for a long time ago. And Interstate Commerce—what *is* Interstate Commerce, anyhow?

HENDERSON   *(Business of a look at* GRANDPA. *With murderous calm, crosses and places his hands on table)* There are forty-eight states—see? And if there weren't Interstate Commerce, nothing could go from one state to another. See?

GRANDMA   Why   not?   They   got fences?

HENDERSON   *(To* GRANDPA*)* No, they haven't got fences. They've got *laws!* *(Crossing up to arch* L.*)* My . . . , I never came across anything like *this* before!

GRANDPA   Well, I might pay about seventy-five dollars, but that's all it's worth.

HENDERSON   You'll pay every cent of it, like everybody else! And let me tell you something else! You'll go to jail if you don't pay, do you hear that? That's the law, and if you think you're bigger than the law, you've got another thing coming. You're no better than anybody else, and the sooner you get that through your head, the better . . . you'll hear from the United States Government, that's all I can say . . . (*The music has stopped. He is backing out of the room.*)

GRANDPA   (*Quietly.*) Look out for those snakes.

(HENDERSON, *jumping, exists off* L.)

No Time for Sergeants

by Ira Levin and Mac Hyman

Will Stockdale is a private in the United States Army. His blundering and naive behavior have disrupted Army routine, so his sergeant has sent Will to the base psychiatrist hoping that the doctor will recommend that Will be transferred. In the following scene, Will responds to the doctor's questioning in an innocent, but sensible, manner.

(PSYCHIATRIST, *a major, signs and stamps a paper before him, then takes form from* WILL, *seated next to desk.* PSYCHIATRIST *looks at form, looks at* WILL. *A moment of silence.*)

WILL   I never have no dreams at all.

PSYCHIATRIST   (*a pause. He looks carefully at* WILL, *looks at form.*) Where you from, Stockdale?

WILL   Georgia.

PSYCHIATRIST   That's . . . not much of a state, is it?

WILL   Well . . . I don't live all over the state. I just live in this one little place in it.

PSYCHIATRIST   That's where "Tobacco Road" is, Georgia.

WILL   Not around my section. (*pause*) Maybe you're from a different part than me?

PSYCHIATRIST   I've never been there. What's more I don't think I would ever *want* to go there. What's your reaction to that?

WILL   Well, I don't know.

PSYCHIATRIST   I think I would sooner live in the rottenest pigsty in Alabama or Tennessee than in the fanciest mansion in all of Georgia. What about that?

WILL   Well, sir, I think where you want to live is your business.

PSYCHIATRIST *(pause, staring)* You don't mind if someone says something bad about Georgia?

WILL   I ain't heared nobody say nothin' bad about Georgia.

PSYCHIATRIST   What do you think I've been saying?

WILL   Well, to tell you the truth, I ain't been able to get too much sense out of it. Don't you know?

PSYCHIATRIST   Watch your step, young man. *(pause)* We psychiatrists call this attitude of yours "resistance."

WILL   You do?

PSYCHIATRIST   You sense that this interview is a threat to your security. You feel yourself in danger.

WILL   Well, kind of I do. If'n I don't get classified Sergeant King won't give me the wrist watch. (PSYCHIATRIST *stares at* WILL *uncomprehendingly.)* He *won't!* He said I only gets it if I'm classified inside a week.

PSYCHIATRIST   *(turns forlornly to papers on desk. A bit subdued)* You get along all right with your mother?

WILL   No, sir, I can't hardly say that I do—

PSYCHIATRIST   *(cutting in)* She's very strict? Always hovering over you?

WILL   No, sir, just the opposite—

PSYCHIATRIST   She's never there.

WILL   That's right.

PSYCHIATRIST   You resent this neglect, don't you?

WILL   No, I don't resent nothin'.

PSYCHIATRIST   *(leaning forward paternally)* There's nothing to be ashamed of, son. It's a common situation. Does she ever beat you?

WILL   No!

PSYCHIATRIST   *(silkily)* So defensive. It's not easy to talk about your mother, is it.

WILL   No, sir. She died when I was borned.

PSYCHIATRIST   *(a long, sick pause)* You . . . could have told me that sooner . . .

WILL   *(looks hang-dog.* PSYCHIATRIST *returns to papers.* WILL *glances up at him.)* Do you hate *your* Mama? *(*PSYCHIATRIST'S *head snaps up, glaring.)* I figgered as how you said it was so common . . .

PSYCHIATRIST   I do not hate my mother.

WILL   I should hope not! *(pause)* What, does she beat you or somethin'?

PSYCHIATRIST   *(glares again, drums his fingers briefly on table. Steeling himself, more to self than* WILL.*)* This is a transference. You're taking all your stored up antagonisms and loosing them in my direction. Transference. It happens every day. . . .

WILL *(excited)* It does? To the Infantry?

PSYCHIATRIST *(aghast)* The Infantry?

WILL You give Ben a transfer, I wish you'd give me one too. I'd sure love to go along with him.

PSYCHIATRIST Stop! *(The pause is a long one this time. Finally* PSYCHIATRIST *points at papers.)* There are a few more topics we have to cover. We will not talk about transfers, we will not talk about my mother. We will only talk about what *I* want to talk about, do you understand?

WILL Yes, sir.

PSYCHIATRIST Now then—your father. *(quickly)* Living?

WILL Yes, sir.

PSYCHIATRIST Do you get along with him okay?

WILL Yes, sir.

PSYCHIATRIST Does he ever beat you?

WILL You bet!

PSYCHIATRIST Hard?

WILL And how! Boy, there ain't nobody can beat like my Pa can!

PSYCHIATRIST *(beaming)* So *this* is where the antagonism comes from! *(pause)* You hate your father, don't you.

WILL No . . . I got an uncle I hate! Every time he comes out to the house he's always wantin' to rassle with the mule, and the mule gets all wore out, and *he* gets all wore out . . . Well, I don't really *hate* him; I just ain't exactly partial to him.

PSYCHIATRIST *(pause)* Did I ask you about your uncle?

WILL I thought you wanted to talk about hatin' people.

PSYCHIATRIST *(glares, drums his fingers, retreats to form. Barely audible)* Now—girls. How do you like girls?

WILL What girls is that, sir?

PSYCHIATRIST Just girls. Just any girls.

WILL Well, I don't like just any girls. There's one old girl back home that ain't got hair no longer than a hounddog's and she's always—

PSYCHIATRIST No! Look, when I say girls I don't mean any one specific girl. I mean girls in general; women, sex! Didn't that father of yours ever sit down and have a talk with you?

WILL Sure he did.

PSYCHIATRIST Well?

WILL Well what?

PSYCHIATRIST What did he say?

WILL *(with a snicker)* Well, there was this one about these two travelin' salesmen that their car breaks down in the middle of this terrible storm—

PSYCHIATRIST Stop!

WILL   —so they stop at this farmhouse where the farmer has fourteen daughters who was—

PSYCHIATRIST *Stop!*

WILL   You heared it already?

PSYCHIATRIST *(writing furiously on form)* No, I did not hear it already . . .

WILL   Well, what did you stop me for? It's a real knee-slapper. You see, the fourteen daughters is all studyin' to be trombone players and—

PSYCHIATRIST *(shoving form at* WILL*)* Here. Go. Good-by. You're through. You're normal. Good-by. Go. Go.

WILL   *(takes the form and stands, a bit confused by it all)* Sir, if girls is what you want to talk about, you ought to come down to the barracks some night. The younger fellows there is always tellin' spicy stories and all like that.

The Teahouse of the August Moon

by John Patrick

The setting of the play is Okinawa, where United States Armed Forces were based during World War II. Captain Fis-

by's main responsibilities are to teach the Tobiki villagers the principles of democracy and to help them learn to be more independent. In the following scene, Captain Fisby is packing for the trip to the village of Tobiki. He dislikes his new assignment and is irritable. Sakini, the local interpreter, is a shrewd rascal who knows how to take the best advantage of Captain Fisby and the United States Army.

(The jeep is piled with Fisby's belongings. Perched high on top of this pyramid sits a very old and very wrinkled NATIVE WOMAN. SAKINI *pays no attention to her as he goes around the jeep test-kicking the tires. And the* OLD WOMAN *sits disinterested and aloof from what goes on below her.)*

FISBY   Hey, wait a minute! What's she doing up there? *(He points to her. The* OLD WOMAN *sits with her hands folded serenely, looking straight ahead.)*

SAKINI   She nice old lady hear we go to Tobiki Village. She think she go along to visit grandson.

FISBY   Oh, she does. Well, you explain to her that I'm very sorry but she'll have to take a bus.

SAKINI   No buses to Tobiki. People very poor—can only travel on generosity.

FISBY   I'm sorry, but it's against regulations.

SAKINI   She not fall off, boss. She tied on.

FISBY   Well, untie her and get her down. She'll just have to find some other way to visit her grandson.

SAKINI   Her grandson mayor of Tobiki Village. You make him lose face if you kick old grandmother off jeep.

FISBY   She's the mayor's grandmother?

SAKINI   Oh yes, boss.

FISBY   Well, since she's already tied on, I guess we can take her. *(He looks at the bundles.)* Are all those mine?

SAKINI   Oh, no. Most of bundles belong to old lady. She thinks she visit three or four months so she bring own bed and cooking pots.

FISBY   Well, tell her to yell if she sees any low branches coming. *(He starts to get in.)* Let's get started.

SAKINI   Oh, can't go yet, boss.

FISBY   Why not?

SAKINI   Old lady's daughter not here.

FISBY   *(glances at watch)* We can't wait for a lot of good-byes, Sakini!

SAKINI   *(looking behind* FISBY*)* Oh, she come now—right on dot you bet.

*(*CAPTAIN FISBY *turns to witness a squat young* NATIVE WOMAN *come on pushing a wheelbarrow loaded with bundles. She stops long enough to bow*

The Teahouse of the August Moon *by John Patrick has many comic scenes for young actors.*

low to FISBY—*then begins to tie bundles onto the jeep.)*

FISBY   Sakini, can't the old lady leave some of that stuff behind?

SAKINI   Not her things, boss. Belong to daughter.

FISBY   Wait a minute. Is the daughter planning on going with us, too?

SAKINI   Old lady very old. Who take care of her on trip?

FISBY   Well, I—(THE DAUGHTER *takes the wheelbarrow and hurries off.)* Hey—you come back! Sakini— tell her to come back. We can't carry any more bundles.

SAKINI   *(calmly)* Oh, she not go to get bundles, boss. She go to get children.

FISBY   Come here, Sakini. Now look— this sort of thing is always happening to me and I have to put a stop to it some place. This time I'm determined to succeed. It's not that I don't *want* to take them. But you can see for yourself, there's *no room left for kids!*

SAKINI   But daughter not go without children and old lady not go without daughter. And if old lady not go, mayor of Tobiki be mad at you. *(Turns to see the* DAUGHTER *hurry back with three children in tow. They all politely bow to* FISBY. *Their mother then piles them on the hood of the jeep.)*

FISBY   For Pete's sake, Sakini, how

does she expect me to see how to drive!

SAKINI   Old lady got very good eyesight. She sit on top and tell us when to turn. *(At this point one of the* CHILDREN *climbs off the hood and points offstage.)*

The Master Builder

by Henrik Ibsen

Solness, "The Master Builder," came into prominence largely through unscrupulous maneuverings. In his drive to the top, he unseated his past employer, Brovik. Now Brovik and his son, Ragnar, work for Solness. In the following scene, Brovik pleads with Solness to help Ragnar develop as a builder, but Solness, as unmoving as ever, refuses to give any assistance.

BROVIK   *(Lowering his voice a little)* I don't want the poor children to know how ill I am.

SOLNESS   Yes, you've been looking very poorly of late.

BROVIK   It will soon be all over with me. My strength is ebbing from day to day.

SOLNESS   Won't you sit down?

BROVIK   Thanks—may I?

SOLNESS   *(Placing the armchair more*

conveniently) Here—take this chair. —And now?

BROVIK *(Has seated himself with difficulty)* Well, you see, it's about Ragnar. That's what weighs most upon me. What is to become of him?

SOLNESS Of course your son will stay with me as long as ever he likes.

BROVIK But that's just what he doesn't like. He feels that he can't stay any longer.

SOLNESS Why, I should say he was very well off here. But if he wants a rise, I shouldn't object to—

BROVIK No, no! It's not *that. (Impatiently)* But sooner or later he, too, must have a chance of doing something on his own account.

SOLNESS *(Without looking at him)* Do you think that Ragnar has quite talent enough to stand alone?

BROVIK No, that's just the heart-breaking part of it—I've begun to have my doubts about the boy. For you've never said so much as—as one encouraging word about him. And yet I can't help thinking there must be something in him—he can't possibly be without talent.

SOLNESS Well, but he has learnt nothing—nothing thoroughly, I mean. Except, of course, to draw.

BROVIK *(Looks at him with covert hatred, and says hoarsely)* You had learned little enough of the business when you were in my employment. But that didn't prevent you from setting to work— *(Breathing with difficulty)* —and pushing your way up, and taking the wind out of my sails—mine, and other people's.

SOLNESS Yes, you see—circumstances favored me.

BROVIK You're right there. Everything favored you. But then how can you have the heart to let me go to my grave—without having seen what Ragnar is fit for? And of course I'm anxious to see them married, too—before I go.

SOLNESS *(Sharply)* Is it she who wishes it?

BROVIK Not Kaia so much as Ragnar—he talks about it every day. *(Appealingly)* You must—you *must* help him to get some independent work now! I *must* see something that the lad has done. Do you hear?

SOLNESS *(Peevishly)* You can't expect me to drag commissions down from the moon for him!

BROVIK He has the chance of a capital commission at this very moment. A big bit of work.

SOLNESS *(Uneasily, startled)* Has he?

BROVIK If *you* would give your consent.

SOLNESS What sort of work do you mean?

BROVIK *(With some hesitation)* He can have the building of that villa out at Lövstrand.

SOLNESS That! Why, I'm going to build that myself!

BROVIK Oh, you don't much care about doing it.

SOLNESS *(Flaring up)* Don't care! I! Who dares to say that?

BROVIK You said so yourself just now.

SOLNESS Oh, never mind what I say. — Would they give Ragnar the building of that villa?

BROVIK Yes. You see, he knows the family. And then—just for the fun of the thing—he's made drawings and estimates and so forth—

SOLNESS Are they pleased with the drawings? The people who've got to live in the house?

BROVIK Yes. If you would only look through them and approve of them—

SOLNESS Then they would let Ragnar build their home for them?

BROVIK They were immensely pleased with his idea. They thought it exceedingly original, they said.

SOLNSS Oho! Original! Not the old-fashioned stuff that *I'm* in the habit of turning out.

BROVIK It seemed to them *different*.

SOLNESS *(With suppressed irritation)* So it was to see Ragnar that they came here—whilst I was out!

BROVIK They came to call upon you—and at the same time to ask whether you would mind retiring—

SOLNESS *(Angrily)* Retire? I?

BROVIK In case you thought that Ragnar's drawings—

SOLNESS I? Retire in favor of your son?

BROVIK Retire from the agreement, they meant.

SOLNESS Oh, it comes to the same thing. *(Laughs angrily.)* So that's it, is it? Halvard Solness is to see about retiring now! To make room for younger men! For the very youngest, perhaps! He's got to make room! Room! Room!

BROVIK Why, good heavens! There's surely room for more than one single man—

SOLNESS Oh, there's not so very much room to spare either. But be that as it may—I will never retire! I will never give way to anybody! Never of my own free will. Never in this world will I do *that!*

BROVIK *(Rises with difficulty)* Then I am to pass out of life without any certainty? Without a gleam of happiness? Without any faith or trust in Ragnar? Without having seen a single piece of work of his doing? Is that to be the way of it?

SOLNESS *(Turns half aside, and mutters)* H'm—don't ask more just now.

BROVIK   But answer me this one thing. Am I to pass out of life in such utter poverty?

SOLNESS *(Seems to struggle with himself; finally he says in a low but firm voice)* You must pass out of life as best you can.

BROVIK   Then be it so. *(He goes up the room.)*

SOLNESS *(Following him, half in desperation)* Don't you understand that I *cannot* help it? I am what I am, and I can't change my nature!

BROVIK   No, no; you evidently can't. *(Reels and supports himself against the sofa-table.)* May I have a glass of water?

SOLNESS   By all means. *(Fills a glass and hands it to him.)*

BROVIK   Thanks.

(He drinks and puts the glass down again. SOLNESS *goes up and opens the door of the draughtsmen's office.)*

SOLNESS   Ragnar—you must come and take your father home.

Whose Life Is It Anyway?

by Brian Clark

Ken Harrison has been totally paralyzed from the neck down as the result of an automobile accident. He is a sculptor and is devastated by the thought that he will never be able to work again. In the following scene, Ken has asked a lawyer, Mr. Hill, to argue on his behalf for release from the hospital.

KEN   Could you come away from the door? Look, do you work for yourself? I mean, you don't work for an insurance company or something, do you? . . .

HILL   No. I'm in practice as a solicitor, but I . . .

KEN   Then there's no reason why you couldn't represent me generally . . . apart from this compensation thing . . .

HILL   Certainly, if there's anything I can do . . .

KEN   There is.

HILL   Yes?

KEN   . . . Get me out of here.

HILL   . . . I don't understand, Mr. Harrison.

KEN   It's quite simple. I can't exist outside the hospital, so they've got to keep me here if they want to keep me alive and they seem intent on doing that.

I've decided that I don't want to stay in hospital any longer.

HILL   But surely they wouldn't keep you here longer than necessary?

KEN   I'm almost completely paralyzed and I always will be. I shall never be discharged by the hospital. I have coolly and calmy thought it out and I have decided that I would rather not go on. I therefore want to be discharged to die.

HILL   And you want me to represent you?

KEN   Yes. Tough.

HILL   . . . And what is the hospital's attitude?

KEN   They don't know about it yet. Even tougher.

HILL   This is an enormous step . . .

KEN   Mr. Hill, with all respect, I know that our hospitals are wonderful. I know that many people have succeeded in making good lives with appalling handicaps. I'm happy for them and respect and admire them. But each man must make his own decision. And mine is to die quietly and with as much dignity as I can muster and I need your help.

HILL   Do you realize what you're asking me to do?

KEN   I realize. I'm not asking that you make any decision about my life and death, merely that you represent me and my views to the hospital.

HILL   . . . Yes, well, the first thing is to see the Doctor. What is his name?

KEN   Dr. Emerson.

HILL   I'll try and see him now and come back to you.

KEN   Then you'll represent me? . . .

HILL   Mr. Harrison, I'll let you know my decision after I've seen Dr. Emerson.

KEN   All right, but you'll come back to tell me yourself, even if he convinces you he's right?

HILL   Yes, I'll come back.

Dial M for Murder

by Frederick Knott

Tony, an ex-tennis pro, married Margot for her money. He solicits the help of Swann, a past classmate from college, to murder Margot. However, things go wrong and Margot kills Swann with a pair of scissors in an attempt to defend herself. Margot is convicted of Swann's murder and sentenced to death. In the following scene, Max, a friend of Margot and a mystery writer, comes up with a plan to save Margot's life. What he must do is convince Tony to go along with the plan.

The same. A few months later. Early afternoon.

The furniture has been rearranged. Curtains open but shutters have been fastened. No light except sharp rays through shutters. On the desk are a bottle of whiskey and a glass. The wastepaper basket is overflowing with odd junk and crumpled newspapers. Next to this there is a paper carrier containing groceries. The oblong table that was behind the sofa in preceding scenes is now U. L. *under bookcase. A small radio is on this table. A bed has been brought into the room* L. C. *It has not been made properly for several days. Against the fireplace is the sofa. Odd clothing and robe are thrown over the sofa. On the floor is Tony's leather suitcase with the lid open, half packed. An electric heater stands on floor between sofa and bed, and is plugged in. A metal ice pick with bottles and glasses are on bottom shelf of* R. *bookcase.*

When the curtain rises the room is in darkness. (NOTE: *During this act Tony, Margot and Hubbard should wear special shoes so that their footsteps can be well heard in the passage, when necessary.) Footsteps are heard in the passage outside and a key turns in the hall door. Tony enters. He wears a raincoat, and carries a small blue fiber attaché case. Tony switches on the lights. He takes key out of door and puts it in raincoat pocket, then takes raincoat off. He puts raincoat on chair in hall. Closes door. He puts attaché case on bed, looks at watch, then crosses to table. He turns on radio. He returns to attaché case and unlocks it.*

He takes out a wad of pound notes, about 50, puts it in pocket and relocks case. Radio fades in. He looks up at the set and listens intently.

TONY By all means, think it over— only I'm going away the day after tomorrow. *(The door buzzer.* TONY *glances anxiously at the door. Quietly.)* Excuse me. I shall have to ring you back. *(He rings off. Goes to hall door and opens it.* MAX *stands in the passage outside. He wears neither coat nor hat. They stare at each other for a moment or two.)*

MAX Hullo, Tony.

TONY Hullo, Max.

MAX May I come in?

TONY Of course, you're quite a stranger.

MAX *(Entering.)* I'm sorry I haven't been around before. I wasn't sure how you felt— after . . .

TONY That's all right. It's rather chilly in here. I'll switch on . . . *(TONY stops short as he sees attaché case on bed.)* I'll switch on the fire. Let's find somewhere for you to sit. *(TONY picks up his robe from sofa and throws it over attaché case to hide it from* MAX.*)* I've hardly seen anyone for weeks. I'm getting quite used to it. I've had to move in here because everybody stops in the street and peers in at the bedroom window. When the appeal failed they started climbing into the garden. You can't blame them, I suppose—it's cheaper than the zoo and far more top-ical.

MAX I—had to come—in case there was anything . . . *(TONY takes a typed letter from his pocket and hands it to MAX.)*

TONY *(Quietly.)* I'm afraid it's settled, Max. Our lawyer received this from the Home Secretary this morning. *(MAX reads letter and hands it back to TONY.)*

MAX You mustn't give up trying. It's not over yet.

TONY I'm afraid it is. *(Sits on bed.)* We've done all we can. I went to the prison this morning to—say good-bye, but she wouldn't see me. I was rather glad—she never did like good-byes. *(Pause. Simply.)* I shan't see her again.

MAX Tony, I take it you'd do any-thing—to save her life?

TONY *(Surprised)* Of course.

MAX Even if it meant going to prison for several years?

TONY *(After a pause.)* I'd do absolutely anything.

MAX I think you can—I'm certain. *(Slowly.)* If you tell the police *exactly* the right story.

TONY The right story?

MAX Listen, Tony. I've been working this out for weeks. Just in case it came to this. It may be her only chance.

TONY Let's have it.

MAX You'll have to tell the police that you hired Swann to murder her. *(Long pause. TONY can only stare at MAX.)*

TONY *(Rises.)* What are you talking about?

MAX It's all right, Tony—I've been writing this stuff for years. I know what I'm doing. Margot was convicted because no one would believe her sto-ry. Prosecution made out that she was telling one lie after another—and the jury believed him. But what did his case amount to? Only three things. My letter—her stocking, and the idea that, because no key was found on Swann, she must have let him in herself. *(Pause.)* Now Swann is dead. You can tell any story you like about him. You can say that you did know him. That you'd met him, and worked out the whole thing together. Now the black-mail. Swann was only suspected of blackmail for two reasons. Because my letter was found in his pocket and because you saw him the day Margot's bag was stolen.

TONY Well?

MAX You can now tell the police that you never saw him at Victoria. That the whole thing was an invention of yours to try and connect him with the letter.

TONY But the letter was found in his pocket.

MAX Because you put it there.

TONY   *(Pause)* You mean I should pretend that I stole her handbag?

MAX   Sure. You could have.

TONY   But why?

MAX   Because you wanted to find out who was writing to her. When you read my letter you were so mad you decided to teach her a lesson.

TONY   But I can't say that I wrote those blackmail notes.

MAX   Why not? No one can prove that you didn't. *(TONY thinks it over.)*

TONY   All right. I stole her bag and blackmailed her. What else?

MAX   You kept my letter and planted it on Swann after he'd been killed.

TONY   Wait a minute—when could I have done that?

MAX   After you got back from the party and before the police arrived. At the same time you took one of Margot's stockings from the mending basket and substituted it for whatever Swann had used. *(TONY thinks it over.)*

TONY   Max, I know you're trying to help but—can you imagine anyone believing this?

MAX   You've got to make them believe it.

TONY   But I wouldn't know what to say. You'd have to come with me.

MAX   No. I couldn't do that. They know the sort of stuff I write. If they suspected we'd talked this out they wouldn't even listen. They mustn't know I've been here.

TONY   Max! It's ridiculous. Why should I want anyone to murder Margot?

MAX   Oh, one of the stock motives. Had Margot made a will? *(Pause.)*

TONY   I—yes, I believe she had.

MAX   Are you the main beneficiary?

TONY   I suppose so.

MAX   Well, there you are.

TONY   But thousands of husbands and wives leave money to each other, without murdering each other. The police wouldn't believe a word of it! They'd take it for exactly what it is. A husband desperately trying to save his wife.

MAX   Well, it's worth a try. They can't hang you for planning a murder that never came off. Face it. The most you'd get would be a few years in prison.

TONY   Thanks very much.

MAX   . . . And you'd have saved her life. That doesn't seem too big a price.

TONY   That's fine coming from you, Max. Her life might not be in danger at all if it hadn't been for you. It was because of your—association with her that she lost the sympathy of the jury.

Don't get me wrong, Max. If there was the slightest chance of this coming off—of course, I'd do it. But it's got to be convincing. How—how could I have persuaded Swann to do a thing like this?

MAX   You'd have to say you offered him money.

TONY   What money? I haven't got any. (*Pause.*)

MAX   You would have Margot's money.

TONY   It would be months before I could lay my hands on that. And people don't commit murder on credit. No, we'll have to think up something better than that . . .

MAX   All right—we will. There is an answer and we've got to find it. (*Pause.*) How much time have we got?

TONY   (*As though he can hardly say the words.*) It's tomorrow morning . . . (*Offstage door slams. Footsteps. Door buzzer.*)

MAX.   Ssssssh! (*They stop and listen. They look at each other.*)

_____

Scenes for Mixed Groups

Blithe Spirit

by Noel Coward

Charles Condomine is a writer. As part of his research on a book, he invited Madame Arcati, a spiritualist, to hold a séance. As a result of the séance, the spirit of Charles's first wife, Elvira, has been brought back. Because Charles is the only one who can see her, he is constantly trying to convince his present wife, Ruth, that he is not crazy or being deliberately rude to her. In the following scene, Elvira has once again popped up, and Charles once again tries to cope with two wives— one a spirit and one very, very real.

(ELVIRA *comes in from the garden, carrying an armful of roses. The roses are as grey as the rest of her.*)

ELVIRA   You've absolutely ruined that border by the sundial—it looks like a mixed salad.

CHARLES   O my God!

RUTH   What's the matter now?

CHARLES   She's here again!

RUTH   What do you mean? Who's here again?

CHARLES   Elvira.

RUTH   Pull yourself together and don't be absurd.

ELVIRA   It's all those nasturtiums— they're so vulgar.

CHARLES   I like nasturtiums.

RUTH   You like what?

ELVIRA   (*putting her grey roses into a vase*) They're all right in moderation but in a mass like that they look beastly.

CHARLES   Help me, Ruth—you've got to help me—

RUTH   (*rises*) What did you mean about nasturtiums?

CHARLES   Never mind about that now— I tell you she's here again.

ELVIRA   You have been having a nice scene, haven't you? I could hear you right down the garden.

CHARLES   Please mind your own business.

RUTH   If your behaving like a lunatic isn't my business nothing is.

ELVIRA   I expect it was about me, wasn't it? I know I ought to feel sorry but I'm not—I'm delighted.

CHARLES   How can you be so inconsiderate?

RUTH   *(shrilly)* Inconsiderate—I like that, I must say—

CHARLES   Ruth—darling—please . . .

RUTH   I've done everything I can to help—I've controlled myself admirably—I should like to say here and now that I don't believe a word about your damned hallucinations—you're up to something. Charles—there's been a certain furtiveness in your manner for weeks— Why don't you be honest and tell me what it is?

CHARLES   You're wrong—you're dead wrong—I haven't been in the least furtive—I—

RUTH   You're trying to upset me—for some obscure reason you're trying to goad me into doing something that I might regret—I won't stand for it any more— You're making me utterly miserable— *(She bursts into tears and collapses on sofa.)*

CHARLES   Ruth—please— *(sits on sofa beside* RUTH*)*

RUTH   Don't come near me—

ELVIRA   Let her have a nice cry—it'll do her good.

CHARLES   You're utterly heartless!

RUTH   Heartless!

CHARLES   *(wildly)* I was not talking to you—I was talking to Elvira.

RUTH   Go on talking to her then, talk to her until you're blue in the face but don't talk to me—

CHARLES   Help me, Elvira—

ELVIRA   How?

CHARLES   Make her see you or something.

ELVIRA   I'm afraid I couldn't manage that—it's technically the most difficult business—frightfully complicated, you know it takes years of study—

CHARLES   You are here, aren't you? You're not an illusion?

ELVIRA   I may be an illusion but I'm most definitely here.

CHARLES   How did you get here?

ELVIRA   I told you last night—I don't exactly know—

CHARLES   Well, you must make me a promise that in future you only come and talk to me when I'm alone—

ELVIRA   *(pouting)* How unkind you are—making me feel so unwanted. I've never been treated so rudely—

CHARLES   I don't mean to be rude but you must see—

ELVIRA   It's all your own fault for having married a woman who is incapable of seeing beyond the nose on her face—if she had a grain of real sympathy or affection for you she'd believe what you tell her.

CHARLES   How could you expect anybody to believe this?

ELVIRA   You'd be surprised how gull-
ible people are—we often laugh about
it on the other side.

(RUTH, *who has stopped crying and
been staring at* CHARLES *in horror,
suddenly gets up*)

RUTH   *(gently)* Charles—

CHARLES   *(surprised at her tone)* Yes,
dear—

RUTH   I'm awfully sorry I was cross—

CHARLES   But, my dear—

RUTH   I understand everything now, I
do really—

CHARLES   You do?

RUTH   *(patting his arm reassuringly)* Of
course I do.

ELVIRA   Look out—she's up to something—

CHARLES   Will you please be quiet?

RUTH   Of course, darling—we'll all be
quiet, won't we? We'll be as quiet as
little mice.

―――――――

Liliom

by Ferenc Molnar

Liliom *is the drama on which the musical* Carousel *is based.* Liliom *is a merry-
go-round barker at an amusement park.
Julie and Marie are both maids. They are
still young, innocent teenagers. Liliom
has just been fired by the carousel owner,
Mrs. Muskat, after he insulted her. In the
following scene, Marie and Julie are
waiting for Liliom's return because he
offered to take them out.*

MARIE   Are you sorry for him?

JULIE   Are you?

MARIE   Yes, a little. Why are you looking after him in that funny way?

JULIE   *(sits down)* Nothing—except I'm
sorry he lost his job.

MARIE   *(With a touch of pride)* It was on
our account he lost his job. Because
he's fallen in love with you.

JULIE   He hasn't at all.

MARIE   *(confidently)* Oh, yes! he is in
love with you. *(Hesitantly, romantically)* There is someone in love with
me, too.

JULIE   There is? Who?

MARIE   I—I never mentioned it before,
because you hadn't a lover of your
own—but now you have—and I'm
free to speak. *(Very grandiloquently)*
My heart has found its mate.

JULIE   You're only making it up.

MARIE   No, it's true—my heart's true love———

JULIE   Who! Who is he?

MARIE   A soldier.

JULIE   What kind of a soldier?

MARIE   I don't know. Just a soldier. Are there different kinds?

JULIE   Many different kinds. There are hussars, artillerymen, engineers, infantry—that's the kind that walks—and———

MARIE   How can you tell which is which?

JULIE   By their uniforms.

MARIE   *(After trying to puzzle it out)* The conductors on the streetcars—are they soldiers?

JULIE   Certainly not. They're conductors.

MARIE   Well, they have uniforms.

JULIE   But they don't carry swords or guns.

MARIE   Oh! *(Thinks it over again; then)* Well, policemen—are they?

JULIE   *(With a touch of exasperation)* Are they what?

MARIE   Soldiers.

JULIE   Certainly not. They're just policemen.

MARIE   *(Triumphantly)* But they have uniforms—and they carry weapons, too.

JULIE   You're just as dumb as you can be. You don't go by their uniforms.

MARIE   But you said———

JULIE   No, I didn't. A letter-carrier wears a uniform, too, but that doesn't make him a soldier.

MARIE   But if he carried a gun or a sword, would he be———

JULIE   No, he'd still be a letter-carrier. You can't go by guns or swords, either.

MARIE   Well, if you don't go by the uniforms or the weapons, what *do* you go by?

JULIE   By———*(Tries to put it into words; fails; then breaks off suddenly)* Oh, you'll get to know when you've lived in the city long enough. You're nothing but a country girl. When you've lived in the city a year, like I have, you'll know all about it.

MARIE   *(Half angrily)* Well, how *do* you know when *you* see a real soldier?

JULIE   By one thing.

MARIE   What?

JULIE   One thing———*(She pauses.*

MARIE *starts to cry)* Oh, what are you crying about?

MARIE   Because you're making fun of me. . . . You're a city girl, and I'm just fresh from the country . . . and how am I expected to know a soldier when I see one? . . . You, you ought to tell me, instead of making fun of me———

JULIE   All right. Listen then, cry baby. There's only one way to tell a soldier: by his salute! That's the only way.

MARIE   *(Joyfully; with a sigh of relief)* Ah—that's good.

JULIE   What?

MARIE   I say—it's all right then—because Wolf—Wolf——— *(JULIE laughs derisively)* Wolf—that's his name. *(She weeps again)*

JULIE   Crying again? What now?

MARIE   You're making fun of me again.

JULIE   I'm not. But when you say, "Wolf—Wolf—" like that, I have to laugh, don't I? *(Archly)* What's his name again?

MARIE   I won't tell you.

JULIE   All right. If you won't say it, then he's no soldier.

MARIE   I'll say it.

JULIE   Go on.

MARIE   No, I won't. *(She weeps again)*

JULIE   Then he's not a soldier. I guess he's a letter-carrier———

MARIE   No—no—I'd rather say it.

JULIE   Well, then.

MARIE   *(Giggling)* But you mustn't look at me. You look the other way, and I'll say it. *(JULIE looks away. MARIE can hardly restrain her own laughter)* Wolf! *(She laughs)* That's his real name. Wolf, Wolf, Soldier—Wolf!

JULIE   What kind of a uniform does he wear?

MARIE   Red.

JULIE   Red trousers?

MARIE   No.

JULIE   Red coat?

MARIE   No.

JULIE   What then?

MARIE   *(Triumphantly)* His cap!

JULIE   *(After a long pause.)* He's just a porter, you dunce. Red cap . . . that's a porter—and he doesn't carry a gun or a sword, either.

MARIE   *(Triumphantly)* But he salutes. You said yourself that was the only way to tell a soldier———

JULIE   He doesn't salute at all. He only greets people———

MARIE   He salutes me. . . . And if his name *is* Wolf, that doesn't prove he ain't a soldier—he salutes, and he wears a red cap and he stands on guard all day long outside a big building———

JULIE   What does he do there?

MARIE   *(Seriously)* He spits.

JULIE   *(With contempt)* He's nothing—nothing but a common porter.

MARIE   What's Liliom?

JULIE   *(Indignantly)* Why speak of him? What has he to do with me?

MARIE   The same as Wolf has to do with me. If you can talk to me like that about Wolf, I can talk to you about Liliom.

JULIE   He's nothing to me. He put his arm around me in the carousel. I couldn't tell him not to put his arm around me after he had done it, could I?

MARIE   I suppose you didn't like him to do it?

JULIE   No.

MARIE   Then why are you waiting for him? Why don't you go home?

JULIE   Why—eh—he *said* we were to wait for him.

(LILIOM *enters. There is a long silence.*)

LILIOM   Are you still here? What are you waiting for?

MARIE   You told us to wait.

LILIOM   Must you always interfere? No one is talking to you.

MARIE   You asked us—why we———

LILIOM   Will you keep your mouth shut? What do you suppose I want with two of you? I meant that one of you was to wait. The other can go home.

MARIE   All right.

JULIE   All right. *(Neither starts to go)*

LILIOM   One of you goes home. *(To* MARIE*)* Where do you work?

MARIE   At the Breier's, Damjanovitsch Street, Number 20.

LILIOM   And you?

JULIE   I work there, too.

LILIOM   Well, one of you goes home. Which of you wants to stay? *(There is no answer)* Come on, speak up, which of you stays?

MARIE   *(Officiously)* She'll lose her job if she stays.

LILIOM   Who will?

MARIE   Julie. She has to be back by seven o'clock.

LILIOM   Is that true? Will they discharge you if you're not back on time.

JULIE   Yes.

LILIOM   Well, wasn't I discharged?

JULIE   Yes—you were discharged, too.

MARIE   Julie, shall I go?

JULIE   I—can't tell you what to do.

MARIE   All right—stay if you like.

LILIOM   You'll be discharged if you do?

MARIE   Shall I go, Julie?

JULIE   *(Embarrassed)* Why do you keep asking me that?

MARIE   You know best what to do.

JULIE   *(Profoundly moved; slowly)* It's all right, Marie, you can go home.

MARIE   *(Exits reluctantly, but comes back, and says uncertainly)* Good night. *(She waits a moment to see if* JULIE *will follow her.* JULIE *does not move.* MARIE *exits. Meantime it has grown quite dark)*

The Diary of Anne Frank

by Frances Goodrich and Albert Hackett

The Franks and the Van Daans, two Jewish families, are in hiding in a secret attic above a warehouse in Amsterdam during World War II. They are hoping to escape Nazi capture and the inevitable imprisonment in a German concentration camp. In the following scene, both families celebrate Hanukkah, also called the "Feast of Lights," a Jewish ceremony.

ANNE   *(singing)* "Oh, Hanukkah! Oh, Hanukkah! The sweet celebration."

MR. FRANK   *(rising)* I think we should first blow out the candle; then we'll have something for tomorrow night.

MARGOT   But, Father, you're supposed to let it burn itself out.

MR. FRANK   I'm sure that God understands shortages. *(Before blowing it out)* "Praised be Thou, oh Lord our God, who hath sustained us and permitted us to celebrate this joyous festival."

(He is about to blow out the candle when suddenly there is a crash of something falling below. They all freeze in horror, motionless. For a few seconds there is complete silence. MR. FRANK *slips off his shoes. The others noiselessly follow his example.* MR. FRANK *turns out a light near him. He motions to* PETER *to turn off the center lamp.* PETER *tries to reach it, realizes*

he cannot and gets up on a chair. Just as he is touching the lamp he loses his balance. The chair goes out from under him. He falls. The iron lamp shade crashes to the floor. There is a sound of feet below, running down the stairs.)

MR. VAN DAAN   *(under his breath)* God Almighty! *(The only light left comes from the Hanukkah candle.* DUSSEL *comes from his room.* MR. FRANK *creeps over to the stairwell and stands listening. The dog is heard barking excitedly.)* Do you hear anything?

MR. FRANK   *(in a whisper)* No. I think they've gone.

MRS. VAN DAAN   It's the Green Police. They've found us.

MR. FRANK   If they had, they wouldn't have left. They'd be up here by now.

MRS. VAN DAAN   I know it's the Green Police. They've gone to get help. That's all. They'll be back!

MR. VAN DAAN   Or it may have been the Gestapo, looking for papers.

MR. FRANK   *(interrupting)* Or a thief, looking for money.

MRS. VAN DAAN   We've got to do something—Quick! Quick! Before they come back.

MR. VAN DAAN   There isn't anything to do. Just wait. *(MR. FRANK holds up his hand for them to be quiet. He is listening intently. There is complete*

silence as they all strain to hear any sound from below. Suddenly ANNE *begins to sway. With a low cry she falls to the floor in a faint.* MRS. FRANK *goes to her quickly, sitting beside her on the floor and taking her in her arms.)*

MRS. FRANK   Get some water, please! Get some water! *(MARGOT starts for the sink.)*

MR. VAN DAAN   *(grabbing* MARGOT*)* No! No! No one's going to run water!

MR. FRANK   If they've found us, they've found us. Get the water. *(MARGOT starts again for the sink.* MR. FRANK, *getting a flashlight)* I'm going down. *(MARGOT rushes to him, clinging to him.* ANNE *struggles to consciousness.)*

MARGOT   No, Father, no! There may be someone there waiting. It may be a trap!

MR. FRANK   This is Saturday. There is no way for us to know what has happened until Miep or Mr. Kraler comes on Monday morning. We cannot live with this uncertainty.

MARGOT   Don't go, Father!

MRS. FRANK   Hush, darling, hush. *(MR. FRANK slips quietly out, down the steps and out through the door below.)* Margot! Stay close to me. *(MARGOT goes to her mother.)*

MR. VAN DAAN   Slush! Slush! *(MRS.

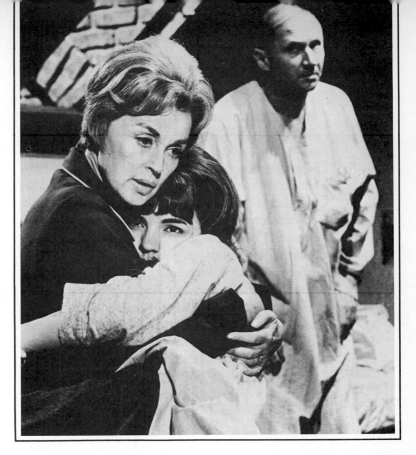

A scene from The Diary of Anne Frank, *with Lily Palmer (Mrs. Frank), Diana Davilla, and Donald Pleasence*

FRANK *whispers to* MARGOT *to get the water.* MARGOT *goes for it.)*

MRS. VAN DAAN Putti, where's our money? Get our money. I hear you can buy the Green Police off, so much a head. Go upstairs quick! Get the money!

MR. VAN DAAN Keep still!

MRS. VAN DAAN *(kneeling before him, pleading)* Do you want to be dragged off to a concentration camp? Are you going to stand there and wait for them to come up and get you? Do something, I tell you!

MR. VAN DAAN *(pushing her aside)* Will you keep still! *(He goes over to the stairwell to listen.* PETER *goes to his mother, helping her up onto the sofa. There is a second of silence, then* ANNE *can stand it no longer.)*

ANNE Someone go after Father! Make Father come back!

PETER *(starting for the door)* I'll go.

MR. VAN DAAN Haven't you done enough? *(He pushes* PETER *roughly away. In his anger against his father* PETER *grabs a chair as if to hit him with it, then puts it down, burying his face in his hands.* MRS. FRANK *begins to pray softly.)*

ANNE Please, Please, Mr. Van Daan. Get Father.

MR. VAN DAAN Quiet! Quiet! *(ANNE is shocked into silence. MRS. FRANK pulls her closer, holding her protectively in her arms.)*

MRS. FRANK *(softly, praying)* "I lift up mine eyes unto the mountains, from whence cometh my help. My help cometh from the Lord who made heaven and earth. He will not suffer thy foot to be moved. He that keepeth thee will not slumber . . ." *(She stops as she hears someone coming. They all watch the door tensely. MR. FRANK comes quietly in. ANNE rushes to him, holding him tight.)*

MR. FRANK It was a thief. The noise must have scared him away.

MRS. VAN DAAN Thank God.

A Raisin in the Sun

by Lorraine Hansberry

Walter is struggling to retain his self-esteem in the face of family and financial obstacles. He lives in a small apartment with his wife, Ruth, their son, Travis, his sister, Beneatha, and his mother. The close quarters and the money problems create tensions and conflicts among the family members. In the following scene, Walter is trying to assert himself by attacking his sister's ambition to be a doctor.

BENEATHA *(Her face is in her hands— she is still fighting the urge to go back to bed. Sits R. of table.)* Really— would you suggest dawn? Where's the paper?

WALTER *(Senselessly.)* How is school coming?

BENEATHA *(In the same spirit.)* Lovely. Lovely. And you know, Biology is the greatest. *(Looking up at him.)* I dissected something that looked just like you yesterday.

WALTER I just wondered if you've made up your mind and everything.

BENEATHA *(Gaining in sharpness and impatience prematurely.)* And what did I answer yesterday morning—and the day before that—?

RUTH *(Crossing back to ironing board R., like someone disinterested and old.)* Don't be so nasty, Bennie.

BENEATHA *(Still to her brother.)* And the day before that and the day before that!

WALTER *(Defensively.)* I'm interested in you. Something wrong with that? Ain't many girls who decide—

WALTER and BENEATHA *(In unison.)* —"to be a doctor." *(Silence.)*

WALTER Have we figured out yet just exactly how much medical school is going to cost?

BENEATHA *(Rises, exits to bathroom. Knocks on the door.)* Come on out of there, please! *(Re-enters.)*

RUTH   Walter Lee, why don't you leave that girl alone and get out of here to work?

WALTER   *(Looking at his sister intently.)* You know the check is coming tomorrow.

BENEATHA   *(Turning on him with a sharpness all her own. She crosses D.R. and sprawls on sofa.)* That money belongs to Mama, Walter, and it's for her to decide how she wants to use it. I don't care if she wants to buy a house or a rocket ship or just nail it up somewhere and look at it—it's hers. Not ours—hers.

WALTER   *(Bitterly.)* Now ain't that fine! You just got your mother's interests at heart, ain't you, girl? You such a nice girl—but if Mama got that money she can always take a few thousand and help you through school too—can't she?

BENEATHA   I have never asked anyone around here to do anything for me!

WALTER   No! But the line between asking and just accepting when the time comes is big and wide—ain't it!

BENEATHA   *(With fury.)* What do you want from me, Brother—that I quit school or just drop dead, which!

WALTER   *(Rises, crosses down back of sofa.)* I don't want nothing but for you to stop acting holy around here—me and Ruth done made some sacrifices for you—why can't you do something for the family?

RUTH   Walter, don't be dragging me in it.

WALTER   You are in it—Don't you get up and go work in somebody's kitchen for the last three years to help put clothes on her back—?

(BENEATHA rises, crosses, sits armchair D.R.)

RUTH   Oh, Walter—that's not fair—

WALTER   It ain't that nobody expects you to get on your knees and say thank you, Brother; thank you, Ruth; thank you, Mama—and thank you, Travis, for wearing the same pair of shoes for two semesters—

BENEATHA   *(In front of sofa, falls on her knees.)* WELL—I DO—ALL RIGHT? THANK EVERYBODY— AND FORGIVE ME FOR EVER WANTING TO BE ANYTHING AT ALL—FORGIVE ME, FORGIVE ME! *(She rises, crosses D.R. to armchair.)*

RUTH   Please stop it! Your Mama'll hear you.

WALTER   *(Crosses U.C. to kitchen table. Ties shoes at chair R. of table.)* — Who . . . told you you had to be a doctor? If you so crazy 'bout messing around with sick people—then go be a nurse like other women—or just get married and be quiet—

BENEATHA   *(Crossing toward L. end of sofa.)* Well—you finally got it said— It took you three years but you finally

THESEUS   Pyramus draws near the wall. Silence!

PYRAMUS   O grim-looked night! O night with hue so black!
O night, which ever art when day is not!
O night, O night! Alack, alack, alack,
I fear my Thisby's promise is forgot!
And thou, O wall, O sweet, O lovely wall,
That stand'st between her father's ground and mine!
Thou wall, O wall, O sweet and lovely wall,
Show me thy chink, to blink through with mine eyne!

(WALL *holds up his fingers.*)

Thanks, courteous wall. Jove shield thee well for this!
But what see I? No Thisby do I see.
O wicked wall, through whom I see no bliss!
Cursed be thy stones for thus deceiving me!

THESEUS   The wall, methinks, being sensible, should curse again.

PYRAMUS   No, in truth, sir, he should not. "Deceiving me" is Thisby's cue. She is to enter now, and I am to spy her through the wall. You shall see it will fall pat as I told you. Yonder she comes.

(Enter THISBY.)

THISBY   O wall, full often hast thou heard my moans,
For parting my fair Pyramus and me!
My cherry lips have often kissed thy stones.
Thy stones with lime and hair knit up in thee.

PRYAMUS   I see a voice: now will I to the chink,
To spy an I can hear my Thisby's face.
Thisby!

THISBY   My love thou art, my love I think.

PRYAMUS   Think what thou wilt, I am thy lover's grace;
And, like Limander, am I trusty still.

THISBY   And I like Helen, till the Fates me kill.

PYRAMUS   Not Shafalus to Procrus was so true.

THISBY   As Shafalus to Procrus, I to you.

PRYAMUS   O kiss me through the hole of this vile wall!

THISBY   I kiss the wall's hole, not your lips at all.

PYRAMUS   Wilt thou at Ninny's tomb meet me straightway?

THISBY   'Tide life, 'tide death, I come without delay.

(Exeunt PYRAMUS *and* THISBY.)

WALL   Thus have I, Wall, my part discharged so;
And, being done, thus wall away doth go. (*Exit.*)

Cyril Ritchard as Oberon and Jerry Dodge as Puck in the 1967 production of the fantasy A Midsummer Night's Dream *at The American Shakespeare Festival Theatre in Stratford, Connecticut. Ritchard directed the play.*

THESEUS Now is the moon used between the two neighbors.

DEMETRIUS No remedy, my lord, when walls are so willful to hear without warning.

HIPPOLYTA This is the silliest stuff that ever I heard.

THESEUS The best in this kind are but shadows; and the worst are no worse, if imagination amend them.

HIPPOLYTA It must be your imagination then, and not theirs.

THESEUS If we imagine no worse of them than they of themselves, they may pass for excellent men. Here come two noble beasts in, a man and a lion.

(Enter LION *and* MOONSHINE.*)*

LION You, ladies, you, whose gentle hearts do fear

The smallest monstrous mouse that creeps on floor,
May now perchance both quake and tremble here,
When lion rough in wildest rage doth roar.
Then know that I, as Snug the joiner, am
A lion fell, nor else no lion's dam;
For, if I should as lion come in strife
Into this place, 'twere pity on my life.

THESEUS   A very gentle beast, and of a good conscience.

DEMETRIUS   The very best at a beast, my lord, that e'er I saw.

LYSANDER   This lion is a very fox for his valor.

THESEUS   True; and a goose for his discretion.

DEMETRIUS   Not so, my lord; for his valor cannot carry his discretion, and the fox carries the goose.

THESEUS   His discretion, I am sure, cannot carry his valor; for the goose carries not the fox. It is well. Leave it to his discretion, and let us listen to the moon.

MOONSHINE   This lanthorn doth the hornèd moon present—

DEMETRIUS   He should have worn the horns on his head.

THESEUS   He is no crescent, and his horns are invisible within the circumference.

MOONSHINE   This lanthorn doth the hornèd moon present; Myself the man i' th' moon do seem to be.

THESEUS   This is the greatest error of all the rest. The man should be put into the lanthorn. How is it else the man i' th' moon?

DEMETRIUS   He dares not come there for the candle; for, you see, it is already in snuff.

HIPPOLYTA   I am aweary of this moon. Would he would change!

THESEUS   It appears, by his small light of discretion, that he is in the wane; but yet, in courtesy, in all reason, we must stay the time.

LYSANDER   Proceed, Moon.

MOONSHINE   All that I have to say is to tell you that the lanthorn is the moon; I, the man i' th' moon; this thorn bush, my thorn bush; and this dog, my dog.

DEMETRIUS   Why, all these should be in the lanthorn; for all these are in the moon. But, silence! here comes Thisby.

(Enter THISBY.*)*

THISBY   This is old Ninny's tomb. Where is my love?

LION   Oh—(*The* LION *roars.* THISBY *runs off.*)

DEMETRIUS   Well roared, Lion.

THESEUS   Well run, Thisby.

HIPPOLYTA   Well shone, Moon. Truly, the moon shines with a good grace.

(The LION *shakes* THISBY's *mantle, and exit.)*

THESEUS   Well moused, Lion.

DEMETRIUS   And then came Pyramus.

LYSANDER   And so the lion vanished.

(Enter PYRAMUS.*)*

PYRAMUS   Sweet Moon, I thank thee for thy sunny beams;
I thank thee, Moon, for shining now so bright;
For, by thy gracious, golden, glittering gleams,
I trust to take of truest Thisby sight.
   But stay, O spite!
   But mark, poor knight,
What dreadful dole is here!
   Eyes, do you see?
   How can it be?
O dainty duck! O dear!
   Thy mantle good,
   What, stained with blood!
Approach, ye Furies fell!
   O Fates, come, come,
   Cut thread and thrum;
Quail, crush, conclude, and quell!

THESEUS   This passion, and the death of a dear friend, would go near to make a man look sad.

HIPPOLYTA   Beshrew my heart, but I pity the man.

PYRAMUS   O wherefore, Nature, didst thou lions frame?
Since lion vile hath here deflow'red my dear:
Which is—no, no—which was the fairest dame
That lived, that loved, that liked, that looked with cheer.
   Come, tears, confound;
   Out, sword and wound
The pap of Pyramus;
   Ay, that left pap,
   Where heart doth hop. *(Stabs himself.)*
Thus die I, thus, thus, thus.
   Now am I dead,
   Now am I fled;
My soul is in the sky.
   Tongue, lose thy light;
Moon, take thy flight.

(Exit MOONSHINE.*)*

   Now die, die, die, die, die. *(Dies.)*

DEMETRIUS   No die, but an ace, for him; for he is but one.

LYSANDER   Less than an ace, man; for he is dead, he is nothing.

THESEUS   With the help of a surgeon he might yet recover, and yet prove an ass.

HIPPOLYTA   How chance Moonshine is gone before Thisby comes back and finds her lover?

THESEUS   She will find him by starlight. Here she comes; and her passion ends the play.

(Enter THISBY.)

HIPPOLYTA Methinks she should not use a long one for such a Pyramus. I hope she will be brief.

DEMETRIUS A mote will turn the balance, which Pyramus, which Thisby, is the better; he for a man, God warr'nt us; she for a woman, God bless us!

LYSANDER She hath spied already with those sweet eyes.

DEMETRIUS And thus she means, videlicet:

THISBY Asleep, my love?
　　What, dead, my dove?
　O Pyramus, arise!
　　Speak, speak. Quite dumb?
　　Dead, Dead? A tomb
　Must cover thy sweet eyes.
　　These lily lips,
　　This cherry nose,

These yellow cowslip cheeks,
　　Are gone, are gone.
　　Lovers, make moan.
His eyes were green as leeks.
　　O Sisters Three,
　　Come, come to me,
With hands as pale as milk;
　　Lay them in gore,
　　Since you have shore
With shears his thread of silk.
　　Tongue, not a word,
　　Come, trusty sword,
Come, blade, my breast imbrue! *(Stabs herself.)*
　　And, farewell, friends.
　　Thus Thisby ends.
Adieu, adieu, adieu. *(Dies.)*

THESEUS Moonshine and Lion are left to bury the dead.

DEMETRIUS Ay, and Wall too.

Monologues for Women

As You Like It

by William Shakespeare

Rosalind is the daughter of a banished duke. Her Uncle Frederick has wrongly seized her father's dominions and has cast out Rosalind from court. In order to reach her father safely, Rosalind must masquerade as a young man to travel through the forest. In the following monologue, she scolds a young shepherdess, Phoebe, for rejecting a young shepherd, Silvio.

ROSALIND *(Advancing.)*

And why, I pray you? Who might be
 your mother,
That you insult, exult, and all at
 once,
Over the wretched? What though you
 have no beauty—
As, by my faith, I see no more in
 you
Than without candle may go dark to
 bed—
Must you be therefore proud and piti-
 less?
Why, what means this? Why do you
 look on me?
I see no more in you than in the ordinary
Of nature's sale-work. 'Od's my little
 life,
I think she means to tangle my eyes
 too!
No, faith, proud mistress, hope not
 after it;
'Tis not your inky brows, your black
 silk hair,
Your bugle eyeballs, nor your cheek of
 cream,

That can entame my spirits to your
 worship.
You foolish shepherd, wherefore do
 you follow her,
Like foggy south, puffing with wind
 and rain?
You are a thousand times a properer
 man
Than she a woman. 'Tis such fools as
 you
That makes the world full of ill-
 favour'd children.
'Tis not her glass, but you, that flatters
 her;
And out of you she sees herself more
 proper
Than any of her lineaments can show
 her.
But, mistress, know yourself. Down
 on your knees,
And thank heaven, fasting, for a good
 man's love;
For I must tell you friendly in your
 ear:
Sell when you can; you are not for all
 markets.
Cry the man mercy, love him, take his
 offer;
Foul is most foul, being foul to be a
 scoffer.
So take her to thee, shepherd. Fare you
 well.

Saint Joan

by Bernard Shaw

According to legend, Joan of Arc was an illiterate girl who heard voices and led soldiers into battle. In Shaw's Saint Joan, *Joan is portrayed as an independent, courageous visionary who wanted to lead a man's life. In the following monologue, Joan is addressing her inquisitors, who have just sentenced her to life imprisonment instead of to burning at the stake.*

JOAN   *(Rising in consternation and terrible anger)* Perpetual imprisonment! Am I not then to be set free?

. . .

Give me that writing. *(She rushes to the table; snatches up the paper; and tears it into fragments)* Light your fire; do you think I dread it as much as the life of a rat in a hole? My voices were right.

. . .

Yes; they told me you were fools *(the word gives great offense)*, and that I was not to listen to your fine words nor trust to your charity. You promised me my life; but you lied *(indignant excla-*mations). You think that life is nothing but not being stone dead. It is not the bread and water I fear: I can live on bread: when have I asked for more? It is not hardship to drink water if the water be clean. Bread has no sorrow for me, and water no affliction. But to shut me from the light of the sky and the sight of the fields and flowers; to chain my feet so that I can never again ride with the soldiers nor climb the hills; to make me breathe foul damp darkness, and keep from me everything that brings me back to the love of God when your wickedness and foolishness tempt me to hate Him; all this is worse than the furnace in the Bible that was heated seven times. I could do without my warhorse; I could drag about in a skirt; I could let the banners and the trumpets and the knights and soldiers pass me and leave me behind as they leave the other women, if only I could still hear the

Cornelia Otis Skinner as Anne of Cleves and as Jane Howard in her one-woman show The Wives of Henry VIII.

wind in the trees, the larks in the sunshine, the young lambs crying through the healthy frost, and the blessed blessed church bells that send my angel voices floating to me in the wind. But without these things I cannot live; and by your wanting to take them away from me, or from any human creature, I know that your counsel is of the devil, and that mine is of God.

. . .

His ways are not your ways. He wills that I go through the fire to His bosom; for I am His child, and you are not fit that I should live among you. That is my last word to you.

The Belle of Amherst

by William Luce

The Belle of Amherst *is a one-character play about Emily Dickinson. In this opening monologue of the play, Emily sets the stage for the evening's entertainment. She gives glimpses of her past and reveals her independent nature.*

EMILY   *(She enters, carrying the teapot. She calls back over her shoulder)* Yes, Vinnie, I have the tea, dear!

(She places the tea on the tea cart, then looks up wide-eyed at the AUDIENCE. *Slowly she picks up a plate with slices of dark cake on it, walks shyly downstage, and extends it to the* AUDIENCE*)*

This is my introduction. Black cake. My own special recipe.

Forgive me if I'm frightened. I never see strangers and hardly know what I say. My sister, Lavinia—she's younger than I—she says I tend to wander back and forth in time. So you must bear with me. I was born December tenth, eighteen thirty, which makes me—*fifty-three?*

Welcome to Amherst. My name is Emily Elizabeth Dickinson. Elizabeth is for my Aunt Elisabeth Currier. She's father's sister. Oh, how the trees stand up straight when they hear Aunt Libbie's little boots come thumping into Amherst! She's the only male relative on the female side.

Dear Aunt Libbie.

But I don't use my middle name anymore—since I became a *poet*.

Professor Higginson, the literary critic, doesn't think my poems are—no matter. I've had seven poems published—anonymously, to be sure. So you see why I prefer to introduce myself to you as a poet.

Here in Amherst, I'm known as Squire Edward Dickinson's half-cracked daughter. Well, I am! The neighbors can't figure me out. I don't cross my father's ground to any house or town. I haven't left the house for years.

The soul selects her own society—then—shuts the door. Why should I socialize with village gossips?

*(*EMILY *turns to the window, still holding the cake)*

There goes one of them now—Henrietta Sweetser—everyone knows Henny. She'd even intimidate the anti-

Christ. Look at her! She's strolling by the house, trying to catch a glimpse of me. Would *you* like that?

So I give them something to talk about. I dress in white all year around, even in winter. "Bridal white," Henny calls it.

(She mimics back-fence gossips)

"Dear, dear! Dresses in bridal white, she does, every day of the blessed year. Year in, year out. Disappointed in love as a girl, so I hear. Poor creature. All so very sad. And her sister Lavinia, a spinster too. Didn't you know? Oh, yes. Stayed unmarried just to be at home and take care of Miss Emily. Two old maids in that big house. What a lonely life, to shut yourself away from good people like us."

Indeed!

You should see them come to the door, bearing gifts, craning their necks, trying to see over Vinnie's shoulder. But I'm too fast for them. I've already run upstairs two steps at a time. And I hide there until they leave. You can imagine what they make of that!

One old lady came to the door the other day to get a peek inside. I surprised her by answering the door myself. She stammered something about looking for a house to buy.

(Mischievously)

To spare the expense of moving, I directed her to the cemetery.

A Raisin in the Sun

by Lorraine Hansberry

Mama's son, Walter, has accused her of not trusting his judgment in handling money. In the following monologue, Mama admits that she has misjudged her son and will hand over to him the insurance money given to her on her husband's death.

MAMA *(Crosses R. to WALTER.)* Listen to me now. I say I been wrong, son. That I been doing to you what the rest of the world been doing to you. *(She turns off RADIO.)* Walter—*(She stops and he looks up slowly at her and she meets his eyes evenly.)* what you ain't never understood is that I ain't got nothing, don't own nothing, ain't really wanted nothing that wasn't for you. There ain't nothing as precious to me—there ain't nothing worth holding on to, money, dreams, nothing else— if it means—if it means it's going to destroy my boy. *(Crosses U.R.C. to buffet for her pocketbook and money. He watches her without speaking or moving.)* I paid the man thirty-five hundred dollars down on the house. That leaves sixty-five hundred dollars. Monday morning I want you to take this money and take three thousand dollars and put it in a savings account for Beneatha's medical schooling.

(WALTER rises, crosses U.C.)

The rest you put in a checking account—with your name on it. And from now on any penny that comes out of it or that go in it is for you to look after. For you to decide. *(Puts money on coffee table and drops her hands a little helplessly.)* It ain't much, but it's all I got in the world and I'm putting it in your hands. I'm telling you to be the head of this family from now on like you supposed to be.

▬▬▬▬▬▬▬

A Member of the Wedding

by Carson McCullers

Frankie's brother is getting married and Frankie is having difficulty adjusting to the idea. In the following monologue, Frankie comes up with her solution to the problem of her brother's marriage and her fears of separation.

FRANKIE   Don't bother me, John Henry. I'm thinking.

. . .

About the wedding. About my brother and the bride. Everything's been so sudden today. I never believed before about the fact that the earth turns at the rate of about a thousand miles a day. I didn't understand why it was that if you jumped up in the air you wouldn't land in Selma or Fairview or somewhere else instead of the same back yard. But now it seems to me I feel the world going around very fast. *(FRANKIE begins turning around in circles with arms outstretched . . .)* I feel it turning and it makes me dizzy. . . . *(Suddenly stopping her turning.)* I just now thought of something.

. . .

I know where I'm going.

(There are sounds of children playing in the distance)

I tell you I know where I'm going. It's like I've known it all my life. Tomorrow I will tell everybody.

. . .

(Dreamily) After the wedding I'm going with them to Winter Hill. I'm going off with them after the wedding.

. . .

Just now I realized something. The trouble with me is that for a long time I have been just an "I" person. All other people can say "we." When Berenice says "we" she means her lodge and church and colored people. Soldiers can say "we" and mean the army. All people belong to a "we" except me.

. . .

Not to belong to a "we" makes you too lonesome. Until this afternoon I didn't have a "we," but now after seeing Janice and Jarvis I suddenly realize something.

. . .

I know that the bride and my brother are the "we" of me. So I'm going with them, and joining with the wedding. This coming Sunday when my brother and the bride leave this town, I'm going with the two of them to Winter Hill. And after that to whatever place that they will ever go. *(There is a pause)* I love the two of them so much and we belong to be together. I love the two of them so much because they are the *we* of me.

▬▬▬▬▬▬▬

Monologues for Men

Cyrano de Bergerac

by Edmond Rostand

A boorish young man has attempted to insult Cyrano by stating, "Your nose is rather large." Cyrano responds by suggesting all the imaginative descriptions a more perceptive person might have used.

CYRANO   Ah, no, young sir!
You are too simple. Why, you might
    have said—
Oh, a great many things! Mon dieu,
    why waste
Your opportunity? For example,
    thus:—
AGGRESSIVE: I, sir, if that nose were
    mine,
I'd have it amputated—on the spot!
FRIENDLY: How do you drink with
    such a nose!
You ought to have a cup made special-
    ly.
DESCRIPTIVE: 'Tis   a   rock—a
    crag—a cape—
A cape? say rather, a peninsula!
INQUISITIVE: What is that recepta-
    cle—
A razor-case or a portfolio?
KINDLY: Ah, do you love the little
    birds
So much that when they come and sing
    to you,
You give them this to perch on! INSO-
    LENT:
Sir, when you smoke, the neighbors
    must suppose
Your chimney is on fire. CAUTIOUS:
    Take care—

A weight like that might make you
    topheavy.
THOUGHTFUL: Somebody fetch my
    parasol—
Those delicate colors fade so in the
    sun!
PEDANTIC: Does not Aristophanes
Mention a mythologic monster called
Hippocampelephantocamelos?
Surely we have here the original!
FAMILIAR: Well, old torchlight! Hang
    your hat
Over that chandelier—it hurts my
    eyes.
ELOQUENT: When it blows, the
    typhoon howls,
And the clouds darken. DRAMATIC:
    When it bleeds—
The Red Sea! ENTERPRISING: What a
    sign
For some perfumer! LYRIC: Hark—the
    horn—
Of Roland calls to summon Charle-
    magne!—
SIMPLE: When do they unveil the
    monument?
RESPECTFUL: Sir, I recognize in you
A man of parts, a man of promi-
    nence—
RUSTIC: Hey? What? Call that a nose?
    Na na—
I be no fool like what you think I be—
That there's a blue cucumber! MILI-
    TARY:
Point against cavalry! PRACTICAL:
    Why not
A lottery with this for the grand
    prize?
Or—parodying Faustus in the play—
"Was this the nose that launched a
    thousand ships

Christopher Plummer as Cyrano de Bergerac in Rostand's sentimental drama of that name

And burned the topless towers of Ilium?''

These, my dear sir, are things you might have said

Had you some tinge of letters, or of wit

To color your discourse. But wit,—not so,

You never had an atom—and of letters,

You need but three to write you down—an Ass.

Talley's Folly

by Lanford Wilson

It is July 4, 1944, in the early evening. Matt Friedman is outside the boathouse on the Talley place in Lebanon, Missouri.

He has come to persuade Sally Talley to marry him. Matt's opening monologue ends as Sally calls from outside the boathouse.

A Victorian boathouse constructed of louvers, lattice in decorative panels, and a good deal of Gothic Revival gingerbread. The riverside is open to the audience. The interior and exterior walls have faded to a pale gray. The boathouse is covered by a heavy canopy of maple and surrounded by almost waist-high weeds and the slender, perfectly vertical limbs of a weeping willow. Lighting and sound should be very romantic: the sunset at the opening, later the moonlight, slant through gaps in the ceiling and walls reflecting the river in lambent ripples across the inside of the room.

The boathouse contains two boats, one turned upside down, buckets, box-

es, no conventional seating. Overhead is a lattice-work attic in which is stored creels, bamboo poles, nets, seines, minnow buckets, traps, floats, etc., all long past use.

At opening: All this is seen in a blank white work light; the artificiality of the theatrical set quite apparent. The houselights are up.

MATT *(Enters in front of the stage. MATT FRIEDMAN is forty-two, dark, and rather large. Warm and unhurried, he has a definite talent for mimicry. In his voice there is still a trace of a German-Jewish accent, of which he is probably unaware. He speaks to the audience)* They tell me that we have ninety-seven minutes here tonight—without intermission. So if that means anything to anybody; if you think you'll need a drink of water or anything . . .

You know, a year ago I drove Sally home from a dance; and while we were standing on the porch up at the house, we looked down to the river and saw this silver flying thing rise straight up and zip off. We came running down to the river, we thought the Japanese had landed some amazing new flying machine, but all we found was the boathouse here, and—uh, that was enough.

I'll just point out some of the facilities till everybody gets settled in. If everything goes well for me tonight, this should be a waltz, one-two-three, one-two-three; a no-holds-barred romantic story, and since I'm not a romantic type, I'm going to need the whole valentine here to help me: the woods, the willows, the vines, the moonlight, the band—there's a band that plays tonight, over in the park. The trees, the berries, the breeze, the

When delivering a monologue, the actor must be intensely involved with the character.

sounds: water and crickets, frogs, dogs, the light, the bees, working all night.

Did you know that? Bees work—worker bees—work around the clock. Never stop. Collecting nectar, or pollen, whatever a bee collects. Of course their life expectancy is twenty days. Or, in a bee's case, twenty days and twenty nights. Or possibly "expectancy" is wrong in the case of a bee. Who knows what a bee expects. But whatever time there is in a life is a lifetime, and I imagine after twenty days and twenty nights a bee is more or less ready to tuck it in.

(In a craggy, Western, "Old-Timer" voice) "I been flyin' now, young sprout, nigh-on to nineteen days an' nineteen nights."

(Imitating a young bee) "Really, Grandpa Worker Bee?"

(Old-Timer) "An' I'm 'bout ready to tuck it in."

(Slight pause. Reflectively) Work. Work is very much to the point. *(Showing the set)* We have everything to help me here. There's a rotating gismo in the footlights (do you believe footlights) because we needed the moon out there on the water. The water runs right through here, so you're all out in the river—sorry about that. They promise me moonlight by the baleful, all through the shutters. We could do it on a couple of folding chairs, but it isn't bare, it isn't bombed out, it's rundown, and the difference is all the difference. And valentines need froufrou.

We have a genuine Victorian folly here. A boathouse. Constructed of louvers, and lattice and geegaws. I feel like a real-estate salesman. Of course there's something about the term "real estate" that strikes me wrong. Estate maybe, but real is arguable. But to start you off on the right foot . . . Everybody ready? This is a waltz, remember, one-two-three, one-two-three.

There was a time—or, all right, I think that has to be: Once upon a time—there was a hope throughout the land. From the chaos of the Great Depression, people found strength in union, believing their time had come. But even as this hope was perceived, once again a dark power rose up from the chaos in another land. Once again this country pitched its resources and industry into battle. Now, after almost three years of war, it has become apparent that the battle is turning. Once again we are told that "peace and prosperity" are in the air. But in the midst of battle, that "hope" the people had known has been changed into the enemy. Peace, and—more to the point—prosperity, is our ally now. Once again, we are told the country has been saved by war.

Now, you would think that in this remote wood, on this remote and unimportant, but sometimes capricious, river—that world events would not touch this hidden place. But such is not the case. There is a house on the hill up there, and there is a family that is not at peace but in grave danger of prosperity. And there is a girl in the house on the hill up there who is a terrible embarrassment to her family because she remembers that old hope, and questions this new fortune, and questioning eyes are hard to come by nowadays. It's hard to use your peripheral vision when you're being led by the nose.

Now I know what you're thinking. You're saying if I'd known it was going to be like this, I wouldn't have come. Or if I'd known it was going to be like this, I would have listened. But don't worry, we're going to do this first part all over again for the late-comers. I want to give you and me both every opportunity. So. Okeydokey. *(Checks pocket watch)* Oh, boy, this has gotta be fast. So: *(Deep breath, then all in a run)* They tell me that we have ninety-seven minutes here tonight without intermission so if that means anything to anybody if you think you'll need a drink of water or anything I'll just point out some of the facilities till everybody gets settled in if everything goes well for me tonight this should be a waltz one-two-three, one-two-three a no-holds-barred romantic story and since I'm not a romantic type I'm going to need the whole shmeer here to help me the woods the willows the vines the moonlight the band there's a band that plays tonight over in the park the trees the berries the breeze the sounds water and crickets frogs dogs the light the bees . . . *(Pauses. With a slight hill accent)* Frogs, dogs . . . *(To stage manager in sound booth)* Could we have a dog? I'd like a dog. *(He listens a second. Nothing. Then a furious, yapping, tiny terrier is heard)* Fellas! Fellas! A *dog!* *(Beat. Then a low, distant woof-woof-woof that continues until* SALLY's *entrance.* MATT *listens a beat, pleased)*

Oh, yeah. Old man Barnette kicked out Blackie and called in the kids, and about now the entire family is sitting down to supper. Even Blackie, out by the smokehouse. But a car pulled off the road about a mile downstream, and

someone got out. And at this hour it begins to be difficult to see, the chickens have started to go to bed, and noises carry up the river as though there was someone there in the barnyard. And Blackie wants to let everybody know the Barnette farm is well guarded. *(Beat. Then back to run-on narration)*

Working all night did you know that bees work worker bees work around the clock never stop collecting nectar or pollen whatever a bee collects of course their life expectancy is twenty days or in a bee's case twenty days and twenty nights or possibly expectancy is wrong in the case of a bee who knows what a bee expects but whatever time there is in a life is a lifetime and I imagine after twenty days and . . .

━━━━━━━━━━━━━━━━

Wine in the Wilderness

by Alice Childress

Bill Jameson is an artist preparing his culminating work, a triptych (three paintings that make up one work). What he is seeking is a female model to represent the third part of the triptych, the lost and abandoned black woman of today. In the following monologue, Bill is talking on the phone to his agent.

BILL . . . *(Phone rings. He finds an African throw-cloth and hands it to her)* Put this on. Relax, don't go way mad, and all the rest-a that jazz. Change, will you? I apologize. I'm sorry. *(He picks up phone)* Hello, survivor of a riot speaking. Who's calling? *(TOMMY retires behind the screen with the throw. During the conversation she undresses and wraps the throw around her. We see TOMMY and BILL, but they can't see each other)* Sure, told you not to worry. I'll be ready for the exhibit. If you don't dig it, don't show it. Not time for you to see it yet. Yeah, yeah, next week. You just make sure your exhibition room is big enough to hold the crowds that's gonna congregate to see this fine chick I got here. *(This perks TOMMY's ears up)* You ought see her. The finest black woman in the world . . . No, . . . the finest *any* woman in the world . . . This gorgeous satin chick is . . . is . . . black velvet moonlight . . . an ebony queen of the universe . . . *(TOMMY can hardly believe her ears)* One look at her and you go back to Spice Islands . . . She's Mother Africa . . . You flip, double flip. She has come through everything that has been put on her . . . *(He unveils the gorgeous woman he has painted . . . "Wine In The Wilderness." TOMMY believes he is talking about her)* Regal . . . grand . . . magnificent, fantastic . . . You would vote her the woman you'd most like to meet on a desert island, or around the corner from anywhere. She's here with me now . . . and I don't know if I want to show her to you or anybody else . . . I'm beginnin' to have this deep attachment . . . She sparkles, man, Harriet Tubman, Queen of the Nile . . . sweetheart, wife, mother, sister, friend. . . . The night . . . a black diamond . . . A dark, beautiful dream . . . A cloud with a silvery lining . . . Her wrath is a storm over the Bahamas. "Wine In The Wilderness" . . . The memory of Africa . . . the *now* of things . . . but

best of all and most important . . . She's tomorrow . . . she's my tomorrow . . .

━━━━━━━━━━━━━━━━━━━

You're a Good Man, Charlie Brown

by Clark Gesner, based on the comic strip Peanuts by Charles M. Schulz

Charlie Brown is alone in the school yard during lunchtime. He is feeling very sorry for himself because he is always alone. During the following monologue, he wonders how a young girl also sitting alone would react if he joined her for lunch.

CHARLIE BROWN   I think lunchtime is about the worst time of the day for me. Always having to sit here alone. Of course, sometimes mornings aren't so pleasant, either—waking up and wondering if anyone would really miss me if I never got out of bed. Then there's the night, too—lying there and thinking about all the stupid things I've done during the day. And all those hours in between—when I do all those stupid things. Well, lunchtime is *among* the worst times of the day for me.

Well, I guess I'd better see what I've got *(He opens the bag, unwraps a sandwich, and looks inside)* Peanut butter. *(He bites and chews)* Some psychiatrists say that people who eat peanut butter sandwiches are lonely. I guess they're right. And if you're really lonely, the peanut butter sticks to the roof of your mouth. *(He munches quietly, idly fingering the bench)* Boy, the

PTA sure did a good job of painting these benches. *(He looks off to one side)* There's that cute little redheaded girl eating her lunch over there. I wonder what she'd do if I went over and asked her if I could sit and have lunch with her. She'd probably laugh right in my face. It's hard on a face when it gets laughed in. There's an empty place next to her on the bench. There's no reason why I couldn't just go over and sit there. I could do that right now. All I have to do is stand up. *(He stands)* I'm standing up. *(He sits)* I'm sitting down. I'm a coward. I'm so much of a coward she wouldn't even think of looking at me. She hardly ever *does* look at me. In fact, I can't remember her ever looking at me. Why shouldn't she look at me? Is there any reason in the world why she shouldn't look at me? Is she so great and am I so small that she couldn't spare one little moment just to . . . *(He freezes)* She's looking at me. *(In terror he looks one way, then another)* She's *looking* at me.

(His head looks all around, frantically trying to find something else to notice. His teeth clench. Tension builds. Then, with one motion, he pops the paper bag over his head)

Amen Corner

by James Baldwin

David is a brilliant young jazz musician. In the following monologue, he decides to leave his home and reject his mother's goal for his future. He decides to go out into the world and become his own man.

DAVID   And if I listened— what would happen? What do you think would happen if I listened? You want me to stay here, getting older, getting sicker— hating you? You think I want to hate you, Mama? You think it don't tear me to pieces to have to lie to you all the time. Yes, because I been lying to you, Mama, for a long time now! I don't want to tell no more lies. I don't want to keep feeling so bad inside that I have to go running down them alleys you was talking about—that alley right outside this door!—to find something to help me hide—to hide—from what I'm feeling. Mama, I want to be a man. It's time you let me be a man. You got to let me go. *[A pause]* If I stayed here—I'd end up worse than Daddy— because I wouldn't be doing what I know I got to do—I *got* to do! I've seen your life—and now I see Daddy—and I love you, I love you both!—but I've got my work to do, something's happening in the world out there, I got to go! I know you think I don't know what's happening, but I'm beginning to see—something. Every time I play, every time I listen, I see Daddy's face and yours, and so many faces—who's going to speak for all that, Mama? Who's going to speak for all of us? I can't stay home. Maybe I can say something—one day—maybe I can say something in music that's never been said before. Mama—*you* knew this day was coming.

BIBLIOGRAPHY

Cohen, Lorraine: *Scenes for Young Actors,* Avon, New York, 1973.
Olfson, Lewy: *50 Great Scenes for Student Actors,* Bantam, New York, 1977.
Price, Jonathan: *Classical Scenes, A Mentor Book,* New American Library, New York, 1979.
Schulman, Michael, and Eva Mekler: *Contemporary Scenes for Student Actors,* Penguin, Baltimore, 1980.

LONG PLAYS FOR PRODUCTION AND STUDY

Alice in Wonderland, adapted for the stage by Eva Le Gallienne and Florida Friebus from Lewis Carroll's *Alice's Adventures in Wonderland* and *Through the Looking Glass*
Anne of the Thousand Days by Maxwell Anderson
Beckett (or The Honour of God) by Jean Anouilh, translated by Lucienne Hill
Berkeley Square by John L. Balderson
Cock Robin by Elmer Rice and Philip Barry
The Corn Is Green by Emlyn William
Daddy Longlegs by Jean Webster
Death of a Salesman by Arthur Miller
Death Takes a Holiday by Alberto Casella
Easter by August Strindberg
Golden Boy by Clifford Odets
Indians by Arthur Kopit
J.B. by Archibald MacLeish
Leave It to Psmith by P. G. Wodehouse
Lilies of the Field by John Hastings Turner
The Lion in Winter by James Goldman
Luv by Murray Schisgal
A Man for All Seasons by Robert Bolt
Mary of Scotland by Maxwell Anderson
The Miracle Worker by William Gibson
Mr. Pim Passes By by A. A. Milne
The Odd Couple by Neil Simon
Outward Bound by Sutton Vane
The Perfect Alibi by A. A. Milne
The Piper by Josephine Preston Peabody
The Pleasure of His Company by Samuel Taylor and Cornelia Otis Skinner
Quality Street by James M. Barrie
The Royal Family by Edna Ferber and George S. Kaufman
R.U.R. by Karel Capek

The School for Scandal by Richard Sheridan
Seventeen by Booth Tarkington
The Show-Off by George Kelly
The Sleeping Prince by Terence Rattigan
Stage Door by Edna Ferber and George S. Kaufman
The Swan by Ferenc Molnar
A Thousand Clowns by Herb Gardner
The Time of Your Life by William Saroyan
A View from the Bridge by Arthur Miller
The Way of the World by William Congreve
The Wild Duck by Henrik Ibsen, revised by Lorraine Cohen
The Winslow Boy by Terence Rattigan
Uncle Vanya by Anton Chekhov, adapted by Lorraine Cohen

Index

Page numbers set in boldface type indicate illustrations.

Photo Credits

Part One Opener   Pp. xvi–1   Jerry Goodstein

3: Mimi Forsyth/Monkmeyer;   **5:** Nancy McFarland;   **9:** New York Public Library/Picture Collection;   **11:** Gerhard E. Gscheidle/Peter Arnold, Inc.;   **17:** Ken Firestone/Peter Arnold, Inc.;   **23:** Laimute E. Druskis;   **24:** Martha Swope;   **27:** Bert Andrews;   **28, 29:** Martha Swope;   **31:** Henry E. Lowenstein/Bonfils Theatre, Denver;   **33:** Theatre Collection/New York Public Library, Astor, Lenox & Tilden Foundations;   **35:** Zodiac Photographers;   **37:** Courtesy of Caedmon Records;   **49:** James Karales/Peter Arnold, Inc.;   **52:** NBC Photo;   **54:** New York Public Library/Picture Collection;   **59:** Jerry Goodstein;   **62, 66, 71, 77, 81:** Martha Swope;   **88:** Carl Davis/Alley Theatre;   **95tl:** Martha Swope;   **95tr:** Roger Greenwalt;   **96bl:** Don McKague;   **96br:** Tass/Sovfoto;   **98:** Zodiac Photographers;   **99:** Martha Swope;   **101:** Bert Andrews;   **103:** Mark Taper Forum;   **105:** Bert Andrews;   **110:** Henry E. Lowenstein/Bonfils Theatre;   **112:** Susan Cook;   **119:** Henry E. Lowenstein/Bonfils Theatre;   **130:** Martha Swope;   **132tl:** Henry E. Lowenstein/Bonfils Theatre;   **132tr:** Bert Andrews;   **132bl:** Martha Swope;   **132br:** Jerry Goodstein;   **135t&bl:** Martha Swope;   **135br:** Henry E. Lowenstein/Bonfils Theatre;   **138:** Hartke Theatre;   **139:** Henry E. Lowenstein/Bonfils Theatre;   **142:** Martha Swope.

Part Two Opener   Pp. 148–149   Martha Swope

152, 155, 157, 158, 162: Don McKague;   **165, 170:** Martha Swope;   **175, 176:** Henry E. Lowenstein/Bonfils Theatre;   **177:** Zodiac Photographers;   **179:** Joseph Schuyler;   **181:** William Nelson/Carnegie-Mellon University;   **183, 186:** Martha Swope;   **193:** Mark Taper Forum;   **196, 197:** Martha Swope;   **200:** Courtesy of Hofstra University;   **205:** D. A. Harissiadis, Athens;   **207:** Don McKague;   **210:** German Information Center;   **212:** Alinari;   **216:** Graphic House, Inc.;   **219, 222, 225, 226:** New York Public Library/Picture Collection;   **230:** Martha Swope;   **231:** Dallas Theatre Center;   **232:** Martha Swope;   **235:** Hartke Theatre;   **236:** Martha Swope.

Part Three Opener   Pp. 238–239   Martha Swope

241: Denver Center Theatre;   **259:** Mark Taper Forum;   **264:** Laimute E. Druskis;   **267:** William Nelson/Carnegie-Mellon University;   **269:** Joseph Schuyler;   **270:** Martha Swope;   **272:** Hartke Theatre;   **279:** Graphic House, Inc.;   **283:** Zodiac Photographers;   **285, 286:** Theatre Collection/New York Public Library, Astor, Lenox & Tilden Foundations;   **294:** Dallas Theatre Center.

Color Insert Section

305, 306: Richard Corson;   **307:** Bruno Zehnder/Peter Arnold, Inc.;   **308:** Martha Swope;   **309, 310:** New York Public Library/Picture Collection;   **311t:** Robert Capece/McGraw-Hill;   **311b:** Martha Swope;   **312:** Robert Capece/McGraw-Hill.

325: Zodiac Photographers;   **329:** Coleman Photography;   **333:** Jerry Goodstein;   **337:** Plymouth Theatre;   **338:** Martha Swope;   **341:** Bruce Siddons/Yale Repertory Theatre;   **342:** Zodiac Photographers;   **346:** Martha Swope;   **375:** Ken Firestone/Peter Arnold, Inc.; **386:** Courtesy of Harvey Sabinson;   **389:** NBC Photo;   **391:** Courtesy of The Stratford Festival Theatre, Stratford, Ontario, Canada;   **400, 402:** Dallas Theatre Center;   **405:** Martha Swope;   **406:** Zodiac Photographers;   **411:** Plymouth Theatre.

Part Four Opener   Pp. 414–415   Joseph Schuyler

447: Dallas Theatre Center;   **476:** Martha Swope;   **483:** NBC Photo;   **501:** Zodiac Photographers;   **507:** Courtesy of The American Shakespeare Theatre;   **512:** Culver Pictures;   **517:** NBC Photo;   **518:** Dallas Theatre Center.